THE
CONSERVATORY GARDENER

THE CONSERVATORY GARDENER

Anne Swithinbank

Photographs by Deni Bown

TODTRI

HALF-TITLE PAGE *Lilium nepalense*

FRONTISPIECE *Brugmansia, Lilium regale,
Ipomoea indica* and *Pelargonium tomentosum*
flourish in this small conservatory

The Conservatory Gardener
Copyright © Frances Lincoln Limited 1993
Text copyright © Anne Swithinbank 1993
Photographs copyright © Deni Bown 1993
except for those listed on page 192.
Illustrations © Frances Lincoln Limited 1993

This edition published by
TODTRI Book Publishers
254 West 31st Street
New York, NY 10001-2813
Fax: (212) 695-6984
E-mail: info@todtri.com

Visit us on the web!
www.todtri.com

ISBN 1-57717-195-0

First Frances Lincoln edition 1993
This United States edition 2001

Contents

Introduction

The modern sunroom could be described as a place where people and plants share an almost symbiotic relationship in the same living space. The contemporary sunroom gardener wants to enjoy a bright, extended living area made more beautiful, inviting, and soothing by the presence of plants. In exchange, he or she needs to be prepared to choose and care for the plants and maintain them in good health, extending their lives and enhancing their appearance. Setting up a sunroom with plants, furnishings, and ornaments is an expression of personal taste and an act of creativity. Plants that thrive are essential to success and the aim of this book is to help foster the delicate marriage between humans and plants.

Discussion of the many different types and styles of sunroom and greenhouse is beyond the scope of this book, as are the intricacies of design and construction. Here, the emphasis is on those elements of planning which most clearly affect the health of plants. In other words, aspiring sunroom gardeners should go ahead with whatever modest or extravagant plans they have in mind. While drawing them up, though, they should read the section on Environments for Plants. This will highlight vital areas such as the provision of adequate ventilation, shading, heating and humidity, and aspects of interior landscaping which relate directly to plant growth. Readers who already have a sunroom or greenhouse may find that minor adjustments can be made to improve growing conditions for their plants. The Plant Care section provides general guidelines and good practices for keeping a varied collection of plants in excellent health.

The largest section of this book is devoted to the plants themselves. There is a vast selection of plants and they have been grouped here according to the most useful method available – that dictated by the role of the plant. In the same way that an outdoor gardener would choose larger trees and shrubs first, to make a framework, adding smaller shrubs, climbers, herbaceous plants, and annuals to build up a balanced planting, so the keen greenhouse gardener, about to stock up with plants or faced with a motley assortment of ill-matched potfuls, needs similar guidance. First a selection of large specimen plants is offered, to give the sunroom or greenhouse its character and backbone. Then the gardener is invited to select climbing plants to dress the vertical, and trailing plants to cascade from hanging baskets and flow over the sides of tables and benches. Finally, gaps are plugged by choosing from a wide range of smaller flowering, fruiting, and foliage plants. Annuals, biennials, and bulbs, and aquatic plants will complete the effect.

Just as the outdoor gardener has to take into account the prevailing climate and the exposure of the plot, which may determine what will thrive and where it is positioned, when choosing greenhouse plants from the various sections, minimum temperature has to be kept very much in mind. Listed under each plant is the minimum temperature at which it will grow. Optimum growing temperatures are usually slightly warmer. Dividing these greenhouse temperatures into categories is an arbitrary matter, but it is useful to distinguish five: unheated – below 38°F(3°C); frost-free – 38-40°F(3-4°C); cool – 40-50°F(4-10°C); temperate – 50-60°F(10-16°C); and warm/tropical – 60°F(16°C) and over. Other books

sometimes omit the first two categories, but unheated or merely frost-free greenhouses and sun porches, properly sited, can be pleasurable even in midwinter. There are many plants that tolerate these low temperatures with the protection afforded by glass, creating effective displays of foliage and even flowers through the cold season; and plants that thrive in low temperatures rarely enjoy warm or tropical temperatures during winter. Lists of plants that can be grown in each temperature category are given on pages 180-84.

In the plant descriptions, the country of origin of each plant is mentioned, whenever possible. Having some idea of a plant's natural home can help in understanding its cultural preferences. Those from tropical rainforests tend to be leafy, enjoying some shade, warm, constant temperatures, and high humidity. Those from Mediterranean regions like lots of light, can usually tolerate temperatures that are just above freezing, and tend to have a long season of flower. Succulent plants from arid regions can survive periods of drought, need plenty of light, and can usually tolerate low winter temperatures.

Some of the well-loved and commonly grown greenhouse plants are poisonous. Oleander contains glycosides, dumb cane (dieffenbachia) and other aroids can cause swelling of the mouth, tongue, and throat if accidentally chewed, and *Primula obconica* can be responsible for an itchy rash. The poisonous nature of some plants is well documented, while for others there is little information; moreover, some people will sometimes show signs of sensitivity or even allergy to generally harmless plants. Here, where plants are known to be poisonous, this has been pointed out in the description. This does not, however, mean that the omission of a warning guarantees that a plant is safe. Always take care when handling plants, wash your hands after contact with them, and keep children and pets under supervision in the sunroom or greenhouse.

Greenhouse plants do represent a commitment and a tie. Regular attention is the key to their well-being and if the greenhouse gardener is not always around to do it, then a well-briefed plant sitter will have to be appointed. The only alternative to this is sophisticated and expensive automation, which is available precisely tailored to meet every aspect of greenhouse management nowadays. Nevertheless, the pleasure and sense of accomplishment to be derived from coaxing a group of plants into healthy growth and flower far outweighs any disadvantages.

Apart from the undisputed aesthetic pleasures that plants bring, the therapeutic value of tending them, and the likelihood that their green presence reduces stress, cultivating them indoors produces other, unseen benefits. Scientific research carried out by NASA has revealed that a wide range of plants can remove pollutants from the air in homes. Pollutants are given off in small amounts, mainly from synthetic materials. Formaldehyde is emitted from foam insulation and soft furnishings and trichloroethylene from some paints and glues, while benzene can be found in tobacco smoke and detergents. Plants such as spathiphyllum, chrysanthemum, and dracaena used in tests were found to absorb these harmful substances and turn them into plant foods. Look after your plants, and it seems that they will look after you!

Environments for plants

The history of the conservatory is inextricably linked with the care of plants, and design has evolved with their well-being in mind until very recent times. Plant collectors and gardeners in regions with severe winters have always been concerned with preserving delicate plants imported from warmer climates through the cold winter months. Conservatories – like the more functional greenhouses – have their origins in very primitive structures for overwintering plants known from as far back as ancient China and the Roman Empire, but a fresh impetus came with the Renaissance fashion for collecting tender plants such as citrus, myrtle, oleander, and pomegranate, when wealthy garden owners needed to preserve these precious but vulnerable possessions from winter frosts. Sometimes plants were grown in containers and moved indoors in winter (just as is done today). In other instances, they were planted in the ground and a heated shelter built over them.

By the seventeenth century, a grand garden might well have an orangery, an ornate structure with large, paned windows along one side where people as well as plants could enjoy shelter. The term "conservatory", signifying a place where plants were conserved through the winter, dates from this time, as does "greenhouse" – a building where "greens" (tender evergreens) were kept. Just as the obsession and fashion for collecting exotic plants grew, so did the structures to accommodate them. The classical lines of these early orangeries lie behind the inspiration of many of today's "traditional" conservatory and greenhouse designs. The early structures were often substantial; plants' need for light as well as shelter was only gradually appreciated, and glass manufacture was primitive.

Nineteenth-century developments made it possible to maximize light by largely dispensing with heavy masonry and by utilizing sheet glass, supported by slim glazing bars of iron or wood, for roofs as well as walls. Reflecting a more sophisticated appreciation of plants' needs, these structures built to house an ever-expanding influx of plants from tropical and sub-tropical zones incorporated all sorts of patent heating devices as well as provision for ventilation, watering, and spraying. Soon both greenhouses and conservatories were to be found even in quite modest gardens: the former generally utilitarian and free-standing, the latter attached to the house and often echoing its architectural style. In these controlled conditions, plant collections proliferated.

The successors of yesteryear's conservatories are today's sunrooms. Many of these nostalgically refer back to the old styles, reinterpreting them in up-to-date materials. Others often reject tradition and are designed on uncompromisingly modern lines. The big difference is that most modern sunrooms are envisaged more as home extensions for people than as accommodation for plants. Plant collectors who build their sunrooms chiefly in order to house and admire their plants are now in the minority. The new breed of sunroom owner often knows little about plants but may dream of sitting in a bright and comfortable, sometimes carpeted room, surrounded by soft furnishings with plants as accessories. Unless some knowledge of plants is acquired, this vision of leafy foliage and bright blooms may never be matched by reality. To learn by trial and error would be an expensive process. Plants are living things with specific needs. Each has its own requirements of light, humidity, and temperature which are influenced by the habitat in which that plant and its ancestors have evolved over the years. If they are not thriving, plants are of no use even as decorative accessories.

In many ways, plants and people need similar sorts of conditions. Designing for plants from the outset will ensure that the sunroom is comfortable for both, and that money spent on plants will not be wasted in the first hot summer or cold winter. Taking into account exposure, light and shade, ventilation, heating, and humidity makes it possible to create an environment that caters for a broad range of human and horticultural tastes. The space can then be landscaped and furnished in detail.

A plant-lover's ideal sunroom would be positioned so as to catch the winter sun. It would have plenty of vents in both roof and sides, and provision for shading and underfloor heating beneath a solid, tiled floor. During summer, the gardener would create plenty of humidity and spray lightly under the foliage of plants to freshen them up and deter spider mite. As labor-saving measures, some plants might be arranged on staging or benches fitted with capillary matting and others grown hydroponically, grouped in large containers, thus reducing the amount of watering necessary during the day. Rather than having to turn on taps, wield hoses, raise or lower blinds, and operate vents manually, a computerized environmental control system could take care of the management of light, shade, temperature, and humidity.

However, life is about compromises and the modern sunroom may often need to double as extra sitting space, a dining room, or an office. Someone may insist on the comfort of carpets. There may be no barrier between house and sunroom, so that the humid atmosphere that would benefit the plants would penetrate into the rest of the house with disastrous consequences. Nevertheless, provided the sunroom has adequate shading and ventilation, growing plants never presents a problem. The advantages of extra light mean that a greater range than just houseplants can thrive. Humidity can be raised locally around the plants by means of gravel trays and misting. Grouping plants together also helps.

Displaying a variety of smaller flowering plants in the sunroom presents something of a challenge. Pots of small plants standing on the floor cannot be seen properly, are a nuisance to maintain, and are liable to be kicked over or damaged. Here, tiered shelves secured to the wall provide an elegant solution. Each shelf stands out further than that above, which not only makes more of the display but is also of practical benefit, as light reaches every plant.

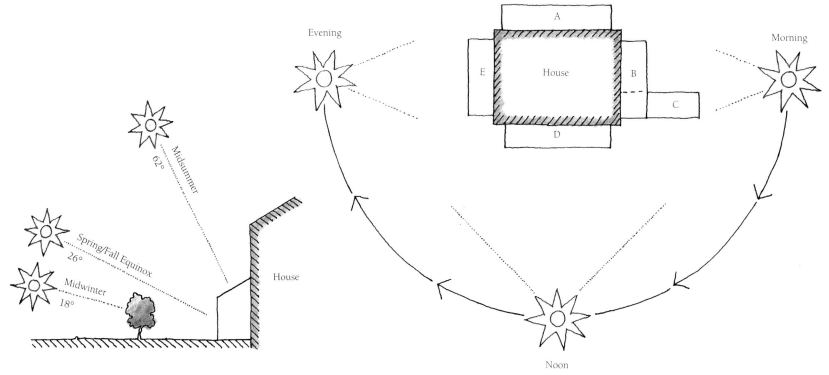

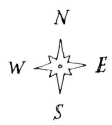

BELOW The sun's rays are weakest when it is low in the sky – that is, at sunrise and sunset in summer, and for most of the day in midwinter. If there is shade from nearby buildings or trees, the sunroom may get almost no sun in winter.

BELOW RIGHT A north-facing sunroom (A) receives direct sunlight only in summer, and then only very early in the morning or in the late evening. A southern exposure (D) benefits from sun for most of the day, year-round. A sunroom that faces west (E) is warmed by the afternoon light. While an east-facing site (B) receives morning light in summer, winter light is restricted. A sunroom at right angles to the wall of the house (C) can absorb light along its south side.

Before choosing plants, knowing the minimum temperature of the room is essential. That warmth-loving plants will be miserable at lower temperatures seems obvious. Conversely, plants which grow happily in frost-free or cool temperatures will often suffer badly if kept too warm. Plants also have different light requirements. A sunroom with inadequate ventilation and shading can still be filled with plants, but these will have to be a collection of cacti, other succulents, and plants from hot, sunny areas of the world. Many, *Tradescantia sillamontana* for instance, are covered with dense hair which helps prevent moisture loss from the surface of the leaves. Sun-loving climbers like bougainvillea and pereskia (a climbing cactus), will eventually provide shade for other plants.

There is even plenty of scope for an unheated sun porch in a cool climate. A fig would grow well trained against the wall and grape vines could be trained overhead or grown as standards in pots. Houseplants could be moved into the sun porch for the summer, while potted camellia and daphne could be brought in for late-winter flowers. Smaller foliage might be supplied by hardy ferns and ivies. Colorful primula and cyclamen would tolerate all but the coldest weather, when they could be moved into the house.

Location

The first clue as to the potential of a sunroom is offered by its siting. The type of plants that can be grown successfully will depend above all on the amount of sun the sunroom receives. Early-morning shafts of sunlight or radiant sunsets, blazing midday sun in summer, or none at all for three long months in winter – these are factors to take into account. They will affect how both people and plants enjoy the space, and what modifications may need to be made.

Orientation and siting

The orientation of the house is a starting point. A conservatory or greenhouse is often positioned at the back or side for privacy, and its layout and design are influenced by factors such as access from the house and what space is available. The exposure of a greenhouse is the direction in which most of the glass faces. Unless it faces due south, a lean-to design positioned against one of the house walls is the most restricted, because it will receive the sun's rays for only part of the day. A structure projecting as a wing captures light (and therefore warmth) from more directions, but has extra surfaces to lose heat at night and in winter, and benefits proportionately less from any warmth emitted by the house wall. A greenhouse in an unsheltered site will have particular problems. A windbreak can provide protection but, unless sufficiently distant from the greenhouse, may obstruct winter light.

Latitude also plays a part. The farther from the Equator, the lower the angle of the sun in winter, and therefore the less likely a conservatory or greenhouse, even one with a fairly sunny aspect, will be to gain maximum benefit from its warmth. It is worth looking in turn at some of the pros and cons of the different points of the compass and seeing how they would affect the functioning of a greenhouse. These brief examples assume a standpoint in the northern hemisphere.

Northern exposures

Since they receive no direct light during three months of the winter, arguably the time when light is most needed by both plants and people, north-facing, lean-to greenhouses are often considered to be the least satisfactory. They do, however, have some advantages. In summer, when people with south-facing conservatories have had to invest in shading and need to work hard to ensure a comfortable atmosphere for their plants, owners of north-facing conservatories are able to enjoy cool, more or less trouble-free conditions without expending too much effort. North-facing sunrooms, then, are worth considering as long as the lack of winter sunshine is appreciated from the outset. They would be more expensive to heat without help from the sun and would be best run on a cool or just frost-free winter minimum. Plant choice would need to be tailored to suit but it is potentially rich. It might include a collection of different-colored Cape primrose (streptocarpus), which suffer in hot temperatures and, like most other gesneriads, will need considerable shade from hot sun. Other candidates are those plants that can take a winter rest at low temperatures, coming into growth and flowering during spring and summer. Among these are sun-loving tender plants which could be placed outside in a brighter spot for the summer. Combine these, for winter interest, with shade-loving plants capable of tolerating low temperatures (a collection of ivies, ferns, fatsia, fatshedera, some bamboos, *Daphne odora*, and some palms, for instance).

Southern exposures

A sunny, southern exposure has enormous advantages in winter, to be set against the difficulties of controlling excess heat in high summer. For those who want to sit and enjoy winter sunshine, this aspect is ideal, to be bettered only by a structure positioned on a corner which manages to face both southeast and southwest, giving a long stretch of brightness from sunrise to sunset. The sun's warmth will reduce heating bills substantially, so this aspect would be ideal for a warmer conservatory. To avoid disappointment, though, it is necessary to take into account the lower angle of winter sun, an issue which becomes more important the farther north one lives. Trees and buildings, such as the house next door, could seriously diminish light received by the glass. Conversely, deciduous trees that cast welcome shade in summer would be leafless, allowing winter sun to reach the conservatory. None the less, this is by far the most favorable exposure to keep plants from sunny, warm climates healthy and flourishing all winter.

Eastern exposures

During summer, this exposure combines the attributes of receiving soft morning light excellent for plant growth, then becoming shaded from harsher afternoon light. Winter light, though, is poor, imposing the same sort of restrictions as a north-facing sunroom. One solution, given sufficient space, would be to run the long axis of the sunroom east to west at right angles to the east-facing wall of the house. Provided nearby buildings offered no obstruction, the sunroom would then absorb light along its south-facing side. In exposed areas this exposure risks the disadvantage of cold east winds taking heat away from the glass and raising heating bills. Unless the site was sheltered and the glass double-glazed, a cool or frost-free sun porch would be the most feasible option.

Western exposures

During summer, intense afternoon sun could easily scorch plants and full provision for shading and reducing temperatures would need to be made, as with a southern exposure. In winter, light would shine in, through the side rather than the roof, all afternoon until the sun sets. The heat absorbed would warm the conservatory for the evening and cut down on heating bills, making this a good candidate for warmer minimum temperatures. An additional bonus of a west-facing conservatory is the opportunity to enjoy pretty sunsets, provided the view westward is open rather than obscured.

Light and shade

It is vital to become thoroughly acquainted with the changing patterns of light and shade in your sunroom or greenhouse. Location, and the proportion of glass in the design, are the main influences on the amount of light available; this may be affected by shade cast by nearby buildings or by trees and shrubs at various times of the day and of the year. Predicting these fluctuations makes it possible to plan shading and ventilation strategies and also to help with siting plants, all of which have their own optimum light levels.

Meeting plants' needs

Bear plants' preferences for light or shady conditions in mind when choosing what to grow and when positioning plants. Some have a confirmed preference for shade. On the whole, green-leaved foliage plants with their origins in tropical jungles are least tolerant of direct light: make sure they are placed in shade as dense as that provided by the tree canopy in their native habitat.

Sun-loving climbers trained overhead may themselves act as shading for the other plants below. Evergreens or semi-evergreens such as thunbergia and passiflora need light to flower well, and can be thinned to allow more light to penetrate in winter. Deciduous climbers such as grape vines shed their leaves and allow precious rays of winter sun to break through to the understory. Depending on exposure and latitude, however, even these climbers may need some light shading in summer.

RIGHT Fabric roller blinds fitted inside the glass are the ideal solution for unusually shaped windows which would be difficult to shade from the outside. The blinds can be raised selectively as the sun moves around the sunroom, providing cool oases for plants and people.

FAR RIGHT Many climbers are tolerant of bright light. In their native habitats they climb mighty trees, flowering only when the upper parts of their stems reach sunlight unfiltered by leaves and branches. We can capitalize on this characteristic in the sunroom by using climbers to provide shade for plants below.

LEFT Exterior blinds are a traditional form of shading and there are a number of good arguments in their favor. In this sunroom a simple arrangement of wood strips shields the glass on the outside, deflecting bright light from the sun and preventing rapid temperature rises while creating an attractive dappled effect underneath.

Only well-adapted plants such as succulents, with their swollen stems and often reduced or waxy-coated leaves, will survive a position in direct summer sunlight. Other plants – even sun-lovers – begin to wilt despite being well watered, as they cannot keep pace with the excessive moisture loss through their leaves, and their foliage eventually becomes yellow and scorched. Raising humidity offers some remedy, but avoid spraying water on plants in full sun, as the water droplets act like magnifying glasses, intensifying the sun's rays and causing burn marks.

Be prepared to move plants around if they show signs of receiving too much or too little light. Signs of deprivation include long, drawn-out growth, weak stems, and refusal to flower.

Providing shade

Any sunroom or greenhouse receiving direct light during summer is going to require shading. Without this, temperatures will soar upward and become unbearable for both plants and people. Special glass can cut down the glare and heat, but a cooling system will be needed to prevent the sun's heat from raising temperatures excessively.

The ideal shading system is one that can respond quickly to changing light levels during the day. This means that plants receive the shade they need, but during dull periods maximum light can enter to great benefit. Shading should be applied or fitted to both roof and any sides which face the sun. Exterior shading is most effective because it intercepts the sun's rays before they pass through the glass and heat the interior. Shading on the inside cuts down on uncomfortable glare, but needs even more emphasis on good ventilation and the provision of humidity to succeed in lowering temperatures.

Exterior shading

The simplest and cheapest expedient is to paint the outside of the glass with a shading compound for use on sunrooms or greenhouses. These products are simple to spray on or apply with a soft broom in spring,

and relatively easy to clean off in fall. Choose the kind that remains white and opaque when dry but becomes transparent when wet, so that extra light can penetrate on dull rainy days. Perhaps the least appealing aesthetically, this purely functional solution can be useful to protect plants while waiting – or saving up – for a set of more attractive fitted blinds. It could also be appropriate in a conservatory where a dense curtain of climbing plants keeps it unobtrusive and makes other shading devices impractical.

Exterior blinds are effective in keeping sunlight from warming the interior; conversely, they also have some potential to keep heat in on winter nights by acting as insulation. Their straightforward rectangular shapes are practical only on simple pitched roofs, and they are not recommended in windy areas or in those areas which experience heavy snowfalls. Usually of a roller or Venetian type, they are made of light materials – thin plastic or wooden slats, for instance – which can ride easily over open roof vents. Exterior blinds are designed to be raised and lowered by hand or by a light-triggered electric motor, although this can entail potentially cumbersome fittings on the ridge of the roof. They are not, however, compatible with cold, bright climates where shading is needed in early spring when heavy snows and frosts can still be expected, as these may jam and damage the shading and its mechanisms.

Interior shading

Blinds that fit individual windows in roof and walls and that can be operated independently offer the greatest flexibility and, with their tailored look, enhance architectural forms. The practicality and expense of having an ornately shaped conservatory fitted with a complete set of blinds is something to be considered in the planning and budgeting stages. With Venetian blinds, complete automation is possible, louvers being opened or closed by means of an electric motor triggered by either a photoelectric cell or a thermostat. Venetian blinds are also ideal as part of a fully integrated computer-operated system. Alternatively, these blinds can be operated by hand. Because they are fixed permanently, they have the disadvantage of cutting out some light in winter.

Roller blinds can be operated manually or automatically. Off-white or pale, straw-toned materials are preferable to harsher blue, red, and green, which discolor both plants and people beneath them and absorb light rather than reflecting it. Traditional linen and rattan have inspired many imitations, including synthetic fabrics which can be cut into virtually any shape. Specialist manufacturers offer a wide range of materials. Sophisticated combinations of synthetic fabric and metal give relief from heat and light, while allowing visibility from the inside and privacy from the outside during daylight.

Effective, attractive shading in the form of curtains can be accomplished without spending a fortune by those who are gifted with invention and flair. A fabric shop is often a good source of inexpensive, light, translucent fabric; fitted with rings and suspended on wires, this can be stretched as awnings overhead and hung as curtains around the sides, to be pulled back and forth with a long pole. The simple effect of such curtaining is perhaps at its most successful in conservatories that are less complicated in shape.

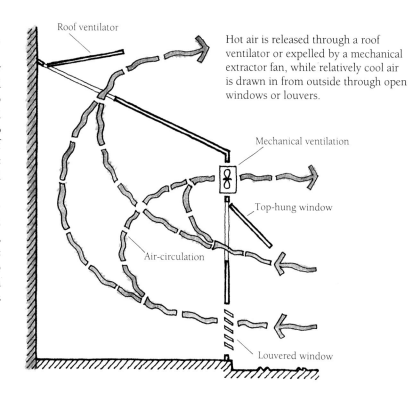

Hot air is released through a roof ventilator or expelled by a mechanical extractor fan, while relatively cool air is drawn in from outside through open windows or louvers.

Ventilation

Ventilation designed to meet the needs of plants often comes low on the priority list of sunroom architects and manufacturers. An efficient system of ventilation is essential both to control temperature overall, and to keep plants healthy by providing fresh air and modifying humidity. Fortunately, where a sunroom has been constructed without adequate vents, it is often possible to replace individual panes of glass with louvers, and to increase the movement of air by installing fans.

Vents positioned in both roof and sides are of paramount importance. The sunnier a site, the more ventilation is needed. On a sunny day temperatures can quickly soar to well over 100°F(38°C) unless vents are open and shading provided. Since heat rises, roof ventilation is necessary to allow hot air to escape, teamed with vents positioned in the lower part of the sides or walls to draw cooler air in. (Make sure, however, that louver designs are draft-free when closed, particularly if situated on a side of a sunroom exposed to cold winds.)

Ventilation that is automatically activated by temperature changes is essential for homes where no one is around to open and close the vents by hand whenever necessary. Simple, unobtrusive automatic controls can be fitted to any vents, including louvers. They can usually be pre-set to work within a given range of temperatures, and most open at about 55°F(13°C).

Plants kept in cold and cool houses really need ventilating at lower temperatures than these, particularly during mild winter periods. Ventilation is needed not simply as protection from excessive heat. Plants need a steady supply of fresh air for the carbon dioxide they absorb during daylight; ventilation also helps to mitigate the effects of humidity – moist stale air offers perfect conditions for the spread of fungal diseases such as powdery mildew and botrytis (gray mold). Most automatic devices can be manually operated when desired. However, beware on bright, sunny winter days when the temperature is balmy inside but freezing cold outside; to open vents then would let in blasts of icy air and spell disaster.

Ventilation can also be assisted by fans. Thermostatically controlled extractor fans are valuable for reducing temperature during summer, and they can also be used in winter to circulate fresh air, preventing the atmosphere from becoming damp and stagnant. Extractor fans specially designed for sunroom and greenhouse use run at low speeds and so do not create damaging drafts. Slow-running overhead fans also help air circulation, and portable everyday electric fans are useful provided plants are not positioned directly in their path. In warmer climates air-conditioning can be installed for the benefit of plants and people.

Just as you consider plants' preferences regarding light when arranging them in the sunroom or greenhouse, so sensitivity to drafts must be taken into consideration, and vulnerable plants screened from sources of cold air.

Heating

Temperature, rather than light or humidity, is the criterion by which we describe a sunroom's potential as a growing environment. The minimum winter temperature governs the choice of plants that may thrive. Achieving and maintaining that minimum depends on balancing the heat loss through the fabric of the structure itself against the amount of heat that can feasibly be generated. Greenhouses can be unheated, (below 38°F(3°C), frost-free 38-40°F(3-4°C), cool 40-50°F(4-10°C), temperate 50-60°F(10-16°C) or warm 60°F(16°C) and over.

Given that sunrooms have by definition large expanses of glass, a notably poor insulator, and that heating is almost universally expensive, it makes sense wherever possible to design a sunroom specifically with a temperature range in mind. Initial outlay and operating costs for a plant-worthy conservatory maintained at constant warm levels will thus both be high. If funds are modest, consider a single-glazed sun porch – unheated, or warmed just enough to keep out frosts. It will still provide an environment where judiciously chosen plants can flourish and give pleasure.

When managing an existing sunroom, a thermometer capable of registering maximum and minimum temperatures is a vital piece of equipment. In winter it will provide proof of whether the heating system is capable of raising the temperature of a large volume of air sufficiently quickly on cold nights. During summer high readings will warn of inadequate shading and ventilation.

Minimizing heat loss

Apart from siting the greenhouse to take full advantage of any winter sunshine and avoid cold winds, most measures to conserve heat consist of some form of insulation. The heat loss through a single layer of glass is enormous. Makeshift improvements to single glazing, such as lining with sheets of bubble plastic, obscure light and entail side-effects such as condensation. Insulation by means of double or triple glazing results in a slight loss of light, but appreciably less heat loss. Drawing blinds or curtains on winter nights also helps keep warmth in.

For sunrooms used as home extensions, heating is important to create a warm atmosphere for family use year-round. A sturdier construction can support the extra weight of double glazing; any low base walls can themselves be insulated, and heat escape through the floor can be cut by incorporating an insulating layer at the building stage. The same construction details would be needed for a sunroom or greenhouse used to grow tropical plants, with added provision for high humidity.

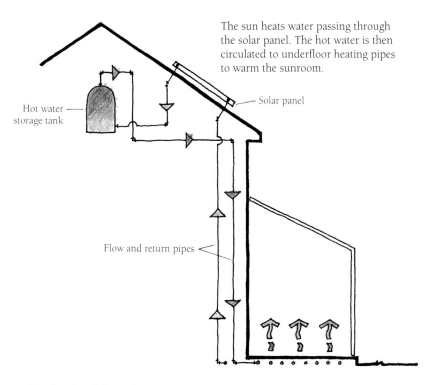

The sun heats water passing through the solar panel. The hot water is then circulated to underfloor heating pipes to warm the sunroom.

Hot water storage tank

Solar panel

Flow and return pipes

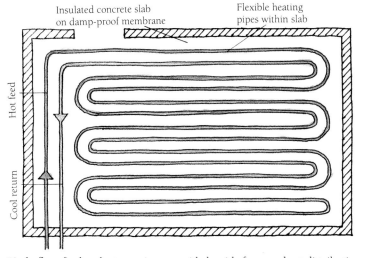

Insulated concrete slab on damp-proof membrane

Flexible heating pipes within slab

Hot feed

Cool return

Underfloor feed and return pipes run side by side for even heat distribution.

Methods of heating

If you are adding a sunroom to your home, the best option is to extend an existing central heating system into the sunroom, providing a separate thermostat so that it is possible to keep up heat levels in the garden area during winter nights when much of the central heating in the main house may switch off. Separate thermostatically controlled gas boilers which have outside balanced flues are an effective and reliable alternative.

Underfloor heating is also a good addition to a conventional system. Flexible piping carrying hot water from a boiler is laid, snake-fashion, on an insulating layer to stop heat loss into the ground, beneath a solid finish such as tiles. Pleasant for feet and roots alike, this warm floor can even double as a large and versatile plant incubator with bottom heat. Pots of seeds or cuttings can be stood on the floor and covered with a glass or plastic case until they have germinated or rooted. Such a floor may be dripped upon with impunity; it may also be spray misted in summer to raise humidity and keep temperatures down.

Another type of underfloor heating can serve as an alternative to radiators or pipes. Here, wider pipes run round the edges and even through the middle of the floor in a channel topped with a decorative grille. Heat is evenly distributed into the room and the channel doubles as a drainage outlet. This is reminiscent of some high Victorian conservatories, where water escaping through ornate gratings onto wide heating pipes made a glorious steam bath, sending up clouds of water vapor to provide plants with humidity. However, many of today's sunrooms and conservatories – full of soft furnishings and linked to the house – cannot be run on these lines; the air must be drier and the plants, from more Mediterranean climates, confined to containers.

Free-standing propane heaters and kerosene heaters have the distinct disadvantage of emitting moisture, and the ventilation they need to prevent condensation and allow escape of fumes reduces their effectiveness. They are, however, handy for use during power outages or other emergencies.

Thermostatically controlled electric fan heaters are a more expensive method of heating a large sunroom, although they are clean, reliable, easy to use, and stir up the air effectively during damp weather. Solar heating is gaining favor, being both economical and ecologically sound. Particularly effective in brighter, warmer countries, it should be designed into the structure of the sunroom from the outset

Water and humidity

A conservatory or greenhouse designed specifically for plants is an environment where water has a considerably higher profile than one which people use as an extra living room. Every plant needs water in some measure, and most require a certain amount of moisture in the air; indeed some will thrive only in a very humid atmosphere. Providing the correct humidity levels for plants is as important as supplying the right amount of light and the correct temperature range. Unless a greenhouse has a solid floor which slopes almost imperceptibly toward a drain, and contains nothing likely to be harmed by moisture, it is better to eschew large numbers of plants from jungle-like habitats that need frequent spraying, and to opt for those from more Mediterranean-type climates, whose requirements can be met in ways more compatible with living-room conditions. Of course, even in a room designed for people, plants that enjoy the same growing conditions can be grouped in attractive displays that facilitate localized watering and misting.

Water supply
Plan the water supply and any special drainage provision for the greenhouse at the outset. Although the main water supply is reliable, it is often cold and in many areas alkaline or "hard". Most plants prefer water at room temperature and some insist on it, responding with leaf spots, poor health, and inability to flower if subjected to icy-cold water. Therefore, leave water to stand in small cans or small covered tanks to bring it up to room temperature to keep these plants happy.

Rhododendrons and most ericas, as well as gardenias and boronias, are acid-lovers and prefer soft water. Failure to supply this can result in mineral deficiencies, mostly of iron, which shows itself in yellowing leaves. To grow such acid-loving plants in any number, it is worth considering collecting rainwater from roof gutters and storing it in an underground tank, from which it can be pumped up for use.

Watering systems
Most conservatories house mixed collections of plants from all over the world. They are different sizes and ages and will have been established in their pots for varying lengths of time. Individual hand watering will suit them best, but is time-consuming. The alternative is to install one of the various automatic watering systems available. These work well with plants of similar size, type, and stage of development, but mixed collections need careful monitoring. Watering systems can be linked to the main water supply, or to a header tank that is topped up manually. Computers installed between the main water supply and the system can be set to turn the water on at given times for specific durations.

For plants spread about on tables, plant stands, and the floor, a system of piped drippers supplied to all the pots can be effective, though the thin tubes can be unattractive. Fine tunings can be effected by adjusting the number of drippers feeding each pot. Staging or benches can be spread with capillary matting (or equipped with trays of moist sand). Plant roots can draw the water they need from this constantly moist surface, but should never be waterlogged. Plastic pots are ideal; clay pots should have a capillary wick tucked into the hole in the base, to link soil with wet matting.

So-called self-watering pots involve modified containers with reservoirs for water, which can be topped up to last longer than usual. Better than these, and the ultimate long-term solution for some plants, particularly those which will remain in the same pot for a long period, are hydroponic systems.

Where moisture-loving plants are grown in profusion, it is essential to have a practical means of raising humidity in the air. In this fern-filled indoor grotto, the floor can be spray misted thoroughly and regularly. Water can drain away through gratings onto underfloor heating pipes.

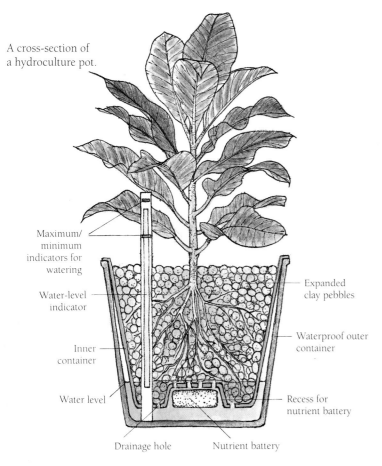

A cross-section of
a hydroculture pot.

Maximum/
minimum
indicators for
watering

Water-level
indicator

Inner
container

Water level

Drainage hole

Expanded
clay pebbles

Waterproof outer
container

Recess for
nutrient battery

Nutrient battery

Hydroponic systems

Hydroculture is the ultimate solution for those who have never mastered correct watering techniques, as all guesswork is removed. This is a method of growing plants in a solution of water and nutrients. To replace the physical support offered by soil, they are potted into sterile, chemically neutral clay pebbles. A water-level indicator monitors how much water sits in the base of the container. Plant roots have access to this, but the clay pebbles can draw moisture up by capillary action. Air in the spaces around the pebbles keeps plant roots healthy, but they also become fleshier than normal and can actually take air from the water. It is better to use plants which have been raised hydroponically from the start, but plants grown ordinarily in soil will adjust.

Start off with young, healthy plants wherever possible. Remove from the pot and stand in lukewarm water for about half an hour, then wash all the soil away carefully. Prepare the pebbles by washing and soaking in water. Specially designed double containers from hydroculture suppliers are ideal. Here, the plant is potted into the inner container, which has slits around the sides as well as holes in the base. Clay pebbles are used in much the same way as soil, with a layer in the bottom, then as filling around the plant. The water-level indicator is inserted into the side of this pot; some units have cartridges of slow-release nutrients which fit underneath. This inner pot is then fitted into the outer, waterproof container so that there is a gap in the bottom where roots can grow out through the holes into the reservoir of water

and nutrients. If a fertilizer cartridge is not integral, sprinkle a special slow-release fertilizer from the hydroculture supplier over the surface of the pebbles; this will last for four to six months. Pour lukewarm tap-water slowly over the surface of the pebbles until the level indicator reads maximum. Wait until the level reads minimum before watering again. It is possible to use large containers filled with several plants in this way, or even to have plants growing hydroponically in a raised bed.

Controlling humidity

Most plants, unless they originate from arid or dry mountainous regions of the world, are accustomed to growing in humid conditions, enjoying the moisture given off by other plants and soil. In the conservatory or greenhouse during summer, temperature rises need to be met with increased humidity. Should the air remain hot and dry, plants are placed under stress because they lose moisture from their leaves faster than they can take it up through their roots. This imbalance can cause wilting, even if the soil is moist. Controlling humidity consists partly of reducing ambient temperatures and partly of adding more moisture to the air.

Temperature reduction is mostly achieved by attention to ventilation and shading. Increasing humidity can be accomplished in a variety of ways. A greenhouse with a solid floor can have its floor and benches hosed and the foliage of plants shaded from the sun misted gently from the underside. Automatic misting devices are available which can be operated by a timer or, even better, actually triggered by falling levels in humidity. In a sunroom where floorings and furnishings are not waterproof, a humidifier is the answer.

On a much smaller scale, foliage plants can be hand-misted regularly. Grouping plants together means that they benefit one another by collectively giving off moisture from leaves and soil. This works even better if plant pots are stood on shallow trays of pebbles. Top the trays up with water to keep them moist, but not so deeply that the plants are standing in water. The trays of pebbles can make an attractive feature in themselves, with interesting stones and shells visible between the pots. Like water in bowls, tanks, or ponds, this all helps to raise humidity.

Humidity should not be encouraged at night or during winter, particularly in frost-free, cool, or temperate sun porches where the temperature remains below 60°F(16°C). Plants will be more prone to botrytis (gray mold), rotting, and the effects of over-watering if their atmosphere is dank and cold. Watering and spraying should be carried out during the morning, leaving the rest of the day for excessive humidity to dry off.

Water features

Pools, even small ones, make an important contribution to maintaining humidity in a conservatory. They can be very attractive and provide an opportunity for a display of water plants (see pp.174-9). Moving water exerts additional fascination, and small fountains are easy to install. The principle can be adapted as part of a planting display – such as a fern grotto in a suitably waterproofed and shady corner, with ferns and selaginellas growing out of pockets in the rock. Water dribbles down the "walls" of the grotto and is filtered through stones at the base, to be collected and pumped back up.

Landscaping

The success of a sunroom or greenhouse is determined as much by the skill employed in its landscaping and decoration, as by the health and vigor of its plants. Whether this is to consist of a few containers or a grandiose scheme involving rock and water, some decisions need to be made at the planning stages. There is no use having vague dreams of jungle-like profusion, with rampant climbers adorning the eaves, if no provision is made for them from the outset. Some plants need a deep root run in order to achieve their full potential and beds to contain these should be marked out in the floor of a greenhouse before a solid base is installed. On the other hand, many plants of tree-like proportions will grow successfully in containers, and the desire to be surrounded by plants can be fulfilled by grouping and combining plants on different levels without major structural upheaval.

Designing with plants

Consider making compositions with plants. A large, bold specimen in a splendid pot might stand on its own, but anyone enthusiastic about plants will want to grow a great variety, and organizing them in a way that suits their various needs and makes the best use of space is a challenge. A mere collection of too many separate items can look cluttered and confusing unless arranged according to some kind of logic. A composition could be a cluster of plants in different pots that look good together, on the floor or on top of pieces of furniture. Sections of "landscape", where functional elements such as containers and growing medium are concealed by trailing greenery, pebbles, or some other natural material, are effective. Not only do well-placed groupings look good, but they can benefit the plants too. Naturally, a grouping that shared the same planting trough or gravel tray would need to enjoy similar cultivation conditions, so watering and spraying tasks would be streamlined. Grouping is also the answer to displaying small but interesting plants that might otherwise pass unnoticed. It suits desert dwellers like cacti and succulents which will thrive in a sunny corner and need special treatment, and curiosities like epiphytic plants, which can be set up to grow on tree branches as they do in nature (see p.19).

Plant displays can be given attractive settings to show them off. *Trompe l'œil* painted on an adjacent wall can be fun, especially as a background for plantings of cacti. Behind the real plants, others depicted on the wall gradually recede into a pictorial desert landscape. Be on the look-out for *objets d'art* to hide among the plants. In a small sunroom a mirror concealed behind plants and ornaments will make the space seem larger and double the apparent depth of the planting. The mirror should be large and fill the wall or echo the shape of an arch to be effective; because it is to be partially masked by foliage, the imperfections of an inexpensive second-hand one will not show.

Props from junk shops and architectural salvage companies – or modern reproductions – can make witty and flattering additions to a planting display and are invaluable for raising plants to different heights. Sometimes they can enhance the ethos of a "traditional" style of conservatory: a glimpse of a piece of classical masonry draped with ivy behind the oleanders and myrtles in a design based on an orangery; a wrought-iron extravaganza swathed in ferns in a Victorian-style conservatory; in other instances they can allude to the style of planting: a lacquer screen as backdrop to oriental bamboos, rattan with tropical rainforest plants, and so on.

Pots and other containers

Any type of container can be considered as a vessel for plants. Old urns, teapots, baskets lined with plastic, copper cauldrons, glass dishes, and even old, hollowed out tree stumps can be used for planting. There need not be drainage holes if a good 1-3in(2.5-8cm) layer of pebbles is placed in the base to act as a reservoir for excess water. The succulent *Ceropegia linearis* ssp. *woodii* (*C. woodii*) will grow in the same tall clay jar with no drainage hole for many years, with its slender stems trailing down for 6ft(1.8m) or more. Plant stands, *jardinières,* and chimney pots are also useful to accommodate trailing plants or to raise particularly attractive smaller specimens to eye level. Baby's tears (*Soleirolia soleirolii*) creeping over the edges of a pot is ideal for this sort of treatment.

Free-standing terracotta pots of various shapes and sizes always make attractive containers for plants. They can be judiciously arranged with larger glazed pots, wooden kegs and half-barrels, although too many contrasting shapes and textures will look messy and cluttered. The overall effect, though mixed, should be harmonious and in keeping with the style of furnishing.

Larger pots can hold several different kinds of plant, chosen because they share the same cultural requirements as well as complementing one another's shape, color of foliage, and flowers. Temporary mixtures of plants can be left in their individual pots and plunged in pebbles or soil. However, if left too long, great wads of roots begin to grow through the base of each pot, making them difficult to move. Large specimens which rise up on a trunk can be underplanted with creeping foliage or with flowering plants which will cover the soil and make a very attractive carpeting surface.

In most sunrooms, pots will have to stand on saucers or trays to catch excess water and keep the floor clean. Make sure these are large enough. Small ones look apologetic, and encourage people to add insufficient water, for fear of its overflowing. Make them into useful and attractive features, filled with moist pebbles or gravel to help raise humidity. Self-watering pots and hydroponic units may be more expensive initially, but are neat and self-contained as well as cutting down on maintenance (see p.15).

Planting beds

Ideally, beds are planned for at the outset, leaving strategically placed gaps in the floor when it is laid. These need not be large. In a small sunroom or conservatory pockets just 18-24in(45-60cm) square are sufficient to give the key climbers a far better root run than any large pot or raised bed. Beds can be accentuated by changing the flooring material around them to make a decorative edge. Indeed, they can be framed with a row or two of bricks to give greater depth and bring small plants into better view.

Fully raised beds are a good alternative and can more easily be added as an afterthought. If they are to be positioned against an existing house

The illustration above depicts an ideal sunroom which is south- or west-facing, cool – 40-50°F (4-10°C) – and well-ventilated. Its features include an overhead paddle fan, hanging baskets, a washstand for plant displays, a bed located in the floor, a window shelf for plants, and a sitting area. Specimen plants give character and focus, while climbers and trailing plants provide a framework, introducing balance and definition by adorning the vertical dimensions, cascading from the hanging baskets and tumbling from the shelf and washstand. Smaller flowering and foliage plants fill the gaps, adding color and completing the leafy backdrop.

1 *Strelitzia reginae*
2 *Agave americana* 'Marginata'
3 *Farfugium tussilagineum* 'Aureomaculatum'
4 *Metrosideros kermadecensis* 'Variegatus'
5 *Pittosporum tobira*
6 *Tibouchina* 'Jules'
7 *Campsis × tagliabuana* 'Madame Galen'
8 *Trachelospermum jasminoides*
9 *Hardenbergia violacea*
10 *Passiflora caerulea*
11 *Bougainvillea*
12 *Hoya carnosa*
13 *Chlorophytum comosum* 'Vittatum'
14 *Ceropegia linearis* ssp. *woodii*
15 *Platycerium* hybrid
16 *Hedera helix*
17 *Saxifraga stolonifera*
18 *Sedum morganianum*
19 *Tradescantia fluminensis* 'Quicksilver'
20 *Punica granatum* var. *nana*
21 *Eucomis bicolor*
22 *Cryptanthus* – various
23 *Boronia* 'Southern Star'
24 *× Fatshedera lizei*
25 *Ferns* – various
26 *Maurandya scandens*
27 *Tulbaghia violacea*
28 *Liriope muscari variegata*

LEFT In this handsome sunroom, water features, impressive urns and planters, and attractive furniture are combined to make a magnificent setting for plants. Here, clivia and azalea are massed beside a rectangular pool, to spectacular effect. The use of decorative pots and planters can be emulated in smaller, less grand sunrooms.

RIGHT In this small sunroom the plants have been skilfully chosen and allowed to grow unchecked into a glorious profusion. Leaf texture – thick waxy hoya, long stems of small columnea leaves, soft foliage of sparmannia and pelargonium – is as important in this composition as the flowers provided by the lilies and angel's trumpets. Soon, though, some selective pruning will be needed to maintain this effect.

FAR RIGHT Here, epiphytic cacti and bromeliads grow much as they would in the wild, attached to a tree branch. These bromeliad "trees" make imposing features, especially when, after a couple of years' growth, the plants develop into large clumps.

or conservatory wall, this needs to be waterproofed, or a separate wall built. The raised bed must have provision for water to drain out of the side, or be lined with a deep layer of pebbles to act as a reservoir for excess water. An alternative would be to run an entire bed according to hydroponics techniques.

Raised beds, like large containers and troughs, bring the planting level more comfortably within reach at sitting height, which allows interesting plant details to be appreciated, and also helps with maintenance. With plants growing in beds of any size, caring for them quickly becomes a matter of full-scale gardening, as opposed to the simpler chores involved when tending plants in individual pots.

Staging and benches

Where sunrooms are built primarily as house extensions, plants have to fit in around furnishings. Staging and benches, which are standard items in greenhouses, are less popular for sunroom use on account of the space they occupy. This is a pity, as they provide great scope for creating artistic arrangements of plants, often in tiers. Here, the smaller flowering and foliage plants, particularly, can be banked into masses of color and greenery. Smaller plants can be raised up, if necessary, by standing them on upturned pots. Never cram plants in, but space generously so that the foliage of one plant just brushes that of its neighbor. As they grow, continuous respacing and re-arranging will be necessary and this should

become part of the maintenance routine.

Old-fashioned Victorian plant benches were often beautiful objects in themselves, but original cast-iron benches are very hard to find and reproductions expensive. Modern-day benches are more likely to be made of wood or aluminum. Aluminum legs, particularly, tend to be utilitarian and ugly. One solution is to conceal them with brick pillars, so that the bench appears to be sitting on the bricks. The pillars can even be allowed to continue upward to provide a support for climbers. Match the brick with that used, perhaps, for a nearby raised bed.

The object is to grow such a profusion of plants that little of the support system is visible. Succulents, bulbs, and other plants which need good drainage prefer to stand on slats so that water has free escape. Those that enjoy good drainage but love humidity can be stood on trays of gravel. Thirsty plants would appreciate capillary matting. In the space beneath eye-level plants, beds of ferns and other shade-loving foliage plants can be grown and will contribute to a humid atmosphere.

If plant benches seem too formal, plants can be grouped on other surfaces. Tables, chests, even old tiled washstands can also be used to gain height. An old dresser could be stood against the back wall and colonized with plants. Train the twining stems of ivy, kangaroo vine (*Cissus antarctica*), and sweetheart plant (*Philodendron scandens*) around its shelves, securing them now and again to small nails. During summer, climbers such as purple bellflower (*Rhodochiton atrosanguineus*), canary

creeper (*Tropaeolum peregrinum*), and *Mina lobata* can be added for their flowers, and can use the foliage plants as their climbing frame.

The vertical dimension

There are so many lovely climbers to grow that even a small sunroom or greenhouse should not be without one or two of the more restrained types. In a large space, extra vertical room can be made for them by creating additional uprights. As well as walls and wires, they can be offered brick or wooden pillars up which to climb. Choose materials in harmony with the style of sunroom or greenhouse and with other fittings. Pillars can rise up from the edges of raised beds, with wooden beams overhead to make an indoor pergola. Bougainvillea, hoya, *Petrea volubilis,* or passion flowers could make this their home, wreathing it with their stems and dangling their flowers down to be admired. Trellis attached to walls makes the training of climbing plants a lot easier, as stems can be neatly tied in, obviating the need for nails and wire. Free-standing trellis also makes a useful screen to divide up larger sunrooms or greenhouses into separate compartments.

Other vertical features add interest to plant displays. Epiphytic plants such as some ferns, orchids, and bromeliads can be "planted" to grow as they would in the wild. One method is to find an old tree branch or log and to set this in the ground at its most attractive angle. This might require concrete, or may be anchored by digging a hole, positioning the base of the branch, then compacting large chunks of rubble around the base to secure it. A more formal alternative is to make a column by securing a length of wide plastic pipe into the ground, then binding sphagnum moss around it using nylon fishing line. Lower mounds, rather like tree stumps, can be made from chicken-wire frameworks similarly covered with sphagnum moss. Even better would be a real old tree stump, dried off for a period, then set into the bed.

Plants can be attached to these "trees" by taking them out of their pots, gently removing excess soil and binding them to their support. Tie moist moss in place first, gently hold the roots against this, cover them with another handful of moss, and secure with nylon line. This works effectively for epiphytic aroids such as anthurium as well as ferns like davallia, some orchids, and bromeliads. Plants like epipremnum and philodendron can be planted against the base and will quickly climb, clinging with their aerial roots. Attach air plants (*Tillandsia* spp.) to the upper parts of "trees" so that drips will not land on them. As they have no root systems and absorb all that they need from the air about them (see pp.47-8), they should not be attached with moss. Instead, use a special type of non-toxic adhesive available from air-plant specialists. This sets slowly, so secure the plant in place with cotton thread while the glue strengthens. An alternative to glue is to tie them in place permanently using mono-filament; the barely visible threads hold the delicate plants in place, with less likelihood of their being accidentally knocked off.

Plant care

Gardening in a sunroom or greenhouse offers wonderful advantages: for while the outdoor garden may be at the mercy of the climate, within the shelter provided by the glass roof and walls of the greenhouse the gardener can create ideal conditions for plants. However, this also has its down side. In this protected environment all plant needs have to be met by the gardener rather than by natural sources, and many conditions are exaggerated to extreme proportions. No rain falls in a greenhouse and roots, even in borders, are more restricted. The air is.generally less humid and there are far greater and more rapid fluctuations in temperature. During summer the glare of the sun can scorch leaves which have grown delicate, yet in winter glass reduces the amount of light able to penetrate. Outside, most plants can survive adequately with minimal additions of fertilizer to the soil, but inside, the supply of nutrients available in any planting medium is quickly exhausted, and plants will stop growing if supplementary fertilizer is not given.

To some, the ownership of a greenhouse marks the fulfilment of a specific gardening ambition. Here, at last, is the ideal vehicle to house their beloved collection of tender plants. To them, cultivating those plants will be much more of a pleasure than a hardship. Their previous experience of plant care will give them a head start as they explore the new environment. However, the sunroom owner who merely wants a pretty house extension, and has chosen plants primarily as green decoration, may have a lot to learn. For plants are *not* just ornaments and can decline quickly unless given the right treatment.

There is a lot of talk about gifted gardeners having green thumbs. One even hears stories of growers who sing, talk, and play music to their plants in the belief that they will grow better. Even the most sceptical must concede that any ruse which concentrates the mind on the well-being of one's plants must lead to greater observation and thus to a better understanding of their needs.

This is the key point which governs success or failure. Probably more important than technical accuracy is a feeling for plants and an understanding of how they grow. There must be a desire for plants to thrive, so that the sudden unfurling of a new leaf or gradual opening of a flower gives real pleasure. Sheer curiosity can also bring its own rewards. The sunroom gardener who enjoys watching such phenomena is in a good position to monitor any adverse plant behavior.

In the search for information, the technically minded can read book after book on exactly how to water, govern the environment, prune and propagate their plants. What is needed to accompany these hard facts is

The secret of creating and maintaining an attractive sunroom, like this one, lies in providing conditions where the plants will flourish. Having chosen the right plants for the minimum winter temperature, it is important to keep to a regular, workable routine for watering, feeding, and grooming. The rewards of seeing plants thrive make these simple tasks seem well worthwhile.

practice at looking after plants themselves. Looking *at* plants is the first step. Learning to be observant is essential. Ultimately, one should only have to make a brief check of the greenhouse to be able to sense whether the atmosphere is too hot and dry or too damp and cold. A quick glance around the plants should be all that is needed to detect signs of ill health. Just as people sometimes look tired and ill, so do plants. The limp-leaved, yellowish appearance of an overwatered plant, the starved look of one that is in need of fresh soil, or the drooping leaves of a plant in need of a drink should all be instantly recognizable.

Some plants will probably be sacrificed to inexperience, but realizing why one plant died is part of a learning process which will help others to survive. Choosing the right plant for the greenhouse is important, especially when it comes to matching them with the minimum temperature. Try not to confuse losing plants as a result of bad cultivation techniques with being unable to provide the right conditions for them.

Introducing a workable care routine is vital to the success of the greenhouse and health of plants. The best time to water plants is morning. This means that in summer they are taken care of for most of the day, and in winter, excess moisture has time to dry out before lower night temperatures combine with humidity to produce unfavorably damp conditions. A typical morning routine would start with cleaning dead leaves and flowers off plants. Next, young plants could be spaced farther apart if necessary and others moved around to enhance the appearance of newly opened blooms. Notice any signs of pest and disease while inspecting plants. Sweep up, take trash away, then water as necessary. In summer, either spray mist or improve humidity in other ways, check ventilation and shading according to the weather forecast, and make sure automatic systems are working. Non-automated greenhouses will need checking again in the middle of the day and finally in late afternoon or evening. During fall and winter, it is important to close vents during mid to late afternoon to trap heat from the sun before temperatures begin to drop.

Although this might sound like hard work, the morning tidy-up need only be brief if it is carried out routinely. The rewards include a well-presented greenhouse full of plants basking in good health, and the chance to deal with potential pest and disease problems before they become epidemics. Besides which, puttering in the greenhouse can be a relaxing interlude in a busy day.

Caring for greenhouse plants is fun. The processes are not difficult, yet they are demanding enough to be interesting. Good results will bring a tremendous sense of achievement. Having successfully mastered the art of keeping them alive, it is only a short step to more daring projects. Soon, even a novice will be training standards and trying out some of the many different kinds of propagation. The same basic philosophy of always having the welfare of plants or cuttings firmly in mind will ensure success with the more complicated techniques as well as the simple ones.

Watering

Determining when to water a plant and how much to give it is a skill which comes with practice. The notes in the plant catalog chapters include a broad indication of each plant's preferences and mention any particular likes or dislikes. Unfortunately for the novice greenhouse gardener, there are no definite rules to follow. Requirements will vary according to the type of plant, the length of time it has spent in its pot, the time of year, and the conditions in the greenhouse. Cacti and other succulents can last longer without water than other, leafier plants and during their growing season can wait until at least the top half of the well-drained potting mixture has dried out. They could become totally dry without suffering, provided this neglect did not continue for a long period. At the other end of the scale are plants like maidenhair ferns. At the slightest hint of dryness their fronds begin to shrivel and they may never recover. They require the difficult balance of being constantly moist without becoming waterlogged.

With most plants, the potting mixture should be allowed to dry out on the surface before more water is given. This usually means that roots will be sufficiently moist, but air can circulate in the soil around the roots, enabling them to breathe. If the air spaces around soil particles are constantly filled with water, the roots may suffocate and die. Should this happen, the plant will be unable to take up water and will begin to wilt. At this point, it is easy to mistake these symptoms for underwatering, and to give another, usually fatal, dose of water.

When a plant has been overwatered, act cautiously. Do not remove the plant from its pot to dry out or, worse, repot. Instead, allow at least the surface of the soil to dry out before the next watering. This reduces the risk of further damage to already suffering roots.

When plants are overwintering at low temperatures, they almost stop growing until conditions of improved light and warmth resume in spring. During this period, they cannot be allowed to dry out completely unless they naturally die down to a storage organ. They need to be watered sparingly, allowing the top two-thirds to dry out in between times. This applies to plants such as mandevilla between fall and spring.

A dry, wilting plant where the potting mixture has shrunk away from the sides of the pot needs emergency treatment. Immerse the pot in a bucket of water until bubbles have stopped escaping and the pot and soil feel heavy and saturated.

If a regularly watered plant seems to be suffering from drought, this might be caused by giving too little water too often. Water thoroughly, so that it penetrates to all the roots, with a little excess running out into the saucer. Most plants can be watered from above, but some, notably gesneriads like African violets and Cape primrose, with rosettes of leaves close to the soil's surface, are best watered from below. Fill the saucer with water, emptying any excess after about an hour.

Give plants water at room temperature; this is not particularly important to some plants, but others suffer badly if the water is too cold. Some plants, gardenias and rhododendrons for example, need soft water; collect rainwater or give them cooled, boiled water. Should these plants have to be given hard, alkaline water regularly, use half-strength liquid fertilizer formulated for acid-loving plants. For hydroponics see p.15.

Fertilizers

Newly potted plants usually have enough fertilizer in their soil to last about two to three months. Once this is used up, they require regular fertilizing to maintain healthy growth. The three main chemical elements necessary for plant growth are nitrogen, phosphorus, and potassium. In addition, plants need minor or trace elements, which should also be present in a well-balanced fertilizer. Look on the fertilizer bottle or box for an analysis of the relevant amounts of the major three elements as well as a list of trace elements. Nitrogen (N, nitrates) promotes fresh leafy growth, phosphorus (P, phosphates or phosphoric acid) encourages healthy root systems, and potassium (K, potash) helps the production of flowers and fruit, including the maturing of stems in preparation for flowering. The relative amounts of N:P:K are always listed in the same order, so that one can tell whether the fertilizer is best for leafy foliage plants, is a good all-purpose one, or will encourage a hoya to bloom. Special fertilizers are also available to meet the specific needs of groups of plants like orchids, cacti, and African violets. Generally fertilizers containing varying amounts of NPK are given according to season. During short days plants need less nitrogen and more phosphorus and potash. In spring, as the days lengthen, more nitrogen can be given. Flowering plants require high-potash feeds as their buds form.

Liquid fertilizers

Of all the different methods of applying fertilizers to plants, the most common is liquid feeding, where the fertilizer is diluted with water and applied as the plants are watered. As a general rule, most established plants benefit from a feeding every one or two weeks during the growing season. Where many plants are grown, it saves time to invest in a dilutor or injector. These may vary in size but usually consist of a small drum filled with concentrated liquid fertilizer, fitted between tap and hose, which is calibrated to pick up the right dose of fertilizer into a given pressure of water so that the fertilizer comes out of the hose at the correct dilution rate. Plants should not be fertilized when their soil is already saturated with water, nor when dry, as this might damage the roots. A root system needs to be active in order to benefit from liquid fertilizer. If a plant has been pruned hard, suspend fertilizing until new shoots have begun to sprout.

Foliar fertilizers

Foliar fertilizers are quick-acting tonics which are sprayed onto the leaves and absorbed by them. While for some plants they can be used as a quick pick-me-up, they can be the staple diet for those that grow epiphytically in the wild. Because epiphytes are adapted to growing up in the trees, clinging to branches, or flourishing in niches, they tend not to have such extensive and active root systems as terrestrial plants. As such, they will absorb their food more readily through leaves. Plants with large, smooth leaf surfaces will benefit more from liquid fertilizer than those with succulent or hairy leaves.

Slow-release fertilizers

Finding time to administer fertilizer regularly to a large group of plants is not always possible for a busy person. The solution here is to use slow-release fertilizers in the form of pills, capsules, or spikes. These, pushed into the soil, will release nutrients slowly over three to six months, after which they can be renewed or the plant returned to a regime of liquid fertilizing; or use slow-release fertilizer granules, which can be mixed into potting soil when repotting.

The planting medium

There are many ready-made potting mixtures to choose from, all of which will grow plants well provided they are watered and fertilized correctly. To help the grower, specialized mixtures are available for different groups of plants. Of major importance is acidic soil mix for plants which dislike an alkaline or even neutral soil. The specific needs of aquatic plants, cacti and other succulents, orchids, and African violets are also catered for. Some mixtures are formulated to suit different stages of a plant's development, including seed and cutting starter mixtures.

Choice of general-purpose potting mixture for most plants is largely a matter of personal preference and experimentation. The majority of mixtures fall into one of three categories, and are described as soil- or loam-based, peat-based, or peat substitutes, depending on the material that makes up the greater part of the volume. However they also include varying quantities of nutrients and proportions of other bulk ingredients. Each type of potting mix has its pros and cons, its enthusiasts and its critics; each can be bought ready-made and adapted at home, or mixed from the separate constituents by the gardener.

Soil- or loam-based potting mixtures
Soil mixtures are based on loam, with the addition of coarse aggregates and organic matter. Their particular advantage over soil-less mixtures is that they remain nutritious over a longer period. They also have more weight and substance and so they are often a good choice for large plants, which require a more stable potting medium. Plants that need a winter rest at a low temperature, while being watered very sparingly, are also easier to manage in a soil-based potting mix, as soil mixes shrink less from the sides of the pot, and take up water more readily when the dormant period is over.

The loam in a soil mixture should comprise two parts by bulk sharp sand, two parts silt, and one part clay. Avoid loam that is saline, very acidic, or extremely alkaline. It should not have been treated with herbicides, yet it must be as weed-free as possible, so some form of sterilization is needed. Loam that has been sterilized by steam aeration is preferable to that subjected to the regular steam treatment, as with aeration fewer beneficial organisms are killed and fewer toxic chemical compounds are released.

Rather than using a soil-based potting mix on its own, it is often a good idea to add some extra peat and sharp sand. Three parts by bulk of soil-based potting mix combined with one part of well-moistened medium-grade peat moss and one part of sharp sand will give excellent results and ensure that the mixture is well-drained.

Peat-based mixtures
Mixtures based on granulated peat were developed when the demand from horticulture became too great for loam-based potting mixtures to satisfy. The demand for peat in its turn has led to fears that finite natural resources will be exhausted, and many alternative materials are being explored. All seek to imitate as closely as possible the desirable qualities of peat. Light and reliable, peat-based mixtures suit most plants and are convenient to use. Both moss peat (largely derived from sphagnum moss) and sedge peat (from the decomposed roots of sedges and other plants) are widely used in the planting mediums. Peat is available in various grades: fine is useful for seed starter mixes, medium for most potting mixtures, and coarse grade for epiphytic plants such as orchids and bromeliads. By mixing two or three parts by bulk of peat with one part of coarse sand or medium-grade perlite and adding the appropriate amount of suitable fertilizer and lime, mixtures can be home-made. There are usually several brands of fertilizer on garden-center shelves which can be used as constituents in potting mediums. They should always state how much lime needs to be added to make a neutral, not acidic, mix. Peat is naturally acidic, but by adding specific quantities of lime with the fertilizer mixtures can be balanced to neutral.

Peat substitutes
For conservation reasons or to experiment, some growers like to try the ever-expanding range of alternative bulk materials and to use reduced-peat or completely peat-free soils. Some have coconut fiber as a major constituent. This can make a very good potting medium, though there are two main points to be aware of. Coconut fiber mixes seem to run out of nutrients faster than normal, so fertilizing is of paramount importance, though phosphates tend to be retained for a longer time than normal, so low-phosphate liquid fertilizers are best. Secondly, the surface of the soil appears to be dry when lower levels are still quite moist, which can deceive some growers into over-watering their plants. Potting mixes based on pulverized bark seem to share the problem of low nutrients, making supplementary fertilizing essential. There are various other bulky organic waste materials which have been treated and marketed as planting mediums. Basically, most plants will grow in any neutral, non-toxic substrate if they have access to the correct amount of water and minerals. Certain plants, usually epiphytic, can grow against the surfaces of cork oak sections, tree fern sections, osmunda fiber, or tufa rock, which are fibrous and/or porous, thus allowing roots to penetrate or attach themselves. Carnivorous plants like live sphagnum moss, which absorbs water like a sponge.

Cutting starter mixtures
Cuttings need a well-drained potting medium and equal amounts by bulk of peat (or peat substitute) and sharp sand work well. An alternative to peat is peat-based soil, which offers some nutrients to the developing plants after roots have formed. This is particularly useful to leaf cuttings of streptocarpus, where time must elapse before the individual plantlets can be separated. Fine sand can be substituted for half of the sharp sand. Inert perlite or vermiculite could replace the sand as useful alternatives for keeping the texture open and ensuring good drainage.

Repotting

Sooner or later, every plant will reach the point where it needs a larger pot and fresh soil. Again, there are only general guidelines governing when to pot up, because plants vary according to their type, health, and vigor.

Plants raised from seed or cuttings need to be repotted regularly, so that their roots never become cramped. This would halt their development, possibly resulting in premature flower production before reaching full size. Regular inspections by gently tapping a plant out of its pot should reveal when roots are penetrating to the sides of the pot and time has come for a move.

Once longer-lasting plants reach an appreciable size, they can remain in their pot for several years. Some palms, shrubs, and many foliage plants might last as long as six or seven years before signs of stress – usually yellowing of leaves and a disinclination to grow – signal the need for a larger pot. Sometimes the signs are not so subtle. The large, fleshy root systems of plants like asparagus ferns, sansevieria, and aspidistra often crack their old pots. When transplanting to a larger pot is not practical, top-dressing can be carried out instead. As much soil as possible is broken away from the surface and replaced with a rich potting mix. If this is impossible, remove the plant and cut away some of the old roots, then repot into the same-sized pot.

Pot plants up only when they are in good health and enjoying active growth, otherwise they will not be ready to push new roots out into the fresh soil. If growth and subsequent take-up of water are slow, then there is a danger of the plant dying from overwatering at this stage. For this reason, most plants are repotted during late spring and early summer, when they are in their prime state of growth. Prune first if necessary, potting up only after new growth has started.

How to repot

With a large collection of plants, it is a good idea to have a potting session in late spring. Prepare a clean surface and collect together the potting mixtures required, a selection of clean pots, and a watering can fitted with a misting attachment. The process is simple (see right).

The new pot should be two sizes larger than the old, so that plants move from a 3in(8cm) to a 5in(13cm) pot, a 4in(10cm) to a 6in(15cm), a 5in(13cm) to a 7in(17cm), and so on. These measurements are the diameter at the top of the pot. Attempts to economize on pots and effort by moving a plant from a 3in(8cm) to a 7in(17cm) pot, for example, are likely to be met with failure.

Plastic pots and smaller clay pots do not need crocking but larger clay pots should be crocked by placing pieces of broken pot over the drainage hole, to prevent it from being blocked by the soil. For plants which enjoy good drainage, a layer of pebbles can also be added.

For the less dextrous, there is a method which ensures that no air spaces are left around the old root ball (though this does not work with pot-bound plants). The old pot serves as a mold. Having removed the plant, put the old pot into the new, larger one as shown on p.25. When you take it out, the hole will fit the plant like a glove. This is particularly useful for prickly cacti and plants with low rosettes of leaves.

Repotting a plant
When repotting a small plant, place one hand over the top of the pot, to support the plant and the soil surface. Up-end the pot, tap the rim against the edge of a bench or table, and slide the pot off with the other hand (**a**). Large, stubborn plants are best placed on their sides on the floor. Tap around the rim with a block of wood, and the pot should be loose enough to ease off.

Gently tease out the roots (**b**) to encourage new roots to penetrate the fresh potting mix.

Place some soil in the bottom of the new pot and stand the plant on top (**c**). Add or remove soil until the plant is at the correct height. Fill in around the old root ball, firming gently. The plant should be upright and central in the pot, with the old soil surface just covered by new. Tap the pot gently to settle the soil, then water in (**d**) .

Planting a hanging basket
Stand the basket on a plant pot to hold it steady. Line the base and sides with a generous layer of sphagnum moss (**a**) and half-fill it with potting mix. A 10-12in(25-30cm) basket will hold five 3½in(9cm) pots. Knock the plants out of their pots and plant the pots into the basket (**b**). Fill the basket with soil, firming it gently around the pots, then remove the pots and drop the plants straight into their tailor-made holes (**c**).

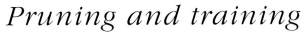

Hanging baskets

This last method can also be used to position plants in hanging baskets filled with potting mix. Choose a basket in scale with the plant, for instance a large 10-12in(25-30cm) basket is ideal for subjects like fuchsia and columnea. Five young plants in 3½in(9cm) pots will be required for one basket. With correct training, the plants will soon spill outward over the edge. Hanging-basket plants set on their edges, although giving a trailing effect more quickly, sometimes leave an ugly gap between the edge and the middle. For carpeted sunrooms, solid plastic baskets with saucers fitted to catch water are a good choice, though wire baskets lined with sphagnum moss are more attractive. Plant saucers can be suspended beneath, to catch drips.

Planting in beds

Before planting, fork the soil over, adding fresh potting mix and slow-release fertilizer if necessary. Plant so that the top of the old soil ball will be level with the surface without burying plant stems or crown, or leaving roots exposed. Small specimens can be arranged informally in groups for greater effect.

Pruning and training

Some greenhouse plants need regular pruning to keep their height and spread under control and others to prevent them from becoming straggly. Others – climbers and plants of lax habit – need to be tied in to supports in order to grow upward and even overhead. Free-standing plants grown in formal shapes are popular for the greenhouse. Ivies and other climbing plants can be trained over hoops of wire into circles and fancy loops. Tightly sheared shrubs in topiary shapes or flowering plants trained as standards make attractive focal points.

Pruning

Major pruning jobs on plants as diverse as bougainvillea and pelargoniums are best tackled in spring, as plants come into growth. However, some shrubs and climbers – *Plumbago auriculata* (*P. capensis*), for instance – can be quite a tangle by the end of summer. The correct pruning time may well be spring, but some thinning and shortening of stems is a good idea for a fall tidy-up. Spring-flowering plants like boronia and cytisus should be pruned immediately after flowering.

In all cases, whether pinching back a shoot tip with finger and thumb or sawing through a thick woody stem, cut above a node. New growth

Identifying a node
When pruning a stem, always cut above a node, that is, the point from which a leaf grows or used to grow. This is often indicated by a slight swelling.

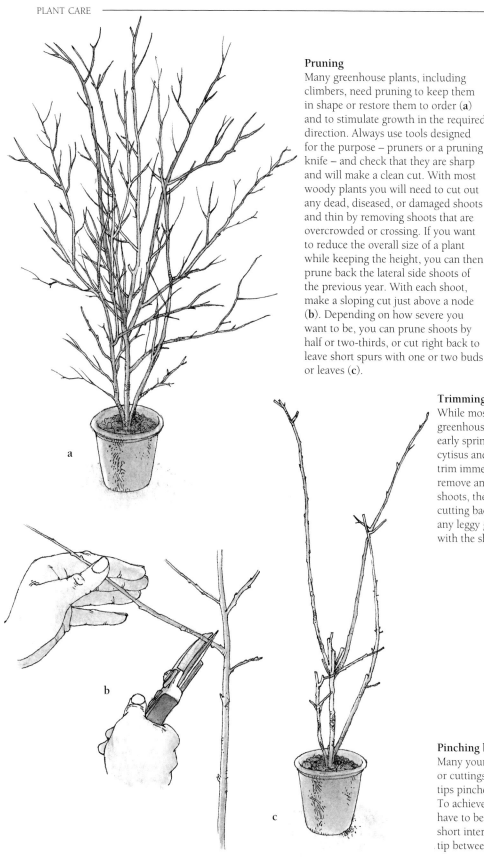

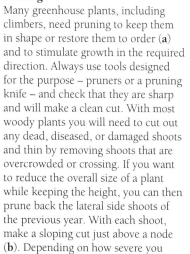

Pruning

Many greenhouse plants, including climbers, need pruning to keep them in shape or restore them to order (**a**) and to stimulate growth in the required direction. Always use tools designed for the purpose – pruners or a pruning knife – and check that they are sharp and will make a clean cut. With most woody plants you will need to cut out any dead, diseased, or damaged shoots and thin by removing shoots that are overcrowded or crossing. If you want to reduce the overall size of a plant while keeping the height, you can then prune back the lateral side shoots of the previous year. With each shoot, make a sloping cut just above a node (**b**). Depending on how severe you want to be, you can prune shoots by half or two-thirds, or cut right back to leave short spurs with one or two buds or leaves (**c**).

Trimming

While most major pruning of greenhouse plants is best undertaken in early spring, some plants, such as cytisus and boronia, benefit from a trim immediately after flowering. Just remove any dead, damaged, or diseased shoots, then trim the plant all over (**d**), cutting back the flowering stems and any leggy growth until you are satisfied with the shape (**e**).

Pinching back

Many young plants grown from seed or cuttings need to have their growing tips pinched back to induce bushiness. To achieve a rounded shape, this may have to be done two or three times at short intervals. Pinch back the growing tip between finger and thumb (**f**).

will invariably arise from this point. Where considerable height reduction is needed (with a large yucca, for example), then cut low down on the stem to be sure of regenerative growth coming from close to the base.

Training a standard

As well as classic foliage plants such as bay, some varieties of fuchsia, heliotrope, coleus (*Solenostemon*), and others can be trained satisfactorily into standards. The aim is for a good bushy head of growth at the top of a long, straight stem. Training begins by selecting a sturdy cutting, which is encouraged to grow upward by removing any side shoots (leaves stay on) and by attaching it to a slender cane. Look after the plant well by fertilizing, potting up when necessary, and replacing thin canes with longer, stouter ones. Once the desired height is reached, pinch back the growing tip, leaving the top four side shoots to develop into the head. For a fuchsia, these should be pinched back again after about two pairs of leaves, but for a heliotrope, pinch back after either four or five leaves. Thereafter, training consists of pinching back as for an ordinary bush shape (see p.26).

Standards will develop a lot quicker if allowed to grow during winter at 50-55°F(10-13°C). Once established, fuchsia and heliotrope standards can be kept from year to year, overwintering at 40°F(4°C). Prune the head hard back in spring to promote new growth. *Heliotropium arborescens* and *H.* 'Chatsworth' make good standards. Almost any fuchsia can be grown as a standard, including the trailing varieties with their heads trained over an upturned wire hanging basket secured to the top of their cane. *F.* 'Swingtime', *F.* 'Taffeta Bow', *F.* 'Pink Marshmallow', and *F.* 'Devonshire Dumpling' all look marvelous grown in this way.

Bonsai

Indoor bonsai specimens are becoming increasingly popular. Techniques are much the same as for outdoor bonsai, with roots being restricted to small, shallow containers. Young plants in their formative years are usually potted annually in spring, sometimes into a slightly larger pot, but more often back into the same one. Roots have to be disentangled and pruned back by up to one-third. Place gravel in the bottom of the container and use a well-drained potting mix. Older plants can often last several years without disturbance. Because of their restriction, attention to watering and fertilizing is important. Pruning and wiring the top of the plant is necessary to achieve the desired shape. To do this, one end of annealed aluminum or copper wire is anchored to the soil and coiled around the main stem or trunk of the plant. There are various styles, copied from nature, to be observed when training. These include the formal and upright, informal, cascade, leaning and windswept, root over rock, and a grove of small trees.

The following are good candidates for indoor bonsai: Norfolk Island pine (*Araucaria heterophylla*), Japanese azalea (but stand this outside during summer), camellia, false cypresses *Chamaecyparis pisifera* 'Plumosa' and *C.p.* 'Squarrosa', jade plant (*Crassula ovata*), *C. sarcocaulis*, *Cuphea hyssopifolia*, eucalyptus, *Ficus benjamina*, fuchsia (small-flowered), crape myrtle (*Lagerstroemia indica*), myrtle (*Myrtus communis*), olive (*Olea europaea*), stone pine (*Pinus pinea*), pittosporum, pomegranate (*Punica granatum*), *Serissa foetida*, and Chinese elm (*Ulmus parviflora*).

Propagating

Filling a greenhouse with plants could be an expensive process, if it were not for the many kinds which can be propagated at home. Growing plants from seed or from cuttings is a way of expanding a collection, but is also useful for plants that grow rapidly and need replacing with smaller specimens, and for annuals, or perennials grown as annuals, where fresh plants are grown each year. Remember that plants grown from seed do not always come true, whereas vegetative methods produce new plants identical to the parent plant.

Plants from seed

While some seeds germinate reliably given a general set of instructions, others need more specialized treatment. Instructions are usually supplied along with the seed and, if followed, should give good results. As a plant collection grows, there will be opportunities to collect seed at home. Snip off the seed heads when they become dark and ripe, dry thoroughly, clean, and store in a dry, cool place. Some seeds, like that of *Clivia miniata*, *Scadoxus multiflorus* ssp. *katherinae*, ardisia, and lapageria should be sown as soon as ripe. Because they have not become dormant, they will germinate far more readily.

Most seeds begin germination when moisture penetrates their seed coat and the temperature is optimum. Some need to be soaked for 24 hours, in order to wash away the germination inhibitors found naturally in their seed coats. Other seeds, usually large types with hard coats, take water up faster if they are scratched or grazed with sandpaper. Light is usually necessary for germination, but some seeds require darkness and should be covered.

Sowing seeds
Collect together seeds, washed pots and seed flats, seed starter mix, boards and pressers to level the surface, labels, and a pencil.

Assess the size of container necessary for the number of seeds to be sown. Overfill the pot with starter mix, level off with a board, and press down with a flat piece of wood (**a**).

Place the pot on a level surface and water the soil (**b**). Leave the water to soak in. The surface should now be fine, smooth, and moist. Sow the seed evenly and thinly, sowing large seeds individually (**c**) and sprinkling small seeds straight from the packet (**d**).

Scatter a little soil over the top of large or medium-sized seeds (**e**). Leave fine seeds uncovered, but press them down gently into the soil. Stand the pot in a plant incubator or a loosely knotted plastic bag (**f**).

Thinning

As soon as germination takes place, remove the pots of seedlings from the plant incubator or plastic bag. When they are large enough to handle, with fully developed seed leaves (the first pair) and two true leaves, they can be transferred into a larger flat or single pots. Where a batch of celosia or schizanthus is required, a flat would be sensible. For plants like passiflora or erythrina, where only a few of each species are required, plant seedlings in individual pots. Always handle seedlings by their leaves, as holding the stems may damage them.

When planting in a flat, start by marking out a grid where the holes will be. Holding each seedling carefully by one of the larger leaves, use a pencil to pull it loose from the seed starter mix (**g**). With the pencil, make a hole big enough to hold the roots of the seedling.

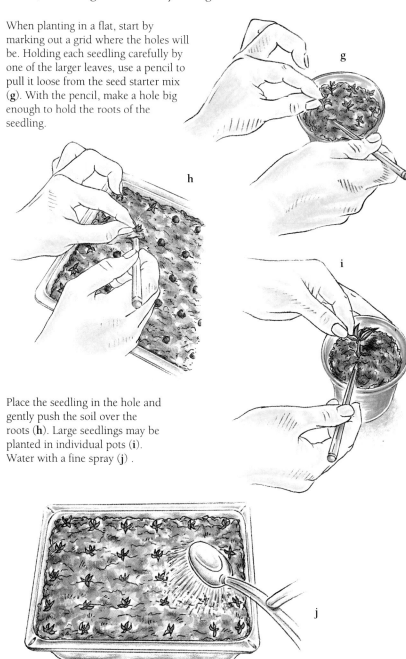

Place the seedling in the hole and gently push the soil over the roots (**h**). Large seedlings may be planted in individual pots (**i**). Water with a fine spray (**j**).

28

Growing ferns from spores

As ferns mature, look for rusty-brown spots, lines, or patches under the oldest fronds (**a**). Cut the frond from the fern and put it in an envelope or paper bag (**b**). After a few days, dust-like spores will have been shed. Fill a pot with a mixture of three parts moist peat moss and one part sharp sand, sifting the top 1in(2.5cm) to give a fine finish.

Press down lightly but firmly. Cut a disk of absorbent paper to fit the top of the pot. Pour boiling water onto the paper (**c**) so that it filters through evenly to sterilize the soil. Scatter the fern spores evenly over the surface (**d**) and cover the pot with a plastic bag (**e**). After two to six months, the spores germinate into prothalli (**f**). It may be another six months before the fronds begin to develop. When they are large enough to handle, gently lever them out with a pencil and transfer them, three in a pot (**g**). Once they reach a height of about 1in(2.5cm), ferns can be separated and grown on.

Vegetative propagation

Vegetative propagation creates young plants which are clones of the parent plants and is therefore completely different from propagation by seed or spores, which give rise to variable progeny. Raise most new plants during late spring and early summer. This makes use of maximum light and naturally warm temperatures, allowing young plants to grow and become strong before the lower light levels and colder temperatures of winter. Most plants need to be kept warm and humid while they produce roots. Unless otherwise stated, most cuttings will root best in a heated plant incubator. Failing this, stand the pot or flat in a loosely knotted plastic bag and shade from bright light or stand out of the sun. However, there are exceptions to this general rule. Succulent and hairy-leaved plants (including pelargoniums) dislike a close, humid atmosphere and should not be covered. Similarly, although most cuttings will root better and faster if dipped into fresh hormone rooting powder or liquid, there are a few plants, notably pelargonium and ficus, on which hormone rooting compound should not be used.

a

b

Stem cuttings

Cut shoots 2-4in(5-10cm) long and, using a sharp knife, trim each just below a leaf node. Remove the bottom leaves (**a**) and on large-leaved plants shorten the remaining leaves by half to two-thirds (**b**), to avoid overcrowding and cut down on moisture loss. Dip the cuttings into fresh hormone rooting compound (**c**), then plant them in pots of cutting starter mix. They will root better if several are crowded in a pot (**d**). Place the pots in a plant incubator or loosely knotted plastic bags shaded from hot sun.

c

d

Long stem cuttings

Plants with, long stems – epipremnum, syngonium, and heptapleurum, for instance – can have cuttings taken all along the stem. Each cutting should contain at least one but preferably two nodes. Cut above the top node and below the bottom one (**f**), and root the cuttings in cutting starter mix (**g**).

e

Rooting in water

Some cuttings, of tradescantia, impatiens, and maranta, for example, will root in water. Take a cutting in the usual way and stand it in a jar of water (**e**). Pot up when the roots have grown.

f

g

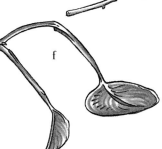
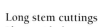

Heel cuttings

To take a heel cutting, grip the bottom of a side shoot between the thumb and forefinger. Pull down sharply so that the shoot comes away with a sliver of tissue from the old stem (**a**). Trim the long tail of the heel and plant the cutting in cutting starter mix.

Leaf cuttings

A number of plant leaves will root readily from leaf stalks or sections of leaf inserted into soil.

BEGONIAS

Begonia rex and *B. masoniana* can be propagated by any of three methods. One way is to select a healthy leaf, turn it upside down on a board, and make cuts across all the major veins. Place the leaf, the right way up, on moist cutting starter mix and weigh it down with pebbles (**e**). Alternatively, cut the leaf into square sections, each containing a portion of major vein. Lay the squares on the soil surface to root (**f**). Or cut triangular sections from th healthy leaf, each with a portion of that point where the main vein joins the leaf stalk. Plant them upright in cutting starter mix (**g**).

Hardwood cuttings

Hardwood cuttings are taken from mature stems of plants such as bougainvillea, and grape vines during winter. Choose a young shoot and cut a 4-8in(10-20cm) length from the stem. Trim the cutting above a node at the top and below at the bottom (**b**). Insert the cutting into soil to a depth of two-thirds of its length. Overwinter in a cool greenhouse or a cold frame.

Stem sections

Plants such as *Begonia manicata*, dieffenbachia, and draecena can be propagated from short chunks of stem. Cut so that each piece contains two nodes (**c**). Plant the tip upright. Nestle the other cuttings horizontally in soil (**d**).

Some small-leaved rhizomatous begonias like *B.* 'Tiger Paws' can be propagated from leaves. Remove a leaf, trim the stalk, leaving about 1in (2.5cm) as an anchor, and push it into the soil, so that the whole leaf is in contact with the surface (**h**).

PEPEROMIA

Peperomias will root from leaves. *P. caperata* can be propagated in the same way as *Begonia* 'Tiger Paws' (see p.31). To propagate *P. argyreia*, cut the leaves across and insert them upright in soil (**a**).

SANSEVIERIA

   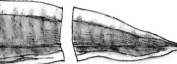

Chop a healthy leaf into sections 2in(5cm) long, making sure that top and bottom do not become confused (**d**). Plant several in a flat of cutting starter mix (**e**). Do not cover the flat but keep it out of direct light, and they will root, sending up small plants. *S. trifasciata* 'Laurentii' will lose its yellow leaves when propagated this way.

SAINTPAULIAS/AFRICAN VIOLETS

Saintpaulias also root from leaf stalks. Select a healthy leaf from the middle band of leaves, pull it away, and trim the stem, making a slanting cut with a sharp knife or razor blade (**b**). Leave 1-1½in(2.5-4cm) of stalk if rooting in cutting starter mix and 2-3in(5-8cm) if rooting in water. In neither case is there any need for hormone rooting compound. In mix, insert two leaves back to back so that they support each other, with the leaf blades sitting on top of the mix (**c**). To root in water, fit a piece of silver foil over the top of a water-filled jar. Make some small holes in the foil and push the leaf stalks through, so that their bases make contact with the water and the blades rest on the foil. When, after six to eight weeks, roots have formed, remove the leaves and pot them up. Separate the plantlets when they are 1½-2in (4-5cm) high. Set them three to a 3½in (9cm) pot, and wait until they have filled this before potting them separately. After every root disturbance the vulnerable young plants should be covered with plastic or a plant incubator until they are established. In the lead-up to potting time, give the plantlets a dilute liquid fertilizer.

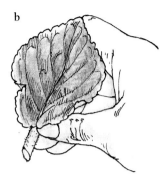

STREPTOCARPUS

There are several different ways of rooting the leaves of Cape primrose. Whichever way you prefer, always choose a fresh young leaf approaching maturity. The easiest method is simply to insert the leaf upright in one piece, perhaps just trimming the end (**f**). Roots form readily from the thick midrib at the base. To make more plants from one leaf, divide it into three pieces, cutting across the leaf, and insert all three (**g**). The further the cutting from the leaf base, the less likely it is to root, but with luck all three will strike. For even more plantlets, place a leaf upside down on a board and cut along both sides of the midrib. Discard the midrib and insert both halves on edge, cut veins down, in a flat of cutting starter mix (**h**). Plantlets will form along the cut veins.

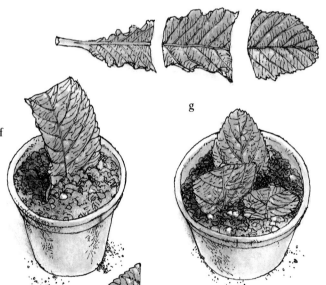

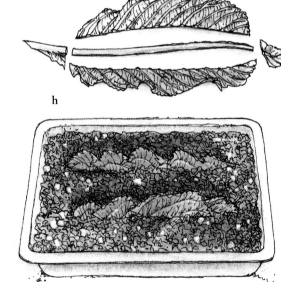

Division

This is arguably the most straightforward method of propagation. At the same time as potting, clump-forming plants can be divided and potted separately. Some have distinct crowns of growth, which need to be identified and pulled apart in such a way that damage is avoided. Others, sansevieria and aspidistra, for instance, have underground rhizomes which need to be cut with a knife. Where large root masses are too thick to separate, drive two forks, back to back, into the middle and use as levers against each other, much as when dividing herbaceous plants. You may even need to take a saw to the pot-bound roots of an *Asparagus densiflorus* 'Sprengeri', but both halves can survive.

Air layering

This technique enables roots to be formed on the new plant before it is severed from the old. Carried out most frequently on rubber plants (*Ficus elastica*) and Swiss cheese plants (*Monstera deliciosa*), this is a useful alternative to stem cuttings.

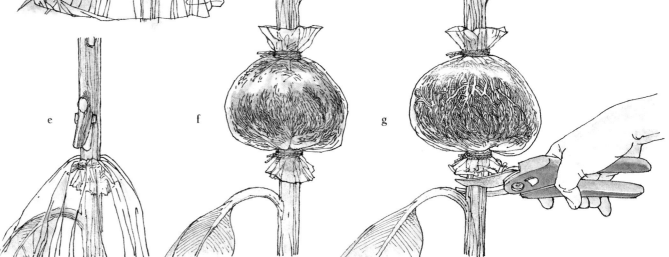

Dividing a plant
Having removed the plant clump from its container, pull it apart by hand (**a**), to give two, three, or more separate plants (**b**).

Air layering
Strip the leaves from a length of stem about 12in(30cm) down from the tip. Slit a plastic bag to make a "sleeve". Slip this over the prepared stem and tie the lower end (**c**). Make a ½in(1cm) upward-slanting cut half-way into the stem, stopping just under a node (**d**). Wedge the tongue open with a sliver of wood (**e**). Pull the plastic up, pack moist sphagnum moss or cutting starter mix around the cut, then tie the plastic tightly at the top (**f**). After six to eight weeks, when new roots have grown, cut through the stem below the roots (**g**), remove the plastic, and pot the new plant.

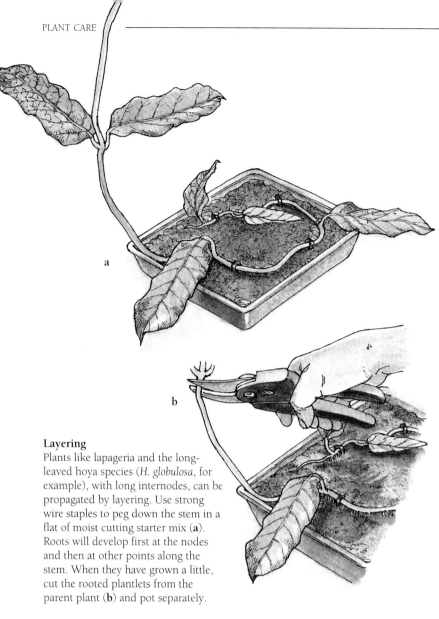

Layering
Plants like lapageria and the long-leaved hoya species (*H. globulosa*, for example), with long internodes, can be propagated by layering. Use strong wire staples to peg down the stem in a flat of moist cutting starter mix (**a**). Roots will develop first at the nodes and then at other points along the stem. When they have grown a little, cut the rooted plantlets from the parent plant (**b**) and pot separately.

Offsets

A simple method of propagation, offsets are small plants produced directly from the parent plant, which can be pulled or cut away and potted up. These are common on bromeliads, cacti, and some bulbs. Remove the parent plant from its pot in order to bring as many roots as possible away with the offset. Sometimes there will be no roots and the offset will have to be treated like a cutting. Either way, allow offsets to reach a reasonable size before attempting to detach them.

Plantlets

Some plants produce small replicas of themselves which can be pulled off, with or without roots, and grown on. These are great fun to grow but can be a nuisance when their plantlets fall off and root where they are not wanted. Simply detach the small plants when large enough to handle and push them, spaced apart, into cutting starter mix, water, treat them like small cuttings and they will soon grow strongly.

Pests and diseases

Regular, routine inspection of plants is essential to spot pest infestations as soon as they begin and to recognize symptoms of disease as early as possible. If necessary, examine particularly prone plants with a magnifying glass for signs of small pests like spider mite. It is often easier to find evidence of their presence than to see the pests themselves. Many pests (aphids, mealy bugs, and scale insects, for instance), secrete sticky honey-dew, which drops down and coats the leaves below. Sooty mold grows on this, turning leaves black and masking them from the light. Some problems are merely unsightly, others severely disfiguring or even fatal. Some affect specific plants, others spread indiscriminately. It is good practice if possible when acquiring a new plant to give it a period of quarantine before introducing it into a well-stocked greenhouse, to make sure it is not harboring any pests.

Healthy plants, like healthy people, have more chance of fighting off diseases. Far greater problems will be experienced when plants are neglected, underfertilized, incorrectly watered, or weakened by pests, and where the greenhouse is inadequately ventilated.

Chemical control

Specific chemical controls are not recommended here, because they are constantly changing, with new products coming onto the market and older ones being removed. Diagnose the problem correctly, then seek advice and guidance from a garden center or store. Most pesticides require more than one application to effect control. The instructions usually state that the spray or other treatment should be repeated again, at least once, after a given period of days. To follow this precisely is vital in order to kill successive generations of the pest as they hatch out.

Individual plants with problems can be removed from the greenhouse, sprayed, and returned when the spray has dried. Needless to say, this can only be carried out when weather conditions permit, and plants should never be sprayed in full sun.

Biological control

This method of pest control, also known as natural control, is where predators or parasites of the pests are introduced into the greenhouse. These do not usually eradicate the pests completely, but keep them at manageable levels. Unfortunately, most die off during the lower temperatures of winter and need to be reintroduced in spring, just as the pests become noticeable again.

Many of the chemicals which kill pests would also kill the biological control, so before changing from chemical to biological control methods, a period must be observed during which pesticide residues wear off or are washed away from plant leaves. Usually, a pesticide-free winter is sufficient. If outbreaks do occur, they will have to be dealt with using insecticidal soap.

Once biological controls are introduced, chemicals can no longer be used unless they are selective, in other words specifically targeted. The organic Margosan-O kills only mealy bugs, thrips, sweet potato and greenhouse whitefly, aphids, and leaf miners. Some fungicides can be used sparingly, where there is biological control.

Pests

In the lists below, pests are grouped broadly by the part of the plant they are most likely to attack.

Sap-sucking pests

APHIDS

These sap-sucking insects, commonly known as greenfly or blackfly, attack the leaves and flower buds of a wide range of plants. They can transmit viruses from one plant to another, which makes their control doubly important. They can be controlled by specific aphicides. Biological controls are available, but they do not seem particularly effective.

WHITEFLIES

Having developed immunity to many pesticides and capable of rapid breeding, whiteflies are hard to control. They can be seen as small white flies dancing around the plant and settling under leaves to suck sap and deposit their scale-like young. If plants which are prone to whitefly attack are grown (for example, *Lantana camara* or *Brugmansia* cvs.), then one should either be committed to a regular spraying program or use biological control by introducing the parasitic wasp *Encarsia formosa* when the whitefly is first noticed. This lays its eggs in the scales of the whitefly. They hatch out into tiny wasps which are barely noticeable, do not bite humans, and remain in the greenhouse provided there are still a few whiteflies for them to eat. Where there are not too many whiteflies, yellow cards covered in sticky grease attract and trap large numbers if plants are ruffled regularly to set them flying.

RED SPIDER MITES

Just visible to the naked eye, these mites often go unnoticed until they have bred to plague proportions. During warm, dry periods, webs are formed at the tops of plants. To make them even harder to spot, the insects are not usually red but pale yellow with black markings. Look out for a fine speckling of the foliage and a dry, scorched look to the leaves. Inspect the back of the leaf for clusters of mites. Spider mites are hard to control

by spraying, but biological control is effective if introduced while numbers are still small. Slightly larger, more sprightly, red-colored predatory mites (*Phytoseiulus persimilis*) are introduced, which run around eating the spider mite. It pays to position infected plants close together, in order to allow the predator to travel from one to another.

SCALE INSECTS

Hemispherical scale has reddish-brown shells and soft scale has flatter, yellow-brown scales, both about 1/4in (5mm) long. Under their protective shell, the insects feed on sap, clustering around stems and leaf veins. There are no males and before they die, females lay hundreds of eggs which are left behind under the protective shell. At this stage they are protected from chemical sprays, becoming vulnerable only when the eggs hatch into tiny crawlers which disperse before settling down to feed. They can be difficult to spot, but look for stickiness and sooty mold on leaves below. Common on citrus, grape vines, and coffee plants. A small parasite (*Metaphycus helvolus*) provides natural control, but their release, in spring, needs careful coordination and they require high temperatures – above 72°F(22°C) for several hours every day – to be really effective.

MEALY BUGS

These grayish-pink flattened bugs live in colonies, secreting mealy or wool-like waxy fibers around themselves and their eggs for protection. When spraying, hold the nozzle close to the pests and blast them to penetrate the mealy wool. Some plants, notably ferns, can be damaged by the chemicals used against mealy bugs; these can be treated with a brush or cotton twist dipped in alcohol. Biological control consists of a predatory ladybug (*Cryptolaemus montrouzieri*), which resembles a giant mealy bug. Root mealy bugs are difficult to control, because the infestation becomes extreme before signs of ill health force one to examine the roots of the plant. Good hygiene, particularly thorough pot washing, will prevent the spread of this pest. Control

consists of drenching the soil or, alternatively, dunking the whole plant into a solution of the relevant pesticide. Cacti, succulents, and streptocarpus are frequent victims.

LEAF HOPPERS

The pinhead-sized white dots on leaves, particularly those of primula, are easier to spot than the insects that cause them. Pale-colored leaf hoppers move around a lot, often leaving only their white shed skins behind, earning the name ghost flies. They can be controlled by spraying.

TARSONEMID MITES

This group of mites, invisible to the naked eye, infests the growing points of certain susceptible plants. Their feeding at this crucial part of the plant affects the development of new shoots, resulting in distorted and scarred stems, leaves, and flower buds. Unfortunately no effective chemicals are available to the amateur, but detection is crucial. Burn infested plants to prevent spread. Cyclamen, ivy, impatiens, and saintpaulia are all vulnerable plants. Anybody who houses a large collection of saintpaulia or begonia, for example, would be well advised to place any new plants in quarantine for a period of weeks. Spray damage can cause similar symptoms but plants usually recover quickly from the latter. Bulb scale mites infest the necks of plants like hippeastrum, causing curved, distorted leaves with saw-toothed scars and notches on leaves and flower stems. There could be confusion with virus symptoms, but in both cases, the best solution is always to dispose of the plant.

Pests that attack flowers, fruit, and foliage

SLUGS

Usually associated with damage to outdoor plants, slugs that enter greenhouses and sunrooms cause havoc among seedlings. They feed at night and lurk beneath pots by day. Slug pellets applied around the seedlings will protect them. Choose aluminum sulfate-based products where animals and children may be present.

THRIPS

Greenhouse thrips can do a lot of damage to leaves and flowers if unchecked. Long, thin, pale yellow or brown insects are winged, but are more likely to jump than fly. They rasp and suck at leaves and petals, leaving behind persistent, silvery streaks. Palms are particularly prone. Western flower thrips, which damage growing tips and flowers, are common greenhouse pests. Fortunately there is effective biological control in the form of a predatory mite called *Amblyseius cucumeris*. Thrips can be responsible for transmitting viruses from one plant to another, making their control doubly important.

LEAF MINERS

These begin as white spots on the leaves, made by the female fly laying eggs. Larvae mine within the leaves, leaving squiggly patterns behind as they go and eventually pupate between leaf tissues. Catch infestations early, and controls will be effective. Alternatively, squash small outbreaks of larvae by hand.

TORTRIX MOTHS

The caterpillars of the carnation tortrix moth have brown or green bodies and dark heads. They make a nest for themselves out of a curled leaf, or several leaves tightly bound together by webbing. Undetected, they can cause a lot of unsightly damage to a wide range of plants, injuring both leaves and flowers. Learn to spot their nests, peel them open, and squash the small caterpillar before it can wriggle backward and escape. The alternative is spraying, which is not very successful as the caterpillars are so well protected.

Pests that attack roots

SPRINGTAILS

If, when watering, the soil surface seems to be alive with small, white, jumping insects, these are springtails. Wingless, they resemble tiny terrestrial shrimps. Like sciarid flies, they usually do no harm, only occasionally attacking the plants. Rarely found in sterilized soil, they can be controlled with a soil drench of the appropriate insecticide.

Aphid

Whiteflies

Red spider mites

Scale insects

Leaf hopper damage

Tarsonemid mites

Slug

Thrips

Tortrix caterpillar

Springtails

Sciarid fly larvae

Woodlice

Powdery mildew

Damping-off

Botrytis

Sooty mold

Geranium rust on pelargonium leaf

Blackleg

Leaf gall

Virus on palm leaves

Mealy bug

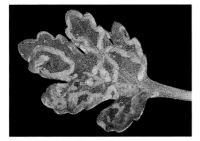

Leaf miner damage

Vine weevil larva

Cineraria rust

Pelargonium leaf curl virus

SCIARID FLIES

Also known as fungus gnats, these are small black flies which lay their eggs in the surface of potting mixes, especially peat-based kinds. These hatch into tiny, almost see-through maggots which eat the rotting organic matter or the remains of plants killed by overwatering. They rarely harm plants but sometimes eat roots and are generally irritating. An alternative to pesticide sprays is biological control using *Bacillus thuringiensis*. Deter them by placing a layer of gravel or vermiculite over the soil's surface.

VINE WEEVILS

Adult vine weevils are small black beetles with long "snouts" and elbow-like antennae. While these bite circular pieces out of leaf edges, it is their pale, c-shaped grubs with darker heads that do the real damage. These eat plant roots, going undetected until the plant collapses and dies. Eggs are laid during summer, with the grubs hatching and destroying roots during fall, winter, and early spring. If certain plants like cyclamen, kalanchoe, and saxifrage are regularly affected, it is best to drench the soil in their pots with the relevant pesticide as a preventive measure. A biological control consists of a nematode which infests the vine weevil grub and kills it. This is best introduced in late summer, after a few grubs have been spotted by tapping susceptible plants out of their pots for inspection. Apply as a drench through a watering can. Female vine weevils cannot fly, so if plants and benches are clean, standing the legs of a bench in wide saucers of water makes a moat which the egg-bearing females cannot cross.

WOODLICE

Although woodlice (also known as pill bugs) usually feed only on rotting organic matter, they can begin to attack the roots of seedlings and even to eat holes in leaves. They feed at night, hiding in crowds under old seed flats, pots, and other debris during the day. To discourage them, clean out hardware and trash, pour boiling water where they congregate, and, if still infested, apply pesticide.

Diseases

Plants are threatened by disease organisms which can be divided into the three following categories.

Fungi

POWDERY MILDEW

One of the commonest of diseases, this is first noticeable when the spores appear on the surface of the leaves, like ghostly white powder. Discourage by good ventilation and adequate watering. Spray with the appropriate fungicide. Begonia, grape vine, and *Cissus rhombifolia* 'Ellen Danica' are particularly vulnerable.

DAMPING-OFF

This disease, closely related to blackleg, attacks seedlings at the point where their stems emerge from the soil, and is caused by soil- and water-borne fungi. Once it begins to occur regularly, one can assume the worst and take precautionary measures. Water the seed starter mix with Truban before sowing, water it into the soil just before planting seedlings, and water the seedlings with it afterward. This is a particular problem with small seedlings, especially when sown too close together. The use of porous soil mixes and clean pots and general attention to hygiene will help avoid infection.

BOTRYTIS

Gray mold is encouraged by cold, damp conditions, usually when the greenhouse is not ventilated sufficiently during winter and dull periods. This fungal disease, which is distinguished by its gray fluffy appearance, begins by feeding on dead matter but can spread to live plants. Remove infected material and spray early on a dry day, when the vents can be opened to dry out the plants.

SOOTY MOLD

These are black, soot-like fungi which grow on the honeydew secreted by pests like aphids, mealy bugs, scale insects, and whitefly. Although it does not feed off plants itself, the sooty covering deprives the leaf of light. The only cure is to control the pest and wipe away the sooty mold.

RUST

This first shows itself as orange to dark brown pustules, usually on the undersides of leaves. Plants like zonal pelargonium, fuchsia, pericallis (*Cineraria*), and carnation are affected. Remove and burn badly infected leaves or whole plants and spray the remainder with the appropriate fungicide as soon as possible, repeating the spray as advised. Rusts overwinter on leaves, so strip the foliage from infected pelargoniums or fuchsias in fall and overwinter them leafless at low temperatures.

BLACKLEG

Affecting pelargonium cuttings, this disease turns the base of the stem black. Do not use hormone rooting compounds when taking cuttings of pelargoniums, and pay attention to hygiene. Sometimes the tip of the cutting can be re-struck successfully.

Bacteria

LEAF GALL

There is no cure for this bacterial gall which causes masses of distorted, dwarfed, fasciated shoots around the base of plants like chrysanthemums and pelargoniums. The only answer is to destroy the plants and sterilize both their pots and the ground or bench.

Viruses

Viruses affect a wide range of plants and are responsible for a variety of symptoms. Leaves may become mottled, striped, or blotched, with leaves, stems, and flowers distorted and stunted. The only course of action is to destroy the plants before the virus spreads. Many viruses are carried from plant to plant by sap-sucking insects such as aphids and thrips. Particularly virulent is Tomato Spotted Wilt Virus (TSWV), affecting a wide range of indoor ornamental plants. Symptoms include ringspots, dark purple-brown sunken spots, browning of stems, and stunting of growth. This is spread from plant to plant by western flower thrips, which possess considerable resistance to chemicals. Routine control of thrips and immediate destruction of infected plants are the only ways of checking this virus.

Specimen plants

In a well-planted greenhouse, specimen plants are the key plants, striking enough in their stature or sheer visual impact to stand alone or form the climax to a plant grouping. It is not simply a question of size, although a single, bold specimen might fill and furnish an entire area very effectively on its own. It is also a matter of distinction: a specimen has qualities that make it stand out from the crowd and draw the eye with handsome foliage, a dramatic profile, or conspicuous flowers. The principle of using specimens as focal points works whatever the scale. It applies equally in a large permanently planted bed and in an arrangement of half-a-dozen smaller plants on benches or table-top.

Most specimens are long-lasting plants that set the scene for other, secondary planting. In the garden outside, trees and large shrubs are chosen to make up a permanent framework or backbone. Selected for impact of foliage, flower-color, or shape, they add substance, act as a backdrop for smaller plants, and also provide a succession of interest throughout the year. Choose greenhouse specimens with the same careful thought. Since they need to be the first acquisitions, it is vital to envisage the desired effect at the planning stages.

Specimen plants should be long-lasting and chosen with the style of the greenhouse in mind. Traditional conservatories which have classical proportions reminiscent of an orangery might be appropriately dressed with the strategically placed greenery of citrus, bay, cupressus, and camellia. In some greenhouses an oriental atmosphere can be created through the use of various bamboos, including sacred bamboo (*Nandina domestica*). In a modern-style sunroom with clean, fluid lines, give emphasis to plants with architectural shape or foliage. Deploy fewer, larger plants so that their silhouettes are clearly displayed against a plain background rather than massed greenery. Mediterranean-style plantings for bright sunrooms might well include large bush-like bougainvillea, oleander, hibiscus, and senna. For pretty, cottage-style informality, use subjects with delicate foliage like smaller-leaved pittosporums and acacias.

A more dramatic option is to encourage jungle-like profusion in sunrooms where humidity levels will not damage furnishings. A tropical rainforest consists of several stories of growth: tall trees form the main canopy, with palms and large shrubby plants making one or more understories, which in turn provide shade for the forest-floor plants. It may seem far-fetched to reproduce this in a small sunroom, but shading takes the place of the leafy canopy. Tall specimens like palms and tree-like ficus can be used to form an understory, providing shade for smaller foliage and flowering plants beneath. When a tall tree falls in the rainforest, light is admitted, enabling other sorts of plants like bananas (*Musa*) and some climbers to grow, a profusion which is easy to mimic in the sunroom.

To some extent, the status of specimen plants fluctuates with the seasons. Just as some framework plants offer only seasonal interest in the outside garden, certain large shrubby specimens are chosen for their flowers indoors. Plants like callistemon, *Erica canaliculata,* and luculia blend into the background when not in bloom. To sustain interest, intersperse them with bolder foliage specimens or smaller plants with eye-catching flowers or fruit, which thus assume a starring role.

The classification of specimens is a very elastic one, encompassing plants from other chapters when in peak performance or when trained in certain ways. Some examples of the smaller flowering and fruiting plants, for instance, make temporary but bold displays when grouped together. *Clivia miniata*, with deep, evergreen leaves and bright orange flowers in spring, eventually makes large, bold clumps; for instant impact, pot three individual plants together. Plants can be juggled all the time, if they are grown in pots. Any good smaller foliage, flowering, or fruiting plant enjoying its season of glory could be brought forward into a position of prominence and earn itself the title of a temporary specimen. Some, normally grown as small bushes – such as fuchsia, lantana, and heliotrope – can be elevated to true specimen status by being trained as standards. Climbing plants like monstera, philodendron, and epipremnum, which produce aerial roots, can be trained around a free-standing moss pole that is fitted in a bed or planted in a pot to make a distinctive specimen feature.

Long-lived specimens represent a considerable investment – either of money, or of time and expertise spent in growing them onto larger sizes – but potentially play their part for many years. At the planning stage, assess how best to meet the cultivation needs of such large plants, at the same time considering their long-term role in the greenhouse. Whether to grow plants in beds or containers is one decision you'll need to make. For a really permanent backbone, beds are always the best option. Large specimens are likely to be healthier and more vigorous when given a good root run. These plants demand care when first planted. Space them sufficiently far apart to account for their eventual size; but take care when plugging the gaps with more temporary plantings not to crowd or distort the growth of the young giants.

Over the years the sunroom gardener may want several changes of scene. This is more easily accomplished with plants grown in pots than when they have developed large root systems in beds. Specimens confined to the same large pot for many years rely heavily on fertilizers: keep them in a healthy state by adding slow-release fertilizer to the soil in the pot and by regular liquid fertilizing.

The character and style of a sunroom are determined as much by the choice of plants as by the design and construction. Focal points are provided by specimen plants like this flamboyant bird of paradise (*Strelitzia reginae*), either rising above groups of smaller plants or shining out among them. Flowering plants nearby should be carefully chosen to support the specimen plant without upstaging it: the pretty *Primula* × *kewensis* works beautifully in this position. The soft effect of foliage, provided here by delicate maidenhair ferns, is always welcome.

Abutilon 'Kentish Belle'

Abutilon

(Malvaceae)

These showy plants are often called flowering maples, but only the leaves are maple-like; the flowers are clearly related to hibiscus and hollyhock. All require good light, plenty of water in summer, and prefer loam-based soil. Rapid growers, most have lax stems which can be wall-trained. However, handsome free-standing specimens can be grown by supporting the main stems with canes. Prune in spring, cutting back all side shoots by at least two-thirds so that new growth will regenerate close to the older main stems. Ungainly plants can be trimmed back in fall. Cuttings 3-4in(8-10cm) long, of half-ripe wood, root easily during summer. Mixed hybrids and species can be grown from spring-sown seed.

Abutilon hybrids need warm greenhouse conditions to perform well – whitefly can be a problem. Many have hanging, bell-like flowers. Some have plain green foliage and flowers of white, red, yellow, or orange; others have the added interest of variegated leaves. *A.* 'Cannington Carol' is a short, sturdy plant with golden-yellow mottling on bright green leaves and brilliant orange-red flowers; *A.* × *h.* 'Savitzii' is a shorter, more elegant variegated type; *A.* 'Kentish Belle' has orange-yellow petals and a dull red calyx; *A.* 'Souvenir de Bonn' has pinkish-red flowers and a creamy-yellow edge to the leaf.
40°F(4°C) H&S:5-6ft(1.5-1.8m)

A. megapotamicum Unlike those of most hybrids, the leaves of this Brazilian species are narrow, pointed and dainty. *A.m.* 'Variegatum' has leaves so brightly marked with yellow that the pretty red and yellow bell-shaped flowers hardly register. Good grown against a wall, but free-standing specimens make attractive features.
32-40°F(0-4°C) H&S:6-7ft(1.8-2m)

A. pictum 'Thompsonii' This variegated form of a Brazilian species will, unpruned, grow vigorously into a tall shrub. Leaves are very maple-like, with heavy mottling of creamy-yellow. Orange flowers are heavily veined.
40°F(4°C) H:7ft(2m) S:5-6ft(1.5-1.8m)

A. × *suntense* Suitable for an unheated greenhouse, this flowering maple is a large deciduous hybrid with splendid saucer-shaped, pale bluish-mauve flowers 2½-3in(6-8cm) wide.
23-40°F(-5-4°C) H:10ft(3m) S:5-6ft(1.5-1.8m)

Acacia

(Leguminosae)

These are the beautiful florists' mimosas, most of Australian origin. Deservedly popular for their show of yellow flowers during late winter/early spring and, in some cases, attractive foliage, they make marvelous additions to a roomy, cool greenhouse. Although most acacias reach 20-30ft(6-9m) in the wild, they

can be restricted by containers and pruning, best carried out after flowering. Whether planted in beds (where they do best) or pots, do not allow the roots to become too dry in winter, which can jeopardize the developing flower buds. Seed of a variety of species is available. For faster germination, cover with boiling water, then allow to soak for two days prior to sowing.
H:8ft(2.5m) S:6ft(1.8m) or more

A. baileyana This is a lovely spreading evergreen plant with fern-like, glaucous leaves. Both this and *A.b.* 'Purpurea', with purple-tinted leaves, make excellent foliage plants when young. Golden flowers are produced in spring.
32-40°F(0-4°C)

A. dealbata The silver wattle is probably the best known and arguably the hardiest. Dense, silvery-white, feathery leaves contrast beautifully with the globular yellow flowers produced through winter. Although capable of great heights, quick-growing specimens confined in a pot will flower when young.
23-40°F(-5-4°C)

A. paradoxa (*A. armata*) The kangaroo thorn lends itself well to being wall-trained, but also makes an imposing free-standing plant. The stems are covered with small, almost triangular leaf-like phyllodes. Prune back unwanted, wayward shoots after flowering to keep plants in check.
32-40°F(0-4°C)

A. podalyriifolia The Queensland wattle has silver, downy, oval-shaped phyllodes and 4in(10cm) racemes of globular golden-yellow flowers in winter.
32-40°F(0-4°C)

A. pravissima This species has graceful, arching growth and triangular, silvery phyllodes. Frothy, clear yellow flowers appear in early spring. A good candidate for training against a wall.
32-40°F(0-4°C)

A. retinodes 'Lisette' This plant has a long flowering period, often producing its pale yellow, fragrant flowers through winter. Foliage is willow-like.
23-40°F(-5-4°C)

Acalypha
(Euphorbiaceae)
Hippocrates used the name acalypha for the nettle, a good comparison, as this unrelated genus does resemble flamboyant nettles. The cultivated species share a love of warm, humid conditions, which also help deter red spider mite; regular spray misting, especially under the foliage, and general vigilance are necessary precautions. Leggy specimens will respond to pruning by two-thirds in spring. Avoid cutting into old wood by leaving short spurs of younger side shoots from which new growth can be made. Cuttings 3-4in(8-10cm) long root easily.

A. hispida The chenille plant or red hot cat's tail from

Acalypha hispida

New Guinea will grow better the more heat and humidity you can give it. Well-tended plants produce 12-24in(30-60cm) long crimson tassels composed of many tiny flowers virtually year-round. Grown by an indoor pond, plants will love the extra humidity. (There are also miniature forms suitable for hanging baskets.)
55°F(13°C) H:6ft(1.8m) S:4-6ft(1.2-1.8m)

A. wilkesiana Jacob's coat, fire dragon, and copperleaf are names reflecting the bright leaf color of this Pacific Islands species. Beginning green, they turn a rich copper mottled and splashed with red. Leaves of *A.w.* 'Godseffiana' are shiny green, edged with cream. Those of *A.w.* 'Marginata' are an unblotched, shiny copper, edged with serrations of coral-pink. More rounded than the species, the leaves curl around each other as if fighting for space. Lower temperatures of 45°F(7°C) can be tolerated during winter if plants are watered sparingly but they will probably drop all their leaves. Prune back in spring as growth re-starts.
55°F(13°C) H&S:6ft(1.8m)

Acca
(Myrtaceae)
A. sellowiana (*Feijoa sellowiana*) The pineapple guava is from Brazil and Uruguay. Even when not in flower, the oval leaves are an attractive shiny green on top with greenish-white felted undersides. Bushes

Acca sellowiana

begin to flower only after several years but the summer flowers are worth the wait. Four purple-pink petals, dark at the center but fading to white at the edges, turn back from a boss of long dark red stamens peppered with yellow anthers. Edible egg-shaped fruits, strictly berries, are 2in(5cm) long. Enjoys good light. Propagate by spring-sown seed or in summer by cuttings.
38°F(3°C) H:7ft(2m) S:5ft(1.5m)

Agapanthus
(Liliaceae/Alliaceae)
The African lilies, from South Africa, are particularly suited to growing in large tubs, and flower earlier and more spectacularly under glass, sending up tall stems bearing rounded heads of funnel-shaped flowers in shades of blue or white. Pairs of tubs look particularly fine set either side of a door. When plants become crowded, divide in spring: remove the plant from its pot and use two forks to separate the clump into portions. African lilies prefer a well-drained, loam-based soil and are easily raised from seed but take several years to flower. *A. africanus*, 32-40°F (0-4°C), is arguably the best-known species, with evergreen, leathery leaves and magnificent heads of blue flowers. *A.* Headbourne Hybrids have beautiful large flowers and strong healthy but deciduous foliage. These are the hardiest of the agapanthus.
H:24-48in(60-120cm) S:24in(60cm)

Alpinia zerumbet

Alyogyne huegelii 'Santa Cruz'

Allamanda

(Apocynaceae)

The climbing species, *A. cathartica*, is spectacular and well known (see p.79) but greenhouse owners should not overlook shrubby *A. schottii* (*A. neriifolia*) from Brazil. Handsome, evergreen leaves make a backdrop for golden-yellow, funnel-shaped flowers 1¹/₂in(4cm) long produced throughout summer. Shade lightly from full sun. Hardly any pruning is required but plants can be thinned in spring. Propagate by seed or by cuttings taken in spring.
50-55°F(10-13°C) H:3-6ft(1-1.8m)
S:30-48in(75-120cm)

Alpinia

(Zingiberaceae)

Growing into fine clumps of tall, leafy stems, alpinias can make imposing specimens. When restricted in a pot, plenty of water and liquid fertilizer are needed in summer. Planted in borders they can become rampant, sending tough rhizomes in all directions. Slight shade protects leaves from scorching and prevents stunted growth; too much inhibits flowering. Humidity is essential, so spray mist the undersides of the leaves during dry conditions. Propagate by dividing the rhizomes in summer. All parts of the plant give off a pleasant gingery smell.

A. purpurata The Pacific Islands red ginger has rich green leaves and racemes of red bracts which arch over as they elongate with age. Almost concealed by the bracts are small white flowers.

45-50°F(7-10°C) H:6ft(1.8m) S:3ft(1m)

A. vittata (A. sanderae) The variegated ginger from New Guinea has leaves striped with white so that the green parts look like arrow-heads. This striking foliage plant remains smaller than most of its relatives, so is useful where space is restricted. Unfortunately, flowers are rare.
45-55°F(7-13°C) H&S:24in(60cm)

A. zerumbet (A. speciosa, A. nutans) The names shell ginger and pink porcelain lily describe the fragrant flowers held in bending racemes: pale pink, bell-shaped calyces tipped with red each sport a yellow and red petal.
45-50°F(7-10°C) H:5-10ft(1.5-3m) S:6ft(1.8m)

Alyogyne

(Malvaceae)

A. huegelii 'Santa Cruz' This relative of the hibiscus is graced with small deep green lobed leaves and pretty pink flowers, up to 3in(8cm) across on well-grown plants. Finding the best time to prune is difficult as this Australian native is rarely out of flower, but it can be postponed until late winter or early spring. Be vigilant against whitefly and spider mite.
40°F(4°C) H:6-7ft(1.8-2m) S:5ft(1.5m)

Araucaria

(Araucariaceae)

These stately evergreen trees, close relatives of the monkey puzzle, make good – albeit large – greenhouse plants of great character. They attain 200ft(60m) high in the wild, but adapt well to living for long periods restricted in a pot. Plants grow easily from rather beautiful seeds. Keep at 70°F(21°C) until germination, then cool down as the seedling emerges properly.

A. angustifolia This marvelous conifer, from Brazil to Argentina, has the same appeal as the monkey puzzle, but the leaves are softer and, although tiered, are not arranged in so rigid a pattern.
36-40°F(2-4°C) H:6-10ft(1.8-3m) S:4-5ft(1.2-1.5m)

A. heterophylla (A. excelsa) The Norfolk Island pine is probably the most popular greenhouse choice. Leaves are soft and a superb bright green. The overall shape is far less rigid and tiered than the monkey puzzle's. Branches 3ft(1m) long are held out from the main stem, dip down, then rise up slightly at the tips.
40°F(4°C) H:6-8ft(1.8-2.5m) S:4-5ft(1.2-1.5m)

Ardisia

(Myrsinaceae)

A. crenata (A. crenulata) This small, neat, shrubby plant from the East Indies is perennially attractive, its glossy evergreen leaves making a handsome backdrop to an abundance of bright red berries following small pink flowers. Plants appreciate light shade and good humidity: spray mist around the plant, especially the foliage. Plants will grow in 6-7in(15-18cm) pots for some time, making splendid specimens. The contents of ripe berries, squashed straight onto the surface of moist seed starter mix, will germinate readily. Alternatively, take cuttings, preferably 3-4in(8-10cm)

long shoots with a heel, in spring or summer. Lower temperatures can be tolerated but new growth will turn pale and sick-looking if these are prolonged.
45-50°F(7-10°C) H:36in(90cm) S:24in(60cm)

Asplenium
(Aspleniaceae)

There are two aspleniums of quite different appearance that, given time, will build themselves up into fine specimen ferns. They could also be used *en masse* as underplanting for larger shrubby plants. Both, but particularly *A. nidus*, should be kept moist.

A. bulbiferum The mother spleenwort or hen and chicken fern from Australia and New Zealand has prettily divided fronds. As these mature, bulbils or miniature plants are produced along them; pull these off and insert into loose potting mix to grow their own roots. Where light is poor or the temperature too low, plants grow slowly and remain small. Given a warmer minimum of 50°F(10°C), plants grow large and strong.
40°F(4°C) H&S:24in(60cm)

A. nidus The bird's nest fern from Australia and tropical Asia requires shade if its shiny, lance-shaped fronds are not to scorch. Warmth, humidity, and time will combine to give large plants, which in the wild would live epiphytically, rooted into niches in tree boughs. Mature specimens produce spores which often germinate in the soil around the plant. More precise sowings can be made in separate pots (see p.29).
55°F(13°C) H&S:36in(90cm)

Bamboos

Bamboos grown in borders or tubs can make an effective mass of foliage that lends a distinctly oriental feel to the environment. As even tropical bamboos will withstand frost if they are watered sparingly during winter, these are ideal for the unheated greenhouse. The leaves of these amazingly resilient plants, members of the family Gramineae, curl inward during periods of drought to reduce transpiration. However, most have the capacity to bounce back into health as soon as they are watered. Shade from hot sun and provide high humidity during warm periods. Tall-growing bamboos can be restricted by cutting their stems back to the desired height. Propagate by division in early spring before the new shoots develop (these are delicate and easily broken), or in fall. Tropical bamboos like *Bambusa vulgaris* can be propagated by stem cuttings. Cut through a three-year-old stem on either side of a node and place it at an angle of 30-40° in a large tub of potting mix, so that the node is mostly below soil level. Given temperatures of 60-70°F(16-21°C), roots and new shoots should form in eight to twelve weeks, but the success rate is only about 50 percent. Watch out for spider mite, aphids, and thrips.

Ardisia crenata

Phyllostachys nigra

Chimonobambusa marmorea

× *Hibanobambusa tranquillans* 'Shiroshima'

Bamboos

Bambusa

B. multiplex (*B. glaucescens*), H:8ft(2.5m), is the hedge bamboo from north China, Asia, and the Himalayas. An attractive evergreen with long stems and narrow leaves 4-6in(10-15cm) long, it is often represented by a more colorful form, *B.m.* 'Alphonse Karr'. This has delicate foliage, often with yellow and white stripes within the leaf. Young stems are yellow, soon becoming striped vertically with green, then flushed and striped with deep pink. The more sun it receives, the brighter this striking bamboo will be. Cold winter temperatures as low as 18°F(-8°C) can be tolerated, but must be accompanied by careful watering (just as the leaves begin to curl through dryness is the time to water again). *B. ventricosa*, the Buddha or Buddha's belly bamboo from India, can reach 28-30ft(8-9m) in its natural habitat. For no apparent reason, it may stop producing straight stems and the shiny green nodes of some or many of its new shoots become swollen and club- or bottle-shaped. Plants can be kept as small as 20in(50cm) and are useful as bonsai, or can be allowed to reach 8ft(2.5m) or more.
32-45°F(0-7°C)

Chimonobambusa

C. marmorea from Japan is a pretty bamboo with attractively marbled stems, quite wide leaves, and a shrubby appearance. Young canes are pale green, their culm (cane) sheaths mottled with brown and silvery-white, striped with pink, sometimes turning purple in very good light. A beautiful variegated form has leaves striped with white. The Chinese species *C. quadrangularis* has very attractive, square jade-green stems. Both of these produce new shoots in fall.
27-45°F(-3-7°C) H:6-7ft(1.8-2m)

× Hibanobambusa

× *H. tranquillans* 'Shiroshima' is a truly magnificent variegated bamboo. The leaves are large, marked with yellow and light and dark green.
27-45°F(-3-7°C) H:6-7ft(1.8-2m)

Phyllostachys

P. aurea is the robust fishpole or golden bamboo from China. This strong grower is pretty when young but older, well-kept, and well-fed specimens become magnificent with age. Stately 1-1½in(2.5-4cm) wide stems can reach 12ft(3.5m) if given headroom. Its most notable feature is the strange shape of the lower internodes which, shortened and swollen, push the old sheathscars into interesting zigzag patterns toward the bases of the stems. *P. nigra*, the black bamboo from China and Japan, is also distinguished by its stems which, though green when young, turn black. These, plus a graceful arching habit, make a dramatic and eyecatching addition to the greenhouse.
27-45°F(-3-7°C) H:6-8ft(1.8-2.5m)

Banksia

(Proteaceae)
The Australian honeysuckle trees are not easy to grow. They germinate easily from seed but young plants seem to die for no apparent reason, turning first pale yellow and then brown. They need a sunny, bright position, good ventilation, and a well-drained potting mix (equal parts of peat and sharp sand), without added fertilizer. Give only rainwater or tap water which has been boiled and cooled. Other dislikes include phosphates and, to an extent, nitrates (both present in most fertilizers), so grow in a low-nutrient mixture of peat and sand with a little dried blood. Feed occasionally throughout summer with weak liquid fertilizer containing magnesium sulfate and nitrogen in the form of urea or dried blood. When flourishing, banksias are wonderful plants, making rather wayward shrubs with long, leathery, tooth-edged, distinctive leaves. Dense, cone-shaped flower heads (sometimes composed of over 1,000 individual flowers each) are an incredible sight and really give one a sense of achievement. Cuttings of well-ripened shoots will root. Grow in containers.

Leaves of *B. coccinea* are more rounded than is usual, with small teeth around the edge. Late-winter and early-spring flowers are sensational, making a structured, bright scarlet head. *B. grandis* is a striking sight in bloom, when 6in(15cm) long cylindrical spikes of yellow flowers appear in spring, surmounted by bright, grayish-green leaves with triangular teeth. *B. hookeriana* is a spreading shrub, with flower spikes of a subtle honey color. Serrated-edged leaves have an almost golden appearance. In *B. spinulosa collina*, short, toothed leaves are dark green with beautiful silver undersides, and flower heads are rusty-brown and purple.
40-50°F(4-10°C) H:4-6ft(1.2-1.8m) S:3-4ft(1-1.2m)

Beaucarnea

(Agavaceae)
B. recurvata (*Nolina recurvata*) Pony-tail palm, elephant's foot, and bottle palm are common names that suggest that this native of Mexico is better described as striking than pretty. The swollen base of the stem, like a giant onion, is surmounted by a disorderly rosette of long narrow leaves. These grow out and hang down away from the plant, ending with a spiral twist toward the tip. As leaf tips often trail down below the base of the pot, a pedestal stand is the best method of display. The leaf tips invariably turn dry and straw-colored with age; the tidy-minded could trim them off without causing harm. Eventually, as bottom leaves die, the trunk above the swelling grows, drawing the rosette of leaves higher. Pony-tail palms thrive in full light and, being able to store water, can survive short periods of drought. Allow the top half of the soil to dry out between

waterings, then soak it thoroughly before drying out again. Feed with liquid fertilizer monthly throughout summer, using a formula for cacti and succulents, and use a well-drained potting mix when repotting. Take particular care when handling: leaf edges are rough and can cut if rubbed backward. Branching plants have usually had their tops removed. Offsets and new shoots resulting from such decapitations can easily be rooted to make more plants. Propagate also by seed.
40°F(4°C) H:6ft(1.8m) S:3ft(1m)

Blechnum

(Blechnaceae)

B. gibbum This small attractive, humidity-loving tree fern from New Caledonia has great presence. The short scaly black trunk will grow to 24in(60cm) and develops as the plant grows older. Topped by stiff, shiny fronds, it looks almost palm-like. Shade from direct sunlight and never allow the soil to dry out. Propagate by spores.
50°F(10°C) H:48in(120cm) S:36in(90cm)

Brachychiton

(Sterculiaceae)

B. rupestris The Queensland bottle tree, so called because of the huge bottle-shaped base to its trunk, can reach 60ft(18m) high or more in the wild but will grow happily restricted in a pot. Leaves on the same plant vary from entire to having between five and nine leaflets. A thick trunk forms, even in a pot, and to reduce height, the main stem may have to be pruned hard back in late spring. Two or more new shoots will grow from the stump which can also be pruned. It is possible to buy "cut back" plants with thick bases and several shoots, trained to look rather like a bonsai specimen. Allow the soil to dry out between waterings. Whitefly and spider mite can be a problem. Propagate by seed.
45-50°F(7-10°C) H:7ft(2m) S:4ft(1.2m)

Beaucarnea recurvata

Bromeliads

The fascinating and colorful members of the family Bromeliaceae make excellent greenhouse specimens, prized for their brilliant bracts and flower spikes. A group of these plants attached to a bromeliad log or tree (see p.19) make an interesting focal point.

Most bromeliads are epiphytic, growing on the trunks and branches of trees and shrubs. They derive no nourishment from their hosts, merely using them as anchorage. Some are lithophytic, which means that they grow on rocks. What appears to be a normal, active root system has evolved more for support than the gathering of water and minerals.

Most tropical epiphytic bromeliads form a rosette of leaves which acts like a funnel or urn to collect water. Falling plant and animal debris is also caught and breaks down into a nutritious liquid, which is absorbed through special glands at the leaf bases. Urn plants like aechmea, nidularium, and neoregelia will grow happily in pots but need an open potting mix (ordinary potting mix with added perlite and orchid grade bark). They prefer to be slightly pot-bound and require only modest watering. During summer, keep the funnel topped up with water and feed regularly with weak foliar fertilizer.

Epiphytic bromeliads also grow in forests of higher and cooler regions, festooning limbs of trees. In Mexican deserts tillandsias drape themselves over cacti and in the strange, seasonally fog-bound deserts of Peru, where the air is moist but the ground dry, they can be found just resting on the sand surface. Some tillandsias have no discernible root system at all. Those with silvery, narrow leaves are usually known as air plants, appearing to live on little else; covered with moisture-absorbing scales, they can take all they need from the air surrounding them. There are terrestrial bromeliads that live in the deep, light leaf litter of forest floors. Others come from such diverse habitats as deserts or swamps. Roots of these are important for water and nutrient absorption as well as anchorage.

Mature bromeliads bloom once, then die. Most, though, produce offsets which nourish themselves from the parent plant as it slowly dies. Once these reach a good size, they can be severed from the remains of the original and grown separately. Tropical urn plant types can take a long time to reach flowering size unless in ideal conditions of warmth and humidity.

Aechmea

The handsome urn plant, *A. fasciata* from rainforest areas of Brazil, H:20in(50cm), has gray-green leaves banded and streaked horizontally with silvery-white markings. A spike of pink bracts and blue flowers is held just above the "urn" of leaves. Other species and hybrids are blessed with taller spikes, sometimes with very showy, colorful bracts and flowers. *A. chantinii*, H:15-36in(40-90cm), has well-defined bands of gray-white across rich green leaves and a branched, red-bracted inflorescence with orange flowers. *A.* 'Foster's Favorite', the lacquered wine cup, H:12-24in (30-60cm), boasts lovely wine-red flushed leaves; an even more handsome sport of this popular hybrid has cream edges and stripes running vertically down the leaves. The red and purple flower spike droops.
50-60°F(10-16°C)

Ananas

Making bold upright plants, these bromeliads are terrestrial rather than epiphytic. *A. comosus* var. *variegatus*, H:36in(90cm), is a native of Brazil. To grow in the greenhouse, choose a pineapple with a good, healthy "top". Cut the top off and remove the bottom leaves to reveal a thick stem. Rooted in loose potting mix and potted up, this will grow into an attractive plant that might even flower and fruit, given humidity and temperatures of 70-80°F(21-27°C).

The wild or red pineapple, *A. bracteatus*, native to Brazil and Paraguay, is popularly sold as an ornamental plant. *A.b.* var. *tricolor*, H:36in(90cm),

Aechmea fasciata

Bromeliads

has cream-edged leaves flushed with pink when young and a beautiful flower spike like a colorful miniature pineapple crowned with a tuft of variegated leaves.
55-60°F(13-16°C)

Billbergia

Unlike some bromeliads, this attractive genus will reliably produce flowers year after year, though they are not always long-lasting, and some tolerate low temperatures.

B. nutans, queen's tears, will grow in greenhouses kept just frost-free. Undivided, a plant will build up into a wide clump of narrow rosettes, H:12in(30cm) S:24in(60cm), from which arching flower stems are produced in spring. These bear pink bracts and curious pale green flowers with purple-blue edges. Divide plants after flowering. *B. × windii*, of similar size, is almost as easy to grow, perhaps liking a little more warmth. The individual rosettes are wider and leaf color more a dusty gray-green. Arching flower spikes have wider pink bracts and flowers of similar color but somehow less fine than those of *B. nutans*.

B. pyramidalis var. *striata*, the striped urn plant, H:12-15in(30-40cm), boasts much wider, cream-striped leaves and bears an upright spike of spectacular fleshy-colored bracts and red flowers tipped with blue. This plant also prefers warmth.
38-40°F(3-4°C)

Cryptanthus

The terrestrial earth stars are among the loveliest bromeliads. They are small, but work as bold specimens when they become part of a larger display, such as planted as the base of a bromeliad log. Their low, star-shaped rosettes are ideal for wide shallow pans, terrariums and bottle gardens. Resembling exotic starfish, some are banded horizontally with powdery silver, others streaked or edged vertically with cream suffused with pink. *C. bivittatus* is possibly the most common. Leaves 4in(10cm) long are dark green at the edges and in the middle, with two silvery-gray stripes, sometimes pink-tinged, running the length of the leaf. *C. fosterianus* has leaves 12in(30cm) long of deep maroon banded with irregular silvery markings. One of the most colorful, *C. bromelioides* var. *tricolor*, has spreading 8in(20cm) long leaves with creamy, pink-tinged, often bright pink edges and green and cream stripes running along the length.
50°F(10°C)

Fascicularia

Ideal foliage plants for the frost-free greenhouse, *F. bicolor* and *F. pitcairniifolia*, two almost identical species from Chile, are ground-dwellers and take well to growing in pots. They form a tuft, H&S:24in (60cm), of many silvery-green rosettes of saw-edged leaves. Mature individual rosettes will flower in summer, flattening out to display pale blue flowers surrounded by bright red bracts. The flowers of *F. pitcairniifolia* are somewhat darker than those of

Ananas bracteatus var. *tricolor*

smaller *F. bicolor*, which has longer flowers than flower bracts. The inner leaves of the rosette of *F. bicolor* are red and green at flowering time, while those of *F. pitcairniifolia* are red.
36°F(2°C)

Guzmania

This epiphytic genus contains a good range of species and hybrids. Flower spikes, mainly in orange and red, last for many months. Even when these have faded, glossy foliage, sometimes colored, remains attractive, though unless conditions are warm and humid they are shy of re-flowering. *G. lingulata* var. *minor*, H&S:12in(30cm), is compact; its cultivar *G. l.* var. *m.* 'Red' has really red bract color. Larger plants with taller spikes – flaming swords and flaming torches – include 'Gran Prix' and 'Amaranth'. *G. musaica*, H:24in(60cm) S:30in(75cm), is grown primarily for its attractive foliage, heavily marked, mosaic-like, with dark green against a lighter background. Orange-yellow bracts protrude above the foliage and house a head of yellow flowers.
50°F(10°C)

Neoregelia

Mostly from Brazil, these epiphytic plants are grown primarily for their wonderfully colorful, tooth-edged foliage. Flowers, such as they are, are produced within the rosette, often in the "urn" of water. Top this up regularly until the rosette has reached maturity and flowered; subsequent decay results in stagnation.

N. carolinae f. *tricolor*, known as the blushing bromeliad, H:12in(30cm) S:24in(60cm), has cream-striped leaves that turn bright pink from the center at flowering time. *N.c.* 'Flandria' is similar but has a cream-striped edge. *N. spectabilis*, the fingernail plant (of similar size), restricts itself to turning red just at the leaf tip, like a red-varnished talon. *N. sarmentosa* and *N. marmorata* (the marble plant) have heavy maroon markings, the green showing as mottles and blotches, rather like marbling.
50°F(10°C)

Nidularium

This epiphytic genus from rainforest areas of eastern Brazil is superficially similar to neoregelia: its name means "a little nest". *N. fulgens*, also named blushing bromeliad, H:9in(23cm) S:15-20in(40-50cm), has mottled tooth-edged leaves and when it flowers, a bright red center resembling one of those gift-wrapping rosettes. *N. billbergioides*, H:12in(30cm) S:24in(60cm), has a flower spike that rises some 12in (30cm) away from the center of the plant. This is an acidic color, with leaves a splendid lime-green, as are the tips of the outwardly curved, lemon-yellow bracts concealing white flowers.
50°F(10°C)

Cryptanthus bromelioides var. *tricolor*

Neoregelia carolinae f. *tricolor*

Fascicularia bicolor

Puya

These terrestrials are suitable for a frost-free greenhouse. They come from the Andes of Colombia, Ecuador, Peru, Bolivia, and northern Chile, are the highest-growing bromeliads and have a size range from cushion-like 4in(10cm) high dwarfs to majestic giants like *P. raimondii*, H:33ft(10m), from the Peruvian Andes. Adapted to withstand cold and drought, they dislike being wet at the roots during cold winter spells and need a well-drained soil. Ventilate the greenhouse on fine winter days to avoid a damp atmosphere. Easily raised from seed, they can take many years to flower. They are also suitable for propagation by offsets in spring. In summer, *P. alpestris* can send up incredible 6ft(1.8m) tall flower spikes. Each branched inflorescence is spangled with a long succession of short-stalked, shimmering flowers of an indescribable blue-green. Rosettes of spiny-edged, white-scaled leaves reach up to 3ft(1m) high. *P. chilensis* differs in having a branched, candelabra-like stem, but is blessed with flowers of an equally fascinating yellowish-green color.

36-40°F(2-4°C)

Tillandsia

These are basically divided into two types. Those like pretty *T. cyanea*, H&S:10in(25cm), are epiphytic but have a comparatively well-developed root system and will grow in a pot. Leaves are a dark brownish olive-green. Green bracts, attractively suffused with pink at the edges, make a paddle-shape at the end of the flower stalk. The flowers themselves are striking, surprisingly large, and usually open, one by one, to a glorious deep violet-blue. In contrast, those referred to as air plants are covered in silver or gray furry scales which absorb moisture from the air; often rootless, they can take nourishment from particles of

Bromeliads

dust. They are often sold stuck to shells or pieces of bark. The long skeins of moss-like growth dangling from trees in the mangrove swamps of Florida prove on closer inspection to be hundreds of plants of *T. usneoides* linked together. Their habitat varies from hot, steamy rainforest, through cool, moist cloud-forest to surprisingly dry cliffs.

T. ionantha, H:3in(8cm), from Mexico, Guatemala, and Nicaragua is popular, its compact rosettes slightly bulbous at the base with arching, silvery leaves. Happy plants will produce stalkless purple flowers, when the whole rosette turns red. *T. caput-medusae*, H&S:6in(15cm), is well named, as the twisting leaves arising from their bulbous bases look like the writhing snakes on the head of Medusa. Leaves of *T. argentea*, H&S:4in(10cm), are fine and thread-like as they twist out from the body of the plant. They are not difficult to grow once their way of life is understood. Water with a fine mist spray at least daily during hot summer days and during winter when the air is hot and dry. During cold,

damp spells, spray two or three times a week; water should dry from the plant within a couple of hours, as they are prone to rot in wet and cold. Feed with a half-strength foliar fertilizer every two months. 50°F(10°C)

Vriesea

Vrieseas are among some of the most attractive epiphytic bromeliads, particularly the well-known *V. splendens* from Trinidad, Guyana, and Venezuela, known as flaming sword. Striking foliage is shiny green with dark cross-banding. The spike of red bracts and yellow flowers reaches some 24in(60cm), while the main body of the plant rarely exceeds H&S:12in(30cm). A marvelous one is *V. hieroglyphica*, king of the bromeliads from Brazil; dark markings on the 18in(45cm) long, light green leaves do indeed resemble hieroglyphics. *V. × poelmanii* makes a bold rosette of shiny green, wide strap-shaped leaves spreading to 30in(75cm) across before flowering. The branched spike of red bracts 36in(90cm) high lasts several months. 50°F(10°C)

Brugmansia sanguinea

Brugmansia

(Solanaceae)

The showy angel's trumpets are prized for their huge, often perfumed flowers and virtual indestructibility. The larger species and hybrids will make substantial shrubs, best pruned hard in fall after flowering to sprout back into growth every spring. Well-watered and fed, they will flower throughout summer. Watch for whitefly and spider mite and keep plants clean by promptly spraying or introducing parasites and predators. Many brugmansias are available from seed, often listed under their old name, *Datura*. Cuttings 3-4in(8-10cm) long root easily during summer; pinch back young plants to encourage several stems to form. All parts of the plant are poisonous. Give brugmansias a position of good light, even standing them outside for the summer. Heights and spreads are given for plants pruned annually. 40°F(4°C) H:6-8ft(1.8-2.5m) S:4-5ft(1.2-1.5m)

B. arborea This species from Peru and Chile tends to flower during late summer and into fall. The white, trumpet-shaped flowers, 6-8in(15-20cm) long, have a heady perfume.

B. × candida One of the prettiest angel's trumpets, scented flowers are usually white but can sometimes be creamy-yellow or pink and are a magnificent 8-12in(20-30cm) long. A double form, *B. × c.* 'Plena', is sometimes known as *Datura cornigera* 'Knightii'. *B. × c.* 'Grand Marnier' sometimes seems a lovely subtle, warm apricot; at other times, especially as they age, flowers look merely dull, like white yellowing to parchment color.

B. chlorantha Perfumed yellow flowers are freely produced during late summer and fall.

B. sanguinea This species has delightful warm red flowers with a yellow tube, a familiar sight along roadside clearings in its native Colombia, Chile, and Peru. A plant with similar flowers is sometimes sold under the name of *Datura rosei*.

Tillandsia cyanea

Vriesea splendens

Brunfelsia americana

B. suaveolens A classic angel's trumpet from Brazil to Mexico, the ghostly, scented white flowers are more trumpet-shaped than most, flaring out at the petal edges with the tips pointing up as though wired.

Brunfelsia

(Solanaceae)

These reliable evergreen shrubs from South America and the West Indies need little attention to flower freely. They prefer slight shade during summer, suggesting that their natural home would be under taller trees. Propagate by seed or by 3-4in(8-10cm) long cuttings in summer. Feed with liquid fertilizer regularly during summer months to prevent yellowing of leaves.
50-55°F(10-13°C)

B. americana Lady of the night has butter-yellow flowers, fading to white with age, which are only perfumed after dusk.
H&S:36-48in(90-120cm)

B. pauciflora (B. calycina) The yesterday, today, and tomorrow plant from Brazil and Peru has large scentless flowers, purple-blue on their first day of opening. The intense color fades in roughly three days through pale mauve almost to white. Flowering begins in midwinter and can continue throughout summer, making this a worthy greenhouse shrub. If plants become too tall or unshapely, prune toward the end of summer. Plants that are raised in borders can be left to grow naturally to their full size.
B.p. 'Macrantha' is more vigorous, with larger flowers.
H&S:30-60in(75-150cm)

B. undulata The white rain tree from the West Indies bears clusters of white, scented, wavy-lobed flowers fading to creamy-yellow. Less showy than
B. pauciflora, flowers open at the end of summer, then occasionally throughout the year.
H:48in(120cm) S:36in(90cm)

Cacti and other succulents

Succulent plants are those which have evolved the ability to store water in stems, leaves, roots or all three, in order to withstand long droughts. They include plants from many different families, Cactaceae being one of the most popular and best known. Cacti are characterized by areoles, cushion-like structures on their stems from which spines are produced. Both cacti and other succulents have evolved a wide range of curious and often handsome shapes, and large, well-grown specimens are guaranteed to draw comment from visitors. In a spacious greenhouse a bed turned over completely to a bold composition of cacti and succulents, arranged around a few interesting rocks and with a neat top-dressing of gravel, makes a fascinating and unusual feature.

This group of plants is capable of tolerating short absences by their owners without keeling over from lack of water; thus a large specimen such as a 5ft(1.5m) silver torch cactus could prove a tougher, more worthwhile investment than a weeping fig or palm of comparable size. However, a plant's succulent nature is not an excuse for neglect. Even plants from arid desert regions demand favorable greenhouse conditions and the right kind of care if they are to thrive. Check all plants regularly for mealy bugs, which may attack roots as well as upper parts. Ensure good air-circulation by providing adequate ventilation in summer and in winter when weather conditions permit. Scale insect and spider mite can be a problem.

DESERT CACTI Good light and air-circulation are required for healthy growth, so ventilate well during summer and on mild winter days. From spring to fall, most cacti are in active growth; water regularly, as soon as the top half of the soil has dried out. Feed monthly with special cactus fertilizer. During winter, water plants once or twice to prevent them from shriveling. Most will survive in a greenhouse heated only sufficiently to keep out frost, in which case they are unlikely to need watering at all. Cacti from South America will appreciate a higher winter minimum of 50°F(10°C) and slightly more water than their northern counterparts.

Pot cacti up during late spring, before their roots become restricted, and certainly before spines begin to push against the edge of the pot. Cushioning the bench with loose balls of newspaper and using a soft collar of cloth will protect both hands and delicate areoles, which can easily break off. Use a special well-drained potting mix: three parts of peat (or peat alternative) and one part of sharp sand is a good mix.

Add sufficient fertilizer to make a rich mixture. Alternatively, add peat and sand to a soil-based potting mix.

Should a cactus begin to rot at the base, cut the healthy top part off and leave it exposed to the air for a few hours to a few days, until the cut surface has sealed itself over. Insert what has now become a large cutting upright into nearly dry sand, burying the base by only ⅛in(3mm), and steady the plant with a small cane. Do not cover or water for a few days. After watering, leave until the sand has nearly dried out before repeating. Keep out of full sun and roots should soon form. The process for rooting cuttings is almost identical, but wherever possible remove the cutting at a natural joint, for example where a branch joins the main stem. Sometimes offsets can be pulled away from the parent plant with roots already formed. Cacti are also easily raised from seed.

FOREST CACTI Epiphytic cacti occupy a variety of different habitats, but many grow in humid forests. They prefer warmer conditions, although most will tolerate winter temperatures just above freezing. Shade lightly from hot sun and maintain humidity during high temperatures. Do not allow to dry out completely. Propagate by stem cuttings during spring and summer. For cacti with a trailing habit, see pp.107-9.

OTHER SUCCULENTS Most require good, direct light to succeed, with a few exceptions (for example, *Haworthia* and *Gasteria*), which prefer light shade. Water regularly during summer, adding a cactus fertilizer once a month. Although preferring slightly warmer winter temperatures, most will tolerate temperatures just above freezing, but generally need to be watered a little more than cacti to prevent shriveling. Some succulents make most of their growth during fall and winter; these prefer extra warmth and need modest watering during this period and less in summer. Feed them two to three times during winter with a cactus fertilizer. Pot all succulents up when required just after active growth has started, using the same potting mix as for cacti. Propagate by stem or leaf cuttings, plantlets, seed, or by detaching offsets from rosette-forming species.

Agave (Agavaceae)

These striking rosette-forming succulents make good container plants while young, but are difficult to accommodate as they grow large: most have dangerously spine-tipped leaves. *A. americana*, the century plant from Mexico and its variegated varieties, H&S:3-6ft(1-1.8m), are the most popular. Despite their name, flowering will occur before the age of 100 but only on mature plants and not normally those whose roots have been restricted by containers. It is not uncommon to see roof panes removed from the glasshouses of botanic gardens to

Cacti and other succulents

allow headroom for the spikes of creamy, bell-shaped flowers often 20ft(6m) high. After flowering, the rosette dies, usually leaving both offsets and seed behind. *A. filifera*, the thread agave from Mexico, is also attractive and not quite so lethally spined.
38°F(3°C)

Aloe (Liliaceae/Aloeaceae)
A. arborescens, H&S:3-6ft(1-1.8m), is just one of a group of large aloes which make splendid, unusual specimens, particularly during late winter when they send up their spikes of orange-red flowers.
40°F(4°C)

Beschorneria (Agavaceae)
B. yuccoides, H:3ft(1m) S:5ft(1.5m), forms rosettes of gray-green leaves and can withstand a light frost.
38°F(3°C)

Cephalocereus (Cactaceae)
C. senilis, the old man cactus from Mexico, slowly forms a column of uneven diameter clothed with wild, white hair-like bristles 2-4in(5-10cm) long which form tufts and beards of growth. Plants do better in a lime-rich soil. Take great care not to overwater. Potted plants rarely exceed 3-4ft(1-1.2m), although heights of 20ft(6m) can be found in the wild.
40°F(4°C)

Cereus (Cactaceae)
C. uruguayanus (*C. peruvianus* of gardens, now correctly *C. hildmannianus*) is a plain but handsome columnar cactus, its bluish-green stem eventually becoming much branched. In their native Brazil and Argentina, plants will reach a mighty 33ft(10m) and even in the greenhouse their growth is rapid (for a cactus) and specimens may have to be cut back. Several new stems will arise from the cuts. Many plants sold as *C. peruvianus* prove to be *C. uruguayanus*. True *C. peruvianus*, when mature, produces long white flowers 4in(10cm) across at night.
40°F(4°C)

Cleistocactus (Cactaceae)
One of the best specimen cacti is Bolivian *C. strausii*, the silver torch. Easy, fast growers, the columnar stems reach 3-4ft(1-1.2m) and branch from the base. Should they become too tall, chop off the main stem, and more stems will grow from that point. A mature plant becomes a splendid, multi-stemmed specimen within a few years. White bristles give an overall silvery effect. Once plants reach 3ft(1m), they may produce red tubular flowers 3in(8cm) long, pollinated in the wild by hummingbirds. These project horizontally from the stem and are interesting rather than attractive.

The free-flowering *C. winteri* (*Borzicactus aureispina*) produces pendent stems with golden spines. These stems can reach 3ft(1m), and will begin flowering when half that length. Eventually a great clump forms, like a golden octopus. Difficult to accommodate in a pot and downright lethal in a hanging basket, it looks best tumbling over a well-placed rock in the greenhouse bed. For best results water just a little more in winter than most cacti, and maintain a winter minimum of 50°F(10°C). A plant that is happy will produce its 2in(5cm) wide orange flowers virtually all summer.
45°F(7°C)

Echinocactus (Cactaceae)
The most popular species in this genus is *E. grusonii* from Mexico. Handsome cacti resembling giant pin-cushions stuck with golden pins may grow to H&S: 24in(60cm) in cultivation, but only when over 30 years old. Though common in cultivation, they are extremely rare in the wild. The ribbed body of the cactus is glossy green and the spines, arising from woolly areoles, can vary from almost white to deep gold. These can reach 2in(5cm) on older plants and even on quite a young specimen may be 1in(2.5cm) long. Growth is not rapid, but a plant can increase in size by one-third in its first four years. Yellow flowers appear rarely on mature plants.
40°F(4°C)

Epiphyllum (Cactaceae)
Epiphyllums are epiphytic forest cacti and although most are of modest size, well suited to hanging baskets, *E. oxypetalum* is an intriguing, larger species. From Mexico and Brazil, this will reach a height of 6-7ft(1.8-2m) and a spread of 4ft(1.2m). Growth is upright to begin with, but stems may need the support of canes. Once the desired height has been reached, simply allow the stems to flop over and sprawl out. The huge white, perfumed flowers 9in(23cm) long and 5in(13cm) wide, borne during the night in summer, make up for the untidy growth habit of this epiphytic cactus. To succeed, plants need shade during summer, high humidity, should not be allowed to dry out, and prefer a warm temperature, 50-55°F(10-13°C).
40°F(4°C)

Espostoa (Cactaceae)
These are among the most beautiful of columnar cacti. A dense covering of white hairs hides sharp spines. *E. lanata*, the cotton ball or Peruvian old man cactus, is the best known. Older plants often branch out at the base and may slowly reach 3ft(1m) or more in cultivation.
40°F(4°C)

Furcraea (Agavaceae)
F. foetida 'Mediopicta', the variegated Mauritius hemp, H:4ft(1.2m) S:5ft(1.5m), is a succulent that makes an attractive specimen while young, its spiky rosette of leaves looking rather like a cross between an agave and a spider plant. Plants grow well planted in borders but will eventually become too large for most greenhouses. Grow in pots to restrict their size. Propagate by offsets or seed.
38°F(3°C)

Agave americana 'Variegata'

Echinocactus grusonii

Calliandra haematocephala

Callistemon citrinus

Calliandra

(Leguminosae)

These are evergreen shrubs with attractive foliage and showy flowers. Clusters of promising buds suddenly explode, one by one, long stamens bursting out, to become a rounded pompon of flowers. These are relatively short-lived, but appear in long succession. There are species with red, pink, creamy-yellow, and white flowers. Mature plants are best grown in large pots. When the shoots become too long, prune back by about two-thirds after flowering. Mealy bugs can be a problem.

C. haematocephala This wonderful plant is lovely even when not in flower, as its soft leaves composed of five to ten pairs of leaflets are pink-tinged when young. Flowers, which appear during winter, are a welcome sight, like soft red powderpuffs 2-3in (5-8cm) across. The origin of this plant is thought to be Bolivia. Although plants might survive lower temperatures, they do better at a minimum of 50-55°F(10-13°C). Shade lightly from hot sun. 45°F(7°C) H:6ft(1.8m) S:4ft(1.2m)

Callistemon

(Myrtaceae)

The bottlebrushes from Australia and Tasmania have showy red, yellow, purplish, or green summer flowers which grow in spikes at the ends of shoots, their long stamens giving the bottlebrush effect. Planted out in large tubs or in the greenhouse border, they make fine specimens of wayward habit. The stems continue to grow beyond the old blooms to produce next year's flowers, leaving woody seed capsules behind. These, with the narrow leathery leaves and long branches, can be striking in silhouette. To retain shape and size, cut some of the older, weaker stems close to the base or to a stronger stem in fall. Badly shaped plants can be cut back hard successfully, but may take two years or more to flower again. Grow bottlebrushes in good light and in a well-drained, loam-based soil. Water well during summer but keep drier during cold winter spells, ventilating freely during mild winter weather. Plants should flower in four or five years from seed, available from specialists. Cuttings, 4in(10cm) long,

preferably with a heel, root better with bottom heat. 40-45°F(4-7°C)

C. citrinus The name lemon bottlebrush refers not to the flower color, which is bright red, but to aromatic leaves, lemon-scented when crushed. Young leaves are pinkish-red. Flower spikes are some 4in(10cm) long. Most popular is *C.c.* 'Splendens' with stamens of brilliant crimson.
H:10ft(3m) S:7ft(2m)

C. speciosus The Albany bottlebrush has 5in(13cm) long flower spikes of showy red stamens. Plants can reach great heights when given the root run of the greenhouse border, their long stems arching down.
H:15ft(4.5m) S:9ft(2.7m)

Camellia

(Theaceae)

Camellias make good greenhouse specimens because with the protection of glass their flowers open earlier and are undamaged by frost. *C. reticulata* and its varieties need shelter more than most. The best plan is to bring camellias into the greenhouse in pots or tubs from fall onward. Depending on the warmth available, plants will begin flowering from midwinter. Once danger of frost is past, set plants in an outside bed in a semi-shady position. Pot up in late spring, using a neutral to acidic soil. Do not allow plants to dry out. Feed with a liquid fertilizer for acid-loving plants. Those restricted in tubs or grown against walls will benefit from a little formative pruning after flowering. Planted in the greenhouse border, most camellias would eventually grow as high as the roof. Propagate by 4in(10cm) long semi-hardwood cuttings or leaf-bud cuttings in late summer.

C. japonica must be a magnificent sight in the mountains of Japan and Korea, where it will reach 30ft(9m) in height. In the wild, flowers are red but this species is now represented in cultivation by a large range of cultivars, single, semi-double, and double in shades of red, pink, white, and bicolors. C. reticulata is a Chinese species and has large pink flowers 3-5in(8-13cm) across. There are superb cultivars with even larger, more sumptuous flowers, mostly in shades of pink. The advantage of the Japanese C. sasanqua is that it flowers early, during winter. It would be ideal for bringing winter cheer to a barely heated greenhouse. Small single, occasionally semi-double, flowers are usually white but can be pink or red. Again, there are many cultivars to suit most tastes. C. sinensis, the tea plant, originally from China, is grown for curiosity rather than ornamental value. Flowers, 1in(2.5cm) long, are off-white and slightly fragrant. C. × williamsii, an early-flowering group of hybrids between C. japonica and C. saluenensis, has produced two of the best-known camellias, C. 'Debbie' and C. 'Donation'.
40°F(4°C) H:7-8ft(2-2.5m) S:5ft(1.5m)

Carica

(Caricaceae)

C. papaya Papayas or pawpaws, originally from Mexico and Costa Rica, may be raised by sowing the pips found inside the fruit. To grow plants of any stature, a greenhouse of high temperature and humidity is required. Male and female flowers usually occur on separate plants, so for fruit, grow several young plants in the hope of finding at least one of each sex in the batch and hand pollinate to set the fruit. Even without this they are handsome plants. Tall, pole-like stems taper toward the top, where a cluster of large, divided, lobed leaves, sometimes 24in(60cm) across on tall plants, form a small canopy. Flowers and fruits grow straight out from the stem. C.p. 'Solo' is a self-pollinating cultivar, bearing both male and female flowers.
55-60°F(13-16°C) H:12ft(3.5m) S:7ft(2m)

× Citrofortunella

(Rutaceae)

× **C. microcarpa** (× **C. mitis**) The calamondin is an intergeneric hybrid between Citrus and Fortunella.

Camellia japonica

Carica papaya

Plants are compact and highly ornamental, with glossy foliage and an almost continuous succession of pretty white flowers and small bright orange fruits. Both are often present at once and the fruits can be used for marmalade. With pruning, plants can be kept as small as 24in(60cm). Cultivation is the same as for citrus. × *C.m.* 'Tiger' is attractively variegated in leaf and fruit, the fruits turning bright orange when ripe. 50°F(10°C)

Citrus
(Rutaceae)

Plants with glossy, fragrant evergreen foliage and attractive scented flowers – followed by ornamental, often edible, fruit – could not fail but be popular. Although tolerant of low temperatures, citrus will not grow and fruit well unless a warmer temperature is provided. Grown colder, they frequently drop all their leaves. If this happens, leave them dormant, keeping the soil just moist until spring. Prune back long shoots and they will burst into growth. Citrus are hungry feeders. Leaves of starved plants may turn yellow, while fruit refuses to set or drops prematurely. The cure is a well-balanced liquid fertilizer containing trace or minor elements applied weekly throughout the growing season and an annual top-dressing of rich soil. Too alkaline a soil may cause yellow leaves. Scale insects and sometimes mealy bugs find citrus irresistible: wipe them off if spotted early enough, spray or introduce biological control. Repeated spraying with soft-soap preparations should eventually eradicate these troublesome pests. Failure to do so will harm the plants' health and also result in the growth of sooty mold which feeds on the sticky honeydew secreted by the insects onto leaves below. Citrus respond well to hard pruning, which is a good method of rejuvenating an untidy or infested specimen. Growing citrus from pips is easy and good fun, though plants can take years to flower and may never set fruit. Seeds may take a month or more to germinate and can be polyembryonic: three seedlings sometimes grow from one pip, two arising from embryonic tissue in the mother plant and therefore identical to it, the third being the true hybrid of unknown quality. To be sure of a dependable fruit-bearing plant, buy named varieties from a reputable nursery. Cuttings of 3-4in(8-10cm) long semi-ripe shoots root easily during summer, citron and lemon rooting more readily than grapefruit and orange. The adventurous can try budding their citrus onto one-year-old seedling stocks of a close relative, *Poncirus trifoliata,* in late summer. Heights of greenhouse specimens vary according to whether they are pot- or border-grown and how they are pruned. The heights given are a guide to the optimum for each group. 50°F(10°C)

C. aurantiifolia Limes are a popular choice, their acidic fruits making useful additions to drinks. Varieties include *C.a.* 'Tahiti', which bears large sweet, seedless limes that eventually turn yellow. Hybrids between lemon and lime include *C. aurantiifolia × limon* 'Indian Lime', which yields small, typically lime-flavored fruits, and the prolific *C.a. × l.* 'La Valette'. H:6ft(1.8m) S:4ft(1.2m) restricted by pruning

C. aurantium The bitter oranges are excellent for marmalade, and large flowers make them useful ornamentals for the greenhouse. *C.a.* 'Seville' is well known as the marmalade orange. *C.a.* var. *myrtifolia* 'Chinotto' is a handsome plant graced with prolific blooms, while *C.a.* 'Bouquet' is well worth growing as its flowers are the most scented of any citrus and are used in perfumery. These plants are best given the root run of the greenhouse border. H:6ft(1.8m) S:4ft(1.2m) restricted by pruning

C. limon Lemons have long been popular for the greenhouse, and you can buy large trained specimens. A popular hybrid is *C.* 'Meyer', discovered in China in the early 1900s. Flowers are produced almost continuously throughout the year, yielding medium-sized, juicy lemons. One of the more ornamental choices is *C.l.* 'Variegata', whose fruits and leaves are variegated. H:6ft(1.8m) S:4ft(1.2m) restricted by pruning

C. medica Citrons make excellent cordial, though the fruit is not good to eat. When the thick-skinned, yellow, oval fruits 6in(15cm) are cut in two, the fresh smell is mouthwatering. Citrons, in particular *C.m.* 'Ethrog', gifted with exceptionally thick rind, are used for candying. Of large growth habit, they are best grown in the greenhouse border. H:9ft(2.75m) S:5ft(1.5m)

C. reticulata This group includes the sweet, small-fruited mandarins, clementines, and satsumas. Some of compact, upright growth, others attractively weeping, they make ideal tub plants. H:4-5ft(1.2-1.5m) S:3ft(1m)

Citrus 'Meyer'

× *Citrofortunella microcarpa* 'Tiger'

Citrus sinensis

Clerodendrum speciosissimum

Codiaeum variegatum var. *pictum* 'Carrierei'

C. sinensis The sweet oranges are represented by a wide range including sun-loving blood oranges, whose fruit tend to be small, with very red and sweet flesh. Among other varieties are well-known 'Shamouti' (*C.s.* 'Jaffa'), 'Valencia', and 'Washington'. H:5-6ft(1.5-1.8m) S:3-4ft(1-1.2m)

Clerodendrum

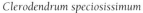

(Verbenaceae)

Grown for their showy flowers, the most popular clerodendrums are those that climb (see p.83), but two make attractive shrubby specimens. Sow seed in spring. When mature plants become ragged, take cuttings of healthy shoots in spring or summer, then cut the remainder of the plant hard back. Given good light, plants will sprout back into healthy, strong growth. Pinch the cuttings back at 3in(8cm) for well-shaped plants with several branches. Shade from hot summer sun.

C. philippinum (C. fragrans pleniflorum) This easy, successful plant from China and Japan deserves wider popularity in greenhouses. Well-grown plants should rarely be without their double flowers which are white suffused with pink. The strong fragrance is pleasantly sweet.

50°F(10°C) H:48in(120cm) S:30in(75cm) restricted in a pot

C. speciosissimum The Javan glorybean, equally easy to grow, begins to open its scarlet flowers during late summer and continues into the winter. They are carried in terminal panicles up to 10in(25cm) high.

Codiaeum variegatum var. *pictum*

Coprosma repens 'Picturata'

Of upright habit, even the large heart-shaped leaves are impressive on their own.
50°F(10°C) H:36in(90cm) S:30in(75cm) restricted in a pot

Codiaeum
(Euphorbiaceae)

Commonly known as crotons, these colorful foliage plants from Malaya and the Pacific Isles are also named Joseph's coat; their leaves certainly are of many colors. The many different colors and shapes are in fact named varieties of *C. variegatum* var. *pictum*. Distinguishing them from one another can be a problem as colors will change with age and quality of light. Warm, stable temperatures are required for healthy growth. Overwatering during winter, sudden drops in temperature, drafts and dry air will result in leaf drop and generally poor health. Shade from hot sun. When old, tall specimens become ungainly, prune them hard, preferably in spring. Cuttings 3-4in(8-10cm) long root easily during spring and summer, benefiting from bottom heat. Air-layering is an alternative.
55-60°F(13-16°C) H:5ft(1.5m) S:3ft(1m)

Coffea
(Rubiaceae)

C. arabica The Arabian coffee makes a handsome evergreen foliage plant of compact habit. White, starry flowers appear during summer and are followed by red fruits containing two seeds which are the coffee beans of commerce. Plants are tough and easy to grow. Shade them from hot sun and be vigilant against mealy bugs and scale insects: tell-tale signs are stickiness on the leaves followed by sooty mold. Cuttings are difficult to root but seed, sown as fresh as possible, germinates easily. *C.a.* 'Nana' is a useful, free-flowering variety for smaller places.
50°F(10°C) H:7ft(2m) S:4ft(1.2m)

Coprosma
(Rubiaceae)

Worthy for their evergreen foliage, these handsome shrubs are easy to grow and remain attractive for many years with little maintenance. Water well during summer, less during winter at low temperatures. Coprosmas, particularly the variegated kinds, appreciate good, though not scorching, light. Cut out some of the taller branches to keep plants compact. 3in(8cm) cuttings root easily during spring and summer. Nurseries specializing in New Zealand plants offer many unusual species.
36-40°F(2-4°C)

C. 'Beatson's Gold' Gold and green variegated leaves brighten up the greenhouse at any time of year.
H:6ft(1.8m) S:4ft(1.2m)

C. repens Variegated forms of this species from New Zealand are the most commonly grown. As the name suggests, growth is creeping at first, becoming upright later. Flowers are insignificant but where male and female plants are grown together, orange-red fruits ¹/₃in(10mm) long will be produced on the females during late summer and fall. *C.r.* 'Marble Queen' has cream leaves, spotted and marked in the center with dark green. *C.r.* 'Picturata' is the other way about, having dark green leaves with central creamy-yellow markings.
H:6ft(1.8m) S:5ft(1.5m)

Cordyline
(Agavaceae)

C. australis The cabbage palm from New Zealand is elegant and suitable for a prominent position in the greenhouse, but needs a lot of space. Older, branched plants may produce panicles of small white perfumed flowers. Light shade is of benefit in summer. Plants are best grown cool during winter, as dry air can scorch leaf tips. Propagate by seed or stem cuttings. Colored-leaved varieties include dark purple *C.a. purpurea*, while even flashier red-leaved and longitudinally striped-leaved versions have flamboyant names like 'Sundance', 'Torbay Dazzler',

and 'Torbay Sunset'. Another species, *C. indivisa*, is similar to *C. australis*, but has slightly wider and longer leaves. Cultivation is the same as for *C. australis*.
40°F(4°C) H:6ft(1.8m) S:4ft(1.2m)

Correa
(Rutaceae)

This distinctive genus of small shrubs flourishes in pots of well-drained, loam-based soil or planted in the greenhouse border. Some have the bonus of producing their bell-shaped flowers during winter. Water well during summer, less during cold winter spells. Prune leggy plants back by half to two-thirds after flowering. *C. alba* is the white correa with pretty, box-like leaves and white flowers. *C. backhouseana* is a favorite, with creamy-colored flowers during spring and early summer. For winter, *C.* 'Mannii' has small, pinkish-red bell-shaped flowers and, similar in color, *C. pulchella* flowers from summer through to winter. *C. reflexa* has prettily reflexed red petals tipped with green. *C.r. virens* is a nice form with green-tinged, pale yellow flowers.
38-40°F(3-4°C) H:36-48in(90-120cm) S:36in(90cm)

Correa backhouseana

Correa pulchella

Crinum moorei

Daphne odora 'Aureomarginata'

Cupressus torulosa 'Cashmeriana'

Crinum

(Liliaceae/Amaryllidaceae)

These bulbous plants with beautiful, often fragrant, flowers make fine specimens in large pots and tubs. Long, strap-shaped leaves are usually evergreen. Allow the long-necked bulbs to multiply and become congested in their containers, as they flower better undisturbed. Top-dress every year and feed occasionally with liquid fertilizer throughout the growing season. Eventually repot in spring, dividing if necessary and leaving the top third of the bulb above the surface of the soil. Propagate by sowing seed as soon as ripe, or by offsets. Shade from summer sun.

Some of the more tropical species require lots of water in summer but less in winter, particularly at lower temperatures. They are all poisonous.

C. asiaticum The Asiatic poison bulb from tropical Asia has lush, shining green leaves and clusters of narrow-petaled sweetly scented flowers, sometimes tinged with pink, in spring and summer. The bulbs themselves become enormous. They were once mashed up as a poison: treat them with caution. 55-60°F(13-16°C) H&S:36in(90cm)

C. bulbispermum Exquisite flowers of pale pink or white with darker pink stripes down the center of each petal are produced from this subtropical

species. The flowers appear in fall. 36-40°F(2-4°C) H&S:36in(90cm)

C. × powellii The tough swamp lily is a hybrid between *C. bulbispermum* and the handsome white- or pink-flowering *C. moorei*. Pink flowers appear reliably every late summer and early fall. *C. × p.* 'Album' has pure white blooms and clumps of both look good either in a border of well-drained soil or in pots. 36-40°F(2-4°C) H&S:36in(90cm)

Cupressus

(Cupressaceae)

Useful evergreens for the greenhouse are always in

demand as foils for the more colorful plants.

C. macrocarpa The Monterey cypress from California is a fast-growing conifer capable of reaching 70ft(20m) when planted outside. The handsome citrus-scented foliage is bright green and produced in dense sprays. Maintain a succession of small plants by regular seed sowings. Allowed to grow tall in a large pot, they will make handsome specimen plants. *C.m.* 'Goldcrest' is a popular golden-leaved variety.
27-45°F(-3-7°C) H:6ft(1.8m) S:30-36in(75-90cm)

C. torulosa 'Cashmeriana' (C. himalaica var. darjeelingensis) The Kashmir cypress is an elegant, regal conifer, suitable for the larger greenhouse (planted in the border, specimens will reach the roof). Pendent sprays of glaucous foliage hang so vertically that they appear to have been draped over the slender branches. Propagate by spring-sown seed. Cuttings can be difficult; in summer try shoots about 4in(10cm) long, with a heel, dipped in hormone rooting powder or liquid, then given gentle bottom heat. They often callus over at the base, then sit for a year before rooting.
27-45°F(-3-7°C) H:7ft(2m) S:3ft(1m) restricted in a large container

Cycas
(Cycadaceae)

Cycads were prevalent 100-160 million years ago. This fascinating group superficially resembles palms but is more closely related to conifers. Many species are protected in the wild but fortunately both plants and seed of the commoner kinds are available in cultivation. Plants are slow-growing and therefore expensive. Partial to long periods of dormancy, specimens will often appear to cease growing for a couple of years, only to begin again when it suits them. Water regularly when in active growth but allow the top half of the soil to dry out while dormant. Good, all-round light is essential while new leaves are developing. These are delicate, so avoid touching them until they toughen up.

C. circinalis The fern palm or sago fern palm from the East Indies has long leaves, freely produced. Knobbly coralloid roots produced at the surface of the soil are thought to enjoy a symbiotic relationship with an alga. Plants grow large comparatively quickly given warmth and humidity. Propagate by seed or by detaching buds formed on the trunks of mature specimens.
50-55°F(10-13°C) H&S:10ft(3m)

C. revoluta The Japanese sago palm is the most common cycad in cultivation, grown for its handsome rosette of leaves, each ranked with pointed leaflets. Several leaves unfurl at once, usually following a period of dormancy, and need all-round light to avoid growing one-sidedly. Eventually, on old specimens, a stout trunk is formed. Propagate by

Cycas revoluta

large seed, sown during spring and summer.
40-50°F(4-10°C) H&S:5ft(1.5m)

Cyphomandra
(Solanaceae)

C. crassicaulis (C. betacea) The tree tomato or tamarillo from Brazil has attractive large, soft evergreen leaves, but is grown for its small whitish flowers and showy edible fruits, rather like pointed red tomatoes (which taste awful). Sow seed in spring. Pot-grown plants should fruit after about a year. Given the root run of a greenhouse border, however, the tree tomato lives up to its name, creating a useful canopy to shade other plants. Guard against whitefly. Prune old, woody plants hard after fruiting or in spring, and new shoots will grow.
45°F(7°C) H:6-20ft(1.8-6m) S:4-10ft(1.2-3m)

Daphne
(Thymelaeaceae)

D. odora 'Aureomarginata' The added protection of a greenhouse guarantees pretty pink and white flowers with a sweet, though not sickly, scent from midwinter to early spring on this handsome evergreen. Leaves are edged with white. *D.o.* 'Walburton' is even better, with broader, brighter variegation. Plants are best grown in pots and stood outside for the summer. Propagate in summer by semi-ripe cuttings over heat.
27-45°F(-3-7°C) H&S:36in(90cm) in a container

Dicksonia
(Dicksoniaceae)

D. antarctica The soft tree fern from eastern Australia

is a superb specimen plant: given the root run of the border, it will eventually outgrow the greenhouse, and can reach 33ft(10m) in the wild. Plants grow surprisingly quickly from spores. A rosette of fronds builds up during the first few years, then growth slows as the trunk forms. Keep humid in summer by spraying the area around the fern with water. Spray mist the trunk, but keep water off the delicate new fronds. A soil containing sufficient peat moss (or peat substitute) is best. Provide shade.
36-40°F(2-4°C) H:6ft(1.8m) S:5ft(1.5m) in a pot

Dombeya
(Sterculiaceae)

These unusual shrubs will flower when quite small and restricted in pots, making them ideal for the greenhouse. Prune hard, reducing newer lateral stems back to within a leaf joint or two of older stems after flowering. Sow seed in spring, or root 3-4in(8-10cm) long cuttings during spring and summer.
45-50°F(7-10°C)

D. burgessiae The bright green leaves alone are attractive, being large, three-lobed, and covered with downy hairs. However, this species from South Africa to Kenya is grown for the clusters of downward-facing, saucer-shaped flowers borne in late summer and fall; these are white, with warm pink centers and veins.
H:6ft(1.8m) S:4ft(1.2m)

D. × cayeuxii The pink snowball is a hybrid between *D. burgessiae* and *D. wallichii* but favors the latter. Planted in the greenhouse border, it will reach the proportions of a small tree if allowed. Hairy leaves are large and vaguely heart-shaped, while the rich pink

flowers hang in downward-pointing clusters.
H:15ft(4.5m) S:10ft(3m)

D. wallichii From Madagascar, this attractive species makes a fine sight when grown as a tall standard and is full of flower in winter, but has three disadvantages. The powder-puff pink flowers smell of slightly rancid margarine and cling ungracefully to the plant long after turning brown, and on large plants the hairs of leaves and stems can irritate when pruning.
H:15ft(4.5m) S:10ft(3m)

Dracaena
(Agavaceae)

Increasingly popular for both house and greenhouse, dracaenas come in two styles. Plants bought as a tuft of leaves on a fleshy young stem or propagated at home will grow into fine specimens retaining their lower leaves for many years. Alternatively, palm-like specimens are produced commercially by taking an older plant with a thick, cane-like stem, pruning this at the desired height and encouraging one or more side shoots to develop into a tuft of leaves at the top. There are several methods of propagation, including seed germination in spring. The shoot tip can be cut off and used as a giant cutting. Alternatively, the shoot can be air-layered, then severed from the parent once roots have grown. Those with thicker stems lend themselves to cane cuttings. Here, chunks

of stem 2-3in(5-8cm) long are laid horizontally onto the loose potting mix and nestled in until buried by half. Results are most satisfactory when two shoots are produced from this chunk, which grow up as a twin-stemmed plant. Keep the parent plant, as the stump will sprout again.

D. cincta (D. marginata) This species from Madagascar is easily accommodated into the greenhouse as its narrow leaves edged with dark red are dainty and the plant slow-growing. There are several colored-leaved varieties, of which *D.c.* 'Tricolor' is the most popular.
50°F(10°C) H:10ft(3m) S:3-5ft(1-1.5m)

D. deremensis This marvelous plant has its origins in tropical Africa. Varieties available have slightly different variegated markings running the length of the leaves. Provide good light, but shade from hot sun.
50°F(10°C) H:6ft(1.8m) S:3ft(1m)

D. draco The dragon tree from the Canary Islands grows too large for a small greenhouse, but young plants remain stemless for some time, consisting of a large tuft of spine-tipped leaves up to 24in(60cm) long. Seed is sometimes seen for sale.
45-50°F(7-10°C) H:6ft(1.8m) S:4ft(1.2m)

D. fragrans The corn palm from tropical Africa has wider leaves than *D. deremensis* and *D. cincta*. As plants mature, their bottom leaves drop, leaving a

clear woody stem. *D.f.* 'Massangeana' is by far the most popular variety. Bright green, glossy leaves some 4in(10cm) wide have a broad central band of gold running their length.
55°F(13°C) H:10ft(3m) S:4ft(1.2m)

D. reflexa (Pleomele reflexa) This sprawling plant is mostly represented by *D.r.* 'Variegata', the song of India, which has gold leaf edges. Support elongating stems with a stout cane. Warmth and humidity are required if this handsome but rather difficult plant is not to drop leaves and stop growing.
55°F(13°C) H:10ft(3m) S:5-6ft(1.5-1.8m)

Echium
(Boraginaceae)

These species from the Canary Islands and Madeira make fascinating flowering specimens for pots or border. Usually obtained from easily germinated seed, some die after flowering. If they set seed, collect this and re-sow to ensure a succession of stately flower spikes. All require a well-drained soil.
38-40°F(3-4°C)

E. candicans (E. fastuosum) The pride of Madeira, a perennial species covered in grayish hair, makes tall spikes of blue flowers in spring.
H&S:3-4ft(1-1.2m)

E. pininana This is one of the largest species. From seed, it builds up as a rosette of long, hairy leaves for two to three years before reaching flowering size. Its finale is to send up a spectacular and long-lasting spike of soft lavender-blue flowers, sometime during summer, after which the whole plant dies.
H:10ft(3m) S:30in(75cm)

E. wildpretii This biennial species is a favorite but possibly the most difficult to grow. In their native Tenerife, plants grow above 6,600ft(2,010m) and are sensitive to humidity. Flowers are produced in early summer. During the first year of growth from seed, plants build up a rosette of long leaves covered in fine hairs. The slightest hint of a damp atmosphere, overwatering, or, worse, moisture dripping into the rosette will make healthy plants rot in the center almost overnight. Perseverance is rewarded in the second year by a beautiful spike of pink flowers which may reach 8ft(2.5m) in the wild.
H:6ft(1.8m) S:24in(60cm)

Erica
(Ericaceae)

E. canaliculata This pretty heath from South Africa becomes an erect shrub but bears its white flowers, sometimes tinged with pink, from early spring to summer even on tiny plants. Cultivate as for other tender heaths (see p.147). This species need not be pruned after flowering, but can be allowed to grow naturally.
40°F(4°C) H:7ft(2m) S:4ft(1.2m)

Dracaena cincta 'Tricolor'   *Eriobotrya japonica*

Echium candicans

Erythrina crista-galli

Eriobotrya

(Rosaceae)

E. japonica The Japanese loquat is often grown from the seed of the edible yellow pear-shaped fruits. Actually from China and Japan, the loquat will reach 30ft(9m) in the wild, bearing small off-white, fragrant flowers followed by fruit. Specimens are worth growing for their 6-12in(15-30cm) long, handsome toothed leaves furred with rusty hairs beneath, but they rarely flower under glass. Soak seed for 24 hours before sowing, and avoid overwatering the soil to prevent the seed from rotting. Plants can be kept smaller when restricted in pots.
40°F(4°C) H:8ft(2.5m) S:6ft(1.8m)

Erythrina

(Leguminosae)

E. crista-galli The splendid coral cockspur tree from Brazil is easily grown from seed, and rapidly builds up a woody root stock. Each year, at the onset of winter and at low temperatures, the plant will die back to the base and should be watered only enough to prevent the soil from drying out completely. In spring, cut the old stems down and the plant will burst back into life. At warmer temperatures, taller stems remain alive. Long, thorned stems produce attractive leaflets and, in late summer, terminal racemes of large, showy, red flowers. Support the stems with canes. Be vigilant for spider mite, which can be controlled if spotted early. Grow in large tubs of loam-based soil or plant in beds. For cuttings, watch for young shoots 3-4in(8-10cm) long on a large plant in spring, and pull one or two away from the woody base with a small heel. Propagate by spring-sown seed.
38-40°F(3-4°C) H:6ft(1.8m) S:3ft(1m)

Eucalyptus

(Myrtaceae)

Easy to raise from spring-sown seed, eucalyptus quickly grow into tall specimen foliage plants for the greenhouse, given a good root run. Leaves are invigoratingly aromatic when crushed. When they outgrow their space, simply replace them with younger plants. They will respond to pruning but if cut close to the base the resulting bush of young shoots is not so easy to accommodate. Watch for aphid attack as the temperature rises in spring. Grayish, mealy aphids colonize the growing tips but are easily controlled.

E. citriodora, the lemon-scented gum from northeastern Australia, has long, slightly hairy leaves which smell of citrus when crushed. E. ficifolia, the red-flowered gum from western Australia, will produce its showy flowers even when restricted to a container. E. globulus, the Tasmanian blue gum, which also comes from southeastern Australia, has long been a popular greenhouse plant and a favorite for sub-tropical beds outdoors during summer. The juvenile leaves for which it is grown are an oval shape and striking glaucous silvery blue-gray. E. gunnii, the cider gum, though more widely used outside, is worth growing for its juvenile foliage, as silvery but even bluer than in E. globulus. Leaves are smaller, stiffer, and rounder. E. moorei nana is a dwarf gum that can achieve its full height of 4ft(1.2m) and produce cream-colored flowers in a small pot.
32-40°F(0-4°C) H:7ft(2m) S:to 4ft(1.2m) unless specified otherwise

Eugenia

(Myrtaceae)

Attractive evergreen foliage, usually a lovely bronze-pink when young, small but interesting creamy-white flowers with showy stamens and edible berries in

Eugenia uniflora

Ficus deltoidea

colors of rose-pink, purple, blue, white, or creamy-yellow according to species, are good reasons for adding a eugenia to your greenhouse collection. It is a good idea to grow these plants as small standards. Propagate by spring-sown seed or by taking cuttings in summer. When necessary, prune back the stems making up the head. Shade lightly from hot sun. While tolerating occasional lower temperatures, plants prefer warmth to do well.
45-50°F(7-10°C) H:6ft(1.8m) S:3-4ft(1-1.2m)

E. brasiliensis This Brazilian species grows to tree-like proportions in the wild. Plants always need plenty of light. In cultivation, they often produce fluffy white flowers but only occasionally set fruit, which is dark red, cherry-sized, and reputed to be sweet to eat.

E. uniflora The pitanga or Surinam cherry is another Brazilian tree. Sweet, edible red fruits are grooved and some 1in(2.5cm) across.

Ficus

(Moraceae)

The ornamental figs include some attractive and popular specimen plants. In their natural habitat they often make large trees, sometimes supported by a mass of stiff and stilt-like aerial roots. At lower temperatures, growth will cease; beware of overwatering. Leaves also tend to be small and curve in slightly at the edges as if cringing at the cold. Plants will grow better in a sustained minimum of 55°F(13°C). Plants need good light, but shade from bright, direct light. During winter, allow the surface of the soil to dry out between waterings, and do not overwater newly potted plants. Propagate by seed, shoot-tip cuttings, air-layering, and, in some cases, stem sections.
45°F(7°C)

F. benghalensis The Bengal fig or banyan from India and tropical Africa has the habit of a branched rubber plant and can be used to fill a large space. Leaves, which can reach 12in(30cm) in length, are covered with rust-colored hairs when young. As plants grow older, aerial roots often form.
H:10ft(3m) S:7ft(2m)

F. benjamina The weeping fig is a great favorite for its comparatively small, glossy leaves and compact, weeping habit. Some leaf drop, particularly in winter, is a natural response to lower light and temperatures;

other causes are drought or excess moisture at the roots. Sometimes, with large plants, insufficient water is given at one time, so that only the top half of the soil is moistened. Sudden drops in temperature or a dry atmosphere could also be suspect. A healthy plant will grow fresh leaves from the tips of shoots in spring to compensate for any loss. The net result of this is a gradually more open plant, which in its native India would grow into a tree. For plants to continue upward growth, select a leading shoot and tie this up to a cane. Air-layering can be used to induce the top section of a plant to form its own roots, so that an old, tall plant can be replaced by its own rooted 24in(60cm) top. There are some attractive varieties with variegated leaves, notably *F.b.* 'Starlight', heavily marked with cream at the edges and *F.b.* 'Golden King', with a narrower, creamy-yellow edge. *F.b.* 'Reginald' has bright yellow and green leaves with a few darker green markings. *F.b.* 'Amstelveen' has a longer leaf, 5-7in(12-17cm), and more open habit. *F.b.* 'Natasja' has small, neat leaves. Many specimens are now sold with attractively plaited stems.
H:7ft(2m) S:4ft(1.2m)

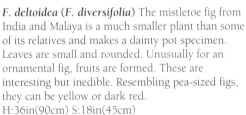

Ficus benjamina and *F.b.* 'Starlight'

Ficus benjamina 'Golden King'

Ficus lyrata

F. deltoidea (F. diversifolia) The mistletoe fig from India and Malaya is a much smaller plant than some of its relatives and makes a dainty pot specimen. Leaves are small and rounded. Unusually for an ornamental fig, fruits are formed. These are interesting but inedible. Resembling pea-sized figs, they can be yellow or dark red.
H:36in(90cm) S:18in(45cm)

F. elastica The rubber plant from tropical Asia makes a single, straight-stemmed plant in the house, but given the extra space, light, and root run of a greenhouse, can begin to resemble the tree it would make in its natural habitat. Plants are fast to grow and easy to propagate when they have outgrown their space. Cuttings of shoots 12in(30cm) long will quickly root. Air-layering will take about eight weeks before the "layer" can be potted. Alternatively, to obtain many plants from one stem, simply cut above and below a leaf. Roll the leaf vertically and secure with a rubber band, insert a cane into a pot of loose potting mix and position the cutting so that the new shoot will be able to grow up from the axil between leaf and stem. Keep in position by tying the leaf to the cane. This can be repeated with all the leaves along

mature, yet not woody, portions of stem. Sticky, white sap will flow briefly from cut surfaces. This seems to do the plant no harm, but could irritate delicate skin and mark floors and furnishings.
F. elastica itself has largely been replaced by *F.e.* 'Decora', and there are some attractive varieties. *F.e.* 'Black Prince' has extremely dark foliage, *F.e.* 'Schrijveriana' is dark green near the central vein but via speckles and splashes of lighter green becomes cream toward the edges. *F.e.* 'Zulu Shield' has bold markings of green, pink, and cream.
H:10ft(3m) S:6ft(1.8m)

F. longifolia Relatively new to cultivation, this elegant fig could be a rival choice to *F. benjamina*, since the habit is similar, if slightly more upright. Pendent deep green, glossy leaves are 6in(15cm) long.
H:7ft(2m) S:4ft(1.2m)

F. lyrata The fiddle-leaf fig from tropical West Africa grows rather like a rubber plant. Leaves, however, are thinner and a distinctive violin-case shape. Remove the growing tip of a single-stemmed plant to form branches. Trim when these branches reach the roof, thus regenerating the head of a large standard.
H:10ft(3m) S:6ft(1.8m)

F. microcarpa The laurel fig from southeast Asia and the East Indies is similar to *F. benjamina*, though growth is slightly more upright and the leaves less pointed. The very popular *F.m.* 'Hawaii' has pretty variegated leaves.
H:6ft(1.8m) S:4ft(1.2m)

F. religiosa The peepul, bo tree, or sacred fig originates from India to southeast Asia. Leaves are up to 6in(15cm) long and are distinguished by long, slightly twisting tail-like tips. Hindus and Buddhists build shrines beneath these unusual figs and refuse to injure or prune the trees in any way.
H:6ft(1.8m) S:5ft(1.5m)

Gardenia
(Rubiaceae)

G. augusta (G. jasminoides) from south China makes a good greenhouse plant. Powerfully scented creamy-white double flowers gradually turn yellow as they fade. Confined in pots and regularly pruned, plants remain small; potted up gradually to large containers or planted in the border, they make small shrubs. Flowers are produced sporadically all year, but even when not in bloom the shiny evergreen

Grevillea banksii

Hedychium gardnerianum

Hibiscus rosa-sinensis

foliage is attractive. Gardenias need soft water and an acidic soil mix. Never allow plants to dry out and feed regularly with a half-strength liquid fertilizer for acid-loving plants. Avoid sudden drops in temperature and drafts. Low temperatures can be tolerated but flowers form more readily at 55-60°F(13-16°C). Propagate in summer by cuttings.
50°F(10°C) H:5ft(1.5m) S:4ft(1.2m)

Grevillea
(Proteaceae)
These interesting evergreen trees and shrubs prefer a well-drained neutral to acidic soil. Take care not to overwater during winter, particularly at low temperatures. Allow the top half of the soil to dry out between waterings. Ventilate well on warm winter days.
G. banksii This is one of the showiest grevilleas, with attractively divided leaves and heads of exquisite flowers that eke out their performance, so that there is rarely a month without a flower. Recurved styles 1½in(4cm) long project from each bright red flower. Plants will set seed in the greenhouse, even in the absence of pollinating honeyeater birds. Though seed germinates readily, seedlings are prone to damping-off disease. Cuttings may be taken in summer; they are not easy to root but, given time, three or four out

of ten may succeed. Be vigilant against mealy bugs.
45-50°F(7-10°C) H:7ft(2m) S:5ft(1.5m)
G. robusta The silky oak is the most popular grevillea grown under glass. Growth from seed is rapid to produce not the tall tree of 100ft(30m) it would make in the wild, but a small, upright specimen – usually single-stemmed to 5ft(1.5m) – bearing fern-like leaves covered with silky hairs on the undersides. The brownish-orange flowers are rarely produced under glass.
45-50°F(7-10°C) H:7ft(2m) S:30in(75cm) in a pot

Hedychium
(Zingiberaceae)
The garland flowers or ginger lilies have tall, showy flower spikes which are fragrant in some species. They grow from large rhizomes which can be lifted and divided as growth starts in late spring and early summer. Plant in large containers or borders of rich soil with the top of the rhizome, laid horizontally, just showing. Give light shade from the sun and water well during summer, less in winter when plants are dormant. In low temperatures foliage may die down almost completely before new growth begins in spring. Soak seed for two hours before sowing. They are all worth growing, but the following species both have fragrant flowers. *H. coronarium*, the

garland flower or butterfly ginger lily from India, has large white flowers. *H. gardnerianum*, the Kahili ginger from northern India, has smaller flowers of lemon-yellow with burnt-orange stamens.
40-50°F(4-10°C) H:4-6ft(1.2-1.8m) S:indefinite

Hibiscus
(Malvaceae)
H. rosa-sinensis The rose of China and its varieties are deservedly popular for their exotic blooms. Flowers are short-lived but produced over a long period in a vivid range including red, pink, orange, yellow, white, and doubles. *H.r.-s.* 'Cooperi' has narrower leaves variegated with white and pink.

Hibiscus are tough plants but can annoy their owners by dropping buds, often a response to the shock of being moved. Other reasons include dryness at the roots, lack of regular feeding during the growing season, or a sudden drop in temperature. Plants can stand temperatures almost down to freezing, but will drop all their leaves and go dormant until spring, when they may be slow to flower again. A temperature of 50-55°F(10-13°C) is necessary to keep plants leafy and flowering almost all year.

Pot up established plants every spring, top-dressing annually once they reach their final pot, and feed with weak liquid fertilizer several times a week.

Specimens given the run of a greenhouse border will grow into large shrubs. Should pot specimens become straggly and lose their lower leaves, prune shoots back to within a bud of older stems. Whitefly can be a problem. Shade lightly from the hottest sun. Cuttings root easily in spring and summer.
40°F(4°C) H:6ft(1.8m) S:4ft(1.2m)

Ixora
(Rubiaceae)

I. coccinea The flame of the woods from India is well worth growing as a specimen shrub in a large pot or border in a warm greenhouse. Terminal flower clusters produced during summer can be pink, apricot, or yellow, but bright red flowers look good against the rich green foliage. Shade plants lightly in summer and keep humid by frequent misting. Plants tend to stop growing in winter. Mealy bugs and scale insects can be a problem. Summer cuttings can be difficult to root, though bottom heat will help.
55-60°F(13-16°C) H&S:4ft(1.2m)

Jacaranda
(Leguminosae)

J. mimosifolia The jacaranda from Brazil has fine, fern-like leaves. It grows readily from seed, so maintain a succession of pot-grown plants to use as a foil for more colorful plants, replacing them when they grow too large. However, where space permits the jacaranda to become a small tree 12ft(3.5m) or more tall – it is capable of reaching up to 40ft(12m) in the wild – it may produce its beautiful panicles of violet-blue flowers in early summer, an event that is greatly encouraged by plenty of light and cool winter temperatures. After flowering, prune back the long shoots to keep size and shape within bounds. Grow tall plants in large containers or, even better, planted in a border. Watch out for aphids and whitefly.
45°F(7°C) H:12-15ft(3.5-4.5m) S:9ft(2.75m)

Juanulloa
(Solanaceae)

J. mexicana (*J. aurantiaca*) This evergreen shrub from Peru is bound to cause interest. Long, stiff shoots furnished with 3-5in(8-13cm) long leaves with felted undersides sometimes need the support of canes. Clusters of curiously shaped, orange, tubular flowers appear during summer and show up well against the leaves. Plants will grow best in warm temperatures, although 45°F(7°C) will be tolerated if accompanied by careful watering. Untidy plants can be pruned by some two-thirds to encourage fresh new stems. Plants are epiphytic in the wild (which explains their wayward habit) and appreciate an open, well-drained soil. Shade lightly from hot summer sun. Propagate in summer by cuttings 3-4in(8-10cm) long.
50°F(10°C) H:4ft(1.2m) S:3ft(1m)

Juanulloa mexicana

Lagerstroemia
(Lythraceae)

L. indica The crape myrtles from China are an easy and rewarding group of deciduous shrubs or small trees, resplendent with terminal clusters of showy, carmine, pink, lilac, or white flowers in summer. The petals bear close inspection, as each is crinkled and flared at the top, then narrows, stalk-like, toward the base. Lower fall temperatures turn the leaves brilliant orange-red before they drop. Water plants well during summer, but sparingly in winter while dormant. To retain a compact shape, prune taller varieties in spring as growth begins. Alternatively, taller varieties can be trained as standards (see p.27). Propagate named varieties by semi-ripe cuttings in summer. Spring-sown seed germinates readily. For smaller plants, opt for *L.* Little Chief Hybrids, which should remain below 12in(30cm).
32-45°F(0-7°C) H:7ft(2m) S:4ft(1.2m)

Laurus
(Lauraceae)

L. nobilis The familiar sweet bay or bay laurel, which has its origins in the Mediterranean region, has attractive, aromatic evergreen foliage that can be scorched by freezing winds during cold spells. Plants that spend the summer outdoors will benefit from

Hibiscus rosa-sinensis 'Natal'

Medinilla magnifica

Musa acuminata 'Dwarf Cavendish'

greenhouse protection in winter, provided they are not overwatered. They can also be kept under glass permanently. Bays in containers are usually sheared to a neat shape; use pruners, not loppers, to do this once or twice during summer. Standard bay trees can be trained from cuttings (see p.27). Propagate by seed or by cuttings taken in summer. Small creamy flowers in the leaf axils are followed, on female plants, by purple-black berries. *L.n.* 'Aurea' is the golden-leaved form. Be vigilant against scale insects.
27-45°F(-3-7°C) H:48in(120cm) S:30in(75cm)

Leea
(Leeaceae)

L. coccinea This is an unusual but attractive foliage plant from Burma. Leaves are composed of many leaflets, giving the plant an interesting shape, particularly in silhouette. Foliage is a bright pink-bronze when young, maturing to rich green. Seed germinates readily and, within a couple of years,

yields specimens approaching 18in(45cm) tall and ready to produce terminal clusters of red buds opening to small pink flowers. Plants prefer warm temperatures. Below 50°F(10°C) they are prone to overwatering with yellowing and dropping leaves.
55-60°F(13-16°C) H:24in(60cm) S:18in(45cm)

L. guineensis 'Burgundy' Similar to *L. coccinea*, this plant is the color of rich burgundy, particularly on young leaves. If exposed to overwatering, fluctuations in temperature, or drafts, its response is to drop leaves. However, given the right set of conditions, the reward is a very striking greenhouse specimen. Plants rarely flower when grown indoors.
55-60°F(13-16°C) H:30in(75cm) S:24in(60cm)

Leptospermum
(Myrtaceae)

L. scoparium The tea tree, from New Zealand and Australia, is an evergreen, shrubby plant which is attractive even when not in flower, for its small, narrow, aromatic leaves. This species is studded with

a profusion of small, white flowers in early summer, but cultivars offer flowers of pink, white, and red, some of them double. Plant in large pots or the greenhouse border. Water well in summer, less during cold winter spells, but never allow to dry out completely. Plants will grow and flower better in good light, so shade only very lightly against the hottest summer sun. Seed germinates readily. Cuttings, preferably with a heel, will root in summer.
27-45°F(-3-7°C) H:6-10ft(1.8-3m) S:3-5ft(1-1.5m)

Luculia
(Rubiaceae)

Luculias make lovely evergreen shrubs for the greenhouse. Given the root run of a border, they will grow large and need little pruning. In pots, prune back by about two-thirds after flowering or in spring. Plenty of water and liquid fertilizer during summer will guarantee a showy and fragrant display of flowers. *L. gratissima* from the Himalayas bears heads of fragrant pale pink flowers during summer.

Propagate by spring-sown seed or by cuttings taken in summer.
45-50°F(7-10°C) H:3-6ft(1-1.8m) S:3-4ft(1-1.2m)

Mangifera

(Anacardiaceae)

M. indica The mango from the East Indies and Malaysia can become a tree of 60ft(18m) in the wild. Restricted in a pot or border in the greenhouse, they are most unlikely to produce fruit, but the foliage is admirable. Leaflets are a wonderful pinkish-orange when young, maturing to glossy green. Grow plants from the large seed extracted from a store-bought fruit. Clean away the fibrous flesh and sow the seed as soon as possible, planting so that the tip is just buried by soil. Place the pot somewhere warm and moist (such as inside a plastic bag in a warm kitchen) until germination, which takes between one and three weeks. The worst enemy of the mango is dry air. Create humidity by using gravel trays and spray misting to prevent ugly brown tips to the leaves. Growth will stop during cold spells. When plants outgrow their space, prune them hard in late spring or start again from seed. Mangos love heat, but shade from hot sun.
55-60°F(13-16°C) H:7ft(2m) S:3ft(1m)

Medinilla

(Melastomataceae)

M. magnifica The rose grape from the Philippines is so called because of its magnificent panicles of flowers like small pink grapes. These hang down under the umbrella of several large, tiered pink bracts, so that the entire structure is up to 12in (30cm) long. Flowers appear in late spring and summer but at other times there is the compensation of handsome foliage. Large, paired leaves are leathery and a deep, glossy green. Stand plants up high so that the exotic beauty of the hanging flowers can be fully appreciated from below. Shade plants from the sun, keep warm and humid. Occasional low temperatures can be tolerated during winter if less water is given.
50-60°F(10-16°C) H&S:36in(90cm)

Metrosideros

(Myrtaceae)

These lovely evergreen trees and shrubs will flower when small, flourishing in pots or borders.

M. excelsus, the New Zealand Christmas tree, is a handsome plant that becomes a spreading tree in the wild. The long, showy bright red stamens of the flowers stand out well against the glossy green leaves, felted with silver on the undersides. *M. kermadecensis* 'Variegatus' is a freely branching shrub. The fresh young stems and leaf undersides are covered with silvery, pale green down. Young leaves have an

irregular broad yellow edge surrounding their bright green centers. Older leaves are predominantly dark green with the yellow fading to cream. The summer flowers have such long, bright red stamens that they manage to assert themselves against the vivid foliage. *M.k.* 'Radiant' is best described as an inside-out version of the latter, in that dark green leaves are marked with a central yellow splash.

Cuttings of semi-ripe wood taken during mid-summer root by fall. Plants enjoy good light and plenty of water during summer.
36-45°F(2-7°C) H:6ft(1.8m) S:5ft(1.5m)

Mitriostigma

(Rubiaceae)

M. axillare Wild coffee from South Africa is a fine shrub with glossy evergreen leaves and fragrant white flowers in spring, reminiscent of a cross between gardenia and coffee. These similarities are acknowledged in the former name of *Gardenia citriodora* and in the common name. An un-complicated plant, it seems less prone to leaf yellowing than gardenia, though it benefits from all the same cultural guidelines. Propagate in summer by making cuttings.
55°F(13°C) H:36in(90cm) S:30in(75cm)

Musa

(Musaceae)

Bananas make striking greenhouse plants, mostly for their tropical-looking foliage but also for their flowers and the prospect of edible fruit. As with giant herbaceous perennials, mature stems die down after flowering to be replaced by suckers which grow around the base. It is best to cut the old stem almost to ground level as soon as it starts to die off. Showy flowers are encased within bright, usually pink bracts.

The fruits form behind the flower. Grow bananas in large tubs or in the border. During summer, shade lightly, give plenty of water and liquid fertilizer regularly. Warm temperatures should be accompanied by high humidity, so spray mist regularly. Spider mite can be a problem. Propagate by removing suckers or, in some cases, by sowing large, hard seed, best soaked for two days before sowing.

M. acuminata 'Dwarf Cavendish' Probably the most popular banana plant in cultivation, this will reach fruiting size, producing edible bananas, in a 24-36in (60-90cm) tub.
60°F(16°C) H:6-8ft(1.8-2.5m) S:4-6ft(1.2-1.8m)

M. basjoo A cool greenhouse can benefit from the tropical effect of the Japanese banana's foliage, though its fruits are not edible. When exposed to cold, this banana will die down; in this case, give only sufficient water to prevent complete drying out at the roots, and ventilate well on warm winter days. Avoid removing brown leaves as some dead foliage acts as insulation. The colder the plant is grown, the smaller it will be.
27-45°F(-3-7°C) H:8ft(2.5m) S:5ft(1.5m)

M. uranoscopus (*M. coccinea*) The flowering or scarlet banana from China and Vietnam is purely ornamental. The flower stalk grows upward and bears yellow flowers within a yellow-tipped, scarlet bract. The yellow fruits that follow are only 2-3in (5-8cm) long.
60°F(16°C) H&S:4ft(1.2m)

Myrtus

(Myrtaceae)

M. communis The common myrtle from western Asia is a handsome evergreen, well worth growing for its foliage and pretty, creamy-white summer flowers with prominent stamens, which are followed by

Leptospermum scoparium cultivar

Myrtus communis

Nerium oleander 'Variegatum'

Ochna serrulata

purple-black berries. *M.c.* var. *tarentina* is more compact and dwarf. *M.c.* 'Variegata' has attractive creamy-white edges to the bright green leaves. Given plenty of light, myrtles are easy to grow. If plants begin to look straggly, simply prune out the offending shoots. Myrtles can be sheared into neat shapes, but at the expense of flowering. Propagate by seed or by cuttings, preferably with a heel, taken in summer.
27-45°F(-3-7°C) H:5ft(1.5m) S:4ft(1.2m)

Nandina
(Nandinaceae)

N. domestica The heavenly or sacred bamboo from China is a hardy evergreen shrub. The youngest parts of the stems are a lovely pink color with a faint gray bloom. Leaves up to 18in(45cm) long, held out horizontally, are composed of many dainty leaflets in a bipinnate or sometimes tripinnate branching arrangement. These leaves are always attractive, especially when coppery-pink with youth and again in fall as they become blotched and tinted with purple-red. Panicles of small white flowers borne in summer can be followed by red fruits. *N.d.* 'Pygmaea' is a dwarf form, and other named varieties have particularly good leaf colors. Provide plenty of water during summer, less in winter. Shade lightly from the hottest sun and maintain humidity at high temperatures. Propagate by seed or in summer by cuttings with a heel.
27-45°F(-3-7°C) H:6-8ft(1.8-2.5m)

Nerium
(Apocynaceae)

N. oleander The oleander originates from Mediterranean regions. These handsome evergreen shrubs produce a profusion of flowers continuously from spring to fall. Flower color is usually pink, but named varieties have red, purple, orange, yellow, or white flowers. Some of the showiest are double-flowered, some bicolored. *N.o.* 'Variegatum' has creamy-yellow edges to the leaves, providing additional interest year-round. All parts of the plant are poisonous. Plants like plenty of light to flower, but are generally unfussy, being able to tolerate low winter temperatures as long as roots are treated to a well-drained, loam-based soil and are not overwatered. Plants usually branch freely once they begin flowering. Pinch back a young plant at the growing point to increase bushiness. To maintain shape and size, prune all stems of mature plants back by about half after flowering. Be vigilant against scale insects and mealy bugs. Propagate by seed or in summer by cuttings, which root easily.
36-45°F(2-7°C) H:6ft(1.8m) S:4ft(1.2m)

Ochna
(Ochnaceae)

O. serrulata The Mickey Mouse plant from South Africa is so called because, when held upright in profile, the receptacle and fruits look like mouse ears, with the old style rising between them like a tail. The evergreen shrub itself is attractive, with coppery-pink young leaves turning a handsome glossy green as they mature. The many pretty flowers produced in spring with short-lived, yellow petals are upstaged by showy, long-lasting fruits. The originally green sepals turn red and curve backward from a large red receptacle, from which project shiny black berries. Thin back some stems to expose more berries to view. Prune long stems hard back after flowering only if plants become too wide or tall. Shade lightly from bright sun, water and feed well during summer. Propagate by seed or in summer by cuttings.
45°F(7°C) H:4-5ft(1.2-1.5m) S:3ft(1m)

Olea
(Oleaceae)

O. europaea The olive is native to the Mediterranean region. Trees can reach 30ft(9m) in warm areas such as the American Carolinas and can live for many years. In the greenhouse mature plants may bear fruit, even when restricted in pots. However, these lovely plants are worth having for the Mediterranean effect of their shape and evergreen foliage alone. Leaves 2-3in(5-8cm) long are a pleasant dull to mid-green above but a delightful silvery-gray beneath. Panicles of small white tubular flowers are fragrant and produced in summer, to be followed by the fruits. *O.e.* 'El Greco' is a good variety. Full sun and a well-drained, sandy soil are appreciated. Propagate by seed or in summer by cuttings. Keep plants cool during winter, or their growth will become too soft.
27-45°F(-3-7°C) H:6-10ft(1.8-3m) S:4-6ft(1.2-1.8m)

Palms

The elegance of palms is compatible with greenhouses of all styles, making the expense of a large and beautiful plant easy to justify in terms of its impact. Members of the family Palmae range from those that tolerate some frost to tropical species that must have high temperatures to do well. Most are easy to care for, provided the minimum winter temperature of the greenhouse suits the sort of palm chosen. Although associated with open, sunny positions, in fact most palms live under the canopy of even taller trees. All will appreciate light shade to protect them not only from scorching but from the dryness caused by excessively high temperatures. Lack of humidity will result in a slow build-up of problems. After a year or two of continuous dry air, the tips of leaflets become dry and brown, and brown marks may spread to kill off whole leaves. Spider mite is also worse when the air is dry. Employ all methods of increasing humidity by spray misting or using gravel trays and grouping other plants around the palm. Keep soil moist, though not saturated, while palms are in active growth. If growth ceases during winter, allow the surface of the soil to dry out between waterings. Feed with liquid fertilizer every month throughout the growing season. Avoid drafts and sudden drops in temperature. Exotic palms like latania and licuala from warm humid countries sometimes fail to adapt well to greenhouse conditions. Before buying these plants, check that the nursery has allowed them to acclimatize for the best part of a year under glass. Propagation is by seed, usually taking up to three months to germinate at 70-80°F(21-27°C). Collecting of seed in the wild is illegal in most countries, but palm nurseries can usually supply seedlings or young palms of unusual species for enthusiasts to raise. Some palms produce suckers around the base of the stem which can be removed and planted separately. Be vigilant against spider mite and thrips.

Butia

B. capitata is the yatay palm or jelly palm from Brazil. Able to withstand a considerable amount of frost – plants can survive 10°F(-12.5°C) – this palm will nevertheless enjoy the protection and good light of a cool greenhouse. The pale, blue-green leaflets are most attractive. However, as the palm ages – it can grow to over 18ft(5.5m) in warm countries – its spread and the spikiness of maturing leaves make it difficult to accommodate.
23-45°F(-5-7°C) H&S:5ft(1.5m)

Caryota

C. mitis, the exotic-looking fishtail palm from southeast Asia, is unlike the usual, classic palm-tree shape. Rather than feathery, its leaflets, 6in(15cm) long and 5in(13cm) wide, are reminiscent of fishtails. This is a suckering palm which will build itself up into a narrow clump of elegant leaves, H:6-8ft(1.8-2.5m) S:3-4ft(1-1.2m), and is easily accommodated. Able to tolerate lower light than some palms, this might be a good choice for a greenhouse with little sun. Warm temperatures above 60°F(16°C) are preferred, coupled with high humidity.
55-60°F(13-16°C)

Chamaedorea

C. elegans, H:36-48in(90-120cm) S:30in(75cm) in a pot, is the popular parlor palm native to Mexico. Its origins, deep in the rainforests, mean that it can tolerate shade, an advantage which has turned it into a highly popular houseplant. In the greenhouse, shade must be provided, as strong sunlight will scorch the leaflets. Mature plants send out straw-colored stems bearing globular yellow-orange flowers. These are often mistaken for seeds, which are rarely produced, as male and female flowers develop on different plants. Another Mexican, *C. seifrizii*, the reed palm, H:5-7ft(1.5-2m) S:3-4ft(90-120cm), is less common. As the name suggests, stems are long, bare at the base for some length and reed-like, surmounted by narrow leaflets. *C. erumpens*, H:5-7ft(1.5-2m) S:3-4ft(90-120cm), from Honduras, is the bamboo palm with much broader leaflets decorating long stems.
50°F(10°C)

Chamaerops

C. humilis, the dwarf or European fan palm, is suitable for the greenhouse while young, but slowly becomes wide-spreading. Large fan-shaped leaves held out on spine-toothed stems are deeply cut into many leaflets. When it finally outgrows its space, capitalize on its cold-tolerance by planting outside, choosing a sheltered spot in full sun.
32-45°F(0-7°C) H&S:5ft(1.5m)

Chrysalidocarpus

C. lutescens (*Areca lutescens*), the areca, golden cane, golden feather, or butterfly palm from Madagascar, makes an unusual and dependable alternative to *Howea belmoreana*. As well as beautifully arching

Chrysalidocarpus lutescens

Phoenix roebelinii and *Rhapis excelsa*

Howea forsteriana

Livistona rotundifolia

Palms

leaves well adorned with light green leaflets, attractive green and gold stems are ringed in a similar way to bamboo canes. Humidity is crucial: a dry atmosphere will lead to slow but certain death. Beware of buying what appears to be a mature, suckering plant cheaply. On closer inspection it may prove to be a cluster of seedlings, some of which will not survive.
50°F(10°C) H:6-10ft(1.8-3m) S:6ft(1.8m)

Howea

The kentia palms are probably the most popular for indoor use. Originating from Lord Howe Island in the southeast Pacific, *H. forsteriana*, the sentry, thatchleaf, or paradise palm, and *H. belmoreana*, the sentry or curly palm, are similar graceful plants. Older leaves have a beautiful, arching habit with

many leaflets hanging down, providing the best way of distinguishing between the species. Those of *H. forsteriana* hang almost straight down, whereas those of *H. belmoreana* reach up, then curve down. Shade plants from bright sun and water well during summer, less in winter. Dryness, whether at the roots or in the air, will result in sick plants.
45°F(7°C) H:6-10ft(1.8-3m) S:3-5ft(1-1.5m)

Hyophorbe

H. lagenicaulis and *H. verschaffeltii*, bottle palms from the Mascarene Islands (hence their former name, *Mascarena*), are unusual palms grown as much for their bottle-shaped trunks as for their attractive, gracefully arching leaves. Despite their exotic appearance, they are surprisingly easy to grow and even reasonably drought-tolerant.
50°F(10°C) H:8ft(2.5m) S:6ft(1.8m)

Latania

L. loddigesii is the unusual and rather difficult silver latan palm from the Mascarene Islands. Fan-like leaves are blue-gray with reddish-brown veins and stalks. Plants prefer a warm temperature, but this must be accompanied by high humidity; a lower temperature would be a better alternative than dry heat. A well-drained soil is appreciated.
60°F(16°C) H&S:5ft(1.5m)

Licuala

L. grandis (*Pritchardia grandis*) is a wonderfully attractive but difficult palm from the New Hebrides. Its leaves are almost circular and pleated like a fan. Like the latan palms, it needs heat and humidity to do well. Again, a well-drained soil will increase chances of success.
60°F(16°C) H:6ft(1.8m) S:4ft(1.2m)

Livistona

These are the beautiful fountain palms with fan-like leaves. In their native countries, they grow to tree-like proportions, particularly *L. australis,* which can reach 80ft(25m). However, the juvenile stage will last some years under glass before the trunk starts to form. Even so, their ever-expanding width, for example H:6ft(1.8m) S:7ft(2m) in pot or border, will outgrow all but the largest greenhouses. Livistonas like good light and plenty of water while in active growth.

L. australis, 40°F(4°C), is known as the Australian or fountain palm, or in its native Australia as the cabbage-tree palm. It is attractive for its shiny green leaflets which droop at the tips. *L. chinensis,* 32-40°F (0-4°C) the Chinese fan or fountain palm, is very similar until it becomes mature (by which time it would need a very large greenhouse), when huge fans of leaflets project up and out from the top of the trunk, their pendulous tips hanging straight down, looking just like a frozen fountain.

L. rotundifolia, 50°F(10°C), is the Malayan footstall palm, prized as a young plant for its almost circular fan-like leaves that droop softly at the edges.

Neodypsis

N. decaryi, the beautiful and elegant triangle palm from Madagascar, is suited to most greenhouses because its leaves, clothed with many leaflets, rise up in a triangular formation rather than projecting outward. The overall effect is of a tall graceful silvery plant. Leaf bases are covered in rusty brown fur. Another advantage of this plant is its relative drought-tolerance.
50°F(10°C) H:7ft(2m) S:3-4ft(1-1.2m)

Phoenix

Surely the palm most often grown from seed by ordinary gardeners is the date palm, *P. dactylifera,* 50°F(10°C), H:6ft(1.8m) S:4-5ft(1.2-1.5m). This palm, originally from North Africa and southwest Asia, where it will reach heights of 100ft(30m), needs light and warmth for growth. In the greenhouse, plants can be accommodated while young, but become large, with stiff, unyielding gray-green leaflets, as they age. There are prettier palms to grow. *P. canariensis,* 40°F(4°C), the Canary Islands date palm, is similarly awkward to accommodate once plants exceed seven or eight years of age. Although these palms are associated with dry areas, correct watering and the provision of humidity are needed to prevent browning leaves. The best phoenix palm for the greenhouse is undoubtedly *P. roebelinii,* the pygmy or miniature date palm, 50°F(10°C) H&S:6ft(1.8m), from east Asia. Plants take some time to reach H&S:3ft(1m) and cannot grow tall until they begin to form a trunk. Better still, the many dainty, long, dark green leaves radiating out from the center

of the palm are not stiff. Each, feather-like, carries soft, slender leaflets.

Ptychosperma

These graceful palms enjoy tropical conditions and are suitable for the warm greenhouse, with light shade and high humidity. *P. elegans* is the solitaire palm from Northern Australia, where it will reach H:22-28ft(7-8m). At any one time there are only six to eight leaves on the palm. These have wide leaflets with rather abrupt ends as if they have been pulled off. The single trunk is attractively ringed with raised leaf scars. In contrast, *P. macarthurii,* the Macarthur palm from New Guinea, H:6-7ft(1.8-2m) S:3-4ft (1-1.2m), makes a clump of green-ringed, cane-like stems not unlike those of a bamboo. The profusion of leaves is well clothed with blunt leaflets, but the overall effect is of a slim, elegant palm.
60°F(16°C)

Rhapis

Two species of lady palms from southern China make excellent greenhouse specimens, lending an oriental atmosphere to their environment. They have been grown in China and Japan for many years. Lady palms are slow-growing and prefer light shade.
45°F(7°C) H&S:3-5ft(1-1.5m)

R. excelsa is variously named ground rattan, broad-leaved or little lady palm, bamboo or miniature fan palm. Fan-shaped leaves are composed of three to ten leaflets. *R. humilis* is the slender lady palm, with leaves divided into 10-20 narrow, more drooping leaflets. The many thin stems are covered in the brown remains of old leaf bases while young and form a bamboo-like clump. *R. excelsa* does not form such a dense thicket of stems. The particularly fine but uncommon variegated form, *R.e.* var. *foliis-variegatis,* has creamy-white stripes running the length of the leaflets. This is the best choice for a dwarf palm as it is very slow-growing and will remain at H:24in(60cm) S:18in(45cm) for many years.

Veitchia

V. merrillii is the Christmas tree palm from the Philippines, H:8ft(2.5m) S:6ft(1.8m), so called because mature plants are hung with bunches of red fruits like Christmas decorations. Its natural habitat is limestone cliffs with very little topsoil, hence its reasonable drought-tolerance. However, to keep plants in top condition, water adequately during active growth. As plants mature and leaves fall off, a beautiful ringed trunk forms, above which is a smooth "crownshaft" of sheathing leaf bases. At the top of this is a tuft of arching leaves with many quite wide leaflets. Shade lightly from the hottest sun.
50°F(10°C)

Paraserianthes

(Leguminosae)
P. distachya (Albizia lophantha) The plume albizia becomes a tree of 45ft(14m) in its native southwest Australia. Foliage is prettily fern-like and the flowers like pale sulfur-yellow bottlebrushes. Plants raised from spring-sown seed grow quickly into elegant small trees, 7ft(2m) high, which flower, in spring and summer, within two to three years. Grow in large pots or in the greenhouse border but maintain a reserve of young plants ready to replace those that have outgrown their space.
32-45°F(0-7°C) H:8-10ft(2.5-3m) S:6-7ft(1.8-2m)

Persea

(Lauraceae)
P. americana (P. gratissima) The avocado plant of commerce originated in tropical America, but there are now hundreds of cultivars. The large seed inside the avocado pear is easy to germinate and, indeed, hard to resist sowing. Clean the seed thoroughly, then set in potting mix, blunt end down, so that the pointed tip is just above the surface. Keep moist and warm. Large plants may produce greenish-yellow flowers but are unlikely to fruit in the greenhouse. However, they are worth growing for their curiosity value and for their quite handsome foliage. Plants love warmth and humidity, some being more prone to brown leaf tips than other. If a bushy plant is required, prune back the side shoots in spring. Shade from hot sun.
50-55°F(10-13°C) H:5-6ft(1.5-1.8m) S:3ft(1m)

Philodendron

(Araceae)
With their spectacular leaves, non-climbing philodendron species make wide-spreading foliage plants, though *P.* 'Imperial Queen' is a more compact hybrid with lance-shaped leaves. The climbing species (for cultivation see p.97) also become first-class free-standing specimens when trained against some support like a moss pole.
P. bipinnatifidum The tree philodendron from south Brazil is a magnificent non-climber that grows quickly from seed. Young leaves are only slightly indented, but a mature plant produces large arrow-shaped leaves, up to 24in(60cm) long and wide, with dramatic, regular incisions. These are held on arching leaf stalks at least as long again. When it outgrows its space, replace with a smaller seed-sown plant.
50-55°F(10-13°C) H&S:4ft(1.2m)

Phormium

(Agavaceae/Phormiaceae)
P. tenax, the New Zealand flax, and *P. cookianum* (*P. colensoi*), the mountain flax, are similar plants. Both these and a number of worthwhile cultivars

have clumps of evergreen, sword-shaped leaves that lend an exotic feel to the cool greenhouse. Dark red, tubular flowers on thick stalks make dramatic shapes among the leaves. Both leaves and flower stems are useful to flower arrangers. Choose plain-leaved phormiums, either green or purple-bronze, or one of the cultivars with dazzling colorful leaves. *P.c.* 'Tricolor' has leaves striped vertically with green, creamy-yellow, and red. *P.* 'Maori Sunrise' has pink leaves striped with bronze. There are dwarf-growing kinds, H&S:12-24in(30-60cm), to suit smaller greenhouses. Phormiums enjoy bright light but will suffer if the air is too hot and dry during summer. Grow them in large containers or in a border. When they become too large, divide the clump in spring (also the time for seed sowing).
27-45°F(-3-7°C) H:4-6ft(1.2-1.8m) S:2-6ft(60cm-1.8m)

Pittosporum

(Pittosporaceae)
Several species of these handsome evergreens are grown in the greenhouse for their decorative foliage but outside they are not reliably hardy in areas with long periods of freezing temperatures. Prune large specimens to retain their shape; the regular removal of stems for flower arrangements is often sufficient. Take cuttings in late summer or propagate by seed sown in spring or fall.

P. crassifolium The karo will reach a tree of 30ft(9m) in its native New Zealand but can be kept smaller in a pot. The young leaves and shoots covered in off-white or brownish felt are attractive. Oblong mature leaves retain this felting on their undersides and are dark green on the surface. Fragrant maroon-red star-shaped flowers borne in spring are small but dramatic. These are followed by rounded, white seed capsules. *P.c.* 'Variegatum' is a variegated form with white-edged leaves.
32-45°F(0-7°C) H:6ft(1.8m) S:3-4ft(1-1.2m)

P. eugenioides The New Zealand lemonwood is a particularly good choice for the greenhouse.

Phormium 'Maori Sunrise'

Plumeria rubra f. *acutifolia*

Narrow, pale green wavy-edged leaves 2-4in(5-10cm) long are lemon-scented when crushed. Small yellow-green flowers are clustered into umbels and are honey-scented. *P.e.* 'Variegatum' has leaves edged with pale yellow.
32-45°F(0-7°C) H:6ft(1.8m) S:3-4ft(1-1.2m)

P. tenuifolium Probably the best known of the pittosporums, this species from New Zealand has dainty oblong leaves with wavy edges. The contrast of the pale green leaves with the almost black stems is popular with florists and flower arrangers. Dark purple flowers are borne in May. The plain-leaved species is decorative, but there are several handsome varieties. *P.t.* 'Atropurpureum' has superb purple-bronze foliage. Among silvery, gold, and variegated sorts, *P.t.* 'Irene Paterson' has most unusual foliage, nearly white, with only a few specks of green. This is a slow-grower and most suitable for a pot. *P.t.* 'Tom Thumb' is a dwarf variety with purple-bronze foliage in winter.
27-45°F(-3-7°C) H:3-6ft(1-1.8m) S:3-4ft(1-1.2m)

P. tobira The Japanese pittosporum from China and Japan is frost-tender. Handsome deep green, leathery leaves 4in(10cm) long make a reliable evergreen background for smaller flowering plants, but the flowers, produced in spring, are also quite noticeable, not least for their sweet perfume. Small and creamy-white, they combine to make terminal clusters some 3in(8cm) across. *P.t.* 'Variegatum' has silvery-green leaves irregularly edged with cream.
36-45°F(2-7°C) H:6ft(1.8m) S:4ft(1.2m)

Plumeria

(Apocynaceae)

P. rubra (P. acuminata) The frangipani, West Indian jasmine, temple or pagoda tree from Central America becomes tall and branching even when grown in large containers. Leaves are paddle-shaped, usually green but sometimes tinged with red, especially when young. Frangipanis have an ungainly thick-stemmed shape but clusters of exquisite, perfumed, five-petaled flowers are produced during summer at the ends of shoots. Rose-pink with a yellow eye, each petal overlaps the next, windmill fashion. *P.r.f. acutifolia* has white flowers with yellow eyes and *P.r.f. lutea*, yellow flowers. The secret of success lies in a winter rest. At temperatures as low as 36-40°F(2-4°C), plants may drop most of their leaves and become dormant. From an optimum minimum of around 50-55°F(10-13°C), plants "wake up" faster in spring and begin flowering sooner. The cooler plants are, the drier the roots can become between waterings, but never allow to dry out completely. Water well during summer while plants are in active growth, and shade lightly from full sun. Propagation from seed is easy, plants taking three to four years to flower, or take cuttings in spring. The white sap

which exudes from cut surfaces is poisonous.
45-50°F(7-10°C) H:8ft(2.5m) S:5ft(1.5m)

Podocarpus

(Podocarpaceae)

This unusual group of conifers contains some half-hardy species, mostly with longer leaves, that make distinguished and unusual specimens, comparable to yews or umbrella pines, for the cool greenhouse. They need good light, but shade lightly from direct sun. Avoid hot, dry air and ventilate the greenhouse whenever possible during winter. Propagate by seed or 3-4in(8-10cm) cuttings in spring or summer. Provide a stake to keep the main branches upright.

Pittosporum eugenioides 'Variegatum'

Pittosporum tenuifolium 'Atropurpureum'

To encourage dense growth, cut back lateral branches by half in summer.

P. latifolius An important timber tree up to 100ft (30m) tall in its native South Africa, when small this species has longer leaves up to 3in(8cm), and does well in pots. Prune to restrict size. Young leaves are bright green, darkening to dull green.
32-45°F(0-7°C) H:6-7ft(1.8-2m) S:4-5ft(1.2-1.5m)

P. macrophyllus The Buddhist pine or Japanese yew will reach 25ft(7.5m) in its native China and Japan, but can be kept as small as 24in(60cm) in a pot. The flat, bright green needle-like leaves are up to 4in(10cm) long, glaucous beneath, and yew-like.
32-45°F(0-7°C) H&S:3-6ft(1-1.8m)

Pittosporum tenuifolium 'Irene Paterson'

Pittosporum tobira 'Variegatum'

Polyscias

(Araliaceae)

These exotic evergreen shrubs are unusual but well worth cultivating if warm, humid, draft-free conditions can be maintained during winter. Shade plants from hot sun during summer. Cuttings taken in summer root easily, provided the wood is not too hard.

55-60°F(13-16°C) H:36in(90cm) S:24in(60cm)

P. filicifolia The fern-leaf aralia has delicate light green foliage, especially when young. This contrasts nicely with dark, purple-tinged stems and leaf stalks.

Plants are relatively slow-growing and possibly the most sensitive to cold, drafts, overwatering, and temperature changes. Symptoms to watch out for are leaves turning yellow and wilting and a generally drooping attitude.

P. guilfoylei The wild coffee or geranium leaf aralia from Polynesia grows to 15ft(4.5m) in the wild. Few branches are produced and the comparatively large leaves are composed of three to seven leaflets, each of which is toothed and can be irregularly lobed. They usually have narrow white edges and are sometimes smudged with gray.

P. scutellaria 'Balfourii' (P. balfouriana) The dinner-plate or Balfour aralia from New Caledonia has rounded, often trifoliate leaves, irregularly toothed and some 3-4in(8-10cm) long. Stems are green, attractively speckled with gray. Most often seen in cultivation is P.s. 'Marginata', its leaves graced with irregular white edges. P.s. 'Pennockii' has leaves mottled with creamy-white.

Prostanthera

(Labiatae)

The shrubby evergreen Australian mint bushes are a delightful sight when in full flower, mostly during spring and early summer. They have a pleasant smell, not necessarily of mint, when brushed against or crushed. Both leaves and flowers are small and dainty. Plants appreciate good light, but shade from the hottest sun. Grow in large pots or borders of well-drained soil. Keep the earliest flowerers moist during winter as dryness jeopardizes developing flower buds. Shorten shoots after flowering to reduce size, but plants will stay compact without pruning. Propagate by spring-sown seed or in summer by cuttings. Watch out for whitefly in summer.

36-45°F(2-7°C)

P. cuneata This is probably the hardiest mint bush, making a low spreading shrub liberally sprinkled with purple-spotted, white flowers in June. Its strong, aromatic perfume is more eucalyptus than mint. H&S:24in(60cm)

P. lasianthos The Christmas bush or Victorian dogwood flowers for Christmas in its native Australia and Tasmania. Leaves 2-4in(5-10cm) long are large for a prostanthera. Flowers are white, spotted with purple, and have a fragrance reminiscent of eucalyptus.

H:6ft(1.8m) S:3ft(1m) or more

P. melissifolia The balm mint bush is the most floriferous and fragrant of the mint bushes. The profusion of dainty flowers can be violet-colored or purple. Although capable of growing into a large bush, this species will flower when small and restricted in a pot.

H:6ft(1.8m) S:3ft(1m) or more

P. nivea The snowy mint bush, one of the smaller species, has white flowers, sometimes tinged with lilac.

H:2-6ft(60cm-1.8m) S:24-36in(60-90cm)

P. rotundifolia Rather similar to P. melissifolia, this has smaller, rounder, sweetly mint-scented leaves. Purple-blue flowers are profuse.

H:6ft(1.8m) S:3-4ft(1-1.2m)

Psidium

(Myrtaceae)

The guavas are grown for their evergreen foliage, small white flowers with prominent stamens in

Prostanthera melissifolia

summer, and nutritious fruits. *P. guajava* from tropical Central America bears rounded, yellow fruits; *P.g.f. pyriferum* is similar but with pear-shaped fruits. *P. littorale* var. *littorale* from Brazil is the strawberry guava and *P. littorale* var. *longipes* (*P. cattleianum*) is the pineapple or purple guava. Plants will grow happily in large, well-drained pots or in the border. Stake specimens if they become straggly. Mealy bugs and scale insects are attracted by their glossy leaves. Propagate from seed, best soaked for 24 hours before sowing, or in summer by cuttings, preferably with a heel of older wood.
45-50°F(7-10°C) H:4-6ft(1.2-1.8m) S:3-4ft(1-1.2m)

Punica

(Punicaceae)

P. granatum The pomegranate originates from the Balkans to the Himalayas, making scrubby thickets of small semi-evergreen trees or shrubs 18-20ft(5.5-6m) high, and is naturalized in Mediterranean regions. It is worth growing in the border or in a large pot of well-drained potting mix for its bright green foliage and unusual, orange-red summer flowers some 1½in(4cm) across. Plenty of light is appreciated – and necessary for fruits to mature. Prune wayward plants as growth is starting in spring. Seed germinates easily in spring or whenever extracted from a fruit. Alternatively, take cuttings in summer. Giving pomegranates a warm winter minimum temperature both encourages fruiting and helps plants retain some leaves: they become deciduous at low temperatures. *P.g.* 'Plena' is a double form. A useful dwarf variety, *P.g.* var. *nana*, H&S:24-36in(60-90cm), makes an attractive ornamental pot plant and can flower in under a year from seed. The whole plant is a miniature version of its larger relative, even down to the setting of small fruits, but these will not ripen.
32-45°F(0-7°C) H:6-7ft(1.8-2m) S:3-4ft(1-1.2m)

Ravenala

(Strelitziaceae)

R. madagascariensis The travelers' tree from Madagascar is so called because water is held in the sheaths at the base of the leaf stalks. At first, this striking plant resembles a banana or a palm. Long-stalked leaves up to 10ft(3m) long fan out opposite each other in two ranks, and the leaf blades, like those of bananas, become split. In the wild, ravenala becomes a tall tree, a trunk gradually building up from parts of the leaf stalks as they fall, but height is restricted if plants are grown in large pots. Allow plants in the border to grow until they reach the roof. As plants mature, white flowers rather like those of strelitzia (bird of paradise) appear in leaf axils during summer. Propagate by seed in spring or by suckers from around the base.
55°F(13°C) H&S:12ft(3.5m)

Rhododendron

(Ericaceae)

There are some beautiful tender rhododendron species from warm temperate climates which deserve to be used more often in the greenhouse. Many of these and their hybrids have deliciously perfumed spring flowers. *R. ciliicalyx* from China, *R. lindleyi* (Himalayas), *R. maddenii* (Himalayas), and *R. taggianum* (Burma) have predominantly white flowers. *R. maddenii*, H&S:6ft(1.8m), planted in a large ceramic or terracotta pot or a half-barrel can fill the whole greenhouse with the rich perfume of its beautiful, pink-flushed white blooms. Out of flower, evergreen leaves and papery, colorful bark are still desirable. Of the hybrids, *R.* 'Countess of Haddington' (pink), *R.* 'Fragrantissimum' (white, tinged pink), *R.* 'Lady Alice Fitzwilliam' (white, stained yellow), and *R.* 'Princess Alice' (white, flushed pink) are the most popular.

Vireya rhododendrons, H&S:4ft(1.2m), are a subgenus of tender, mostly epiphytic species with their origin in the mountains and rainforests of the Far East. Their requirements are similar to other greenhouse-grown rhododendrons, except that because of their epiphytic nature, some orchid-grade bark can be mixed into their soil. They dislike being pruned but are otherwise easy to grow. Many have brightly colored orange or bright pink flowers and some are perfumed. *R. brookeanum* from Borneo and *R. javanicum* from throughout southeast Asia possess orange flowers, while those of *R. macgregoriae* from New Guinea are yellow.

Water with soft rainwater whenever possible; if tap water is alkaline, add at every watering a weak liquid fertilizer formulated for acid-loving plants. Never allow plants to dry out, yet waterlogging should also be avoided; keep the atmosphere humid and well ventilated. Pot in acidic soil mix. Whether plants are grown in pots or in a border, it is critical to make sure they are planted no higher or lower than before. They must be protected from hot summer temperatures by shading and spray misting. During summer, plants can be placed outside in a semi-shaded spot. Propagate by ripened shoots of current season's growth in late summer or fall, or by layering young shoots at any time of year.
38-45°F(3-7°C) H&S:3-10ft(1-3m)

INDOOR AZALEAS The rhododendron most likely to find a place in the greenhouse is the so-called Indian azalea, really from China; often listed as *R. simsii*, the popular plants are beautiful single- and double-flowered hybrids. Young plants are in plentiful supply during the winter months. They are usually pot-bound, with little room for watering at the top, so water them extra carefully and always use rainwater or boiled, cooled water. Keep plants cool and bright, then once all danger of frost is past in

Punica granatum var. *nana*

early summer, place outside in a semi-shaded position. Bring indoors well before the onset of cold fall weather. Repot in spring when necessary and the plants can last for years.
38-45°F(3-7°C) H:24in(60cm) S:30in(75cm)

Rosa

(Rosaceae)

During Victorian times, whole greenhouses were given over to growing roses, so that blooms were available throughout winter and spring. To revive this fashion, choose tender or late-flowering hybrids like Tea, China, Noisette and Bourbon roses. It is best to grow greenhouse roses in pots; they do much better if they can spend the summer outdoors. Pay particular attention to watering, feeding, spray misting and pest and disease control to create good plants. For good winter blooms, disbud in late summer. Move plants inside in midfall, keeping cool and ventilating well. Allow flower buds to form from late fall, flowering as they will. After flowering, in early spring, they can be pruned as necessary. Stand outside when all danger of frost is past. Alternatively, leave the roses in pots outdoors until midwinter, prune, bring indoors and enjoy early blooms in the spring. Plants may need another pruning when they are placed outside for the summer. Some of the marvelous climbing varieties mentioned below can be planted in a bed and trained up the roof like vines. After flowering, cut back the laterals growing from the rods running up the roof, leaving only short stubs of a few nodes on the main horizontal stems at the base.

Experiment with varieties, as well as methods. Tea

Sparmannia africana

The color of their small, dainty flowers intensifies rather than pales with age.
40-50°F(4-10°C)

Schefflera
(Araliaceae)

Handsome foliage plants with interesting leaf shapes, the scheffleras make bold specimen features. Shade them from hot sun and protect from cold drafts. Propagate the first two by cuttings, including stem sections containing two nodes, or by air-layering. Propagate *S. elegantissima* by seed.

S. actinophylla (Brassaia actinophylla) The Queensland umbrella or octopus tree can reach 40ft (12m) in the wild. Olive-green leaves are composed of five to sixteen leaflets up to 12in(30cm) long.
50°F(10°C) H:6-8ft(1.8-2.5m) S:3ft(1m)

S. arboricola (Heptapleurum arboricola) The parasol plant is similar, but tends to have more leaflets especially when young. Individually, they are slightly smaller and narrower. There are numerous varieties, some with striking gold variegations. *S.a.* 'Trinette' has bright, irregular, yellow markings and deep green leaves. *S.a.* 'Janine' is compact with small crinkled leaves unevenly marked with greenish-cream mostly on the margins. Some leaflets are green, others cream.
50°F(10°C) H:4-6ft(120-180cm) S:2-3ft(60-90cm)

S. elegantissima (Heptapleurum elegantissimum, Aralia elegantissima, Dizygotheca elegantissima) This New Hebridean species is quite dissimilar in appearance to the others. Admirable for its striking juvenile foliage, it will vary in habit according to temperature. Leaves are coppery when young and composed of seven to ten narrow, dark green, almost black, toothed leaflets. Given a minimum of 60-65°F (16-18°C), growth is rapid, usually single-stemmed or loosely branched with large leaves. Grown cooler, plants will still succeed if not overwatered or exposed to violent fluctuations in temperature; however, growth will be more compact and leaves smaller.
50°F(10°C) H:2-5ft(60cm-1.5m) S:24-36in(60-90cm)

Senecio
(Compositae)

S. grandifolius (Telanthophora grandifolia) This Mexican shrub has large, dramatic leaves and wide terminal heads composed of many small yellow flowers in winter. Plants in borders respond well to spring pruning; alternatively, cuttings taken in spring root easily and pot-grown plants will flower at about 30in(75cm) tall. Good light is appreciated.
45°F(7°C) H:6-7ft(1.8-2m) S:5-6ft(1.5-1.8m)

Senna
(Leguminosae)

These shrubby plants (formerly in the genus *Cassia*) are well worth growing for their long season of

roses are in the parentage of – and look like slender versions of – modern Hybrid Teas; the fact that they are easily spoiled by frost and bad weather when grown outdoors recommends them for greenhouse use. *R.* 'Catherine Mermet' (1869) has buds of exquisite shape, blush-pink tinged with lilac, while *R.* 'Perle des Jardins' (1874) has flowers of faint, straw-colored yellow. Climbing Tea rose *R.* 'Niphetos' (1889) has large, slightly hanging white blooms. Another climbing form, *R.* 'Devoniensis' (1858), once called the magnolia rose, has delightful creamy-white, pink-flushed flowers with growing apricot centers. In pots, these need not grow too tall

and can be tied up a central cane. Very popular for indoor use is *R.* 'Maréchal Niel', a Tea-Noisette dating from 1864. Nodding creamy-yellow flowers have a ravishing, almost fruity fragrance. A climber capable of reaching 15ft(4.5m), this too will keep smaller in a pot. Other essentially climbing types include *R.* 'Gloire de Dijon' (1853), a wonderful old Noisette with fragrant, buff-yellow blooms suffused with warm pink. The climbing form of *R.* 'Souvenir de la Malmaison' (1843) is a beautiful Bourbon with blush pink, quartered blooms some 5in(13cm) across when mature, with Tea-rose fragrance. China roses, with their light growth to about 6ft(1.8m), are worth a try.

cheerful flowers. Attractive foliage in some species is covered with silvery down. Prune thoroughly after flowering, cutting long wayward stems back to within a spur of older wood, to keep plants compact. Sennas enjoy full light and plenty of water during summer. Take cuttings in late spring, or sow seed, first grazing it with sandpaper.

S. alata (Cassia alata) The candlestick senna from Brazil can be restricted to a flowering plant of some 4ft(1.2m) in a pot. Upright spikes of golden-yellow flowers, black in bud, appear during winter. Foliage is prettily pinnate.
50°F(10°C) H:6ft(1.8m) S:5ft(1.5m)

S. artemisioides (Cassia artemisioides) The well-named silver senna from Australia is covered with silky white down and bears its flowers in short racemes.
40-45°F(4-7°C) H:6ft(1.8m) S:5ft(1.5m)

S. corymbosa (Cassia corymbosa) This Argentinian species is probably the most popular and undemanding. Leaves consist of four to six oval leaflets. Rich yellow flowers appear during mid- to late summer and would be well complemented by a tub of blue agapanthus.
40°F(4°C) H&S:5-6ft(1.5-1.8m)

Sparmannia
(Tiliaceae)

S. africana The African hemp or house lime can reach 20ft(6m) in South Africa. Specimens planted in the greenhouse border aspire to similar heights and need annual pruning after flowering. Large, lobed, hairy leaves are lime-green, making an attractive foliage plant. Flowers, produced during spring, have white petals with a bunch of prominent yellow stamens, changing to red toward the tips; tickle these stamens and they will open outward as if by magic. Propagate in spring or summer by cuttings, pinching back growing tips for a bushy plant, though too much pinching retards flowering. Plants are prone to whitefly attack.
45°F(7°C) H:5-6ft(1.5-1.8m) S:3-4ft(1-1.2m)

Strelitzia
(Strelitziaceae)

S. reginae The impressive bird of paradise from South Africa can survive the harsh light of an unshaded, sunny greenhouse. Leathery leaves are held on long stalks, with the flowers peeping through them during spring and summer just like the heads of birds. The beak part is a red-rimmed, green bract out of which appear crest-like orange sepals and smaller blue petals. Whether in pots or in the border, plants will build up into clumps. Propagate by seed or by dividing the clumps. Small plants will take up to six years to begin flowering. Water well during summer.
38°F(3°C) H:3-5ft(1-1.5m) S:24-36in(60-90cm)

Tetrapanax
(Araliaceae)

T. papyrifer (Fatsia papyrifera) The rice paper plant from China will rapidly grow from seed into a handsome, stately specimen with dramatic long-stalked leaves gracing tall, suckering stems. In shape, leaves are like a large version of *Fatsia japonica* but with more lobes. They are white-felted on the undersides, sage-green on the surface, making a lovely contrast. Sprays of creamy flowers may appear in summer. Shade plants lightly from hot sun. Cut down stems that are too long and leggy at the end of summer, and new stems will be sent up in spring. Propagate by seed or suckers in spring.
38-45°F(3-7°C) H&S:6-10ft(1.8-3m)

Yucca
(Agavaceae)

Yuccas can make dramatic specimen plants for the greenhouse and are tolerant of bright light. Many have vicious, spine-tipped leaves and should never be positioned where adults, children, or animals can walk or run into them and damage their eyes. Propagate by seed, or cut or pull offsets away from the parent in spring to root like a cutting. Yuccas usually respond well to pruning, sending up a cluster of new shoots from the cut stem. The section that has been removed can be shortened and treated like a giant cutting. If too many new shoots are formed, carefully pull away those not wanted and root them too.

Y. aloifolia The Spanish bayonet or dagger plant is from southern USA, Mexico, and the West Indies. As might be gathered by its vicious-sounding names, this species has unyielding, sharply pointed leaves. There are some attractively variegated varieties. *Y. elephantipes* is similar and probably a safer choice.
38-40°F(3-4°C) H&S:3-6ft(1-1.8m)

Y. elephantipes The arching leaves of the spineless yucca from Mexico, up to 3-4ft(1-1.2m) long, are softer and safer than the above. As plants grow, the base of the tough stem becomes swollen. Plants can become tall and wide. For a small greenhouse, choose a plant whose main, woody stem has been chopped off, resulting in the growth of several smaller shoots.
38-40°F(3-4°C) H:6-7ft(1.8-2m) S:4-6ft(1.2-1.8m)

Y. whipplei Our Lord's candle from Mexico and California has the advantage of possibly flowering in a container. Many more leaves are produced than in the more familiar species. Narrow blue-green leaves 12-36in(30-90cm) long are spine-tipped and edged with fine but sharp teeth. Long panicles of greenish-white, sometimes purple-flushed flowers are fragrant, but can reach 12ft(3.5m) in height. Plants die after flowering.
32-40°F(0-4°C) H&S:4-6ft(1.2-1.8m)

Tetrapanax papyrifer

Schefflera actinophylla

Climbing and wall plants

After the specimen plants, the next important group to create impact in the sunroom or greenhouse consists of the climbing plants and their allies. These can scale verticals such as posts and pillars, curtain trellising, and host plants or dangle their trailing stems down from the roof. This chapter includes both plants whose natural habit is to climb, twine, or otherwise haul themselves up toward the light, and shrubby plants with lax, arching branches that can be trained on supports to perform in the vertical plane.

True climbing plants have developed a variety of methods by which they cling to their supports. Apart from some gentle guidance in the right direction, these climbers need little assistance in their ascent. Some scramble, sending out long stems at right angles, which weave through shrubs and trees in the wild, often latching on with hooks. Others cling by stem roots, which insert themselves into fissures and crevices or secrete fluid which dries to cement the plant to its support. Clematis, canarina, and maurandya have sensitive twining leaf stalks. Gloriosa has leaf tips which elongate into tendrils and mutisia produces leaf tendrils formed by extensions of the midrib veins. Some tendrils wrap themselves around their support and others, those of *Macfadyena unguis-cati*, for instance, cling by branched, hook-like tendrils.

Twiners wrap their stems, snake-like, about those of other plants and, in the greenhouse, any kind of supporting framework. Almost all coil either clockwise or counter-clockwise and any attempt to start them off in the other direction results in confusion, with the stem having to turn itself around to twine the other way. Most are anti-clockwise, twining to the right away from the sun, but some twine clockwise, to the left following the sun.

A number of plants with no such natural mechanisms can be induced to "climb" in the greenhouse. There are "sprawlers" and tall, rather leggy shrubs that are malleable enough to be trained against a wall. These need judicious pruning and tying up to encourage fan-like growth for even coverage and an attractive shape. Some make a more emphatic vertical accent: cestrum will clothe a pillar, and the long branches of *Hibiscus schizopetalus* can be tied up overhead to form an archway.

Where any kind of climber needs provision for tying up to the shell of the greenhouse, horizontal wires positioned at regular intervals across walls and ceiling are ideal. These are reasonably straightforward to fit against solid walls but need to be stretched tight. The glass sides and roofs of greenhouses can pose problems if the glazing bars are not made of wood. Materials such as aluminum, for example, need special fittings which clip into the glazing bars. Where fitting a series of wires seems difficult, a section of trellis might prove an alternative. Some plants can be damaged when supporting wires become too hot in summer and burn the stems that twine around them. Plastic-coated wire obviates this problem.

Plants with twining stems can be supplied with their own climbing frame by pushing three or four tall, upright canes around the outside of the pot and drawing them together at the top to make a wigwam-like structure. Stems can be either trained straight up or wound around. One or more circles of wire are also useful for plants like hoya and ivy. Plants with slender stems like gloriosa and *Bomarea caldasii* can be secured with strings. Fit individual lengths near the base of the plant, wind the string loosely around the stem or stems, and tie above the plant.

During summer a climbing profusion of abundant foliage and flowers is easily achieved. Grown up walls and under the roof of the conservatory, a canopy of sun-loving climbers makes a living sun shade, shielding both people and other plants from the scorching rays. Passion flowers are particularly adept climbers, though young plants can take a couple of years to become established. Stems should be fitted away from the glass so that leaves do not touch it, as it would certainly scorch them. For a quick grower, sow cup and saucer vine (*Cobaea scandens*) in spring to produce its strange flowers by late summer. Yellow golden trumpet (*Allamanda cathartica*) and blue trumpet vine (*Thunbergia grandiflora*) make stunning cascades from the roof of a warm greenhouse.

Plants that cling and climb are particularly useful in winter, when many smaller plants are out of season. Some have the added attraction of delicious scent, which is even more inviting if allowed to waft into other parts of the house. One of the most popular is *Jasminum polyanthum*, which climbs to 10ft(3m) or more. In warmer temperatures its pink buds open to pure white flowers in the depths of winter, but grown cooler, the buds will remain tantalizingly closed for weeks before gradually opening in spring. The sweet, almost overpowering fragrance is apt to mask other, more subtle perfumes. *Buddleja asiatica* is a scented climber capable of covering a large wall in a sunroom. Long panicles of sweetly perfumed white flowers drape gracefully from a handsome silvery plant.

Most climbers make rampant growth, and a sound knowledge of their pruning is essential to control this and to stimulate new growth in the lower reaches of the plant which otherwise becomes bare and leggy. Pests will often colonize the upper parts, remaining unseen until they reach plague proportions. Regular pruning permits close inspection as well as removing a considerable quantity of stems and leaves which possibly harbor pests and their eggs. The upper reaches of climbers are difficult to spray, making biological control an ideal solution (see p.34).

The aim of most sunroom or greenhouse plantings is to achieve the effect of abundant foliage and flowers. To create a real indoor garden, much of the interior needs to be filled with leafy shoots and the dangling stems of flowers. Once specimen plants have been chosen, climbing plants can be introduced to adorn the vertical surfaces. Some, like this *Bougainvillea* 'Miss Manila' hybrid (shown here with *Convolvulus sabatius*), need to be tied up to their support, even though hooks in their leaf axils help them to grip. Other climbers cling by means of aerial roots or strong tendrils.

Actinidia

(Actinidiaceae)

A. deliciosa (A. chinensis) The Chinese gooseberry or kiwi fruit has its origins in the forests of southern China. Although *A. deliciosa* is considered hardy, the protection offered by a greenhouse will guarantee better and more regular fruiting. Vine-like deciduous climbers, they are ornamental as well as fruitful. Large heart-shaped leaves have downy undersides and grow from hairy shoots. Until recently both male and female plants have been required for fruiting: a good "couple" is made by *A.d.* 'Hayward', a female variety, and *A.d.* 'Tomuri', a male which flowers at the same time for pollination. Clusters of creamy-white flowers with prominent stamens are produced in summer, to be followed by large, brown, hairy egg-shaped fruits. A newer self-pollinating variety, *A.d.* 'Jenny', is said to yield up to 500 fruits a year when mature. These, at 1½in(4cm) long, are smaller than usual, but the flowers will pollinate other, larger-fruited varieties. As plants are large – rambling to 30ft(9m) – prune regularly to keep them within bounds. Thin out or shorten some of the older stems every year, just as the leaf buds begin to grow in spring. Shade lightly from hot sun, maintain humidity in summer, and watch out for mealy bugs. Train against a wall or trellis.
27-45°F(-3-7°C) H&S:10ft(3m)

Agapetes

(Ericaceae)

These unusual plants are best described as sprawling evergreen shrubs. Many are probably epiphytic or

Agapetes macrantha

Allamanda cathartica

Agapetes serpens

semi-epiphytic in the wild. Left to themselves they make rather awkward specimens, unless planted as part of a landscape where they will drape themselves over rocks or old tree stumps. However, tied up to a framework of canes or offered some other support, they will make an effective display. Shade from full sun and maintain humidity. A potting mix for acid-loving plants and watering with soft rainwater will be appreciated. Propagate by cuttings of firm but young wood.

A. macrantha This species from Burma has exquisite, tubular, pale pink flowers nearly 2in(5cm) long. Divided into five sections by white ribs, each is marked with a vertical line of dark pink chevrons. Greenish-colored tips curl back. On closer inspection these strange clustered blooms are even more unusual, as they are held on small pink stalks straight out of both old and young wood. Flowers open in midwinter.
50°F(10°C) H:3-5ft(1-1.5m) S:3ft(1m)

A. serpens This more sprawling species from western China sends out long stems covered with small, pointed, shiny leaves. In spring, like lanterns strung from a line, clusters of red tubular flowers with darker red chevron markings appear. These are similar in shape to those of *A. macrantha*, but smaller.
40°F(4°C) H:6-8ft(1.8-2.5m) S:6ft(1.8m)

Allamanda

(Apocynaceae)

A. cathartica The golden trumpet grows wild in mangrove swamps and along waterways in Brazil and Guyana: in cultivation this evergreen climber does best in warm greenhouses spray misted several times a day to create a similarly moist atmosphere. Less humidity would be required during lower winter temperatures. Confined in a pot, the golden trumpet will be restricted in size, but planted in a bed it will need plenty of space. The plant twines, but will need some wires to help its ascent. Unless the greenhouse is very tall, it is best to construct a "ceiling" of wires, so that having reached a vertical limit it can be trained overhead. Then, as flower buds form at the ends of the long stems, these can be drawn down through the wires to make a most attractive display. Showy yellow flowers are 4in(10cm) wide, vanilla-scented, with five overlapping petals. After summer flowering, plants can be pruned back. Thin out some main stems, then shorten the laterals, cutting them back to within one or two nodes of remaining main stems. *A.c.* 'Hendersonii' is more vigorous with larger, more golden flowers. There are brown veins on the flower and five white spots, one where each petal fuses to make the tube. *A.c.* 'Williamsii' is an unusual double-flowered form. Propagate in spring by cuttings.
55°F(13°C) H:15ft(4.5m) S:6-7ft(1.8-2m)

Ampelopsis

(Vitaceae)

A. brevipedunculata The porcelain berry from China, Korea, and Japan bears small greenish flowers followed by blue berries. Deciduous, its vine-like leaves 2-5in(5-13cm) long are heart-shaped or three-to five-lobed. Left to itself it will climb up to 18ft(5.5m) by means of twining tendrils. More useful for a pretty sunroom with a cottage-style interior is *A.b.* 'Elegans', H&S:36in(90cm); more diminutive in all respects, its cream, green, and pink variegated leaves will mingle with a motley of other foliage and flowering plants. Allow it to ramble or offer it a climbing frame of canes or trellis. Shade lightly and mist regularly to ward off spider mite. Propagate in summer by making cuttings.
32-45°F(0-7°C)

Anemopaegma

(Bignoniaceae)

A. chamberlaynei This yellow-flowered robust climber from Brazil is ideal for the larger greenhouse. Less prone to spider mite than others in its family, it makes long stems clothed with opposite leaves, each composed of two leaflets and a long tendril. This ends in three tendrilar hooks, so that if you run a finger slowly along its length, it will cling gently at the tip. A young plant may need some help early in its ascent but will then cling well unassisted. The best plants are those given the root run of a bed, their growth trained up and across the roof, so that flower stems hang gracefully down. Tubular, foxglove-like flowers are soft primrose-yellow and appear mostly in summer, but sporadically throughout the year. Shade lightly from the hottest sun. Prune in spring when necessary. Propagate in summer by making cuttings.
50°F(10°C) H:15-20ft(4.5-6m)

Araujia

(Asclepiadaceae)

A. sericifera From Brazil and Peru, this woody, evergreen, twining climber is capable of covering a greenhouse wall when support is provided. Leaves are pale and downy on their undersides. Summer flowers, initially flushed with pink but clearing to white, are waxy and fragrant; they trap visiting moths with their glutinous pollen. Flowers are followed by large pods shaped like avocado pears, which split to reveal silky threads and small seeds. Plants are easily raised from spring-sown seed or by making cuttings in summer. Because cut stems exude a milky sap, replacing leggy specimens with new plants is usually preferable to pruning back.
32-45°F(0-7°C) H:7-15ft(2-4.5m) S:7ft(2m)

Aristolochia littoralis

Aristolochia

(Aristolochiaceae)

These climbers are worth growing for their strange, though handsome flowers, produced, mostly, during summer and fall. Their unusual shape, dark purplish-maroon mottling and often spicy, sometimes rotting smell attract and temporarily trap flies for cross-pollination. Some are large or graced with long, twisting tails. There are species to suit most temperature ranges and all germinate readily from seed. Smaller species can be grown in large pots of well-drained potting mix; the larger kinds will need the root run of a greenhouse border. Plants respond well to spring pruning, but the continuous removal of one-year-old stems will prevent flowering in some species. Shade lightly from summer sun. Small, thin-leaved species are prone to spider-mite attack, while larger-leaved, thick-stemmed species are more attractive to mealy bugs.

A. gigantea From Brazil, this species has huge hooded flowers up to 8in(20cm) across of sinister brownish-purple, with no smell. Plenty of humidity and a good root run will assist flowering.
60°F(16°C) H:20ft(6m) S:8ft(2.5m)

A. grandiflora The pelican or duck flower from the lowlands of Mexico to Panama and the West Indies needs tropical heat to grow its long stems from a woody root stock. Its flowers are outrageously large and pungent, with veined brownish-purple blades 6-24in(15-60cm) long and twisted tails to 36in(90cm)

Billardiera longiflora

Bougainvillea 'Scarlett O'Hara'

long. Plants are usually cut back after flowering and start again from the base the following year.

A. littoralis (A. elegans) The calico flower from Brazil is one of the best known aristolochias. Although capable of 20ft(6m), it can be kept much smaller in a pot. Given canes or a pillar to climb, twining stems of small leaves somewhere between kidney- and heart-shaped soon rise up and produce flowers of comparative charm. A small, curved, pale green tube flares out into a white-marbled, rich maroon bowl up to 3in(8cm) across.
55°F(13°C) H&S:6ft(1.8m) in a container

A. saccata This plant from India is altogether different. Although quite rare, it makes a lovely plant for the warm greenhouse, 50°F(10°C). Large, hairy heart-shaped leaves are attractive. Small furry, purple-red and creamy-yellow flowers often sprout out of old wood and the base as well as from newer shoots.

Beaumontia
(Apocynaceae)

B. grandiflora This magnificent climber from northern India thrives naturally where a hot, rainy season is followed by a cool, dry season. The greenhouse should be able to provide this, resulting in clusters of huge white fragrant trumpet-shaped flowers, 4-5in(10-13cm) wide, in summer. Prune immediately after flowering if space is restricted. Even when not in flower, beaumontias make handsome foliage plants, their large, deep green leaves have brown hairs on the undersides. Propagate in summer by cuttings. Although plants will easily reach 25ft(7.5m), given the run of a border, they can

be restricted by containerizing and pruning. Water well and feed with liquid fertilizer in summer.
45°F(7°C) H:6-10ft(1.8-3m) S:4-6ft(1.2-1.8m)

Bignonia
(Bignoniaceae)

B. capreolata The cross vine or trumpet vine from the USA is an evergreen climber, with leaves consisting of paired leaflets and branched, twining tendrils. A dainty plant with tubular, burnt-orange flowers in summer, it needs a lot of care to do well. Leaflets quickly turn yellow if feeding is not attended to and plants are prone to attack by spider mite, aphids, and mealy bugs, resulting in sooty mold if not treated. Grow in a border if a large plant 15ft(4.5m) or so high is required to train up walls and across roofs, or grow plants in pots. Prune untidy plants in spring. For pot specimens this can be fairly rigorous, reducing all shoots to about 6in(15cm). In the case of tall plants, cut lateral stems back to within one or two nodes of main stems. Propagate in summer by making cuttings.
45°F(7°C) H:10ft(3m) S:4-5ft(1.2-1.5m)

Billardiera
(Pittosporaceae)

B. longiflora The purple apple berry from Australia and Tasmania at first sight appears mundane, but the profusion of slender woody twining stems will eventually form a column or fan of small, pointed, evergreen leaves up to 2in(5cm) long. In summer, pale greenish-yellow or creamy bell-shaped flowers, flushed with purple inside, are produced. These are followed by ornamental purple-blue fruits, which are

inedible. Grow in pots of well-drained potting mix, and train the stems up a cane: the first stems will need some help to start climbing but successive stems will cling to one another. For plants in the border, try fixing a wire or string from the base of the plant to a point above it. Plants are best raised from spring-sown seed or cuttings in late summer.
32-45°F(0-7°C) H:6ft(1.8m) S:30in(75cm)

Bomarea
(Liliaceae/Alstroemeriaceae)

B. caldasii This plant from Ecuador and Colombia is rather like a refined, climbing type of alstroemeria (or Peruvian lily). The long slender twining stems end in terminal umbels of flowers 1½in(4cm) long in summer. Elegant and shaped like long bells, they are basically pinkish-orange and yellow, sprinkled with dark speckles. Though they can be grown in large pots, the extra root run of a border will result in better, taller, more floriferous plants. Canes or strings must be supplied for the stems to ascend, although after a while they will climb up one another. Divide established plants carefully in summer, pulling apart the fleshy roots. Spider mite and aphids can sometimes be a problem, as can western flower thrips. Old stems may turn yellow, then brown and wither away; cut these off at ground level as they become unsightly.
38°F(3°C) H:6ft(1.8m) S:36in(90cm)

Bougainvillea
(Nyctaginaceae)

Guaranteed to create a luxuriant effect in the greenhouse, bougainvillea boast showy bracts surrounding small creamy flowers. Originally from South America, species like cerise-purple *B. glabra* and red-purple *B. spectabilis*, though handsome and vigorous, have been overtaken in cultivation by the many flamboyant hybrids. Flower colors include pink (*B.* 'James Walker'), pink and white (*B.* 'Mary Palmer', syn. *B.* 'Surprise'), magenta (*B.* 'Barbara Karst', *B.* 'Scarlett O'Hara'), orange (*B.* 'Alabama Sunset', *B.* 'Jamaica Orange', *B.* 'Isabel Greensmith') and white (*B.* 'Jennifer Fernie', *B.* 'Summer Snow'). There are double-flowered kinds and some with variegated foliage (*B. glabra* 'Variegata', *B.* 'Raspberry Ice'), though these tend not to be as vigorous as plain-leaved types. All flower throughout the summer and often into the fall and winter. Varieties with more bush-like growth are less suitable for covering vast expanses of wall or climbing up pillars. Although hooks in their leaf axils help them to climb, bougainvilleas will need to be tied up to their support.

A good system is to train as many main stems as possible, pinching them at the required length to encourage the production of flowering lateral shoots. Prune these laterals back to within a node or two of the older stems in late winter to keep the plants neat and compact. After a summer of particularly profuse growth, stems of vigorous hybrids may need shortening in fall too. Bougainvilleas grown in pots will never reach the size of those given a better root run. Virtually any temperature regime will suit them but they generally flower better after a cool winter. However, if they have to endure temperatures close to freezing they can be very slow in returning to growth, and flowering may be delayed until late summer. During cold temperatures, leaves will drop; keep the soil in pots or borders on the dry side. Full light is appreciated. Whitefly and aphids can be a minor nuisance, but mealy bugs on mature plants are the worst pest offender. Semi-ripe cuttings in summer root easily. Hardwood cuttings made during winter are less reliable.
32-45°F(4-7°C) H&S:5-20ft(1.5-6m)

Buddleja
(Loganiaceae)
Tender buddlejas make excellent, often fragrant greenhouse plants, their rather lax habit ideal for tying up to canes, a trellis, or wires. Large species can be accommodated by restricting their roots to containers and by hard pruning carried out after flowering. Taller specimens trained to cover a large area are best pruned by cutting laterals back to within one or two nodes of older, main stems. Cut back occasional old stems to be replaced with new. Propagate by seed or in summer by cuttings. Plants are prone to whitefly. The following are evergreen.
B. asiatica Arguably the best buddleja for the cool

greenhouse, this elegant, ethereal species originates from the East Indies and China. Once the main stems have been trained upward, the laterals drape downward, ending, in late winter and early spring, in pendent panicles 6in(15cm) long of small, white, fragrant flowers. Stems are covered in white down, as are the undersides of long, grayish-green leaves.
32-45°F(0-7°C) H&S:10ft(3m)
B. auriculata This native of South Africa has fragrant cream-colored flowers with yellow throats. Packed into rounded panicles 2in(5cm) across, they appear throughout fall and winter. Though without the draping elegance of *B. asiatica*, this species is still lax enough to train against a wall.
32-45°F(0-7°C) H&S:6-9ft(1.8-2.75m)
B. lindleyana This Chinese species is more upright and less easy to train against a wall or trellis. Velvety purple flowers held in upright racemes up to 8in(20cm) long are borne in summer.
32-45°F(0-7°C) H:10ft(3m) S:8ft(2.5m)
B. madagascariensis (Nicodemia madagascariensis) Of lax habit, this pretty Madagascan species is a fast grower and needs either a large area or rigorous pruning to keep it under control. Take care when carrying this out, as the felted hair on shoots and under leaves rubs off and can irritate skin and throat. Small orange flowers are borne in tapering panicles 6in(15cm) long during spring.
45-50°F(7-10°C) H&S:12ft(3.5m)
B. officinalis This more upright species from China has soft, woolly gray stems and undersides of leaves, contrasting well with the yellow-throated mauve flowers. These are honey-scented and of great value in the greenhouse during fall and winter.
32-45°F(0-7°C) H:6-9ft(1.8-2.75m) S:6ft(1.8m)
B. tubiflora Of upright habit, this species from Brazil grows more slowly than the others, is the best suited to growing in pots, and requires more skill in its cultivation. While not wanting too cold a temperature, it dislikes the humidity that is often associated with warmth and will die back if there is too much moisture in the air or at the roots. Good care will be rewarded by a handsome plant. The overall appearance is of softness, with downy shoots and velvety leaves. Compact, upright spikes of bright orange flowers are striking during winter.
45-50°F(7-10°C) H:5ft(1.5m) S:3ft(1m)

Campsis
(Bignoniaceae)
The trumpet vines or creepers are showy deciduous climbers which cling rather like ivies, by means of short aerial roots. Foliage is pretty, leaves consisting of several pairs of leaflets. Frost-hardy, they will flower well in sunny positions outdoors during late summer, or in summer in the greenhouse.
C. grandiflora from China has large flowers held in

pendent or horizontal terminal racemes. Individually they are 2¹⁄₂in(6cm) long, opening rose-pink but turning rich rose-apricot as they mature, their tubular shape flaring out into five petal lobes. *C. radicans* from North America is similar, with slightly smaller orange-scarlet flowers. *C.* × *tagliabuana* 'Madame Galen' is a hybrid between the two species and carries pinkish-orange flowers. The root run of a border containing well-drained soil will provide a taller flowering plant than the constriction of a pot. Prune in spring if required. Propagate by semi-ripe cuttings in summer, or raise species from seed.
32-45°F(0-7°C) H:15-30ft(4.5-9m)

Canarina
(Campanulaceae)
C. canariensis The Canary Island bellflower is a fascinating and worthwhile plant to grow. It has a lax habit and at home in the Canary Islands will scramble through shrubs, but some support is required in the greenhouse. Pale green stems are

Bougainvillea glabra

almost succulent and rather brittle, graced with glaucous, vaguely triangular leaves. Bell-shaped flowers are striking, 1½-2½in(4-6cm) long and reddish-orange with darker red veins. Canarina dies down to a tuberous root stock in spring, remains more or less dormant during early summer and sprouts into fresh growth in late summer. Flowers are produced during fall or winter. Keep plants very much on the dry side when dormant. Give plenty of light during winter. Propagate by seed or by cuttings.
45°F(7°C) H:36-48in(90-120cm) S:30in(75cm)

Cestrum
(Solanaceae)

The best way to grow these useful shrubs with a lax, rambling habit is to secure their stems to a wall or, even better, around a pillar. Although plants can be grown in pots, they will become taller and flower more profusely when given the run of a border. Shade lightly from the hottest summer sun. Whitefly can be a problem and aphids sometimes attack young shoots. Propagate by seed or in summer by cuttings. Regular pruning carried out after flowering or in spring, cutting older stems hard back, and shortening laterals, will prevent cestrums from becoming untidy. The plants described are evergreen.

C. aurantiacum This species from Guatemala can also be grown as a free-standing shrub without support. Bright golden yellow tubular flowers appear during summer. Although individually quite small, they are borne in clusters which create some impact.

Cestrum 'Newellii'

A certain amount of leaf fall is normal.
45°F(7°C) H&S:6ft(1.8m)

C. elegans (C. purpureum) This Mexican species offers a long period of interest from late spring through until fall, when successions of reddish-purple tubular flowers are followed by long-lasting berries of the same color. Deep green leaves are downy. The habit is of robust, upward-growing stems; tie these up to a support. They become arching, so that the flowers, borne toward the ends of shoots, hang down. *C.* 'Newellii' is a hybrid very similar to *C. elegans*, which is almost certainly one of its parents. One would not want to grow both as they are so alike. With much pruning, a wall-trained specimen can be kept to H&S:5ft(1.5m).
32-45°F(0-7°C) H:10ft(3m) S:6ft(1.8m)

Cissus
(Vitaceae)

Although more commonly grown as houseplants, cissus make excellent foliage climbers provided they are well shaded from bright sun. Coolness and humidity during summer are necessary to prevent spider-mite attack and yellowing and browning of leaves. Although they will spread high and wide if planted in beds, all will remain at about 6ft(1.8m) when restricted in a pot. Propagate by seed or, more conventionally, by cuttings in spring or summer. Make plenty of these, as it is a good idea to pot several together. Tied up to a cane or encouraged to climb a support, they will quickly become a feature. Plants exceeding their boundaries can be trimmed

Cissus rhombifolia

back in spring. However, if a cissus has become bare and untidy at the base, cut back all the growth to within a few inches; plants almost always sprout fresh new shoots, but make cuttings as insurance.

C. antarctica The kangaroo vine from Australia looks good trained against the back wall of a shady greenhouse, providing attractive evergreen leaf shape against the bricks. For added summer color, raise canary creeper (*Tropaeolum peregrinum*) from seed and allow this yellow-flowered annual climber to mingle with the cissus. Pointed, oval leaves are toothed at the edges. Opposite each is a forked tendril to assist the plant's ascent. As it is less inclined to branch than other cissus, pinch back shoot tips to encourage bushiness.
45°F(7°C) H&S:10-15ft(3-4.5m)

C. discolor Begonia vine or rex begonia vine from Cambodia and Java is not as easy to grow as most other cissus, but is arguably the most impressive. Pointed, deep green leaves are very dark toward the middle, marked with silver between the veins, and maroon undersides. Tendrils and stems are an attractive deep red. When plants are given the warmth and humidity they demand, kept draft-free, and not overwatered, these beautiful leaves will grow unblemished to 4-6in(10-15cm) long. Unless optimum conditions can be guaranteed, the plant will be miserable and not worth growing.
60°F(16°C) H:6-8ft(1.8-2.5m) S:36in(90cm)

C. rhombifolia Grape ivy is flimsier than *C. antarctica* but equally easy to grow. This species has a wide natural distribution from Mexico to Brazil and the West Indies. Leaves are composed of three glossy, toothed leaflets, covered in fine silvery hairs when young. Unless given a support to climb, this plant will flop and trail. *C.r.* 'Ellen Danica' is similar, with lobed leaflets, but is susceptible to powdery mildew, particularly if soil dries out too much between waterings.
45-50°F(7-10°C) H:10ft(3m) S:5-7ft(1.5-2m)

Clematis
(Ranunculaceae)

Protection of glass means that the more tender, evergreen clematis can be cultivated without the effects of frost, wind, and rain damaging the perfection of their dainty flowers. Planted in borders, these climbers can be trained against pillars or indoor arches where they will cling with their sensitive petioles. They can also be restricted in pots (which can be plunged into the border if desired) and tied up to trellis or wire supports. Container-grown plants may need annual top-dressings as they mature. Keep cool and well ventilated. Take care not to overwater during winter, but give plenty of water and liquid fertilizer in summer. Prune by simply cutting out dead or encroaching stems after flowering.

Propagate in summer by cuttings. Species can be raised from fall-sown seed.

C. cirrhosa From southern Europe, this species makes an evergreen climber with pretty three-lobed leaves. Nodding, creamy-yellow flowers are borne, usefully, in winter. *C.c.* ssp. *balearica* has finely cut leaves and creamy flowers marked and spotted inside with dusty pinkish-red.
32-45°F(0-7°C) H:6-10ft(1.8-3m) S:3ft(1m)

C. indivisa This evergreen species from New Zealand has leathery, blunt-ended, trifoliate leaves. Flowers, borne in spring, are pure white stars decorated with a cluster of yellow stamens with pink anthers at their centers. Separate 3in(8cm) male and fragrant 2in(5cm) female flowers are borne on each plant. Potential giants, their size can be restricted by planting in containers and pruning regularly.
32-45°F(0-7°C) H&S:10ft(3m)

C. napaulensis From northern India and China, this evergreen species bears clusters of small silky yellow bell-shaped flowers with purple anthers. These appear during winter and spring on plants capable of reaching 30ft(9m). Plant in containers and prune to restrict to a manageable size.
32-45°F(0-7°C) H&S:10ft(3m)

Clerodendrum

(Verbenaceae)

These showy evergreen climbers from tropical West Africa need light shade. They will grow best in a well-drained soil. Pruning can be simply a matter of cutting away dead or ragged stems and generally thinning out the growth. When plants become too large and untidy, cut hard back to within 24-36in(60-90cm) of the base (this probably means sacrificing the flowers for that year). Propagate by cuttings in spring and summer. Plants seem to do better after a winter rest.

C. splendens This climbing species needs to grow tall before it will produce its bright red flowers with persistent calyces. Although it is mainly summer-flowering, there are often flowers at other times of the year as well.
55-60°F(13-16°C) H:10ft(3m) S:7ft(2m)

C. thomsoniae The twining bleeding heart vine or glory bower begins producing its exotic summer blooms when small. Clusters of crimson flowers project from the inflated white calyces, against the backdrop of massed pointed leaves. After the flowers have fallen, the calyces persist, becoming flushed with pinkish-purple. Sometimes blue fruits are formed.
55-60°F(13-16°C) H:10ft(3m) S:7ft(2m)

C. ugandense The scrambling blue glory bower has showy blue flowers during summer and fall and small, neat leaves.
40°F(4°C) H:10ft(3m) S:7ft(2m)

Clerodendrum thomsoniae

Clerodendrum splendens

Clianthus puniceus 'Roseus'

Dregea sinensis

Gloriosa superba

Clianthus
(Leguminosae)

C. puniceus Parrot's bill or lobster claw is a pretty shrub from New Zealand. It has no climbing mechanisms, but tends to spread and drape itself about, so is best tied up to a support. Leaves are attractively pinnate, making a dainty background for clusters of scarlet flowers borne in late spring and early summer. These are some 4in(10cm) long with a ridged petal. There is a pink- and a white-flowered form. Attack by spider mites is a persistent problem; avoid hot, dry conditions, and take control measures as soon as mites appear. Propagate by seed or in summer by cuttings with a heel.
38-45°F(3-7°C) H&S:6ft(1.8m)

Cobaea
(Polemoniaceae)

C. scandens The cup and saucer vine from Mexico is often grown as an annual climber outdoors. In the greenhouse, planted in a border or large pot, it will, with little help, cover a tremendous area in just one season from seed. The strange flowers open cream but mature to violet-purple. Each sits in its pale green calyx like a cup on a saucer. A prodigious climber, cobaea clings with much-branched tendrils, ending in small recurved hooks. There is a white-flowered form. Good light is appreciated: this is a

good plant to grow under the roof to shade others beneath. It is best to discard the whole plant after flowering and start again from seed the following year. It is possible, however, to cut plants back hard, to resprout in spring.
38-45°F(3-7°C) H&S:12-15ft(3.5-4.5m)

Dioscorea
(Dioscoreaceae)

D. elephantipes (Testudinaria elephantipes)
Tortoiseshell plant, tortoise plant, and hottentot bread are descriptive names for this South African species. It produces a large swollen tuber that rises up above the soil, looking rather like a tortoise shell (*testudo*) or an elephant's foot (*elephantipes*). From the top of this, every year, a climbing stem will rise, clothed with heart-shaped leaves and eventually producing rather insignificant yellow flowers in fall. Once these have finished, the stem withers leaving the strange "shell" behind. Propagate by spring-sown seed. Grow in well-drained soil as for cacti and succulents. Always water sparingly, and barely water at all during winter dormancy. Give plenty of light, shading only from the hottest summer sun. Spider mite on leaves can be a problem.
40-50°F(4-10°C) H:5-10ft(1.5-3m) S:3ft(1m)

Dregea
(Asclepiadaceae)

D. sinensis (Wattakaka sinensis) This evergreen twiner from China is not unlike a hoya in general appearance. Leaves 4in(10cm) long are soft and velvety underneath. Umbels of starry, five-petaled, creamy-white flowers flushed and speckled with pink appear in summer. These are delicate, honey-scented and sometimes followed by interesting seed pods. Grow in well-drained soil. Water carefully in winter, especially during low temperatures, allowing the top half of the soil to dry out before more water is given. Plants can be grown in pots or borders. Shade lightly from summer sun. Propagate by spring-sown seed or cuttings in summer.
38-45°F(3-7°C) H:6-10ft(1.8-3m) S:3ft(1m)

Eccremocarpus
(Bignoniaceae)

E. scaber The Chilean glory flower from the southern Andes of Chile and Argentina is a short-lived perennial climber. This cheerful, attractive plant brightens up foliage climbers during summer and into fall. This is when racemes of small, tubular, orange-red flowers are produced. Plants cling well to their support and to other plants by means of much branched tendrils at the ends of bipinnate leaves. Once flowering is finished, plants can be cut almost

down to the base from which they will sprout again the following spring, or replace annually by spring-sown seed. There are forms with crimson and golden-yellow flowers as well as numerous seed strains.
32-45°F(0-7°C) H:6-10ft(1.8-3m) S:3-5ft(1-1.5m)

Epipremmum
(Araceae)

E. aureum (Scindapsus aureus) Devil's ivy is deservedly popular as a houseplant, tolerating low light, a certain amount of dryness at the roots, and cold drafts. In the greenhouse, plants will require shading from hot summer sun and best suit a shady corner. In a warm, humid atmosphere, this reliable evergreen takes on a larger-leaved, more rampaging habit, sending out aerial roots from its stems – a reminder that in its native Solomon Islands it would reach some 40ft(12m) with leaves 12-18in(30-45cm) long. On small plants leaves rarely exceed 6in(15cm). These are deep green marbled with creamy-yellow. Some varieties have gold or silver markings. One of the newer kinds has leaves of pure gold and looks lovely grown against the speckles of *E. aureum*. Overwatering can prove fatal and dry air often causes ugly brown marks on the leaves. Encourage plants to climb by tying them up to a support such as a moss pole or old tree branch. Cuttings of shoot tips or of stem sections containing two nodes root easily. Plant three or four rooted cuttings around a moss pole in one pot, pinching them at about 4in(10cm) to make them branch and fill out.
50-55°F(10-13°C) H&S:6-10ft(1.8-3m)

× Fatsbedera
(Araliaceae)

× F. lizei The ivy tree, a hybrid between fatsia and hedera, possesses no twining or clinging mechanisms and its tall, unbranching stems are best tied up to a support. Dark green leaves are similar to those of fatsia, though smaller. Healthy, well-grown plants make a handsome sight where their leaf shapes show up against a plain background. Cut out growing tips to encourage branching, or grow three plants in one pot. Shade from full sun, repot or top-dress each year, feed well, and maintain high humidity during summer. Propagate by cuttings, either of the shoot tip or of stem chunks, each containing two nodes, or by air-layering. Prune old, scruffy plants hard back in spring to regenerate into a good bushy shape. × *F.l.* 'Variegata' has creamy-white edges to the leaves.
38-45°F(3-7°C) H:6ft(1.8m) S:3ft(1m)

Ficus
(Moraceae)

F. carica Figs, with their origins in Afghanistan and Iran, have been cultivated since ancient times.

Deciduous and not reliably hardy, they make excellent wall-trained specimens. In winter, when their attractive foliage has fallen, evergreens can be placed in front of the bare stems to hide (but not smother) them. The secret of growing figs is to restrict their roots. A wooden half-barrel, large glazed pot, or planting bed 36in(90cm) square and deep, lined with concrete or bricks, are all suitable. Provide drainage holes, as the free passage of water through the soil and container is essential. Good light is also important. Outdoor figs in areas experiencing frosts lose the tiny embryo figs which are left toward the ends of shoots in fall. With the protection of glass, however, these figs will be able to develop, so that plants fruit on both previous and current seasons' growths. Prune lightly in spring, removing weak or crowding shoots, particularly those which might shade developing fruit. Encourage young, healthy stems from the base to replace those that are old and becoming unproductive. In summer, pinch back fruit-bearing shoots at four or five leaves. There are many named varieties of fig, *F.* 'Brown Turkey' being one of the easiest to find and most popular and well suited to the greenhouse. Its large pear-shaped fruits are brown, tinged with purple. However, it is worth looking for more unusual varieties. The fruits of *F.c.* 'Bourjassotte Grise', 'Brunswick', 'Negro Largo', 'Osborn's Prolific', 'Panachée', 'Rouge de Bordeaux', 'White Ischia', and 'White Marseilles' all have excellent and superior flavor. Propagate by layering in summer or in late summer by 4-6in(10-15cm) long cuttings, preferably with a heel.
32-45°F(0-7°C) H:6-8ft(1.8-2.5m) S:8-10ft(2.5-3m)

Gelsemium
(Loganiaceae)

G. sempervirens The false or Carolina jasmine, a native of the southeastern USA, Mexico, and Guatemala, is grown for its pretty, yellow, fragrant flowers borne in spring and summer. Varying from deep to pale yellow, these are funnel-shaped and 1-1½in(2.5-3cm) long. A slender, twining climber, it has attractive paired leaves. Bright light is appreciated. Propagate by cuttings in summer. All parts of the plant, including flower nectar, are poisonous. *G.s.* 'Flore Pleno' is the double-flowered form.
40°F(4°C) H:10ft(3m) S:3ft(1m)

Gloriosa
(Liliaceae/Colchicaceae)

G. superba The climbing lily from tropical Africa and Asia is a curious plant, with tapering lance-shaped leaves drawn out into spirally coiled tips, which will hook on to twigs in the wild. In the greenhouse they will harness themselves to string, wire, or any similar support. Gloriosas are normally bought as

Eccremocarpus scaber

oddly shaped tubers in spring. Plant these as soon as possible, setting them upright in 6in(15cm) pots; cover with 1in(2.5cm) of potting mix and place in a temperature of 60-65°F(16-18°C), for example in a heated plant incubator. Water tubers in, but subsequently allow the top third of the potting mix to become almost dry before watering again. Even when in full growth, overwatering is the surest way to kill a gloriosa. As soon as plants start growing, provide support: one of the best ways is to secure string at the base of each stem and fix it optimistically 6ft(1.8m) above. Care will be rewarded by large exotic blooms consisting of six reflexed petals which vary slightly in color but are usually red, edged with yellow. Prominent stamens are yellow. After these summer flowers are over, allow the plants to die back and store the tubers dry at 50°F(10°C) for the winter. Propagate by seed (two to four years to flower) or by small tubers separated from the parents in spring at potting time. Watch out for spider-mite attack. Gloriosas are poisonous. 50-55°F(10-13°C) H:6ft(1.8m) S:24in(60cm)

Hardenbergia
(Leguminosae)
These pretty evergreen twiners from Australia are grown for their violet-purple, pink, or white pea-like flowers, which appear in late winter and early spring in the cool greenhouse. Plants need repotting or at least top-dressing every year in summer. If possible, plant them in a border or raised bed. Give plenty of water during summer, shade from bright sun, and keep the atmosphere around them humid to reduce temperatures and ward off spider mite. Even so, plants will become straggly, so prune them back after flowering to retain a compact shape. Propagate by seed or cuttings. *H. comptoniana*, known as wild sarsaparilla, and *H. violacea* are similar plants. *H.v.* 'Happy Wanderer' is a good form, and *H.v.* 'White Crystal' has pure white flowers.
40-45°F(4-7°C) H:6-10ft(1.8-3m) S:3ft(1m)

Hedera
(Araliaceae)
It would be a mistake to write ivies off as being too common for the greenhouse. Used to clothe walls or pillars, they are specimens in their own right or will make bold evergreen backdrops against which other plants can perform. For feature plants, choose large-leaved variegated ivies like *H. colchica* 'Dentata Variegata' or *H. algeriensis* 'Gloire de Marengo'. Smaller-leaved kinds are neater but create less impact. *H. helix* 'Glacier' is excellent for its cream and green leaves. *H.h.* 'Luzii' offers a more mottled, speckled effect, *H.h.* 'Goldchild' has irregular golden markings around leaf edges. For background effect, choose plain, green-leaved ivies: *H. algeriensis* has large, bold leaves. Smaller-leaved kinds include *H. helix* 'Chicago' with well shaped, typical "ivy leaves". *H.h.* 'Parsley Crested' is a wonderful crinkle-leaved ivy, light green in color. *H.h.* 'Königers Auslese' is the needlepoint ivy frequently referred to as *H. sagittifolia* (which is thought to be lost to cultivation). Its leaves are distinctively arrow-shaped with pointed tips. Most ivies cling to their support by aerial roots which grow out of the stems. The exception is *H. algeriensis* (often confused with

Hardenbergia violacea

Hibbertia scandens

H. canariensis, the Canary Islands ivy), which twines and will need more assistance in its ascent. To grow ivies successfully, think about where they grow naturally, trailing beneath and up trees. They prefer some shade and like a cool, moist atmosphere in which to grow. Give them adequate light, though, or growth will be sparse and variegated leaves begin reverting to plain green. Hot, dry air will cause leaves to turn brown and increase the likelihood of spider mite. Regular misting under the leaves is beneficial. Propagate by cuttings, which root easily. Pinch back the growing tips to encourage branching. 38-45°F(3-7°C) H&S:3-8ft(1-2.5m)

Hibbertia

(Dilleniaceae)

These are useful, sometimes rampant, evergreen twiners. Bright lemon-yellow five-petaled flowers are borne mainly in summer and fall but can appear sporadically at other times. With their central boss of stamens, they rather resemble single yellow roses. These are followed by large seed pods which split to reveal the scarlet seeds inside. Shade lightly from the hottest sun. Propagate by seed or summer cuttings. The species described are Australian.

H. cuneiformis This species is relatively shrubby. Even so, its woody stems are long and spreading. Plants can be successfully restricted in pots, but better specimens are those given the root run of a border. The best support is a column, or even a strong length of wire secured to a peg in the ground and fixed some distance above the plant. Pruning is barely necessary, except to thin out and reduce invasive stems in early spring.
40-45°F(4-7°C) H:7ft(2m) S:4-5ft(1.2-1.5m)

H. scandens (H. volubilis) Guinea flower or snake vine really is a rampant climber. With little encouragement, masses of stems, twining about each other, will ascend to great heights or trail along the ground. In a small greenhouse confine it in a pot. Foliage is a rich green, against which the flowers, 2in(5cm) wide, show up beautifully. They tend not be be borne in great profusion, but open here and there over a long period. Pruning a large, wayward plant has to consist of rather brutally cutting away what is not required, usually in winter or spring. Stems become too tangled for thinning. Young plants in containers, thinned on a regular basis, could more easily be kept under control.
40-45°F(4-7°C) H:8ft(2.5m) S:3ft(1m)

Hibiscus

(Malvaceae)

H. rosa-sinensis and its cultivars are so popular, it is perhaps surprising that the climbing hibiscus or Japanese lantern, *H. schizopetalus*, is not more widely grown. An evergreen from East Africa, it is not equipped to climb but has long arching branches which lend themselves admirably to being trained up and over an arch or tied up beneath the roof. Summer flowers of exquisite form hang down on long thin stalks. Each consists of reflexed, fringed petals, from the center of which dangles a long red stamineal column bristling with golden-yellow anthers. Shade lightly from bright sun and provide humidity during hot summer temperatures. Prune in spring if necessary. Propagate in summer by cuttings. Watch constantly for whitefly, taking control measures immediately they are spotted.
50-55°F(10-13°C) H:10ft(3m) S:6ft(1.8m)

Hoya

(Asclepiadaceae)

The beautiful wax flowers, for the most part twining climbers, are well worth cultivating in the greenhouse, where they will usually flower regularly and abundantly. As houseplants, they often frustrate their owners by remaining luxuriantly green and healthy yet refusing to flower. The secret of success is to give them warm, moist conditions in summer, followed by comparative dryness and cool during winter. Although shading in summer is necessary, good light is required for flowering. Feed sparingly as too much fertilizer will produce leaves at the expense of flowers.

Hoyas will flourish in pots or a shallow border. They do not, generally, have large root systems and are best kept slightly pot-bound. Use a well-drained potting mix: three parts of coarse peat to one of sharp sand plus starter fertilizer but no added lime is a good mixture. Hoyas can be trained around a circle of wire, or a tripod of canes. Even better would be a trellis and best of all, a pillar, pergola, or arch with the stems brought overhead so that the exquisite, star-shaped flowers can hang to be admired from below. When winter temperatures drop to 45-50°F(7-10°C) or lower, do not overwater; allow the top third of the potting mix to dry out between waterings, but never let the roots dry out completely. This will result in irreparably shriveled leaves; sad symptoms also caused by exposure to hot, dry air. Though not particularly pest-prone, hoyas are susceptible to mealy bugs.

Propagate by cuttings in summer. These may be unorthodox in shape and size, but provided there is a healthy node in contact with the loose potting mix, roots and shoots will be formed. Protect plants, particularly newly rooted cuttings fresh from the plant incubator, from drafts. Sometimes slender seed pods are produced after flowering. These will split to reveal many seeds, each equipped with a pappus of fine hairs to facilitate dispersal by wind. Pruning consists of thinning and reducing the stems of older plants, either after flowering, which takes place

Hibiscus schizopetalus

mainly during summer, or in the spring. Many species continue to produce flower buds from old flower stalks, so avoid cutting these off after one batch of flowers has faded and dropped. There are some 200 kinds of hoya in cultivation but only a few readily available. *H. lanceolata* ssp. *bella* and varieties of *H. carnosa* are recommended as trailing plants (see p.111).

H. australis This beautiful twining hoya from New Guinea, Australia (Queensland and New South Wales), and Bougainville Island bears abundant umbels of white flowers adorned with five red spots in the center. With a fragrance reminiscent of honeysuckle, a plant in full bloom is a fine sight and smell. One successful way to grow it is in a 7in(17cm) pot, twined around a tripod of canes 30in(75cm) tall. Leaves are a pleasant rounded shape.
45-50°F(7-10°C) H:15ft(4.5m) S:4ft(1.2m)

H. fusca 'Silver Knight' (H. 'Silver Pink') This variety of a Javan species is easily recognizable by the silver blotches on its leaves. Growth is fast and heads of maroon-pink flowers readily produced.
40-45°F(4-7°C) H:15ft(4.5m) S:4ft(1.2m)

H. globulosa This species from the Himalayas has large, wavy-edged leaves dotted with hairs above and with splendidly soft and downy undersides. Creamy-colored flowers have hairy stalks. Young plants sometimes survive temperatures close to freezing, though this is not recommended. An early flowerer, blooms open from early spring to the fall.
40-45°F(4-7°C) H:15ft(4.5m) S:4ft(1.2m)

H. imperialis This impressive twining species from Borneo has large leaves 6-9in(15-23cm) long, which

Ipomoea indica

Hoya multiflora

Jasminum mesnyi

are downy when young. Magnificent, waxy flowers are maroon with creamy-white centers. Individually 3in(8cm) across, there can be eight to ten in each huge umbel. Stems are downy.
55-60°F(13-16°C) H:15ft(4.5m) S:4ft(1.2m)

H. macgillivrayi This species is distinctive for its large, long leaves which are thin and reddish when young but become thicker and green with age. Maroon flowers, eight to ten per umbel, are larger than most and have a sweet nocturnal perfume.
50°F(10°C) H:10ft(3m) S:4ft(1.2m)

H. multiflora From Malacca, this species does not twine but has a habit best described as lax: tie the long stems to a cane. Butter-yellow flowers have recurved petals, giving the appearance of a cluster of small shuttlecocks. Though ornamental, they can be a nuisance by dropping sticky nectar.
50-55°F(10-13°C) H:3-4ft(1-1.2m) S:24in(60cm)

H. pubicalyx 'Red Buttons' While most hoya flowers have subdued shades of cream, pink, or maroon, this desirable variety has brazen flowers of bright red. Leaves blotched with silver are long, thin, and pointed. Young leaves are a deep reddish color.
50°F(10°C) H:10ft(3m) S:3ft(1m)

Ipomoea

(Convolvulaceae)

I. indica (I. learii, I. acuminata, Pharbitis learii) The perennial morning glory and blue dawn flower are beautiful names for a floriferous and attractive evergreen climbing plant from tropical America and the West Indies. Specimens will need support for their long, twining stems which cling with stem tips. Planted in a large pot or a greenhouse border, a plant will make a fine column trained up a wire from floor to ceiling. Heart-shaped, sometimes three-lobed leaves are attractive but it is for the striking purple-blue trumpet-shaped flowers 2½-3½in(6-9cm) wide

that the plant is grown. These are borne during summer and into the fall. As they mature and begin to go over, they turn pinkish-purple, giving a rainbow effect on the plant. Plants appreciate full light, but nevertheless need protection from bright summer sun. Prune back in spring to retain shape and size. This resilient ipomoea will regenerate well even when reduced to a woody stump, provided some spurs of new wood are left in place. Propagate by cuttings – lengths of stem containing nodes, not necessarily including a shoot tip – or by layering. Whitefly and spider mite can be troublesome.
40-50°F(4-10°C) H:15ft(4.5m) S:3ft(1m)

IPOMOEAS GROWN AS ANNUALS Ipomoeas grown from seed are useful for adding color to the greenhouse as well as to the flower garden. Stand their pots among those of foliage or winter-flowering climbers, or plant them in borders alongside the permanent inhabitants. *I. tricolor* 'Heavenly Blue' is well worth growing for its white-throated sky-blue flowers. This superb color seems to blend well with other flowers, avoiding the clashes one risks with pink- and cerise-flowered kinds. *I. alba*, the moon flower, is desirable, with its large white fragrant blooms that open, ghost-like, during the evening and are closed by midday. Varieties with flowers of red, pink, lavender, a strange chocolate-pink, and violet are available. The drawback to some of the pink and white flower colors is that they are reminiscent of bindweed (convolvulus), to which they are closely related. Take care, as some varieties of ipomoea (and particularly the seeds) are poisonous. Warmth is required early in the year, not only to germinate the seed but to grow plants on; at low temperatures their foliage will turn pale and anemic.
50°F(10°C) H:8ft(2.5m)

Jasminum

(Oleaceae)

The jasmines or jessamines must be among the most popular greenhouse climbers, grown for their pretty, often fragrant flowers. Propagate in summer by cuttings, with a heel if possible.

J. mesnyi (J. primulinum) The evergreen, sometimes semi-evergreen, primrose jasmine comes from southwestern China. Not equipped with any particular climbing mechanism, long sprawling stems need tying up to a wall or trellis. At first glance, this yellow-flowered species resembles winter jasmine (*J. nudiflorum*). However, flowers are accompanied by leaves and can be semi-double. They have no perfume but are a wonderfully cheering sight in early spring. Plants can be grown in pots or in the border. Tie up a network of stems to a suitable height and spread, then leave them to cascade, so that in flower they look like a yellow waterfall. After flowering, cut the flowered stems back to within a couple of inches

of the base, or to healthy laterals. Remove old, dead stems at the same time to prevent a dense thicket.
38-45°F(3-7°C) H&S:6ft(1.8m)

J. nitidum Windmill, star, angel-wing, or royal jasmine, originally from the Admiralty Islands off the north coast of New Guinea, is a white-flowered species. Though less floriferous than some other jasmines, compensation lies in the beautifully formed, star-like flowers 1½in(3cm) across, which appear mostly in summer but sporadically year-round and are blessed with a sweet, though not sickly, perfume. These have six to eleven petal lobes and are pink-tinged in bud. Evergreen, simple, tapering leaves are attractive. A poor twiner, plants need support as they grow.
45°F(7°C) H:6ft(1.8m) S:30-48in(75-120cm)

J. polyanthum Pink or Chinese jasmine from western China is the familiar, spring-flowering species widely grown indoors. Florists and garden centers are redolent with its sweet, almost sickly perfume throughout winter and spring. An evergreen or semi-evergreen twining climber, leaves are pinnate with five or seven leaflets, the terminal leaflet being drawn out to a point. Flower buds, maintained at a minimum winter temperature of 38°F(3°C), develop around midwinter but do not open until spring, continuing to give a display right into the summer. Pink-tinged, the buds open to white flowers. Plants kept cool during winter give the most floriferous display: houseplants are sometimes shy of flowering because of high temperatures and low light. Specimens perform well confined in pots and can be trained around a circle of wire or coiled around a tripod of canes some 5ft(1.5m) high. After flowering, loosen all the stems from their support, prune older stems back hard to within 2-3in(5-8cm) of the base, shortening others to where healthy non-flowering laterals have been produced. Tie the remaining stems up, water and feed well during summer and train in subsequent regrowth. Shading in summer will prevent yellowing and brown leaf tips. Take care not to let plants dry out at the roots and never subject them to cold drafts while in bud.
38-45°F(3-7°C) H:5-10ft(1.5-3m) S:2-6ft(60cm-1.8m)

J. rex Named for the king of Siam, this regal jasmine from Thailand and Cambodia has the largest flowers, 3in(8cm) diameter, though sadly scentless. Nevertheless, this vigorous twiner is worth growing as it will produce blooms not only in the fall and winter but sporadically throughout the year. Maintain an even, warm temperature and high humidity.
55-60°F(13-16°C) H:5-10ft(1.5-3m) S:3-5ft(1-1.5m)

J. sambac Arabian jasmine is a beautiful twining jasmine from India to Burma and Sri Lanka. Simple evergreen leaves in opposite pairs are slightly hairy. The white flowers, deliciously fragrant (particularly

Ipomoea alba

at night), make this a desirable greenhouse plant, blooming sporadically throughout the year while temperatures are warm. *J.s.* 'Maid of Orleans' has semi-double white flowers which turn wine-red as they die, and its bushy nature can be encouraged by pruning out the twining stems. The flowers of *J.s.* 'Grand Duke of Tuscany' are fully double, becoming pinkish-maroon before shriveling; this variety is larger and more wayward. Although lower temperatures can be tolerated, plants are happiest at 60°F(16°C).
45-50°F(7-10°C) H:5-10ft(1.5-3m) S:3-6ft(1-1.8m)

Kennedia

(Leguminosae)

These fast-growing trifoliate twiners from Australia with red flowers superficially resemble pole beans. Easily grown from seed, best soaked for 24 hours before sowing, these climbers are worth a try. A well-drained soil and good light is all they require. Mature plants become woody at the base and can sometimes be attacked by mealy bugs. Look out for spider mite. Rejuvenate old, untidy plants by cutting them hard back in spring, leaving spurs of younger wood. Seed is readily set. Planted in a border, plants can grow tall and be trained into fine columns.

K. coccinea Coral vine has scarlet flowers held in long-stalked bunches of up to twelve blooms, borne in spring and summer. Shoots are covered in silky down.
38-45°F(3-7°C) H:6ft(1.8m) S:3ft(1m)

K. macrophylla Planted in beds, this scarlet-flowered species looks splendid trained up a post or wire. Plants become woody and last some years, making a red-studded, green column when in flower in summer. After initial training, plants will cling to themselves.
38-46°F(3-8°C) H:6-10ft(1.8-3m) S:3-4ft(1-1.2m)

K. rubicunda Dusky coral pea is a species whose coral-red flowers have distinctive, long ridged petals and are borne in spring and summer.
38-45°F(3-7°C) H:6-10ft(1.8-3m) S:4ft(1.2m)

Lablab

(Leguminosae)

L. purpureus (Dolichos lablab) The hyacinth bean, or lablab bean from tropical Asia is an interesting twining climber with a wide range of uses such as animal fodder and green manure. Cultivated in China for many years, most parts of the plant are edible and used both fresh and dried (mature seeds contain toxins and must be cooked thoroughly before use). Sow in spring, grow in well-drained soil and provide a climbing frame for the plants, which grow like pole beans. The warmer the temperature, the more the vines will flourish. The pea-like flowers can be any shade from white to deep purple, with green or purple-tinged leaves. Pick the flattish pods, 3-4in(8-10cm) long, continuously while young, as you would a pea or bean. Although lablab is a perennial, clearing plants away at the end of the season and beginning again from seed the following year is the best method.
40°F(4°C) H&S:8ft(2.5m)

Lagenaria

(Cucurbitaceae)

L. siceraria (L. vulgaris) The bottle or calabash gourd from Asia and tropical Africa can be planted in a border and left to climb freely. Canes, wires, or string will quickly become furnished with speedy growth, clinging by means of tendrils. Let them climb up the sides of the glass and under the roof, so that the oddly shaped fruit can hang down. During summer and early fall, white flowers open at dusk; hand-pollinate to be sure of fruit. Female flowers are those with miniature fruits behind them. The quality of fruit is determined by temperature, with warmth encouraging larger, harder-skinned gourds. Some are narrowly bottle-shaped, 24in(60cm) long, others more rounded and about 12in(30cm) long. Germinate seed at 70-75°F(21-24°C) as early as possible in the spring and keep warm for rapid, early growth. Plants can be grown in pots or borders and trained so as not to run riot. Pinch back shoot tips at a height of 5ft(1.5m), training the laterals along wires. Once a flower has formed on a lateral, allow two leaves to form past this, then pinch back. If fruit is not going to form after the flower, cut the whole stem back to the first leaf joint and allow another to grow. This method of controlling leaf and fruit growth will channel energy into just a few fruits, giving them an increased chance of developing. Gourds love as much heat and humidity as they can get.
50-60°F(10-16°C) H:6-15ft(1.8-4.5m) S:4ft(1.2m)

Lapageria

(Liliaceae/Philesiaceae)

L. rosea The Chilean bellflower is the national flower of Chile and surely one of the aristocrats of the cool greenhouse. A twining climber, its handsome, pointed, leathery leaves are smaller toward the shoot tips where the flowers are borne. These beautiful, bell-shaped, waxy blooms measure some 3-3½in (8-9cm) long and consist of three sepals and three petals, which can be carmine pink or white. Plants raised from seed can be flushed, striped, or marbled with pink on white or white on pink, pale pink, or double. Lapagerias do well in pots or planted in beds and are best trained up and under the roof, so that the long-lasting flowers, produced mostly in summer and fall but sporadically year-round, hang down to be appreciated from below. Always use a potting mix formulated for acid-loving plants. During summer, plants appreciate a cool position shaded from hot sun. The roots, too, like to be cool and should never dry out. Plants seem to dislike climbing up wires, which absorb heat and scorch them, but they can be trained to cover a trellis. Edible green fruits form after the flowers. Once the berry becomes squashy, the contents can be squeezed straight onto the surface of prepared seed starting mix and covered lightly. Germination is usually easy when seed is sown fresh like this, becoming more difficult as it ages and dormancy has to be broken. Propagate also by layering, carried out by pegging a portion of long stem down onto a tray of moist, prepared potting mix; roots may take two years to form. Cuttings are difficult and dislike being too warm and humid. Root them outside of the plant incubator, out of the sun. Semi-ripe shoots taken in early summer seem to root best. Aphids can be a problem on young shoots and mealy bugs on older stems and leaves.
32-45°F(0-7°C) H:6-15ft(1.8-4.5m) S:4ft(1.2m)

Lonicera

(Caprifoliaceae)

In the greenhouse, give honeysuckles the root run of a border. They can be trained up walls and under the roof, over arches, or up pillars. Prune in spring if necessary, thinning out congested growth, reducing height, and shortening laterals. However, over-enthusiastic pruning will reduce flowering potential. Although plants will benefit from plenty of water and monthly fertilizing, too much fertilizer will encourage stem and leaf growth at the expense of flowers. Propagate in summer by making cuttings. Aphids can be a problem.

L. hildebrandtiana Giant honeysuckle, an evergreen climber from Burma, has everything on a large scale. The plant is tall, 60-70ft(18-20m) in the wild, and demands plenty of space. Oval leaves are large and the slightly fragrant summer flowers are 4-6in

(10-15cm) long. There are two or three pairs of flowers in each cluster which open creamy-white but turn orange as they mature, then fade.
45°F(7°C) H&S:12-30ft(3.5-9m)

L. sempervirens Trumpet honeysuckle from southern USA makes up for its lack of scent by its flower color. In summer it is studded with bold clusters of reddish-orange flowers, each about 2in (5cm) long. An attractive, slender twiner, it should remain evergreen except at low temperatures, when leaf shedding should not cause alarm.
40-45°F(4-7°C) H:7-20ft(2-6m)

Luffa

(Cucurbitaceae)

L. aegyptiaca (L. cylindrica) The amazing loofah, sponge, or dishcloth gourd is thought to originate from India. The internal, fibrous skeletons obtained from the fruits of this tendril climber are used as bath sponges. Sold flat and dried, they reflate to a cylindrical shape when moistened. Most of the best loofahs of commerce are grown in Japan. They are processed by immersing ripe fruit, which look rather like fat cucumbers, in tanks of running water which gradually washes the outer skin, soft fleshy part, and seeds away. Loofahs can easily be raised from seed, sown as early as possible in the year. Even given the warmth and protection of a greenhouse, a hot summer is required for the fruits to grow and fatten before fall brings a drop in temperature and light. Flowers are yellow. Cultivation requirements are shared with lagenaria (see left).
50-60°F(10-16°C) H:6-15ft(1.8-4.5m) S:4ft(1.2m)

Lycianthes

(Solanaceae)

L. rantonnetii (Solanum rantonnetii) The blue potato vine, originating from Argentina to Paraguay, is a lax shrub that can be supported and treated like a climber. Its deep purple summer flowers are some ½in(1cm) wide, but the species is usually represented by L.r. 'Grandiflora' with flowers up to 1in(2.5cm) wide. Grow in pots or borders. Cultivation is as for solanum (see p.99).
40°F(4°C) H:6ft(1.8m) S:3-4ft(1-1.2m)

Macfadyena

(Bignoniaceae)

M. unguis-cati (Doxantha unguis-cati) The beautiful cat's claw bignonia is a floriferous evergreen that in its native tropical America and the West Indies climbs high up into the trees, covering branches with its draping growth. Leaves are luxuriantly bifoliate, each pair of leaflets equipped with a terminal tendril with hook-like arms. The best way to grow them is to plant into a small bed and train stems up to a good height. The stems can be

Lablab purpureus

Lycianthes rantonnetii

Mandevilla splendens

encouraged to travel under the roof, allowing skeins of cascading growth to hang down like rich green curtains enriched with yellow in spring and early summer. Individual flowers are foxglove-like in shape and a rich golden-yellow. Pruning consists of periodically cutting the growth back to a manageable size after flowering. If necessary, plants can be reduced to within a few nodes of the base, provided some spurs of new growth are left from which new buds will arise. Propagate by spring-sown seed or cuttings in summer of either a stem tip or lengths of stem containing two nodes. Suckers, which can be lifted carefully with some root, are sometimes formed around the base.
40-50°F(4-10°C) H&S:10-30ft(3-9m)

Mandevilla
(Apocynaceae)

These evergreen climbers (formerly in the genus *Dipladenia*) make superb greenhouse specimens. Twisted buds, like furled umbrellas, hold the promise of beautiful flowers, each consisting of a tube which flares out into five "petals", each one overlapping the next, windmill fashion. These summer flowers are produced even on young, small plants, giving the option of keeping plants small, H:24in(60cm) S:12in(30cm), by restriction in pots and regular pruning. Although they respond well to

warmth, mandevillas belie their exotic appearance by being surprisingly tolerant of low winter temperatures, though the colder they are grown, the more vital it is to water sparingly. As warmth increases in spring, plants can be pruned and will burst into new growth. Shade lightly from hot sun and maintain humidity to preserve the beauty of handsome, entire, shiny green leaves. Propagate by seed or by cuttings of short side shoots pulled away from the parent plant in summer. White sap exudes from cut surfaces but soon dries up. Plants are easy to train, twining eagerly up their wires or canes.

M. boliviensis has striking pure white summer flowers with yellow throats. *M. laxa* (*M. suaveolens*), Chilean jasmine from Bolivia and Argentina, is a fragrant, white-flowered semi-evergreen or deciduous species. Flowers are borne in groups of five to fifteen. Long, narrow pods bearing seeds are freely produced, which explains the frequent listing of this species in seed catalogs. *M. splendens*, popular for its rose-pink flowers 4-5in(10-13cm) across and up to four in a group, originates from the Organ Mountains near Rio de Janeiro, Brazil. The fine hybrid *M.* × *amabilis* 'Alice du Pont' probably has *M. splendens* as a parent. Summer flowers are a warm rosy-pink with rich, more intensely colored throats suffused with golden-yellow. They can be up to 4in(10cm) wide.
45-50°F(7-10°C) H:6-10ft(1.8-3m) S:4-5ft(1.2-1.5m)

Manettia
(Rubiaceae)

M. luteorubra (M. inflata) The firecracker plant from Brazil is a twining evergreen climber with brilliant orange-red, yellow-tipped, bristly, tubular flowers, somewhat inflated at the base. Although only ³/₄in(2cm) long, they are a welcome sight, lighting up the plant in spring and summer. Encourage plants to twine up a tripod of slender canes. Leaves have an irritating habit of turning brown at the tips as they grow older. If raising humidity provides no antidote, be suspicious of overfeeding. Propagate in spring and summer by cuttings. Whitefly can be a problem. Old or straggly plants can be cut back hard in spring, but the best plants are those raised from fresh cuttings.
50°F(10°C) H:48in(120cm) S:24in(60cm)

Maurandya
(Scrophulariaceae)

The small size, free flowering, and bright color of these pretty perennial evergreen climbers and trailers from Mexico make them suitable for any greenhouse. Easy to grow from seed, plants from sowings made early in the year should be flowering by midsummer, carrying on into the fall. Promising buds open to tubular flowers shaped like those of antirrhinum, in rich shades of pink and purple.

Michelia figo

Provide supports but not ties, as the stalks of the triangular leaves are twining. Prune mature plants back to within 6in(15cm) of the base in early spring to encourage fresh new growth. Watch for aphids. Cuttings can be taken during summer.

M. barclayana (Asarina barclayana) Apart from the sepals which are covered with glandular hairs, this dainty species is not hairy. The flowers are a rich, deep violet, but can be white or pink.
40°F(4°C) H:48in(120cm) S:24in(60cm)

M. erubescens (Asarina erubescens) A larger plant in all respects than *M. barclayana*, this species is also covered in soft white glandular hairs. Both flower stalks and young stems will twine around their supports, but stems are also happy to trail downward. Flower color is magenta.
40°F(4°C) H:6-10ft(1.8-3m) S:3ft(1m)

M. scandens (Asarina scandens) No part of this species is hairy, not even the sepals. Flower color is usually pale lavender with a white throat, but can be reddish-rose.
40°F(4°C) H:6ft(1.8m) S:3ft(1m)

Michelia
(Magnoliaceae)
M. figo Left to itself, this would make a tall, rounded shrub. In the greenhouse, plant it in a bed and train against a wall to keep its size within bounds. Otherwise, restricted in a pot, it will rarely exceed H&S:36in(90cm). A handsome Chinese native, it is closely related to magnolia. Leaves up to 4in(10cm) long are deep, glossy green. Interesting spring flowers are creamy-green, crisply edged with maroon. They are only 1-1½in(2.5-4cm) across but are strongly scented, inviting comparisons with bananas (banana shrub is one of its popular names). Specimens begin to flower while still young and, given warm conditions, felted buds will open early in the year. Propagate in summer by cuttings. Grow plants in an acid soil mix and use liquid fertilizer formulated for acid-loving plants. Shade lightly from hot sun.
40-45°F(4-7°C) H:5-10ft(1.5-3m) S:4-6ft(1.2-1.8m)

Mikania
(Compositae)
M. dentata (M. ternata) The plush vine indeed looks like a member of the vine family. This Brazilian native is a scrambling climber whose stems need to be tied up to a support. Hairy, greenish-purple leaves composed of five leaflets are its main attraction. Yellow, daisy-like flowers which appear during summer are full proof of its true family allegiance. A useful plant, the purple tones of its leaves show up among green foliage. Confined in a pot, it can be restricted to 6ft(1.8m). Pruning consists of cutting back stems in danger of invading other plants' territory in spring. Humidity is appreciated, but keep water off foliage. Propagate in summer by cuttings.
50°F(10°C) H:6-10ft(1.8-3m) S:4-6ft(1.2-1.8m)

Mina
(Convolvulaceae)
M. lobata (Quamoclit lobata, now correctly Ipomoea lobata) This perennial, best grown as a colorful annual, is native to an area from Mexico to South America, where it is widely cultivated. Sow the seeds in spring, plant in 3in(8cm) pots, then later, pot three plants together into a 7-8in(18-20cm) pot. Train the twining stems up a tripod of canes or other support. The mass of three-lobed leaves is attractive, but it is for the startlingly colored summer flowers that this plant is grown. Long inflorescences project away from the foliage, each ending in a terminal bud with a branch on either side, furnished with two rows of outward-facing buds and flowers. Scarlet at first, the pointed buds become orange, then finally pale yellow, fading to cream and white as they open – the colors of strawberries, peaches, and cream. Spider mite can be a problem.
50°F(10°C) H:4-6ft(1.2-1.8m) S:30in(75cm)

Mitraria
(Gesneriaceae)
M. coccinea This evergreen climber from Chile has long, trailing stems capable of clinging to a support by means of small roots. Although shiny, toothed leaves are handsome, it is for their curious, showy scarlet-orange flowers that plants are grown. Just over 1in(2.5cm) long, they are tubular and slightly inflated, opening to five lobes. These appear in late summer and are quite substantial to touch. Leaves and whole shoots have an annoying tendency to turn brown and die if plants are even slightly unhappy. They like an acid soil mix, prefer soft rainwater, and like to be shaded from hot summer sun. High temperatures combined with dry air are certainly not appreciated. If these cannot be avoided, grow plants in pots and stand them outside for the summer. Propagate in summer by cuttings.
38-45°F(3-7°C) H&S:3-5ft(1-1.5m)

Monstera
(Araceae)
M. deliciosa The ubiquitous Swiss cheese plant, its large lobed leaves complete with "cheesy" holes as plants mature, lends a lush, tropical atmosphere to the planting in the greenhouse. In their native countries, from Mexico to Central America, plants flourish under the canopy of tall trees, climbing up them to 20ft(6m) or more; they thus like warm humid conditions and shade from the sun. A plant merely surviving will have stunted growth and small, yellowing, scorched leaves; thriving specimens will have shiny leaves up to 24in(60cm) across, well indented and furnished with holes. The ideal method of training is to provide a stout, tall moss pole kept moist by regular spraying. In the wild, tall plants are supported and nourished by long aerial roots which both cling and scout for pockets of moist leaf mold in which to grow fibrous feeding roots. If these roots cannot be pushed back into the pot or attached to a moss pole, they can be cut off with no detriment to the plant. Prune plants hard back if they become too tall, carrying this out in spring and bearing in mind that regrowth will arise from the highest node left on the stem. Take cuttings of the tips and also of stem sections, each bearing two nodes. Air-layering is an alternative method. Plants may produce cream-colored flower spathes, followed by edible, pineapple-flavored fruits. *M.d.* 'Variegata' is the variegated form.
50-55°F(10-13°C) H:10ft(3m) S:5ft(1.5m)

Mutisia
(Compositae)
Climbing gazanias, with long-lasting, daisy-like flowers, originate from high up in the Andes of tropical America. These interesting climbers prefer well-drained soil and should receive plenty of light to flower well. Roots prefer to be cool. These are good plants for the greenhouse wall, where tendrils assist their ascent. Propagate by cuttings in summer or spring-sown seed. The three species described are from Chile.

M. decurrens This sometimes difficult, orange-flowered mutisia has interesting leaves which extend down the stem to the top of the next leaf. Leaf tips are drawn out into tendrils. Flower heads, borne in summer, are some 5in(13cm) across. Can be propagated by suckers.
38-45°F(3-7°C) H:6ft(1.8m) S:3ft(1m)

M. ilicifolia Pretty pink and yellow flower heads some 2-3in(5-8cm) across are borne mostly in late summer and fall. Leathery, holly-like leaves with woolly undersides are toothed and end in a tendril. Stem, veins and tendrils are reddish in color. Stems have toothed wings.
38-45°F(3-7°C) H:6ft(1.8m) S:3ft(1m)

M. oligodon Long-stalked, satiny, silvery-pink ray flowers have darker veins. Tooth-edged leaves are shiny on the surface but white-felted on the undersides. Buds and new growth are also woolly. The central leaf vein continues into a fine tendril. Flowers appear during late summer and fall.
38-45°F(3-7°C) H:3-5ft(1-1.5m) S:24-36in(60-90cm)

Pandorea
(Bignoniaceae)

These attractive evergreen twining climbers are tall but not too overwhelming for the average greenhouse. Best trained up wires and under the roof, their pretty funnel-shaped flowers are a delight in spring and summer. Prune after flowering if necessary, but plants will flower better if left alone. Propagate by spring-sown seed or cuttings in summer.

P. jasminoides, the bower plant, comes from Queensland and New South Wales. This beautiful species has pinnate, shining green foliage and white or pale frosted-pink flowers with dark pinkish-purple throats 2½-3in(6-8cm) wide. The contrast between the two colors is striking. P. pandorana, wonga wonga vine from New Guinea, eastern Australia, and Tasmania, has smaller, pendent flowers of pale buff-yellow or pale pink, their throats spotted and streaked with pinkish-red. They may not be able to match P. jasminoides in color, but are fragrant and plentiful enough to attract both nose and eye. Seedling and juvenile foliage is much more fern-like than the adult leaves, which are pinnate with three to nine leaflets.
40°F(4°C) H:15ft(4.5m)

Passiflora
(Passifloraceae)

The passion flowers are such marvelous climbers that every greenhouse should have at least one. The species and hybrids in cultivation suit a range of temperature regimes from unheated to tropical. Like hoyas, they are very collectable. Climbing easily, clinging with their tendrils to any support offered,

Mitraria coccinea

plants can be restricted in pots and trained up tall canes or wires. The best plants, though, are planted in shallow borders (some root restriction enhances flowering), then trained up and under the roof so that flowering stems can dangle downward. These are first-class plants for creating a canopy to shade smaller plants (and people) beneath. The larger kinds will need regular pruning, ideally in spring, but during winter if necessary, to restrict their growth and tidy the plants. This can consist of pruning back lateral shoots to main stems; however, if more drastic action is required, whole stems can be cut back almost to the base. Always leave spurs of new wood containing healthy nodes behind. To cut right into old wood, leaving thick stumps behind, is to invite failure.

Most species have exceptionally showy, sometimes fragrant flowers, usually in summer. Some bear edible fruit, and others are grown for their attractive foliage. Propagate in summer by cuttings. Species can be propagated by seed, which is a good way of obtaining new plants. Keep vigil against spider mite and on older, woodier plants against mealy bugs.

Passion flowers are the only food plants for a group of beautiful butterflies called heliconus. This unenviable position has led to the evolution of various ruses to avoid caterpillar damage. Yellow dots on the leaves of some species resemble heliconus eggs, deterring the female butterfly from laying on a leaf which already appears to have its fair share of eggs. Nectar secreted by leaf petioles attracts caterpillar-eating ants and wasps, and variable leaf shapes help to confuse the butterflies.

P. alata Originally from Brazil, the wing-stemmed passion flower has square stems and can appear similar to the more widely cultivated *P. quadrangularis*. Fragrant flowers are slightly smaller, the sepals and petals being rich, dark crimson on the inside and white on the outside. The fruits are good to eat.
38-45°F(3-7°C) H:10-15ft(3-4.5m) S:3-5ft(1-1.5m)

P. × allardii (P. caerulea 'Constance Elliott' × P. quadrangularis) With white sepals and pink petals appearing alternately around the flower, here is a most attractive hybrid dating from the early 1900's. The subtle flowers will not clash with other colors and are produced from spring into fall.
45°F(7°C) H:10-15ft(3-4.5m) S:3-5ft(1-1.5m)

P. amethystina A pretty passiflora from Brazil, with flowers of a jewel-like amethyst color. As with amethysts, the color varies according to how much light is received; maximum light will see rich purple flower color, while most greenhouse specimens have blooms of an even lovelier pale mauve. Many flowers are produced throughout summer and fall on a plant easily restricted to 6ft(1.8m).
38-45°F(3-7°C) H:10-15ft(3-4.5m) S:3-5ft(1-1.5m)

P. antioquiensis The stunning red banana-fruited passion flower from the mountainous regions of Colombia has shocking-pink blooms, up to 5¹⁄₂in(14cm) wide with tiny corona filaments that barely show at all. Plants begin to flower as young potted specimens, but let loose, will climb tall and flower profusely. Both small and large plants may die back suddenly during summer for no apparent reason – possibly because of extremes in watering, with drought followed by sudden over-zealous soaking. Hand-pollination is required to set edible golden-yellow fruits resembling small bananas.
45°F(7°C) H:10-15ft(3-4.5m)

P. × belotii (P. × alatocaerulea, P. 'Empress Eugenie', P. 'Impératrice Eugénie', P. alata × P. caerulea) This hybrid has large, up to 2in(5cm) wide, pale pinkish-purple and white fragrant flowers with white-banded, purple filaments, which are easy to accommodate with other colors. The plant is prized for its reliability and floriferous nature.
40°F(4°C) H:10-15ft(3-4.5m)

P. caerulea The blue passion flower is probably the most widely grown of the passifloras. In many areas, this hardy species from central and western South America can be grown in a sheltered position outdoors. Fragrant flowers some 3-4in(8-10cm) across have green-tinged, white petals and sepals overlaid with purple-blue filaments. These abundant flowers are followed by egg-shaped orange fruits which, though edible, are not particularly palatable. *P.c.* 'Constance Elliott' has beautiful, pure white, fragrant flowers.
27-45°F(-3-7°C) H:10-15ft(3-4.5m)

P. × caeruleoracemosa (P. caerulea × P. racemosa) Although its parents are beautiful in their own right, this lovely hybrid has the advantages of delicate reddish-purple flowers 4-5in(10-13cm) wide, combined with tolerance of low temperatures. Pendent branches hang down gracefully, strung with promising buds which open in succession. This plant is tough, highly floriferous, and highly recommended.
38-45°F(3-7°C) H:10-15ft(3-4.5m)

P. cirrhiflora This amazing species from Guyana and French Guiana has bizarre-looking flowers with enormous stigmas, apricot-flushed yellow petals, and rather dirty yellow sepals. The corona filaments look like the legs of some crazed insect, zigzagging from deep red bases, through white middles to yellow tips. Even stranger, the 2¹⁄₂-3in(6-8cm) flowers are produced in pairs halfway along its tendrils. Even the leaves are unusual, having five to seven leaflets.
55°F(13°C) H:10-15ft(3-4.5m)

P. coccinea Red granadilla, from tropical South America, is another species which needs warmth to do well. Flowers are bright scarlet and 4-5in (10-13cm) wide. Leaves have short hairs, are entire, and irregularly toothed. One way to grow this is to create a criss-cross canopy of wires under the roof.

Train the main stems up, then let growth drape over this canopy. When flower buds begin to form, climb up some stepladders and gently pull the long flowering stems down through the wire canopy. The effect is breathtaking. Never prune this species back into hard wood or it is likely to die. An established plant simply needs a little thinning from time to time. The flowers need to be hand-pollinated for successful fertilization. You can also enjoy the edible fruits on this evergreen climber. Some 2in(5cm) across, they have mottled orange-yellow skin decorated with six green stripes. In Guyana they call these "monkey guzzle".
55°F(13°C) H:10-20ft(3-6m)

P. coriacea Again for the warm greenhouse, the wonderful bat-leaved passiflora from South America is grown more for its unusual foliage than its flowers. Only 1-1¹⁄₂in(2.5-3cm) across, these are pale greenish-yellow and insignificant when compared to the showier passifloras. In warm and humid conditions, leaves can eventually reach as much as 12in(30cm) across and do look like a bat in flight. While conventional leaves tend to be longer than they are wide, here the situation is reversed. They are deep green with paler green and yellow mottling. As an added bonus, this species is shade-tolerant.
50°F(10°C) H:10-15ft(3-4.5m)

P. edulis The purple passion fruit or purple granadilla is the species whose dark purple fruits are widely sold in supermarkets. Cut one open and you are faced with dark seeds surrounded by orange-colored juicy pulp. Both seeds and pulp are wonderfully tangy and fragrant. This species is easy to grow from seed and will produce flowers and fruit in abundance without hand-pollinating. Flowers are not among the showiest in the genus, being 3in(8cm) across with short greenish-white petals and sepals overshadowed by comparatively long corona filaments purple at the base and white at the tips. These are hectic and crinkled as though heat-singed. From tropical South America, *P. edulis* is now cultivated in most tropical and subtropical countries.
40-50°F(4-10°C) H:10-15ft(3-4.5m)

P. incarnata May pops, May apple, or apricot vine is native to the USA and has variable, fragrant flowers 3-3¹⁄₂in(8-9cm) wide. Colors of soft greenish-white, mauve and lilac make a delightful combination compatible with those of other plants. Fruits ripen to lime-green or yellow and are said to taste good either fresh or used in preserves. Under glass, hand-pollination is recommended to be sure of a good set of fruit. Do not be concerned if plants appear to die back during winter at cold temperatures; they will reappear vigorously in spring. To be grown cold, they are probably best planted in borders of well-drained soil.
32-45°F(0-7°C) H:10-15ft(3-4.5m)

Passiflora antioquiensis

Passiflora caerulea

Passiflora × caeruleoracemosa

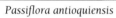

Passiflora coccinea

Passiflora mollissima

Passiflora racemosa

P. 'Incense' (*P. incarnata* × *P. cincinnata*) This hybrid is grown primarily for its dazzling beautiful fragrant flowers, some 4-5in(10-13cm) wide. Petals and sepals are a lighter violet than the corona filaments,which are banded with white toward the base, paler and crimped toward the outside. Hand-pollination is necessary to obtain edible fruits.
32-45°F(0-7°C) H:10-15ft(3-4.5m)

P. ligularis Sweet granadilla has perhaps the sweetest and best fruit of all the passifloras, though for a more tart flavor, *P. edulis* might be preferred. *P. ligularis* must be allowed to grow large and become quite mature before fruits will form. These are a little over 3in(8cm) long, orange when ripe and full of white, sweet pulp. They need fairly warm conditions to flower and fruit well. From Mexico to Venezuela, Peru, and Bolivia, this is a large-growing species with robust rounded stems and roughly heart-shaped leaves 3-6in(8-15cm) long, delicately purple-hued when young. The flowers are not particularly showy, being about 3½in(9cm) wide, with greenish-white petals and sepals and prettily purple-banded filaments, like the tentacles of a sea anemone. There is no need to prune back this passiflora, train it high and allow the long flowering and fruiting stems to dangle.
45-50°F(7-10°C) H:10-20ft(3-6m)

P. manicata This attractive, red-flowered species from Venezuela, Colombia, and Peru is usually found at high altitudes and, though happy to grow in the greenhouse, can sometimes be shy of flowering unless the air is fresh and cool in summer. This, with good light, is not an easy atmosphere to create.
45°F(7°C) H:10ft(3m)

P. mollissima The banana-fruited passion flower is well worth growing. The flowers of this species, 3in(8cm) across, are a wonderful soft pink, uncomplicated by showy corona filaments – which are so reduced as to be almost non-existent. Yellow fruits are shaped like small bananas.
40°F(4°C) H:10-15ft(3-4.5m)

P. quadrangularis The giant granadilla from tropical America is arguably the showiest, most amazing of the passion flowers. Fragrant flowers, 4½in(11cm) wide, have purple-red sepals and petals and incredible, banded filaments which stand away from the flower. The huge, edible fruits are, at 8-12in (20-30cm) long, the largest of the genus and are greenish-orange when ripe. Hand-pollination is recommended for a reliable set of fruit. Warmth and light will be required for them to mature. Keep this rampaging climber in check by regular pruning, and resort to pot culture if necessary.
45-50°F(7-10°C) H:10-30ft(3-9m)

P. racemosa From Rio de Janeiro, this elegant, crimson flowerer is distinctive in that its racemes of flowers are not cluttered by leaves. Train the plant up its supports, then overhead. This way, the flowering stems will hang down and add color to the greenhouse for long periods. Developing buds are as crimson-red as the 4-5in(10-13cm) flowers. Although short spells of lower temperatures are tolerated, warm conditions are appreciated.
50-60°F(10-16°C) H:10ft(3m)

P. vitifolia The vine-leaved passion flower from Central America is arguably the best, most reliable, and free-flowering of the red-flowered species. Its distinctive petals and sepals are pointed, the sepals ending in an awn.
55°F(13°C) H:10-15ft(3-4.5m)

Pereskia
(Cactaceae)

P. aculeata The Barbados gooseberry or lemon vine is a climbing cactus from the West Indies and South America. Long, round, straggly stems dig themselves into their supports by means of recurved spines. In fall abundant flowers 1-1½in(2.5-4cm) across are a wonderful oystershell color of creamy-white, sometimes faintly flushed with pink, with a showy boss of orange stamens in the center. Attractive to the eye, they are also fragrant with the pleasant but pungent scent of wintergreen. Yellowish fruits rather like small, transparent gooseberries are edible. Often deciduous, the glossy leaves may fall during dry, cold winters. *P.a.* var. *godseffiana* has distinctive orange-brown leaves with purple undersides. The best plants are those planted in a border of well-drained soil, given full light, and tied up to a wall or trellis. In the wild, pereskias can reach 30ft(10m); keep plants smaller by pruning some of the older stems back hard after flowering, then reducing side shoots leaving short spurs. Propagate by making cuttings in spring or summer.
40°F(4°C) H:6ft(1.8m) S:4-5ft(1.2-1.5m)

Petrea
(Verbenaceae)

P. volubilis The purple wreath from Mexico, Central America, and the West Indies is a splendid, vigorous, twining climber that becomes woody with age. Once the framework of the plant has been trained up, flowers will be reliably produced every summer. These are like violet-blue stars and are held in racemes 12in(30cm) or more long. After flowering, cut back the flowered stems to within a short spur of the older wood. Good light will be appreciated. Warm temperatures might see plants coming into flower earlier in the year, but cooler temperatures combined with a winter rest are tolerated well. The best plants are probably those planted in beds, but pot culture

Pereskia aculeata var. *godseffiana*

Piper ornatum

keeps size within bounds. Propagate by cuttings in summer or by seed. Mealy bugs can be a problem. 45°F(7°C) H:10-15ft(3-4.5m)

Philodendron
(Araceae)

In their native habitat, deep in the jungles of central and southern tropical America, philodendrons thrive in humid warmth beneath the shade of the tree canopy. This ability to tolerate shade has made them widely popular as houseplants. The often large attractive leaves will create a lush, tropical atmosphere in a warm but sunless greenhouse. Heavy shading from hot sun is vital: yellowing and scorching of leaves are sure reminders that shading is inadequate. Like monsteras, philodendrons send out long aerial roots with which to cling to their supports and also to scout for niches of moisture in which to grow fibrous feeding roots. Sometimes they reach right down to the ground from the tops of tall trees. If these roots become a menace, they can be cut off without causing harm to the plant. Flowers are sometimes produced but these are more curious than showy. Typical of the arum family, they consist of pale green, white, or sometimes red spathes, surrounding a small spadix. Prune and propagate during summer. By cutting overgrown climbing types above a node quite close to the base of stem or stems, they may regenerate. Tips of shoots will root easily like giant cuttings. Stem sections cut below a node at the bottom and above at the top will also root. Air-layering is a useful alternative. Seed of some species is available and easy to germinate. Although lower temperatures might be tolerated, growth will cease; 60-65°F(16-18°C) is optimum. Besides the species listed here, there are many hybrids to choose from. *P.* 'Burgundy' is very popular, with very dark red-tinged leaves. *P.* 'Majesty' and *P.* 'Royal Queen' are excellent cultivars. For *P. bipinnatifidum*, see p.69.

P. angustisectum (P. elegans) The 15in(40cm) long leaves of this climbing philodendron are deeply dissected so as to be almost palm-like. Bold and imposing, they make striking fishbone patterns against their background.
50-55°F(10-13°C) H:6ft(1.8m) S:4ft(1.2m)

P. bipennifolium (P. panduriforme) The fiddle-leaf from southeast Brazil is a climber with handsome leaves 12-30in(30-75cm) long, usually divided into five lobes, the middle one longest so as to form a rough fiddle shape. *P.b.* 'Variegatum' has creamy-white blotches on its leaves.
55°F(13°C) H:6-7ft(1.8-2m) S:30in(75cm)

P. erubescens The blushing philodendron from Trinidad, Colombia, and Venezuela is a climber with leaves to 10in(25cm) long. These are the shape of an arrowhead, deep glossy green above and with coppery-pink undersides. Young stems and leaf

Petrea volubilis

sheaths are purple-pink. *P.e.* 'Red Emerald', *P.e.* 'Imperial Red', and *P.e.* 'Valeria' are good varieties.
50°F(10°C) H:6ft(1.8m) S:3ft(1m)

P. melanochrysum (P. andreanum) The black/gold or velvet philodendron from Colombia is a favorite. The pointed, heart-shaped leaves can, encouraged by warmth and humidity, grow up to 24in(60cm) long on mature plants, though 8in(20cm) is more normal. These dark olive-green leaves have a velvety appearance, the veins and leaf edges picked out in palest green, with purple-pink undersides. The neat arrangement of the leaves, particularly when climbing stems cling tightly to their supports, gives the plant a satisfyingly compact appearance.
55-60°F(13-16°C) H:6ft(1.8m) S:3ft(1m)

P. scandens The heart-leaf or sweetheart plant is one of the most popular philodendrons as it is easily accommodated, whether climbing up a moss pole or allowed to trail. Closely growing, shiny green leaves 4-6in(10-15cm) long are perfectly heart-shaped. Young leaves are a delicate bronze-green. Try pinching back the tips of cuttings to encourage young plants to branch. A good idea is to plant three separate plants in one pot around a moss pole.
50°F(10°C) H:5ft(1.5m) S:30in(75cm)

Piper
(Piperaceae)

P. ornatum This pepper plant from Celebes is the

best choice for showy foliage. Long stems are decorated by heart-shaped leaves 3-5in(8-13cm) long. Basically olive-green, they are attractively patterned with silvery-pink, metallic-looking dots, sometimes fusing into blotches. The pink is more intense on young leaves, turning almost white as they mature. Undersides are rich purple. Probably best grown in a large pot, stems can be trained up around a tripod of canes or a trellis and then allowed to tumble downward. Planted in beds in warmth, plants will reach 10ft(3m). Even warmth, humidity, and shade from summer sun will contribute to success. Propagate by cuttings in spring or summer. As plants have small root systems, three cuttings can be planted in one pot to give a full effect.
55-60°F(13-16°C) H:5-6ft(1.5-1.8m) S:3ft(1m)

Plumbago
(Plumbaginaceae)

P. auriculata (P. capensis) Cape leadwort, a marvelous South African plant, is deservedly popular for its stunning heads of sky-blue flowers, lighting up the greenhouse in summer and fall. The white variety, *P.a.* var. *alba*, while attractive, is not as desirable. Evergreen growth is of a scrambling nature and needs support. Plants are versatile, and can be kept small by tying them around a circle of wire. In early spring, stems which flowered the previous summer can be cut back close to the main stems,

Senecio confusus

leaving small spurs. In larger pots, stems can be tied into tall 5-6ft(1.5-1.8m) canes. Planted against a wall or trellis, they can be fixed to wires or other support. In the latter two cases, prune by thinning out the stems as well as cutting back lateral shoots. Never cut them too hard back into old wood. Provide good light, but shade from hot sun, which can scorch leaves. Propagate in summer by cuttings.
40°F(4°C) H:5-10ft(1.5-3m) S:2-6ft(60cm-1.8m)

Podranea
(Bignoniaceae)

P. ricasoliana This summer-flowering evergreen from South Africa has attractively pinnate foliage with nine to eleven leaflets. Train this plant where the sight and fragrance of beautiful, tubular, pale pink flowers with pale, whitish-yellow throats, 3in(8cm) at the widest, can be appreciated. Prune when necessary by thinning out the stems in spring. Propagate by seed or in summer by cuttings.
45°F(7°C) H:10-12ft(3-3.5m)

Pyrostegia
(Bignoniaceae)

P. venusta The golden shower or Chinese cracker flower, flame flower, or flaming trumpets from Brazil is an evergreen climber much cultivated in the warmer parts of the world. Paired leaflets have a long tendril between them that snakes out and grips any support offered. During fall, buds burst into panicles of bright orange-red tubular flowers. The best way to display this plant is to train it up and under the roof, allowing the flowering stems to hang down. Prune by thinning out stems after flowering. Good light is required for flowering. Propagate in summer by semi-ripe stem cuttings bearing at least two nodes. Plants will be at their best at 55-60°F (13-16°C), though they can be grown satisfactorily at lower temperatures.
45-50°F(7-10°C) H:15-20ft(4.5-6m)

Rhodochiton
(Scrophulariaceae)

R. atrosanguineus The unusual purple bellflower from Mexico is a short-lived perennial that can be grown as an annual vine in frost-free areas. Provide this delicate plant with a support from early days. Both leaf stalks and long flower stalks curl themselves around a cane, securing the slender stem as the plant grows. Dainty, heart-shaped leaves are slightly toothed and complement the strange flowers. These are pendent and consist of a rosy-pink calyx which looks rather like a pink umbrella sheltering the corolla tube underneath. This is darkest purple, flaring out into five rounded lobes, extending to a total of 2in(5cm) in length. Dot these plants around the greenhouse where there are convenient, well-lit

supports for them to climb – preferably on a bench or other high surface, so that the flowers, produced throughout summer, are at eye level or above. Grow three small plants together in a large pot.
40°F(4°C) H:3-5ft(1-1.5m)

Senecio
(Compositae)

S. confusus (Pseudogynoxys chenopodioides) The Mexican flame vine, or orange-glow vine, has flowers of a warm, bright orange, borne in groups at the ends of the stems during summer and intensifying to reddish-orange as they mature. After the flowers fade, they are replaced with fluffy seed heads. At other times of the year, the slightly succulent, toothed leaves of this twining evergreen climber, originally from Mexico and Honduras, are quite attractive, but have an irritating habit of clinging to their stems long after they have turned brown and died. The secret of success here is to prune regularly and clean thoroughly after flowering. Although capable of reaching 10ft(3m), growth can be restricted by pot culture or a small, shallow bed. Watch out for aphid attack. Propagate by seed or cuttings.
45-50°F(7-10°C) H:6ft(1.8m) S:3ft(1m)

S. macroglossus 'Variegatus' Variegated Cape ivy from South Africa is probably the most popular and widely grown of the climbing senecios. This semi-succulent evergreen twiner is often mistaken for a rather fleshy ivy until its yellow, daisy-like flowers 2in(5cm) across appear, usually during fall and winter. Leaves are bright green triangles, edged with creamy-yellow. Plenty of light, coolness, and a well-drained soil should guarantee good results. Propagate by cuttings, which should not be kept too moist or humid.
40-45°F(4-7°C) H:5-6ft(1.5-1.8m) S:30in(75cm)

Solandra
(Solanaceae)

S. maxima The two common names for this Mexican plant, golden chalice vine and cup of gold, hold a promise that is fulfilled by huge, vase-like blooms up to 9in(23cm) long and 6in(15cm) wide. Newly opened flowers are yellow at first, marked with five dark maroon stripes. As the flower matures, however, it deepens in color, so that by the third day it has become golden and the texture of chamois leather. The perfume is reminiscent of pina colada. This evergreen, scrambling climber grows a robust framework of long, stout stems and oval leaves to 6in(15cm) long. Prune by thinning and reducing stems after flowering, in spring and summer. Planted in beds, specimens will slowly grow tall and can be guided up canes or pillars, then along wires strung under the roof. When space is limited keep plants small by restricting them in pots and regularly

pruning them hard. Propagate in summer by cuttings. Mealy bugs and aphids can pose problems.
50°F(10°C) H:5-30ft(1.5-9m)

Solanum
(Solanaceae)

With their abundant purple, blue, or white flowers, these relatives of the potato are an asset to the greenhouse. Most are vigorous climbers flowering in summer and fall, their season of interest often prolonged by attractive berries. Some will grow tall given the root run of a border, but can be restricted by containers and pruning. This is best carried out in spring. Maintain height by reducing lateral shoots to short spurs from the main stems. Occasionally, cut an older stem hard back to encourage new growth from the base. Stems can be trained up walls or pillars and under the roof on wires or over arches. Full light will be appreciated, with light shade from the hottest sun. Whitefly and spider mite can be troublesome. Propagate by making cuttings in summer or spring-sown seed.

S. crispum The Chilean potato tree is a scrambling evergreen shrub that makes an admirable addition to the unheated or cool greenhouse. The clusters of purple-blue flowers ³/₄in(2cm) across are a fine sight. Mostly represented in cultivation by *S.c.* 'Glasnevin', there is also a form with variegated foliage.
27-45°F(-3-7°C) H:12ft(3.5m) S:5ft(1.5m)

S. jasminoides The jasmine nightshade from Brazil is a semi-evergreen species with attractively star-shaped, mauve-blue flowers, each studded with golden-yellow anthers. Leaves sometimes drop during cold periods, often causing unnecessary alarm. *S.j.* 'Album', the white potato vine, is worth growing against a background that will show up its pretty white flowers.
32-45°F(0-7°C) H:15ft(4.5m) S:5ft(1.5m)

S. wendlandii The giant potato vine is an excellent choice for the greenhouse. Originally from Costa Rica, this magnificent scrambling evergreen climber clings to its supports by means of hooked, recurved spines on the leaf stalks, so handle with care during pruning. Secrets of good flowering include plenty of water during summer, with cooler, drier winters. Plants sometimes become semi-evergreen at low temperatures. Beautiful lavender-blue flowers 2¹/₂in(6cm) across in large, long-lasting, floriferous cymes are the reward for fulfilling these requirements. Foliage, handsome during spring and summer, is pinnate, with seven to thirteen leaflets on the lower parts and either heart-shaped or three-lobed higher up.
40°F(5°C) H:15ft(4.5m) S:7ft(2m)

Solanum jasminoides 'Album'

Solanum wendlandii

Stephanotis floribunda

Sollya

(Pittosporaceae)

S. heterophylla (S. fusiformis) Bluebell creeper from western Australia is a delightful twining evergreen climber. Of slender growth, it is easy to slot in between other plants and will grow equally well in borders or pots. Either way, anchor string or wire at the base of the plant and secure above as a guide to the thin stems, or train plants up a tripod of slender canes. During summer and into the fall, plants produce small clusters of nodding, bell-shaped flowers. A fresh sky blue, they make a fine complement to the lance-shaped, deep green leaves. The season of interest is then extended by purple-blue berries. Plants are easily raised from seed and can also be propagated in summer by cuttings. Good light and a well-drained soil will ensure good results from these charming plants.

38-45°F(3-7°C) H:4-6ft(1.2-1.8m) S:12-36in(30-90cm)

Stephanotis

(Asclepiadaceae)

S. floribunda The beautiful Madagascar jasmine or bridal flower is a splendid twining climber but has an irritating habit of remaining luxuriant while refusing to flower. Although this can be a symptom of too much nitrogenous fertilizer, it is more likely to be caused by low light or sudden drops in temperature, both of which can be remedied in most greenhouses. Umbels of six to eight waxy, white, trumpet-shaped flowers some 1½in(4cm) long are sweetly fragrant; one plant will scent the whole greenhouse in summer. Grow plants in clay pots or a small bed, but provide wires, canes, or trellis for them to climb. Trained overhead, they look particularly elegant as stems weighed down with several umbels of flowers become pendent. Train smaller plants on circles of wire around a tripod of canes. Long, unwanted stems can be pruned back to within a couple of nodes of older stems. White sap will ooze from cuts but soon dries up. Even when not flowering, the shiny, slightly fleshy opposite leaves, 3-4in(8-10cm) long, are attractive. Large, established plants sometimes set large, egg-shaped fruit, somehow out of scale with the elegance of the plant. These take about a year to ripen, eventually splitting to reveal plumed seeds. Propagate by seed or by cuttings. Mealy bugs can be a problem.

45-50°F(7-10°C) H:3-15ft(1-4.5m)

Streptosolen

(Solanaceae)

S. jamesonii The marmalade bush from Colombia looks stunning when a large specimen is in full bloom. Planted in a narrow border, and trained 12ft(3.5m) up the glass side of a large greenhouse, it can make a truly magnificent sight in spring. It is smothered in panicles of bright orange flowers borne on long, lax lateral flowering stems which arch downward from the main body of the plant. This evergreen or semi-evergreen can be kept much smaller in pots. Prune annually after flowering to keep plants tidy. It is even possible to grow small standards, supporting the young stem well in the early stages. Shade from hot sun during summer but provide plenty of light during winter. Propagate by soft or semi-ripe cuttings in summer, potting up or top-dressing every spring.

45°F(7°C) H:4-15ft(1.2-4.5m) S:2-6ft(60cm-1.8m)

Syngonium

(Araceae)

The goosefoot or arrowhead vines from tropical America are grown for their decorative leaves. In their natural habitat they are epiphytic climbers, flourishing in hot, humid forests. Although appreciative of shade, warmth, and humidity, they can be surprisingly tolerant of a cooler, drier winter rest period. Given ideal conditions, the neat, compact plant brought back from the garden center quickly changes its character. Stems elongate, reaching out for a tree to climb, and begin to produce aerial roots. Leaves, too, begin to alter, the heart-shaped juvenile leaves becoming more arrowheaded, then five-lobed in the adult form. Plants enjoying tropical conditions eventually sport huge seven- to nine-lobed leaves up to 12in(30cm) long. Propagate by spring and summer cuttings, potting a minimum of three young plants in one pot around a moss pole to achieve a full effect. Pinch back the growing tips to encourage branching.

55-60°F(13-16°C) H:6ft(1.8m) S:24-36in(60-90cm)

S. angustatum (Nephthytis triphylla) From Mexico to Panama, this species has plain green leaves usually with attractive silvery or cream veining, but varieties in cultivation have varying amounts of cream or silver on the leaf.

S. 'Maya Red' (also known as **S. 'Meyers Red'** or **S. 'Red Nerve'**) This pretty goosefoot plant has pink leaves and is a relative newcomer to cultivation. It can tolerate an occasional brief drop to 45°F(7°C) during winter. Water sparingly during cold periods. The play of light on the shrimp-pink leaves is particularly attractive.

Tecomanthe

(Bignoniaceae)

These tall evergreen twiners, mostly from New Guinea, are unusual to grow. Their beautiful foxglove-like flowers are often produced from old woody stems, mostly during summer and fall. This is an advantage, as pruned plants restricted in pots will still produce blooms. Premature bud drop can be brought about by sudden plunges in temperature or cold drafts. Take care never to overwater these fine plants, which thrive in a well-drained soil. Pruning, when necessary, consists of thinning out some of the stems. Propagate by semi-ripe cuttings or by seed.

T. speciosa from the Three Kings Islands north of New Zealand, has glossy leaves composed of three or five leaflets. Flowers are creamy-green colored, with the tips and inside of the tube a darker green.

T. venusta (*T. dendrophila*) ascends tall trees in the wild in New Guinea, draping them with its branches of pinnate leaves. Upright inflorescences sprout from old stems close to the base as well as from the younger branches higher up, where blooms tend to be pendent. There are many flowers to a cluster, each with a pinkish-maroon calyx. The tubes are rose-pink on the exterior, but tipped and colored inside with cream. Although plants flower well in pots, anticipate even better results if roots are allowed more freedom. Even when not in flower, the stems, which often twine about each other, are dotted with raised lenticels and are most attractive.

55-65°F(13-18°C) H:4-20ft(1.2-6m)
S:2-6ft(60cm-1.8m)

Tecomaria

(Bignoniaceae)

T. capensis The Cape honeysuckle from South and southeast Africa is a sprawling evergreen shrub needing support and tying up. The dainty pinnate leaves composed of five to nine leaflets set off the racemes of orange-red tubular flowers produced in spring and summer to perfection. Although good light will benefit flower production, shade plants from scorching summer sun which can bleach both leaves and flowers. Prune by thinning out and shortening lateral stems in spring. Spider mite, whitefly, and aphids can be troublesome. Propagate by spring-sown seed or in summer by cuttings.

50°F(10°C) H:6-10ft(1.8-3m) S:4-5ft(1.2-1.5m)

Tetrastigma

(Vitaceae)

T. voinerianum (Cissus voinerianus, Vitis voineriana) Chestnut vine is a strong, fast-growing foliage climber which will quickly clothe the wall of a new, bare-looking greenhouse. Leaves up to 12in(30cm) across on older plants are usually composed of five toothed leaflets and bear a superficial resemblance to those of the horse chestnut. The undersides of leaves and stems are covered with pale, felted hairs when young, deepening to russet as they mature. Virtually trouble-free, this sturdy vine with its origins in Laos can tolerate low winter temperatures, although growth stops below 55°F(13°C). Always water sparingly during cold periods. Shade from bright summer sun and provide humidity during high temperatures. When this vine has filled its allotted space, train it overhead, allowing the tips of shoots with their handsome tendrils to trail down, creating a jungle-like effect. Even lovers of chaos will need to curb such exuberant growth. Prune in spring. Alternatively raise replacement plants by making cuttings 9in (23cm) long of young wood, not necessarily containing a shoot tip, in summer. Will grow smaller in pots. 45°F(7°C) H&S:6-30ft(1.8-9m)

Thunbergia

(Acanthaceae)

This varied genus contains at least three valuable climbers for the greenhouse. Given initial help, twining stems will cling to one another and make columns of growth rather than needing a wall as support. Propagate from stem sections 3-6in(8-15cm) long containing at least two nodes.

T. alata Black-eyed Susan vine from tropical Africa is a perennial climber usually grown as an annual from seed germinated in spring and provides flower color all summer. The flowers, 1½in(4cm) across and appearing singly from leaf axils, may be the classic orange with black eye, or lemon-yellow, pale yellow, or white, with or without the dark eye. The stalks of pointed, heart-shaped leaves are winged. Allow plants to twine up among other climbers, removing them at the end of the year, or plant three in a pot and train up tall slender canes. Good light ensures the best display. Whitefly and thrips can be a problem. 40°F(4°C) H:6ft(1.8m) S:3ft(1m)

Sollya heterophylla

Streptosolen jamesonii

Thunbergia alata

Tweedia caerulea

T. grandiflora Blue trumpet vine or Bengal clock vine is surely one of the most beautiful and floriferous climbers for the greenhouse. Plants given the root run of a border or large tub will have the vigor to twine up a wire or pillar, making a thick column of growth from floor to ceiling. In summer the dense evergreen foliage is enriched by a profusion of violet-blue, trumpet-shaped flowers with pale yellow throats. Prune if necessary in spring. Propagate by cuttings in summer or by suckers produced around the base. There is a rarer white form.
50°F(10°C) H:6-20ft(1.8-6m) S:3-6ft(90cm-1.8m)

T. mysorensis This striking species from India bears pendent racemes of colorful flowers which can reach 18in(45cm) long. Train stems upward and then along an overhead support, so that the current season's stems can hang down to display the flowers produced at the ends of these shoots during late winter. Worthy of close inspection, each individual flower is yellow, 2in(5cm) long, and marked on the recurved petal lobes with rich, brownish-red. Propagate as for *T. grandiflora*.
55-60°F(13-16°C) H&S:10-20ft(3-6m)

Trachelospermum

(Apocynaceae)

T. jasminoides Star or Confederate jasmine is a scented climber from China and Japan. Although "jasmine" features in both the botanical and the popular names and invites comparisons, *Jasminum polyanthum* is not even a distant relative. While the perfume from these small, white, yellow-centered blooms is indeed similar to that of *Jasminum polyanthum*, it's best to make room for both, as the flowers of trachelospermum begin opening as the last blooms fade from the jasmine. Deep, glossy evergreen foliage makes an admirable backdrop to the flowers. The variegated form *T.j.* 'Variegatum' is desirable for foliage interest but its flowers are camouflaged against the grayish-green and cream background. Trachelospermums, though sometimes slow growers in their early stages, usually become vigorous with age, sending up long, twining stems which will ascend wires or other supports. Specimens restricted in pots remain manageable but when planted in beds, be prepared for a wide column of growth. Good light is best, but shade from hot sun. Prune tall plants if necessary after flowering or in spring. Scale insect and mealy bugs can be a nuisance. Propagate by seed or in summer by cuttings.
32-45°F(0-7°C) H:3-15ft(1-4.5m) S:3-4ft(1-1.2m)

Tropaeolum

(Tropaeolaceae)

There are some fine climbers in this group, better known as the nasturtium family. Good light is necessary for healthy growth and plentiful flowers.

A well-drained soil will encourage healthy roots. Aphids can be a problem.

T. peregrinum Canary creeper from Peru is a cheerful climber with fringed, canary-yellow flowers, best grown as an annual. Sow seed in spring to provide a small crop of creepers to use between other plants, perhaps to add flower color to patches of foliage. Alternatively, grow three plants in one large pot and train their brittle stems of small, five- to seven-lobed leaves up a tripod of 6ft(1.8m) canes.
40°F(4°C) H:6ft(1.8m) S:24in(60cm)

T. tricolorum This Chilean native is an herbaceous climber with tuberous roots. A dainty plant, masses of small leaves each have five to seven leaflets. Sprinkled among them in early summer are cheerful flowers, consisting of yellow petals surrounded by crimson calyces tipped with maroon and ending in long curved orange-red spurs. Poised on their stalks, they look like pixies' hats. After growth has died down tubers should be left dry in their pots to overwinter in frost-free conditions. Begin watering carefully in spring as they come back into growth. Repot every other year into clean clay pots using fresh, well-drained soil. Propagate by dividing the tubers in spring. Cool, light, well-ventilated conditions are ideal.
40°F(4°C) H:36in(90cm) S:12in(30cm)

T. tuberosum This herbaceous, tuberous-rooted species has long, elegant, curved, reddish flower stalks which bend upward from pendent stems. The flowers they bear have orange petals surrounded by darker, orange-red sepals and spur. These usually appear in late summer and fall; the cultivar 'Ken Aslet' begins a little earlier. Grow as for *T. tricolorum*.
40°F(4°C) H:6-8ft(1.8-2m) S:24-36in(60-90cm)

Tweedia

(Asclepiadaceae)

T. caerulea (Oxypetalum caeruleum, Amblyopetalum caeruleum) This small but lovely twining plant from South America is easy to raise from seed. Grow it for the unusual color of its small, 1in(2.5cm) wide flowers. These open in summer and fall, starting off as a cluster of furry pink-tinged buds. The newly opened flower is pale sky-blue but as it matures and fades, turns violet, then lilac before dying. Tweedias may need securing to slender canes. Foliage and stems are soft and hairy. Prune in spring, reducing the plant by some two-thirds, to encourage fresh flowering shoots. Propagate by cuttings in summer or seed. Grow three plants in one pot.
40°F(4°C) H:36in(90cm) S:18-24in(45-60cm)

Vigna

(Leguminosae)

V. caracalla (Phasaeolus caracalla) The snail flower from South America is a twining evergreen climber

Trachelospermum jasminoides

Tropaeolum tricolorum

with extraordinary flowers. Twisted into a fragrant, creamy-white and pinkish-purple spiral shape, each looks like an exotic species of snail. Snail flower is unlikely to bloom in a small pot. Given a wider root run, it produces a number of tall stems furnished with leaves composed of three leaflets. Flowers appear in summer when plants reach some 8-10ft (2.5-3m). Plants seem to cease growth during low winter light levels: water sparingly during this dormant phase, in which case temperatures as low as 45-50°F(7-10°C) can be tolerated. So much growth is made during summer that large plants need cutting in the fall. However, leave the main pruning until spring, shortening as many lateral shoots as required. Propagate by seed. Spider mite can be a problem.
55-60°F(13-16°C) H:10-20ft(3-6m)

Vitis

(Vitaceae)

Dessert varieties of grapes make excellent, productive climbing plants if correctly trained and pruned. Ventilate well to prevent mildew. Some varieties (quick-maturing sweetwaters like white 'Buckland Sweetwater' and black 'Black Hamburgh' and late-producing vinous kinds like white 'Syrian' and black 'Alicante') can be grown in an unheated greenhouse. The best flavored grapes are from muscat varieties such as white 'Muscat of Alexandria' and black 'Madresfield Court'. These need warmth to start them off early, set well, and mature. Plant against the glass wall of the greenhouse in rich, well dug soil. Tie the main stem to horizontal wires fixed 9in(23cm) apart and 12in(30cm) from the glass, starting 36in(90cm) off the ground. Cut off laterals after five leaves and

sub-laterals at one leaf. Tie the laterals down to the wires to prevent crowding. During the winter when leaves have fallen, prune the main stem by removing two-thirds of the summer growth. Prune laterals to one bud. Repeat this every year until the main stem or rod reaches the top wire. Provide a rich top-dressing just as the vine is about to burst into growth, when it should also be watered thoroughly. When the flowers appear, allow two leaves to form beyond, then remove the growing tip. Pinch subsequent side growths at one leaf. Shake the rods or stroke the flowers with the same hand at midday to ensure a good set. Thin developing bunches to between nine and twelve per mature rod, then later thin the grapes with narrow scissors. Keep moist and feed with a high-potash fertilizer every three weeks until the fruit ripens.
32-45°F(0-7°C) H:12ft(3.5m) S:5ft(1.5m)

Trailing plants

The cascading habit of trailing plants adds elegance and a touch of luxury to a sunroom or greenhouse. Dangling out of hanging baskets and bursting forth from wall planters, or simply spilling over the edge of a pot, they provide an extra visual element to complement other forms, particularly those with upright or compact growth. This sort of contrast is important whether plants are growing together in the same bed, massed together on tables or benches, or displayed in a more formal grouping of separate pots. In nature, plants of different shape and form grow together. A similar informal mixture creates an attractive, natural-looking greenhouse planting. In more contrived arrangements, the fluid shapes of trailing plants make a useful contribution to the composition.

Like climbers, trailing plants play a vital role in the vertical dimension. They furnish the middle height of the greenhouse with plant interest and make valuable use of potentially empty spaces overhead or on the upper reaches of walls. Flowers or striking foliage in hanging or wall-mounted containers can provide a focal point at eye-level. A plant trailing out of a jardinière or from a pot standing on a plinth offers a similar focus near table-top height. The tumbling foliage of trailing plants links plants which are growing at different levels, marrying them into a whole.

Long skeins of trailing foliage are especially useful to obscure ordinary or unattractive containers, benches, and furnishings. Trails of foliage and dangling flowers will soften hard edges and sharp outlines, disguising functional, man-made surfaces. Sprawling and trailing plants with dense growth work wonders for utilitarian benches and inexpensive containers, flowing out and over to conceal both pots and stand. But while a thick curtaining of foliage is sometimes appropriate, a lighter web can also be effective: a veil, only partly hiding what lies beneath, creates an air of mystery and allure. A few wisps of foliage or trailing stems may be very flattering to a handsome urn. And, like a screen of trellis, a loose curtain of trailing plants can make an airy room divider.

A wide variety of plants qualify as trailers, their use depending on the way they grow. Some have long flowing stems which pour over the edge of their container and hang straight down. These are useful for high hanging baskets, shelves, and wall planters, but may not perform well when dangling from benches. On plants such as aeschynanthus and columnea, stem tips where flowers are most likely to form, may not receive enough light and will be prone to damage when allowed to sweep the floor. These climbers must have correct watering and regular fertilizing to maintain good, healthy leaves all the way down the stems.

Plants that sprawl over the edges of benches, spill out of jardinières and wall planters, and trail elegantly from hanging baskets, have an important role to play in filling the middle ground in the sunroom or greenhouse. Their tumbling shapes give a necessary balance to the more upright outlines of specimens and climbers. Both the flowers and the foliage of Pelargonium 'L'Elégante', shown here, make a valuable contribution to plant composition.

Plants with elegant, arching growth have also been included in this section. The arching fronds of ladder or Boston ferns (Nephrolepis) look wonderful bursting from a low hanging basket or the top of a stand. Asparagus densiflorus 'Sprengeri' is more abandoned, sending out wild stems of needle-like foliage.

In their natural habitat, many trailing plants are epiphytic, their pendent growth projecting from tree trunks and branches. Epiphyllums make long, heavy, succulent stems which threaten to pull plants over if they are grown in pots. They seem far more at home swinging from a hanging basket and the orchid-like blooms can be admired from below. Stag's-horn ferns (Platycerium) wrap their infertile fronds around their support and dangle antler-like fertile fronds outward. Difficult to grow in pots, they are happier when attached to a slab of osmunda fiber against a board, or grown in a hanging basket.

Some plants fall into more than one category. Many climbing plants, for instance, will trail if deprived of their support. Rabbit or hare's foot fern (Davallia) will cling and climb to the trunks of trees with their hairy rhizomes; however, these ferns are equally at home in (or around) a moss-lined hanging basket, which they quickly colonize. Quite often certain varieties of normally upright plants have a tendency to trail and make useful hanging-basket plants. There are many trailing fuchsias, achimenes, begonias, and even African violets (saintpaulias).

Hanging baskets filled with plants are glorious but demand a high degree of skill in their care and maintenance. Choose plants suited to this method of growing, and hardware suited in style and practicality to the furnishings of the sunroom. Wire baskets lined with sphagnum moss must have a surface beneath that is not harmed by drips. Apart from functional plastic containers, watertight alternatives include attractive hanging planters in which lightweight plant pots can be placed. Always take into consideration the fact that almost all hanging-basket plants will need frequent watering. Using a long lance attached to a hose is convenient where splashing is no problem; where more precise watering is required, baskets can be lowered and raised on a ratchet device installed between basket and hook.

Outdoors, mixtures of different sorts of plants in one basket work well, but this concept rarely succeeds in the greenhouse, where single-subject baskets seem more effective. (It is also much easier to meet the cultivation needs of one type of plant per basket.) Unless the layout is symmetrical, hang baskets at different heights rather than having them all at the same level. A mixture of permanently planted baskets and those planted for seasonal color will work well.

Temporary color can be provided by trailing tuberous begonias and trailing pelargoniums. Make these baskets up in spring and they will flower all summer until taken down in the fall. For the winter, hang baskets of foliage plants like tradescantia and Plectranthus madagascariensis 'Variegated Mintleaf' in their place.

Aeschynanthus
(Gesneriaceae)

These colorful gesneriads make handsome hanging-basket plants, grown mainly for their showy, tubular flowers but also for their attractive foliage. Many are epiphytic in nature with small root systems which need a well-drained soil and careful watering: never allow the potting mix to dry out completely, or to remain soggy. Avoid wetting the foliage. Feed with liquid fertilizer every week at half-strength while in active growth. After several years in a pot or hanging basket, leaves drop and plants begin to look ragged. Take cuttings of healthy shoot tips in spring or summer, then give the whole plant a haircut, pruning all stems close to the top of the basket. Plants usually regrow quickly. Establish rooted cuttings singly in 3-3½in(8-9cm) pots, and remove shoot tips to encourage branching. Plant five young plants in a 10in(25cm) basket. For healthy growth and flowering provide good light but shade from direct,

scorching sun. Although 55°F(13°C) is the ideal winter minimum, plants will happily withstand 45°F(7°C) if watered sparingly. Flowering is generally improved after a cooler winter.

A. marmoratus This epiphytic trailer from Burma and Thailand has prettily marked leaves, purple underneath but green spotted with yellow above. Feed regularly to avoid an anemic appearance. Unusual green flowers with brown markings are produced in summer and fall.
45-50°F(7-10°C) H&S:24in(60cm)

A. 'Mona Lisa' The lipstick vine, one of the most popular aeschynanthus, has dainty leaves which are slightly hairy underneath. Clusters of tubular, dark maroon calyces at the ends of shoots open into 2in(5cm) long red flowers.
45-50°F(7-10°C) H:48in(120cm) S:30in(75cm)

A. speciosus This flashy aeschynanthus from Indonesia bears large clusters of bright orange tubular flowers in summer, which contrast well with

the robust, healthy green foliage.
45-50°F(7-10°C) H&S:24in(60cm)

Alsobia
(Gesneriaceae)

A. dianthiflora (Episcia dianthiflora) The Mexican lace flower makes an admirable hanging-basket plant. Long, trailing stems with rounded, soft green, velvety leaves bear neat plantlets along their length and in summer provide a backdrop for pure white 1in(2.5cm) flowers. These deserve individual inspection, as the edges of the petals have fine, filigree-like indentations. Shade plants from hot sun during summer and avoid wetting the leaves, which spot or scorch easily. Propagate by detaching individual plantlets from the runners and treating them like cuttings. Plant several young plants into one basket for a full effect. A. 'San Miguel' is similar but larger with pink-speckled flowers.
50°F(10°C) H:30in(75cm) S:18in(45cm)

Asparagus
(Liliaceae/Asparagaceae)

A. densiflorus 'Sprengeri' This asparagus fern develops a mass of arching, trailing stems of bright green needle-like "foliage" when mature. Plants are valuable as shapely specimens on their own, act as a green foil to companion flowers or trail to cover the front of a bench. For cultivation see p.119.
40°F(4°C) H&S:30in(75cm)

Begonia
(Begoniaceae)

Several trailing members of this large family make useful candidates for hanging baskets. For cultivation see p.120.

B. 'Cleopatra' Sometimes called maple-leaf begonia, this rhizomatous hybrid has long leaf stems, covered by yellowish-green and pinkish-brown leaves. Pale pink flowers are produced in winter.
50-55°F(10-13°C) H:12in(30cm) S:15in(40cm)

B. procumbens (B. limmingheana, B. glaucophylla) This Brazilian rhizomatous species has light blue-green leaves attractively spotted with white, with purple undersides. Clusters of brick-red flowers are borne in winter. Cuttings root easily; pinch back young plants to encourage branching. Plant several in one basket for a full effect.
50-55°F(10-13°C) H:48in(120cm) S:30in(75cm)

B. serratipetala This shrubby, trailing begonia from New Guinea is striking for its serrated, tapering, deep bronze-red leaves, dotted with raised pink blimps. Small pinkish-red flowers are produced almost continuously at shoot tips. Plant several small begonias in one basket.
50-55°F(10-13°C) H:24in(60cm) S:18in(45cm)

B. solananthera The Brazilian heart vine makes a

Alsobia dianthiflora

Asparagus densiflorus 'Sprengeri'

Aporocactus flagelliformis

Ceropegia linearis ssp.woodii

delightful hanging-basket subject as it is winter-flowering and marvelously scented. Stems are covered with heart-shaped leaves, which provide a backdrop for white flowers with red centers. Feed mature plants monthly with liquid fertilizer during active growth, from late summer to early winter. Propagate by cuttings, pinching back the growing tips of small plants to encourage bushiness. Plant three young begonias in one basket.
50-55°F(10-13°C) H:30in(75cm) S:24in(60cm)
B. sutherlandii This dainty, tuberous-rooted begonia from South Africa makes a lovely summer-flowering hanging-basket or trailing pot plant. The branching stems covered with bright green, red-veined leaves cascade sufficiently to hide their container and bear masses of small orange flowers. Plants die down in the winter; keep dry until growth resumes in spring. Propagate by cuttings or by separating and planting tubers individually in spring. Remove small tubers produced in leaf axils and pot in the same manner.
38°F(3°C) H&S:12-30in(30-75cm)
TRAILING TUBEROUS HYBRIDS Many lovely hybrids of tuberous begonias look superb in hanging baskets. They have thin, trailing stems with single or double flowers in many different colors. Start tubers individually in spring. Pot plants separately until they fill a 3½in(9cm) pot, then plant in baskets. For cultivation see p.140.

Cacti and other succulents

Many trailing succulent plants are best displayed in hanging pots and baskets, wall planters or containers raised on stands. Members of the cactus family with such a trailing habit are often forest dwellers. They grow epiphytically or lithophytically beneath the tree canopy in conditions very different from those of desert cacti. These plants frequently produce such one-sided growth that accommodating them in ordinary pots is difficult. One display option is to attach their roots to dead tree branches, and to provide more humidity and water than for similar pot-grown plants. Like the cacti, trailing succulents from other plant families tolerate more heat and bright light than most other plants, but need good ventilation in summer, and in winter where possible. Water regularly in summer but sparingly during winter. For cultivation see p.49.

Aporocactus (Cactaceae)
In its native Mexico, *A. flagelliformis,* the rat-tail cactus, H:36in(90cm) S:30in(75cm), grows on trees or rocks, producing long, slender, short-spined stems. These will curve over the sides of a hanging

basket most effectively. In spring and early summer, a large specimen in full bloom resembles a Medusa with showy cerise flowers in her hair. Like a desert cactus, only water aporocactus during winter if the stems show signs of shrivelling. Feed monthly throughout the growing season with cactus fertilizer. Propagate by 3-4in(8-10cm) stem tips or sections in spring or summer, as for desert cacti (see p.49).
40°F(4°C)

Ceropegia (Asclepiadaceae)
C. linearis ssp. *woodii* (*C. woodii*), the string of hearts or rosary vine, H:3-7ft(1-2m) S:6-8in(15-20cm), is a useful plant as, although succulent, it tolerates some shade and grows almost anywhere. Its purple stems are strung with opposite pairs of small, kidney- to heart-shaped succulent leaves. These are an attractive feature, being purple on the underside and green, heavily overlaid with silver, on the upper surface. A mature plant has a tumbling mass of stems, 6-7ft (1.8-2m) long, arising from a tuber which forms at the surface of the potting mix. Additional tubers up to ½in(1cm) across form along the stems. Flowers are more curious than beautiful, 1in(2.5cm) long, with a narrow pink tube, inflated toward the base and opening to dark maroon lobes at the top. This amazing plant from South Africa withstands short

Kalanchoe 'Tessa'

Nopalxochia phyllanthoides

Epiphyllum 'Discovery'

Cacti and other succulents

periods of drought very well. Propagate from stem tubers or by 3in(8cm) cuttings. Trim stems if they become too long.
38-40°F(3-4°C)

Epiphyllum (Cactaceae)
Orchid cacti, although beautiful when their large, exotic blooms 4-6in(10-15cm) across are open, are untidy plants, H:12in(30cm) S:24-36in(60-90cm), whose flattened stems project in all directions. Given space to dangle, plants look best in hanging baskets (pots may topple over). Species epiphyllums are night-flowering with lovely white scented blooms. Most plants in cultivation are hybrids with related *Selinicereus* and *Heliocereus* and include white, yellow, red, pink, orange, and purple flower colors. Cut out older ragged stems after flowering.
40-45°F(4-7°C)

Hatiora (Cactaceae)
H. gaertneri (Rhipsalidopsis gaertneri, Schlumbergera gaertneri), the Easter cactus from Brazil, H:6in(15cm) S:8in(20cm), produces orange-red flowers in spring. Stem edges are gently scalloped rather than pointed as in the very similar Christmas cactus (*Schlumbergera*). The many hybrids flower at different times throughout winter and spring. Cooler winter temperatures will delay the flowering of earlier cultivars.
45°F(7°C)

Kalanchoe (Crassulaceae)
K. manginii from Madagascar makes a useful and attractive hanging-basket plant. Able to tolerate more heat and brighter light than most non-succulent plants, it is a natural choice for greenhouses in which shading and ventilation are a problem. Water regularly and feed with a liquid fertilizer every month throughout the growing season. In spring, the wiry branching stems, H&S:24in(60cm), are well furnished with small neat leaves and terminal clusters of red tubular flowers. As flowers fade, plantlets appear. Remove when large enough to handle and place in a pot or box filled with a loose potting mixture to make new plants. Shoot-tip cuttings will also root. Pot several young plants into one basket for a full effect. Once the plantlets have been collected, prune back stems of older plants to the edge of the basket, to regenerate growth. *K.* 'Tessa' (*K. manginii* × *K. gracilipes*) produces a similar effect but has pale orange, tubular flowers.

K. pumila, H:9in(23cm) S:12in(30cm), from Madagascar, bears cool pink flowers in late winter which contrast beautifully with the toothed leaves, their covering of white powder lending them an ethereal silvery-gray hue. The succulent foliage

weighs down the stems to give a trailing appearance suited to hanging baskets or shallow pots. *K.* 'Wendy', H&S:12in(30cm), whose rather clumsy, upright stems also bend downward to make it a contender for basket planting, has an abundance of bell-shaped, pinkish-red flowers ³⁄₄in(2cm) long, tipped with creamy-yellow, which appear in late winter. After flowering, both can be propagated by cuttings.
40-50°F(4-10°C)

Lepismium (Cactaceae)
L. houlletianum, the snowdrop cactus from Brazil, H:24-36in(60-90cm) S:24-30in(60-75cm), produces both round, thin branches and long, flattened, leaf-like types with notched edges. In all, this strange plant looks like a mass of bright green seaweed until small creamy-white flowers appear on the flat branches (hence the common name), followed by red fruits. *L. cruciforme*, H&S:24in(60cm), also from Brazil, has thicker, ribbed stems, white flowers and red fruits.
50°F(10°C)

Nopalxochia (Cactaceae)
N. phyllanthoides from Mexico or Colombia, H:24in(60cm) S:36in(90cm), is closely related to epiphyllum. The parent of many hybrids, the species itself is attractive and well worth growing. Flattened and toothed stems bear many pink flowers in spring and early summer.
50°F(10°C)

Rhipsalis (Cactaceae)
Most of these are dainty plants, H&S:24-36in(60-90cm), with branching, often cylindrical stems. Many bear pale cream or pink flowers in winter or early spring, followed by berries. *R. baccifera (R. cassutha)* has greenish or cream flowers and white fruits which look superficially like mistletoe, hence the name mistletoe cactus.
50°F(10°C)

Schlumbergera (Cactaceae)
Christmas cactus species and hybrids, H:12in(30cm) S:30in(75cm), are possibly the best known of the forest cacti. Flowering time stretches from early fall to early spring and is governed by the hybrid grown and by temperature. Keep plants cool, at 36-40°F (2-4°C), and they flower in spring. Good but not scorching light, sufficient water, and regular feeding during summer ensure good flowers the following winter and spring.
45°F(7°C)

Sedum (Crassulaceae)
S. morganianum, known as donkey's tail, hails from Mexico and is a handsome succulent, best displayed

Sedum morganianum

in a basket or on a stand. Stems of almost cylindrical pale green leaves creep neatly over the top of the container and trail downward, H:24-36in(60-90cm) S:12in(30cm). Rose-pink flowers are produced in summer. Handle carefully, as leaves fall off easily. Propagate by stem cuttings.

S. sieboldii from Japan has stems that arch elegantly but do not trail far, H&S:9in(23cm), making it as suitable for an ordinary pot as for a small basket. Pale pink stems bear rounded, succulent, slightly wavy-edged gray-green leaves in whorls of three. After producing terminal heads of pink star-shaped flowers in fall, the stems die back until spring. *S.s.* 'Mediovariegatum' has attractive cream markings down the center of each leaf. Propagate by division.
38-40°F(3-4°C)

Senecio (Compositae)
S. rowleyanus or string of beads from South Africa, H:36in(90cm) S:9in(23cm), has thin, thread-like stems and spherical, bead-like leaves the size of peas. Long stems trail out of the pot like so many broken necklaces, and small white brush-like flowers appear during summer. Suitable for a hanging basket, this senecio can tolerate light shade. Propagate by cuttings in spring and summer.
38-40°F(3-4°C)

Ficus pumila 'Sonny'

Callisia

(Commelinaceae)

C. repens The trailing stems of this compact, rounded plant from South America quickly fill out to make a small mound of neat apple-green leaves, ideal for small hanging baskets. Use spare plants as infilling between larger specimens on tables and benches. Cuttings 2in(5cm) long root easily in water or potting mixtures. Pinch back the growing tips once established and grow three cuttings in each 3½in(9cm) pot for a fuller effect. Cut back old, straggly plants hard in spring to generate a new flush of shoots. Provide good light, but shade from hot summer sun. Occasional drops in temperature to 45°F(7°C) can be tolerated.
50°F(10°C) H&S:6in(15cm)

Chlorophytum

(Liliaceae/Anthericaceae)

C. comosum 'Vittatum' The ubiquitous spider plant makes a beautiful specimen when grown well. Long narrow green leaves in a dense rosette have a vivid creamy-white stripe running irregularly down the centers. A healthy plant, potted up regularly until it reaches the desired pot size and thereafter well fed, will send out many long stems bearing small but pretty white flowers, followed by plantlets. These little replicas gradually weigh the stems down to make a skirt around the main plant. A less common cultivar, *C.c.* 'Variegatum', has green leaves edged with creamy-white. Shade from hot sun, which scorches the foliage. Propagate by removing plantlets and inserting them individually into small pots.

45°F(7°C) H:36in(90cm) (including plantlets) S:18-24in(45-60cm)

Codonanthe

(Gesneriaceae)

C. gracilis In the mountains of Brazil this dainty plant creeps and climbs over rocks and trees. With its waterfall of small, rather fleshy leaves, it is ideal for a small hanging basket or in a pot on a shelf. Little white flowers with spotted throats appear sporadically year-round and are nicely set off by the dark green foliage. The shallow root system requires a well-drained, open potting mixture and careful watering. Never allow the medium to dry out, or become waterlogged. Shade from hot sun and keep water off the foliage. Propagate by cuttings during spring and summer. Pinch back young plants to encourage bushiness. Plant several cuttings in one basket. Although warm temperatures are preferred, plants tolerate a cool winter if watered sparingly.
50°F(10°C) H:24in(60cm) S:9-10in(23-25cm)

Columnea

(Gesneriaceae)

Goldfish plants, originally from tropical South America, are among the showiest hanging-basket plants. Long stems covered with ranks of neat leaves act as a good background for spectacular tubular, usually scarlet, flowers resembling bright goldfish. The hood-like top petal lobe is often much larger than the others and smaller lobes underneath represent the fins. Many are epiphytes in the wild, which is reflected in their cultivation requirements. Shade from hot sun during summer. Keep humid during high temperatures, but never spray columneas directly with water as their leaves are prone to scorching. Avoid watering with cold water. Although roots should not dry out, they dislike being waterlogged; allow the surface of the potting medium to begin to dry out between waterings. In winter, plants tolerate fairly cool temperatures if watered carefully, and seem to flower better after such a rest. When plants become straggly, take cuttings of shoot tips in spring or summer (usually after flowering), then prune all the growth back to the top of the basket. Pinch back cuttings when small to encourage branching. Pot several young plants in one basket for a full effect.

C. × banksii This hybrid is one of the easiest columneas to grow. Its stiff stems arch upward before trailing, and bear smooth, oval, fleshy leaves, shiny green above and red beneath. Bright red flowers 2½-3in(6-8cm) long appear in winter and spring.

C. gloriosa This exotic-looking Costa Rican species is the most difficult to grow. Leaves are very prone to water scorching and the plant cannot abide

being even slightly overwatered. It demands warmer minimum temperatures of 55-60°F(13-16°C). Given these conditions, the reward is a beautiful plant whose lax stems pour over the edge of a basket and are graced with soft leaves covered with brownish hairs. Bright red flowers 3in(8cm) long with yellow throats and prominent hoods project from the stems during winter.

C. 'Krakatoa' This hybrid is similar in form to *C. × banksii*, in that the stiff stems arch upward before becoming pendent, but its leaves are longer and hairy. Red flowers are freely produced in late winter and spring, then often again in summer.

C. microphylla This Costa Rican species is graceful, with small, rounded leaves. Red flowers 3in(8cm) long with yellow throats appear during winter and spring. The variegated form, *C.m. variegata*, with pretty cream-edged leaves, is more common in cultivation.

C. 'Stavanger' The Norse fire plant is a robust, reliable hybrid making a profusion of trailing stems lined with neat, smooth rounded leaves. Bright red flowers have very pronounced lobes.
45-50°F(7-10°C) H:24-36in(60-90cm) S:30in(75cm)

Davallia

(Davalliaceae)

In an ordinary pot this interesting fern behaves like a veritable Houdini: creeping, scaly rhizomes bearing the newest, healthiest fronds move toward the edges and over the sides, so that eventually all the active growth has escaped to dangle around the outside. Therefore hanging baskets, cork bark or tree-fern fiber are your best choice. *D. canariensis*, from the western Mediterranean, has fronds up to 18in(45cm) long and rhizomes covered with close brown hairs. *D. fejeensis*, from Fiji, with fronds up to 24in(60cm) long, is one of the most attractive. *D. mariesii* from Japan is possibly the hardiest; fronds are 6-8in(15-20cm) long. *D. solida* from Malaysia to northeastern Australia is similar to *D. fejeensis*, but its fronds are less divided. Water plants sparingly during winter, but never allow to dry out completely. Propagate by division or, more easily, by taking 3in(8cm) long sections of rhizome as cuttings. Plant several together for good effect.
38-40°F(3-4°C)

Ficus

(Moraceae)

Creeping figs make decorative trailing and climbing plants for small pots. Shade from hot sun, keep moist but not waterlogged and raise humidity when temperatures are high. They root easily from 3-4in(8-10cm) cuttings (see pp.60-61).

F. pumila (F. repens) This, the most common sort of creeping fig, has small, thin, heart-shaped leaves

Fuchsia procumbens

Fuchsia 'Trumpeter'

Hoya carnosa

which can easily shrivel if the plant dries out at the roots or is subjected to hot, dry air. It likes the same conditions as ivy and can tolerate surprisingly low temperatures. *F.p.* 'Minima' has smaller leaves, *F.p.* 'Variegata' has tiny, creamy-white spots on its leaves and the more popular *F.p.* 'Sonny' has scalloped-edged leaves irregularly edged with creamy-white, particularly down the sides. Even this is remarkably shade-tolerant.
40°F(4°C) H:9-30in(23-75cm) in a pot
F. sagittata (F. radicans) Less petite than *F. pumila*, this fig has lance-shaped leaves 2-4in(5-10cm) long. **F.s. 'Variegata'** is the one most often seen in cultivation and has attractive leaves irregularly edged with creamy-white.
45°F(7°C) H:9-30in(23-75cm) in a pot

Fuchsia
(Onagraceae)
For summer flowers, fuchsias in hanging baskets or half baskets attached to a wall are a joy. Place five young plants grown in 3½in(9cm) pots, which have been pinched and are beginning to branch well, upright in a basket. The plants will soon begin to trail over the edges. As the plants establish and grow, pinch back the shoot tips on the top of the basket after one or two pairs of leaves, but allow the shoots around the edges to grow longer, pinching after two or three pairs of leaves, to encourage the trailing habit. Overwinter plants in baskets at frost-free temperatures and prune back hard in spring. For general cultivation see p.149.

Many trailing and lax-growing varieties are suitable for hanging baskets. Two plants of *F.* 'Marinka' in a half basket will look like a red and purple waterfall when in full flower. Other favorites include *F.* 'Pink Marshmallow', *F.* 'Susan Green', *F.* 'Waverley Gem', *F.* 'La Campanella', *F.* 'Lena', *F.* 'Jack Shahan' and *F.* 'Cascade'. For those who admire triphylla types (with orange-red, long-tubed flowers), new *F.* 'Trumpeter' makes a good basket plant. Quite different from ordinary fuchsias is *F. procumbens*, a species of trailing habit from New Zealand, with long stems covered with small, rounded leaves. Flowers ½-¾in(1-2cm) long are small but striking. The tube is yellow, with maroon sepals and blue pollen. These are followed by large pinkish-red fruits. Happy in pots and baskets of well-drained soil, they can also be grown in tufa rock.
38-40°F(3-4°C) H&S:30in(75cm)

Hoya
(Asclepiadaceae)
Virtually any hoya can be grown as a trailing plant in a hanging basket, but branching, non-climbing species are particularly suitable. The main advantage to basket cultivation is that the exquisite form and delicate fragrance of the flowers can best be enjoyed at eye and nose level. For cultivation see p.87.
H. carnosa Variegated-leaved varieties of the wax flower look particularly good in hanging baskets. *H.c.* 'Variegata' has pink-suffused cream edges to its thick, dark green leaves.
40-45°F(4-7°C) H:5-6ft(1.5-1.8m) S:30in(75cm)
H. lanceolata ssp. bella The miniature wax flower, a non-climbing hoya which is an epiphyte in its native

India, is the most popular choice for a hanging basket. Branching stems arch slightly, then trail downward, making a rather gangly shape at first but becoming beautiful with the fullness of age, and more than compensated for by umbels of eight to ten white flowers with pink centers which appear during summer. The root system is not vigorous; plant in a comparatively small container and avoid repotting. Never allow the roots to dry out or remain waterlogged, as either extreme will result in dying roots and withered leaves. Use two or three young plants in a small hanging basket.
50°F(10°C) H&S:18in(45cm)
H. polyneura Fishtail hoya from the Himalayas is another branching, epiphytic hoya. Leaves are shaped like fishes' tails and loose umbels of six to eight rose-colored flowers are more interesting than showy.
38-40°F(3-4°C) H&S:24-30in(60-75cm)

Lotus
(Leguminosae)
The long stems and delicate, silvery, needle-like foliage of these trailing plants are bound to get noticed. Lotus need good light and careful watering. Allow the potting medium to dry out almost to the point at which the lotus starts to wilt before watering. Propagate by cuttings in midsummer, to yield plants which will flower during the early part of the following summer. Plant several in one basket for a full effect.
L. berthelotii Coral gem or parrot's beak is a native of Tenerife. This magnificent trailer has silvery branches

111

Lotus berthelotii

Nepenthes hybrid

and leaves which act as a perfect foil to the scarlet claw-shaped flowers. *L. maculatus* is similar, with silvery-green leaves; the flowers are a marvelous warm golden-yellow flushed with orange-brown. 36-40°F(2-4°C) H:36in(90cm) S:24in(60cm)

Nepenthes

(Nepenthaceae)
Often called tropical pitchers or monkey cups, these insect-eating plants grow as scrambling climbers in the jungles of the Far East, particularly Borneo. In cultivation, they usually sprawl out of wooden orchid baskets or hanging baskets. These plants are extraordinary, their lance-shaped leaves narrowing at the tip to a long tendril, which in turn ends in a pitcher-shaped structure complete with raised "lid"

and containing digestive fluid. Each plant generally has two sorts of pitcher: those that rest on the ground, and those which hang in the air, with a tendril gripping onto a support.

Originating from areas of high humidity, nepenthes appreciate a light mist-spray around their foliage several times a day and considerably more spray when the weather is hot. Shade from hot sun to prevent leaves and other parts from scorching. Always water from the top, for at no time should the plants be waterlogged. (Drying out at the roots can also prove fatal.) Nepenthes are unusual among insect-eating plants in that they benefit from feeding with a high-nitrogen liquid fertilizer (weekly in summer and monthly in winter). If using orchid fertilizer, apply as a foliar feed at half-strength. Plant in an open potting

mixture of, for example, two parts orchid bark, two parts perlite and one part peat moss. Place a good layer of broken pottery or expanded clay pebbles in the base of pots to improve drainage. Repot with care. Prune back large, ungainly plants in spring to within about 6in(15cm) of the base. Propagate by shoot-tip cuttings (side shoots with a heel give best results), or by stem sections each containing two nodes. Dip the ends into hormone rooting liquid before inserting into live sphagnum or vermiculite, then place in a warm, humid place out of direct light. Layering and air-layering are feasible alternatives, or grow from seed. Scale insect can be troublesome. When purchasing nepenthes, find out whether they are lowland or highland species, as this directly influences their temperature preferences.

LOWLAND NEPENTHES These are easy to grow during summer, provided high temperatures are matched by high humidity. However, winter temperatures need to remain above 60°F(16°C) for plants to continue growing. *N. ampullaria* has large, tub-like pitchers which sit on the ground and needs a large basket (like that used for waterlilies) to accommodate its rhizome. *N. rafflesiana* is perhaps the best choice for a beginner as it is both attractive and relatively easy to grow. Most forms have pale green pitchers spotted with red. The numerous hybrids are best treated as lowland types.
55-60°F(13-16°C) H:3-5ft(1-1.5m) S:3ft(1m)
HIGHLAND NEPENTHES Enjoying higher altitudes in the wild, these plants dislike heat during summer and need ventilation as well as high humidity when temperatures are above 70°F(21°C). Cooler winter temperatures are not only tolerated, but necessary. *N. alata* has narrow pitchers flushed with red. *N. ventricosa* bears a profusion of small pitchers.
46-55°F(8-13°C) H:3-5ft(1-1.5m) S:3ft(1m)

Nephrolepis
(Davalliaceae)
N. exaltata The ladder or Boston fern is an ideal candidate for a hanging basket or a jardinière. Elegant fronds arch out from the center of the plant and drape downward. Basic, ladder-like fronds are attractive enough, but numerous forms have more complicated, often ruffled or lacy-edged fronds. Always keep plants moist at the roots and in a humid atmosphere: hot, dry air will result in scorched, brown frond tips. Runners from the main plant root where they make contact with moist soil. Pot these new plants separately, or propagate by division or by spores (see p.29).
50°F(10°C) H&S:12-36in(30-90cm)

Oplismenus
(Gramineae)
O. africanus 'Variegatus' (*O. hirtellus* 'Variegatus') The variegated basket grass from southern USA to Argentina superficially resembles a tradescantia. Slender stems carry pale green, pointed leaves striped lengthwise with uneven white markings often tinged with pink. Plants trail over the top of a stand or colonize hanging baskets; use in numbers to skirt tables and benches. Eventually, insignificant but typically grass-like flowers reveal its true family identity. Propagate during spring and summer by cuttings, which root easily; plant three in a pot. Shade from hot sun which can scorch the leaves. If older plants become messy, start again with fresh cuttings.
50°F(10°C) H&S:12in(30cm)

Pelargonium
(Geraniaceae)
Trailing ivy-leaved geraniums contribute valuable splashes of summer color to the greenhouse. Each spring, plant baskets or wall planters, each containing one to five cuttings of the same variety. The choice of flower types is wide and there are different sizes of plant: choose more diminutive kinds like *P*. 'Lilac Gem', with its profusion of neat double pink flowers, for smaller containers. *P*. 'L'Elégante' is another favorite. A compact ivy-leaved variety, its variegated leaves are often tinged with pink when the plant is grown in a hot, sunny spot. Single flowers are pale lilac. The Harlequin series are pretty, their flowers, as the name might suggest, consisting of one color combined with white. *P*. 'Harlequin Rosie O'Day', for instance, has rose-pink and white flowers. Single-flowered varieties known as "cascades" or "trailers" include the popular *P*. 'Roi des Balcons Lilas' and shorter-jointed *P*. 'Rote Mini-Cascade'. *P*. 'Snow Queen' has double white flowers with small dots of purple on the upper petals. *P*. 'Tavira' and *P*. 'Yale' are good strong double reds. Different from ivy-leafs, *P*. 'Splendide' has lax trailing flower stems bearing cerise and white blooms. Cuttings can be taken either in spring, from overwintered stock, or during late summer. For cultivation see p.159.
36-40°F(2-4°C) H:12-30in(30-75cm)
S:12-24in(30-60cm)

Lotus maculatus

Platycerium
(Polypodiaceae)
The magnificent stag's-horn and elk's-horn ferns are guaranteed to draw attention. Growing epiphytically, they make two types of fronds. The shield-like infertile fronds wrap themselves around their tree-trunk support, trapping debris falling from the tree canopy above, which rots down into compost from which the plant feeds. Healthy green sterile fronds are a sign that the plant is enjoying the right amount of water, light, warmth and humidity. Some natural dieback occurs in winter, but if in summer they grow little and quickly turn brown, there is clearly a problem. The showy, antler-like fronds, usually covered in white felted scales, are fertile and will bear spores when mature. *P. bifurcatum*, from eastern Australia to Polynesia, and huge *P. superbum* (*P. grande*), from Australia, Java, and Malaysia, are the best known. Grow them in a hanging pot or, even better, against a slab of tree-fern fiber or bark. Hold small ferns in place with fishing line and thin wire. As more fronds form, building up a mass of dead fronds and debris behind the newest and healthiest, they become self-clinging. Shade from hot sun is essential. Feel inside the infertile fronds to determine whether watering is necessary: they should never be completely dry, but should not be continuously wet.

Platycerium bifurcatum

Plectranthus madagascariensis 'Variegated Mintleaf'

Stenotaphrum secundatum 'Variegatum'

Scirpus cernuus

Propagate by spores. Sometimes a small plant can be successfully separated from a colony. Scale insect can be a problem.
45°F(7°C) H:18-60in(45-150cm) S:36in(90cm)

Plectranthus
(Labiatae)
Swedish ivy or candle plants make useful, if not particularly exciting, trailing plants. Both species commonly cultivated become long-stemmed and straggly with age. Cut old plants hard back to generate a flush of fresh shoots, or take fresh cuttings, in spring and summer, and start again. Pinch back the tips of young plants at about 3in(8cm) high to encourage branching. Large baskets may need three or more plants. Spikes of small flowers are usually produced when plants become pot-bound, often to the detriment of the foliage.

***P. madagascariensis* 'Variegated Mintleaf'** Growth of this aromatic plant from southwest India is upright initially, but the brittle stems soon begin to trail downward. The dainty, hairy leaves with irregularly toothed edges have a generous white margin. An easy plant to grow, it can tolerate a certain amount of hot, dry air but appreciates shade from bright sun. Avoid sudden drops in temperature and drafts. Both this plant and *P. forsteri* 'Marginatus' are often wrongly called *P. coleoides* 'Marginatus'.
50°F(10°C) H:36in(90cm) S:18in(45cm)

P. oertendahlii This South African species sends out a chaotic mass of pinkish stems clad with soft, rounded leaves spotted with silver veins and with purple undersides. Shade from hot sun; plants are more tolerant than *P. madagascariensis* 'Variegated Mintleaf' of sudden temperature drops.
50°F(10°C) H&S:30in(75cm)

Portulaca
(Portulacaceae)
P. grandiflora The sun plant from Brazil, Uruguay and Paraguay has brightly colored, sometimes double, five-petaled flowers of white, red, pink, yellow or purple 1in(2.5cm) across, which aptly open in the sun and brighten up the greenhouse. Each flower boasts decorative yellow stamens. Trailing stems and leaves are succulent. Raise this annual from spring-sown seed, or plant pre-started, nursery-grown cuttings. Hang in a bright, sunny spot.
38°F(3°C) H&S:9in(23cm)

Saxifraga

(Saxifragaceae)

S. stolonifera (S. sarmentosa) Mother of thousands, Aaron's beard, roving sailor or strawberry geranium from China and Japan is a mat-forming plant. The numerous rounded olive-green leaves have silver veins, scalloped edges, and reddish-purple undersides. Long branching stolons bearing plantlets are produced from the center of the plant and, when unable to root into the ground, hang down like a long red curtain around the edge, terminating in a fringe of small plants. *S.s.* 'Tricolor' has white- and pink-edged leaves which are smaller and puckered. This variety needs warmer winter temperatures than *S. stolonifera*; avoid overwatering. Both need shade from strong sunlight. Vine weevil can be troublesome. Propagate by pegging runners down in potting medium or by detaching plantlets and placing in a cuttings starting mixture.
36-40°F(2-4°C) H:6-12in(15-30cm)
S:4-9in(10-23cm)

Scirpus

(Cyperaceae)

S. cernuus (Isolepis gracilis) The miniature bulrush is an attractive foliage plant with an arching mass of bright green stems which, when mature, look like a shock of green hair. When pale flowers are produced at the stem tips, it resembles a 1970's fiber optics lamp. This is a good specimen for a small hanging basket. It originates from wetland areas and can be grown in water as long as it is prevented from becoming stagnant. Keep plants moist and shade from hot, scorching sun. Propagate by division: gently pull an older plant into several sections and shorten long, floppy stems. Pot separately into small containers and water carefully while new roots are growing.
45-50°F(7-10°C) H:12in(30cm) S:9in(23cm)

Stenotaphrum

(Gramineae)

S. secundatum 'Variegatum' The variegated buffalo or St Augustine grass, from southern USA and Central and South America, has creeping stems which trail to cover table edges or dangle from a hanging basket. Flat, linear leaves are striped with creamy-white down their length. This plant can survive short periods of drought and bright light before brown patches appear on the leaves. Shading from hot sun is beneficial. Propagate by cuttings in spring and summer. Grow three young plants together.
40-45°F(4-7°C) H:18in(45cm) S:12in(30cm)

Streptocarpus

(Gesneriaceae)

Some caulescent or stem-forming streptocarpus make good trailers for pots and hanging baskets. Chief among these is *S. saxorum*, the false African violet, which originates from tropical East Africa. Plant a group in a medium-sized hanging basket: as they grow, the brittle hairy stems knit together, making mounds of growth which eventually tumble over the edges and trail downward. Oval, hairy leaves are fleshy and fragile. In summer, beautiful pale lilac flowers 1-1½in(2.5-4cm) wide are held away from the stems on long, thin stalks. Propagate by cuttings in spring and summer.
50°F(10°C) H:18in(45cm) S:12in(30cm)

Tolmiea

(Saxifragaceae)

T. menziesii The piggyback plant or youth-on-age from western North America is widely grown for its pretty bright green, hairy leaves and accommodating nature. Plantlets develop at the base of mature leaves and, if left on, weigh the leaves down to become a feature. *T.m.* 'Taff's Gold', with yellow marks on the leaves, needs more light to retain variegation; otherwise, shade lightly from hot sun. Propagate by pegging down a plantlet-bearing leaf until roots have developed. Alternatively, cut the leaf off with about 1in(2.5cm) of stalk attached and insert this into a pot of cuttings medium so that the leaf sits on the surface.
32-40°F(0-4°C) H&S:12in(30cm)

Tradescantia

(Commelinaceae)

Wandering Jews or inch plants are valuable for disguising the front of benches, or cascading from a shelf, wall planter or hanging basket. Although easy to grow, they need constant attention. Variegated sorts tend to revert: remove any green shoots. Pinch back stem tips to encourage branching; even so, old plants become leggy. Take cuttings, prune the old plant back hard and eventually replace it with a newer one. Shade in summer; hot, dry conditions result in scorched leaves. Cuttings root easily, either in water or by placing three cuttings into a 3½in(9cm) pot of potting medium.
50°F(10°C) H:12-36in(30-90cm)
S:12-18in(30-45cm)

T. fluminensis Among the best-known cultivars is *T.f.* 'Albovittata', which has long trailing stems bearing green leaves striped along their length with pale green and cream, good in a hanging basket. *T.f.* 'Quicksilver', with bluish-green leaves striped with silver, is more compact and does well both in a basket and as a foliage plant for benches. White flowers often appear at the ends of stems.

T. pallida 'Purpurea' (Setcreasea purpurea) Purple heart has brittle, wayward purple stems bearing slightly hairy lance-shaped leaves 4-6in(10-15cm) long, also purple and slightly fleshy. Pink flowers appear at the ends of stems in summer. Although brightly colored, this Mexican native is untidy and sprawling. Let it trail out of a wide clay pan.

T. sillamontana White velvet from Mexico tolerates hot dry conditions and is recommended for greenhouses ill-equipped with vents and shading. Both the stems and ranks of stiff leaves are densely covered with white, woolly hair. Upright at first, they flop over and begin to trail. Bright pink flowers contrast nicely with the silvery hairs. When they begin to get ragged, cut all the old stems away to make room for a burst of new shoots at the base of the plant. This species likes a well-drained soil. Root cuttings in equal parts of peat and sand.

T. zebrina (Zebrina pendula) Oval leaves 2in(5cm) long have a silver stripe running down the middle of each side of the leaf, leaving a green stripe down the vein and green edges. The undersides are purple and flowers pinkish-purple. Good in hanging baskets or wide pans.

Tropaeolum

(Tropaeolaceae)

T. majus 'Hermine Grashoff' This choice trailing nasturtium has double red flowers. Propagate by cuttings during late summer or from stock plants in spring. Plant several young plants in a hanging basket for a full effect.
38-40°F(3-4°C) H:18in(45cm) S:12in(30cm)

Tropaeolum majus 'Hermine Grashoff'

Smaller foliage plants

Foliage plants are those which are grown primarily for the effect of their leaves, though many of them will also produce flowers. Some qualify as specimens, at least when fully grown, but there is a whole battalion of useful small foliage plants which fill gaps, create leafy backdrops to highlight the individual blooms, and make a welcome rest for the eye between masses of color. Some of the most successfully planted sunrooms are those where foliage plants predominate, with relatively few flowers to confuse the intricate patterns of leaf and plant shapes. The soothing effect of greenery provides an antidote to stress and is of considerable benefit in any indoor environment.

Although there is dazzling variety among flowers, with their wide range of colors and forms, in many ways there is even greater diversity to be found in foliage. Every shade of green is represented, from the bright young fronds of maidenhair ferns and *Pteris cretica* 'Wimsettii' to the dark, almost black leaves of *Ludisia discolor* (*Anoectochilus discolor*). *Soleirolia soleirolii* 'Aurea' (the golden form of baby's tears) and golden-leaved pelargoniums like *P.* 'Gerald Portas' make pools of brightness between darker plants, creating the impression of continuous sunlight playing through the leaves of taller plants, just as it might through a gap in the forest canopy. Pale, silvery colors are supplied by *Sansevieria trifasciata* 'Moonshine' and the bulbous *Ledebouria socialis*, whose silvery leaves are blotched with olive green.

Leaving aside the tonal contrasts in the green range, foliage can almost match flowers for bright color. Red-leaved plants include *Iresine herbstii* 'Brilliantissima' and some of the stunning varieties of *Cordyline fruticosa*. Others, like coleus (*Solenostemon*), angel's wings (*Caladium bicolor*), crotons, and *Begonia rex* are highly colored, with green, cream, pink, and red predominating, often joined by yellow and orange. Some of these plants (coleus and *B.rex,* for instance) regularly produce flowers, but these detract from the foliage and are usually removed.

Intriguing textures and shapes add to the allure of foliage. Some plants have an irresistibly tactile quality. Soft furry leaves like those of velvet plant (*Gynura aurantiaca*) beg to be stroked and the fern-like leaflets of sensitive plant (*Mimosa pudica*) fold as if by magic at the lightest touch. Foliage can be needle-like in appearance, as in the heaths and various species of asparagus ferns (though these are strictly phylloclades, or modified branchlets). Some are crinkled like the leaves of *Peperomia caperata* and *Pilea involucrata* 'Moon Valley' or imposingly palmate as in *Fatsia japonica*. With their contrasts of lightness or solidity, of well-

defined outlines or more amorphous shapes, these leaf qualities add an extra dimension to the color palette for plant compositions.

Foliage can even compete with flowers in the olfactory stakes. Some leaves are aromatic especially when brushed against or lightly squeezed. Chief among these is lemon verbena (*Aloysia triphylla*) with its exquisite citrus smell. Some of the pelargonium tribe, notably *P. crispum* and *P.* 'Mabel Grey', can also reproduce the smell of lemons, while others are scented with spices, pine, or peppermint. Members of the ginger family (Zingiberaceae) have a different spicy perfume, with *Amomum compactum* one of the sweetest-smelling in both leaf and rhizome.

When smaller foliage plants are used to fill in gaps between larger specimens, or between flowering and fruiting plants, batches consisting of a number of plants of each type will be needed. Equally successful whether grown in small pots – generally up to 4in(10cm) in diameter – or planted in beds, different sorts of foliage can be used to greatest effect as underplantings or to divide one mass of flowering plants from the next. Where large pots brimming with flowers are set out on benches or on tables, foliage plants will fulfil the dual role of providing a green background to accentuate the flowers and of masking the containers.

Small-growers like the peperomias and pileas always look particularly good in groups of three, five, or more – preferably odd numbers – and are especially useful to separate similar small groups of flowering plants. To have a sufficient stock of these plants, a program of regular propagation is needed, with small batches of similarly sized plants being grown on continuously from cuttings or seed. As older plants become irrevocably pot-bound, they can be replaced by a fresh crop.

Other plants in the smaller foliage section deserve more individual treatment. They may not be large enough to qualify for key positions as specimen plants, but should be prominently displayed as they reach their peak of perfection. The many different species of begonia are included here as well as *Radermachera sinica* and *Asparagus densiflorus* 'Myers'. Many of these foliage plants are extremely versatile. A subject like baby's tears (*Soleirolia soleirolii*) can be pot-grown to make a marvelous domed specimen, or used as a diminutive creeping plant to colonize the gaps between flags.

Some predominantly foliage plants are fascinating because of the adaptations they have made in order to survive. Cacti and succulents, even though their flowers can be spectacular, are included in this section. The year-round attraction of their often bizarre swollen stems or leaves cannot be ignored. They are all the more striking when they are grouped together into a "landscape", a strategy which also facilitates meeting their specialized cultivation needs. Similarly, carnivorous plants have evolved various intriguing leaf modifications enabling them to trap and digest insects and other small creatures. The fact that many have either pretty or distinctive flowers is of secondary importance to the perennial fascination of their forms.

Plants grown primarily for their foliage can be as highly prized as those which produce beautiful and exotic blooms and, with such variations in leaf-shape and color, are of considerable ornamental value in the sunroom. Lush, well-grown plants such as these from the Marantaceae family make bold individuals, but are paticularly effective when arranged *en masse* to create a dramatic, jungle-like effect.

Aglaonema commutatum

Alocasia × amazonica

Alocasia cuprea

Adiantum

(Adiantaceae)

The maidenhair fern is prone to drying out at the roots, and will soon turn brown and wither away if neglected. To prevent this, pot newly bought ferns immediately. The fresh potting mix holds more water and there is less chance of drying out. Probably the most popular is the tropical American delta maidenhair, *A. raddianum* (*A. cuneatum*), H&S: 12in(30cm). There are many named varieties. *A.r.* 'Fragrantissimum' is large and vigorous in nature. *A.r.* 'Fritz Luthi' has pleasingly compact, almost lacy fronds. Some, like *A.r.* 'Micropinnulum' and *A.r.* 'Micropinnulum Mist', have much divided pinnae, giving a dainty, ethereal appearance. They prefer warmer temperatures, with a minimum of 45°F(7°C). For a cold or frost-free greenhouse, hardier *A. capillus-veneris*, the common maidenhair, is similar in size and appearance. By contrast, *A. trapeziforme*, H&S:24in(60cm), has long, elegant fronds bearing large, trapeziform pinnules. This needs a warmer minimum of 50-55°F(10-13°C). Provide all plants with shade and humidity. Propagate by spores or division.

Aglaonema

(Araceae)

Known variously as painted drop tongue, Chinese evergreen or golden evergreen, these striking foliage plants grown for their lush ornamental leaves are easily scorched and bleached by the sun. Grow them in a shady greenhouse, or where thick blinds or the leaves of other plants provide shading. Encouraged to grow into clumps by feeding and regular potting up (in spring and summer) they make fine specimen plants. Greenish-cream flowers are insignificant but interesting. Maintain humidity during high summer temperatures and when heating causes dry air in winter. Propagate by cuttings of healthy 4in(10cm) long shoot tips, by detaching a basal shoot with some root attached, or by air-layering. Even 2in(5cm) long chunks of stem will root and sprout if inserted vertically or nestled horizontally into rooting mixture. Old, untidy plants can be cut back hard to within 2in(5cm) of the base in spring: in a light place, the stumps will quickly regenerate.

55-60°F(13-16°C) H:18-24in(45-60cm) S:18in(45cm)

A. commutatum This species, native to the Philippines, has 8in(20cm) long, dark green leaves with silvery markings but is more often represented in cultivation by *A.c.* 'Treubii', whose elegant leaves are grayish-green blotched with yellow. The fast-growing golden evergreen, *A.c.* 'Pseudobracteatum' is also popular for deep green leaves splashed in the middle with cream and marbled with light green and yellow.

A. 'Malay Beauty' A striking foliage color combination of deep green with mottling of white, tinged with green and cream.

A. nitidum 'Curtisii' This Malayan plant is more thick-set, its attractive blue-green leaves overlaid with a silvery feather-shaped pattern.

A. nitidum × A. pictum Hybridizing between these species has given rise to two popular aglaonemas. *A.* 'Silver Queen' has bright green leaves paneled with grayish-silver streaked with green. *A.* 'Silver King' suckers freely, making many short stems crowded with silver-painted green leaves: position this plant low to appreciate its splendid tuft of foliage.

Alocasia

(Araceae)

These amazingly lush foliage plants can look magnificent if given the right combination of heat, humidity, and shade. Although they love moisture at the roots, this can cause problems if the soil is too heavy or the temperature too low. Adding coarse peat (or peat substitute) and sharp sand to their soil is a good plan. Most have underground rhizomes which, planted in a bed, will spread to make a good clump. Propagate by division, by cutting rhizomes into smaller sections, or by removal of offsets in spring.
55-60°F(13-16°C)

A. × amazonica This is arguably the most striking, with arrow-shaped, wavy-edged leaves of shiny, deep green. The veins and leaf edges are picked out with strong white markings.
H:30-36in(75-90cm) S:24in(60cm)

A. cuprea The giant caladium from Borneo has almost oval, dark green leaves with raised, wonderfully metallic greenish-gray areas between the veins. Undersides are purple.
H&S:36in(90cm)

A. korthalsii Also from Borneo, this plant has leaves of a grayish olive-green, the veins outlined in grayish-white in the same manner as *A. × amazonica* but without the scalloped edges. Undersides purple.
H&S:36in(90cm)

A. macrorrhiza The giant elephant's ear or taro is an imposing plant from Sri Lanka and Malaysia. Leaves are a glossy green with prominent veins and wavy edges, reaching up to 36in(90cm) long on stems the same length. These make magnificent plants when grown well, but have an unfortunate habit of flopping over. A variegated form has large cream and gray markings on the leaves.
H:10ft(3m) S:6ft(1.8m)

Aloysia

(Verbenaceae)

A. triphylla (A. citriodora, Lippia citriodora) The lemon verbena, from which verbena oil is extracted, is known for its scented foliage. The mid-green, tapering leaves grow in whorls of three or sometimes in opposite pairs. Panicles of tiny, pale lilac flowers are produced during late summer and fall. Aloysia is

deciduous; when it begins growing in spring, prune back hard to retain a compact shape. Propagate by cuttings taken in spring or summer, or by seed. Watch out for whitefly and spider mite as they can be troublesome.
32-40°F(0-4°C) H:3-6ft(1-1.8m) S:3-4ft(1-1.2m)

Amomum

(Zingiberaceae)

A. compactum (A. cardamomum) This native of Java, with its attractive foliage, blends well into a display of more spectacular plants. Stems grow from a rhizome and are covered with slender, pointed lanceolate leaves. The leaves, rhizome, and roots are sweetly aromatic when damaged. Propagate by division in spring. Plants can be grown in a border or pot. Shade from hot sun and spray mist to increase humidity, which will deter spider mite.
50°F(10°C) H:36in(90cm) S:24-30in(60-75cm)

Anoectochilus

(Orchidaceae)

These beautiful, terrestrial, jewel orchids from tropical Asia, Australia, and Polynesia grow from creeping, branching rhizomes, producing almost velvety-textured leaves with colored veins and other markings. The closely related *Ludisia discolor* (*Goodyera discolor, Anoectochilus discolor*) from China has superb 2-4in(5-10cm) long, dark green, almost black leaves lined along their length with narrow pink veins. Give reasonable, steady warmth and light shade from direct sun. Careful watering is essential, so that roots are allowed almost to dry out between waterings but never remain so for long. Spikes of small, creamy-white and yellow flowers are produced. Ordinary peat-based soil (or a peat alternative) suits them. Pot up when necessary in late spring. Propagate by removing rooted rhizome sections at potting time, or encourage 3-4in(8-10cm) shoot-tip cuttings to root by laying them down in moist, loose potting mixture under warm, humid conditions. *A. setaceus (A. regalis)*, the king orchid from Java and Sri Lanka, is similar but with golden veins.
55°F(13°C) H:6in(15cm) S:18in(45cm)

Anthurium

(Araceae)

A. crystallinum The crystal anthurium from Peru and Colombia is a showy foliage plant that needs more warmth and humidity than the average greenhouse or home can provide. It is an ideal accompaniment to a collection of tropical orchids. An epiphyte, it can be attached to tree branches with a handful of sphagnum moss covering its roots and tied on with nylon fishing line. Plants will grow in pots or beds provided the soil is open and never waterlogged. It produces heart-shaped leaves 10-15in(25-40cm) long, which are

Anthurium crystallinum

pinkish-red as they unfold but become deep green overlaid with a pattern of silvery-white veins. An even temperature is important while a leaf unfolds, as fluctuations can affect the growth of the delicate new blade, though drops to 55°F(13°C) can be tolerated. Shade is vital during summer. Propagate by division in spring.
60°F(16°C) H:30in(75cm) S:24in(60cm)

Asparagus

(Liliaceae/Asparagaceae)

Asparagus are excellent for bringing fern-like foliage into the greenhouse when conditions are too dry or bright for true ferns. The "leaves" are in fact needle-like branches or phylloclades. Insignificant, greenish-white flowers followed by berries are often produced and some species can develop nasty thorns. Roots are fleshy and capable of storing moisture but though drought-tolerant, plants need thorough watering as soon as the soil surface dries out. Plants will tolerate bright light, but light shade will keep leaves an attractive bright green. Seed of most kinds is readily available and easy to germinate. Hard and round, it is best soaked in tepid water for 24 hours prior to sowing at 60-70°F(16-21°C). Divide mature plants in spring or summer.

A. densiflorus 'Myers' The growth of the compact foxtail fern emanates from the center of the plant in dense tails. Best started from seed, pot young plants

Begonia rex 'Vista' and *B.r.* 'Venetian Red'

Begonia masoniana

up to a larger-sized pot each spring.
36-40°F(2-4°C) H:36in(90cm) S:30in(75cm)
A. *falcatus* The sicklethorn from Sri Lanka and South Africa has a very different appearance from some of the more common types. Individual bright green phylloclades are flatter and, coupled with the twining, upright habit of the stems, give the whole plant a somewhat oriental image.
36-40°F(2-4°C) H:8ft(2.5m) S:3ft(1m)
A. *setaceus* (**A.** *plumosus*) Commonly known as asparagus fern, this native of South Africa is popular as a florists' pot plant. The species is a climbing plant and will need a small trellis or a couple of canes. Beware of the sharp, recurving prickles. Flowers are often produced, followed by purplish-black fruits. *A.s.* 'Compactus' and *A.s.* 'Nanus' are not climbing and produce arching stems which are more frond-like.
36-40°F(2-4°C) H:8ft(2.5m) S:3ft(1m) climbing H&S:24in(60cm) not climbing

Aspidistra
(Liliaceae/Convallariaceae)
A. *elatior* This popular houseplant from China will provide handsome foliage for the greenhouse if given shade from bright sun and high levels of humidity. This will help deter spider mite. Plants can be grown in pots or beds and produce lush, dark green, long-stalked leaves up to 36in(90cm) in length. Clumps eventually become crowded and should be divided and repotted in spring. Sometimes strange, small purple flowers are produced at the surface of the soil, which in the wild would be pollinated by slugs. There is a variegated form, with cream stripes of irregular width, but some leaves are hardly variegated at all, while others are half cream, half green.
40°F(4°C) H:36in(90cm) S:24in(60cm)

Begonia
(Begoniaceae)
All begonias produce flowers but some are equally noteworthy for their attractive foliage. They make successful greenhouse plants if given shade from bright sun. Begonias are seldom long-lived and need

frequent propagation or pruning to replace and regenerate old stock. Occasional drops in temperature to 45°F(7°C) or even 40°F(4°C) can be tolerated if the roots are not wet at the time, but warmer minimum temperatures of 50-55°F(10-13°C) are appreciated. Mildew can be a problem.
B. *bowerae* The eyelash begonia is a diminutive rhizomatous species from Mexico. Its small, bright green leaves have dark brown markings toward their edges and a fringe of white hairs. Small white or pink flowers are borne above the foliage in late winter and early spring. Propagate either by dividing the rhizomes, or by leaf cuttings in spring or summer. Cut whole leaves with a portion of leaf stem attached, then insert, so that the underside is in contact with moist, loose potting mixture. Plants are better displayed in pans rather than pots.
B. 'Leopard' and *B.* 'Tiger Paws' are similar.
50°F(10°C) H:4-6in(10-15cm) S:8-10in(20-25cm)
B. × *corallina* '**Lucerna**' This popular "cane" begonia bred in Switzerland is grown for both its leaves and flowers. As a foliage plant, its large, silver-spotted leaves are attractive year-round. Given good light and

growing conditions, large pendent clusters of pink flowers appear sporadically throughout the year. Propagate by cuttings in spring or summer. Plants benefit from hard pruning.
40°F(4°C) H:3-6ft(1-1.8m) S:18-30in(45-75cm)

B. × erythrophylla (B. feastii) The handsome beefsteak begonia has shiny dark green, almost rounded leaves with dark red undersides. Stalks of pale pink flowers rise above the foliage during spring. *B. × e.* 'Bunchii' has crested, frilly leaves. *B. × e.* 'Helix' is the taller whirlpool begonia, with leaves twisted into a spiral. When plants become leggy, use the stem tip as a cutting as well as taking sections of rhizome, each containing at least one node. Nestle horizontally into loose potting mixture until half-buried.
50°F(10°C) H:12in(30cm) S:15in(40cm)

B. masoniana The iron cross begonia, a rhizomatous species from southeast Asia, has bright lime-green, puckered leaves 6-8in(15-20cm) long with a bold, dark brown marking. This is not the easiest of species to grow and will appreciate a warm, humid greenhouse. Avoid overwatering. Propagate by sections of rhizome 2-3in(5-8cm) long in spring or by leaf cuttings in the same way as for *B. rex*.
(10°C)50°F H&S:18in(45cm)

B. metallica The shrubby metal leaf begonia from Brazil is grown for both its foliage and its flowers. Shiny, bronze-green leaves 4-6in(10-15cm) long are veined with dark green on the surface and have reddish undersides. Stems of pale pink flowers with red hairs appear during summer and fall. As growth can be untidy, staking is sometimes required. Propagate by cuttings in spring and summer.
45°F(7°C) H:24-36in(60-90cm) S:18-24in(45-60cm)

B. rex This rhizomatous species from India has large, heart-shaped leaves 6-10in(15-25cm) long. Most of the plants are hybrids raised from seed. They have dark green or maroon leaves with brighter silvery-pink or green markings on puckered areas between the veins. Leaves are slightly hairy and the veins stand out prominently on the undersides. There are a number of excellent named varieties, including 'Raspberry Swirl' with deep red leaves. Most growers remove flowers when they are produced. Although the plants are shade-tolerant, good light is needed for healthy growth. Warmth and humidity encourage large, beautiful leaves. Propagate by leaf cuttings or by surface-sown seed early in the year.
55°F(13°C) H&S:12-18in(30-45cm)

B. scharffii (B. haageana) The elephant's ear begonia from Brazil is worth growing for both foliage and flowers. Pointed, mid-green leaves 4-10in(10-25cm) long are covered in fine hairs. Large bunches of pale pink flowers appear continually throughout the year. Taller plants usually need staking. Propagate by cuttings in spring and summer.
45°F(7°C) H:24-48in(60-120cm) S:24in(60cm)

Cacti and other succulents

A collection of cacti and other succulents, with their variety of shape and character, provides an attraction throughout the year. Most, grown well, have the added bonus of flowers. For cultivation see p.49.

Adenium (Apocynaceae)
The desert rose from east Africa, *A. obesum*, must be a fine sight in its native habitat. In order to grow successfully in cultivation these succulents need a warm greenhouse. They are chunky little plants, H:18-36in(45-90cm) S:12in(30cm), with swollen stems and glossy, deep green leaves. Bright pink flowers like those of mandevilla open in summer.
55°F(13°C)

Aeonium (Crassulaceae)
These succulents, many of which come from the Canary Islands, are worth growing for their pleasingly compact rosettes of leaves as well as their yellow or white flowers. Many make most of their growth between fall and spring, becoming dormant in midsummer. *A. arboreum*, H&S:24in(60cm), from Portugal, Spain, Sicily, Morocco, and Sardinia, has tree-like stems terminating in rosettes of bright green, shiny leaves, with panicles of yellow flowers appearing from late winter to early spring. The purple leaves of *A.a.* 'Atropurpureum' and almost black of *A.* 'Zwartkop' are even more striking. *A. tabuliforme*, H:3in(8cm) S:9-12in(23-30cm), from Tenerife, makes a wide, flat rosette of tightly packed green leaves. In its second or third year, this rises, dome-like, until elongated into a spike of yellow flowers. The plant then dies. As these large rosettes almost always cover the whole surface of the pot, water from below. Leaves can be damaged if water is allowed to settle on the rosette so set the plant at an angle when potting. Propagate by seed or leaf cuttings.
40°F(4°C)

Aichryson (Crassulaceae)
A. × domesticum 'Variegatum' is a variegated hybrid of two Canary Islands species. A small, shrubby plant, H:6in(15cm) S:10in(25cm), the stems are pink with hairy green and cream leaves, arranged in rosettes. Leaves on some rosettes are almost entirely cream and, occasionally, leaves are tinged with pink. Yellow flowers appear in spring and summer. These plants are easy to grow in a well-drained soil. Individual rosettes can be used as cuttings.
38°F(3°C)

Aeonium 'Zwartkop'

Aloe aristata

Astrophytum ornatum

Echinofossulocactus zacatecasensis

Cacti and other succulents

Aloe (Liliaceae/Aloeaceae)

Aloe barbadensis (*A. vera*) is the most commonly available species yet the smaller aloes are also attractive. The South African *A. aristata*, lace aloe or torch plant, H:4in(10cm) S:6-12in(15-30cm), quickly makes a clump of rosettes, each leaf terminating in a thread-like tip. Dark green, they are dotted with white markings and softly toothed along the edges. Orange flowers appear in spring. *A. variegata*, the tiger aloe, is H:12in(30cm) S:7in (17cm). Plump and handsome, it has triangular, white-banded, gray-green leaves. Pink flowers appear in spring. *A. burgersfortensis*, H:8in(20cm) S:18in(45cm), is less well known. Long, thick leaves arch out from the main rosette and bend down, curving under at the tips. Attractive whitish markings run down their length like stretched dots and in full sun they turn reddish-brown. Propagate by seed or offsets.
38°F(3°C)

Astrophytum (Cactaceae)

These fascinating Mexican cacti produce yellow flowers at the top of their globular or cylindrical bodies. Their cultivation is more difficult than that of most cacti. Their root systems tend to be poor and, as

a result, overwatering may prove fatal. *A. asterias*, H&S:3-4in(8-10cm), the sea urchin or sand dollar cactus, looks like a sea urchin without spines or perhaps a pincushion waiting for pins. There are eight ribs, each studded with a line of white areoles. Bright yellow flowers are produced in summer. *A. capricorne*, H:4-8in(10-20cm) S:4in(10cm), is known as the goat's horn cactus, presumably on account of the curved spines sprouting out of the areoles. *A. myriostigma*, H:6-12in(15-30cm) S:4-8in(10-20cm), bishop's cap cactus, usually has five ribs patterned with white scales. *A. ornatum*, H:6in(15cm) S:5in(13cm), the star cactus, is well armed, its eight ribs carrying areoles of five to eleven spines up to 1½in(4cm) long. Astrophytums are propagated by seed.
40°F(4°C)

Cotyledon (Crassulaceae)

These unusual-looking succulents, H&S:12-20in (30-50cm), are mostly represented in cultivation by *C. undulata*, the silver crown from South Africa. Large, wavy-edged leaves look like fans of coral, particularly as they are produced in opposite, almost parallel ranks. When handling, take care not to damage the white floury wax which covers the leaves. Long flower stems bear orange flowers in summer or fall, which marks the beginning of their growing season. Water modestly during winter and enough during summer

to prevent shriveling. Propagate by seed or cuttings.
40°F(4°C)

Crassula (Crassulaceae)

Crassulas make most of their growth during winter. One of the most popular is *C. ovata* (*C. portulacea*, *C. argentea*), H:36in(90cm) S:30in(75cm), known as the money or jade plant. A tree-like stem structure is topped by a "canopy" of succulent, sometimes red-edged, oval leaves. In good light, heads of starry white flowers are produced in fall or winter, which is when most growth takes place. *C.o.* 'Hummel's Sunset' has dramatic yellow-striped leaves edged with orange-red. *C. lycopodioides*, H:12in(30cm) S:9in(23cm), is the extraordinary watch-chain crassula or rat tail plant. Small, pointed leaves overlap each other, scale-like, to hide the long, upright stems. Tiny yellow flowers of rather unpleasant odor appear during spring and summer. Slight shade will prevent leaves from browning in summer. *C. multicava*, H&S:12in(30cm), makes a branching plant grown primarily for its pale pink spring flowers. These make a haze over rather ordinary succulent leaves. As flowers fade, small plantlets sprout from the inflorescence. These can be pulled off and planted in trays of potting mix to root. *C. schmidtii*, H:4in(10cm) S:12in(30cm), is low-growing with small, narrow, neat leaves which turn reddish in hot sun. Spreading to fill its pot, the plant will be smothered in masses of marvelous rose-pink flowers in fall and winter. 38°F(3°C)

Echeveria (Crassulaceae)
This splendid Mexican genus contains handsome plants grown for foliage and flowers. Growth is made during summer. *E. secunda* var. *glauca*, H:2-3in (5-8cm) S:4in(10cm), is the blue echeveria which forms a clump of glaucous, blue-gray rosettes. Spikes of bright red flowers appear during early summer. *E. harmsii*, H:8-12in(20-30cm) S:8-10in(20-25cm), is an upright, branching plant with spatula-shaped leaves which form toward the ends of stems. Quite large, tubular yellow-tipped red flowers appear during early summer. Propagate by seed, stem or leaf cuttings. 38°F(3°C)

Echinocereus (Cactaceae)
These showy cacti from Mexico and Texas have purple-pink flowers 3-5in(8-13cm) across. Although the flowers are similar, there are two forms of this plant, those with dense, comb-like spines virtually covering the whole plant and more open kinds with clear spaces between the spines. *E. pentalophus*, H:12in(30cm) S:24in(60cm), from Mexico has clumps of green stems 1½in(4cm) in diameter bearing bright pink flowers with pale centers 5in(13cm) across. A long, dry winter rest period followed by regular watering and feeding during summer will produce the best flowers. Propagate by seed or cuttings in early summer. 40°F(4°C)

Echinofossulocactus (Cactaceae)
Easy to grow, these wavy-ribbed cacti from Mexico bear their flowers early in the season when surprisingly small and young. They need an earlier start than most cacti, so begin regular watering in late winter. *E. zacatecasensis* (now correctly *Stenocactus multicostatus*), H&S:4in(10cm), found near Zacatecas, is known as brain cactus. A handsome plant with many sinuous ribs, the upper areoles are well furnished with dense white wool. White flowers tipped with pink are 1½in(4cm) across. 40°F(4°C)

Echinopsis (Cactaceae)
The sea urchin cacti, particularly *E. rhodotricha*, from Argentina and Paraguay are widely cultivated and plants readily produce offsets. Blooms are spectacular, being 6in(15cm) long including the tube, 3in(8cm) wide and white, sometimes tinged with pale pink. Easy to grow and flower, plants can reach H:(60cm)24in S:8in(20cm) if potted up when necessary. *E. hertrichiana* (*Lobivia hertrichiana*),

H:4in(10cm), bears scarlet flowers 3in(8cm) long and 2in(5cm) wide. Offsets are readily produced and can be planted in spring or summer. 40°F(4°C)

Faucaria (Aizoaceae)
F. tigrina, H:4in(10cm) S:12in(30cm), known as the tiger jaws plant, hails from the Cape of South Africa. Succulent leaves, vaguely triangular in shape, emerge in pairs from the center of each crown like a pair of tightly clamped jaws with teeth neatly interlocking. Olive-green leaves covered with small white spots are reddish toward the tips and the soft teeth are pink. Yellow, daisy-like flowers appear in fall. Propagate by seed, placing several seedlings together in one large pan. Severing through the short stem and rooting sections to separate is more difficult. 38°F(3°C)

Ferocactus (Cactaceae)
The giant barrel cacti of North American and Mexican deserts are bold plants armed with ferocious spines. *F. latispinus,* devil's tongue, can grow slowly to H:8in(20cm) S:15in(40cm). It has large areoles on the ribs, from which grow three different sorts of spines. The outer and upper six are thin and whitish, the central six are straight, reddish, and needle-like, while the longer, thicker central spine is flattened and

hooked at the tip. Ferocactus thrive on a plentiful supply of water and regular feeding during summer. Pot up when spines touch edge of pot. 38°F(3°C)

Frithia (Aizoaceae)
F. pulchra from the African Transvaal is like a better known but less available plant called fenestraria or baby toes. In the desert, their leaves are almost buried in the soil. These small and stumpy plants leave the minimum amount of surface area exposed to hot, dry air, but can absorb light into the whole leaf through window-like or transparent tops. As light in the greenhouse is not so bright as in the desert, the whole plant (above its roots) should be exposed to light. Growth takes place in winter, when watering should be modest but careful. Water sparingly during summer to prevent shriveling. An established frithia, H:1in(2.5cm) S:3in(8cm), will produce pink flowers ¾in(2cm) across with white centers in summer. Propagate by seed or division. 45°F(7°C)

Gasteria (Liliaceae/Aloeaceae)
There are many gasterias, mostly from southern Africa. *G. carinata* var. *verrucosa*, H:4in(10cm) S:10in(25cm), the wart gasteria or ox tongue, is probably the most common. Two ranks of long,

Echeveria secunda var. *glauca*

Cacti and other succulents

thick, white-speckled leaves with incurved edges are decorated by spikes of orange-green flowers in spring and early summer. *G. bicolor* var. *liliputana*, H:3in(8cm) S:4in(10cm), is smaller, with leaves arranged in more of a spiral rosette. Dark green in color, they are striped, marbled and spotted with pale green and white. *G. batesiana* is a strange sight, its dark leaves spotted with white. Propagate by seed or division.
38°F(3°C)

Haworthia (Liliaceae/Aloeaceae)

These South African succulents vary in shape and form. Some, like *H. pumila* (*H. margaritifera*), the pearl plant, H:3-4in(8-10cm) S:6in(15cm), make neat rosettes. It has rich green leaves spotted with white bumps and looks handsome once a colony of rosettes is established. Others like *H. reinwardtii* have longer stems, in this case 6in(15cm) tall and clothed with long, tapering, incurving leaves dotted with white bumps. Some haworthias look more like geological formations than plants. *H. truncata*, H:³⁄₄in(2cm) S:4in(10cm), has stumpy blue-green leaves which poke through the soil like rocks in strata formation. Propagate by seed or division.
45°F(7°C)

Kalanchoe (Crassulaceae)

Some kalanchoes are tall, making them ideal focal points for groupings with smaller succulents. The following are native to Madagascar. *K. beharensis*, H:48in(120cm) S:24in(60cm), is the majestic velvet leaf. Golden-russet, felted leaves 7in(17cm) long and of roughly triangular shape grow in opposite pairs. They wither and fall from the bottom as plants grow, leaving behind triangular scar patterns. There are two kalanchoes, H:24-36in(60-90cm) S:12in(30cm), which produce plantlets on their leaves. *K. daigremontiana* is the devil's backbone or Mexican hat plant whose toothed and attractively marked leaves sport plantlets all along their edges. Pink flowers appear in winter. *K. delagonensis* (*K. tubiflora*), the chandelier plant, has cylindrical leaves with plantlets at the tips. Pretty orange flowers open in late winter. *K. tomentosa*, H:20in(50cm) S:12in(30cm), earns the name panda plant by having rosettes of oval leaves covered with hairs, which are mostly silver but brown at the edges. Propagate by seed, plantlets, or cuttings.
38°F(3°C)

Kleinia (Compositae)

K. articulata (*Senecio articulatus*),the candle plant, H:12in(30cm) S:8in(20cm), is a strange-looking plant with long- or short-jointed, gray-green stems bearing tufts of similarly colored, three- to five-lobed leaves at the top. Growth is mainly in the winter. For best results water infrequently in summer and modestly

during winter. Use sections of stem as cuttings. Hawkweed-like flowers are produced from spring to fall. *K. neriifolia* (*Senecio neriifolius*), H:4-5ft(1.2-1.5m) S:30-36in(75-90cm), is a bit like a giant version of the candle plant with thick stems and narrow, blue-green leaves at the top. In silvery *K. haworthii* (*K. tomentosa*, now correctly *Senecio haworthii*), H:9in(23cm) S:7in(18cm), both stems and succulent cylindrical leaves are covered in densely woven white felt. Propagate by seed or cuttings.
38°F(3°C)

Lampranthus (Aizoaceae)

L. deltoides (*Oscularia deltoides*, *Mesembryanthemum deltoides*) is a pretty succulent from Africa which has pairs of chunky, glaucous, slightly toothed leaves of a neat, angular shape. They are held on low, sprawling stems. Fragrant pink daisy-like flowers appear in summer. H:6in(15cm) S:30in(75cm). Propagate by seed or cuttings.
38°F(3°C)

Lithops (Aizoaceae)

These are the amazing living stones or mimicry plants which blend into the surface of their pebble-strewn native deserts. Most come from southern Africa. Each stem consists of two swollen leaves fused together with a split in the top. There are many species, which germinate readily from seed. Sow in summer, leaving the seedlings in their pot through winter. The following summer, space small plants in a clay pan of well-drained soil. Top off with a layer of gravel and small stones. In two to three years they will have reached a respectable size, H:1in(2.5cm) S:2in(5cm). Do not water from fall till spring. During summer, water modestly. Soon after their first watering of the season, a new pair of leaves thrusts its way through the split in the old. Some begin to form clumps, with two pairs of leaves pushing through. Daisy-like white or yellow flowers which open in the sun appear in late summer.
40°F(4°C)

Mammillaria (Cactaceae)

There is sufficient diversity within this mostly Mexican genus to build up an interesting collection. Most species are undemanding, needing little encouragement to produce their characteristic rings of flowers around the top of the plant. *M. bombycina* multiplies quickly, given plenty of space, sending up offsets around the base to form a large clump. The white radial spines give them a silvery appearance. Central spines are russet-tipped, the lowest hooked. Small flowers are red. *M. carmenae* is softer, with flattish starbursts of pale gold spines covering the plant. *M. bocasana* is called the powder puff or snowball cactus on account of its many silky hairs.

Rebutia menesesii

Flowers are pale yellow. In contrast, *M. elongata* or lace cactus makes a clump of finger-thick stems densely covered with pale yellow to orange-red spines. One of the most striking in full bloom is the compact *M. zeilmanniana*, the rose pincushion. The dark green body shines through the many white spines and fewer, hook-tipped, reddish-brown spines. Offsets are produced all over the plant. Bright purple-pink flowers, ¾in(2cm) long, are borne in great profusion.
40°F(4°C)

Pachyphytum (Crassulaceae)

The Mexican *P. oviferum*, H:4in(10cm) S:9in(23cm), known as moonstones or sugar almond plant, has crowded egg-shaped leaves of a ghostly glaucous blue color. Interesting flowers appear in the spring. Propagate by stem or leaf cuttings.
45°F(7°C)

Parodia (Cactaceae)

This cactus (formerly classified as *Notocactus*) has its origins in South America. The most widely grown is probably *P. leninghausii*, which, when mature, reaching H:36in(90cm) S:12in(30cm), looks endearingly like a group of owls. Called the golden ball cactus, it does not remain ball-like for long, soon becoming cylindrical. Pale, golden-yellow spines give it a lovely color. *P. magnifica* remains rounded for longer and is beautifully formed with clearly defined ribs of glaucous green. Areoles along the edges make a continuous line of short, creamy-colored wool and relatively soft spines. Both of these species are yellow-flowered but others have blooms of orange, pink, lilac, or purple produced at the top of the plant. Parodias benefit from occasional watering during winter.
40°F(4°C)

Rebutia (Cactaceae)

These cacti (including later-flowering species formerly called sulcorebutias) from Bolivia and Argentina flower when small, producing bright blooms around their base. Individually, flowers are about 1in(2.5cm) in diameter and almost dwarf the diminutive plants. Rebutias start flowering in early spring.
40°F(4°C)

Sedum (Crassulaceae)

Known, generally, as stonecrops, this genus contains some easily recognizable favorites including *S. × rubrotinctum*, known as Christmas cheer. In strong light, leaves turn brilliant red. The jelly bean plant, *S. pachyphyllum*, which has pale green leaves with red tips, is similar. The leaves of both species snap off at the slightest touch and often land in neighboring pots, taking root and growing.
38°F(3°C) H:7in(17cm) S:6in(15cm)

Kalanchoe tomentosa

Lithops pseudotruncatella var. *archerae*

Pachyphytum oviferum

Sedum × rubrotinctum

Caladium

(Araceae)

Most of the beautiful angel's wings in cultivation are hybrids of *C. bicolor* from tropical America and the West Indies. All have spectacular heart-shaped leaves sprouting from an underground tuber on long, colorful stalks. Leaves are paper-thin and can be translucent white with green veins, green with pink veins and spots of white, pink with green veins, green with a glowing pink center, or green with spots and splashes of pink and white. Plants need humid temperatures of 70-75°F(21-24°C) and will fade away if a minimum of 60-65°F(16-18°C) cannot be maintained. Avoid cold drafts. Plant corms 1in(2.5cm) deep in 4-5in(10-13cm) pots, then place in a plant incubator heated to a minimum of 70°F(21°C). Leave here until summer temperatures have risen sufficiently. Although they need good light, shade them from direct sun. At the end of summer, plants die down and can be kept dry. Keep them in their pots at 60°F(16°C). Water once or twice during winter to prevent shriveling. Propagate by removing small tubers in spring.
60°F(16°C) H&S:12-20in(30-50cm)

Calathea

(Marantaceae)

These plants are useful for filling gaps in displays.

Calathea makoyana

Handsome leaves are marked in a variety of ways. Shade and humidity are essential to prevent leaves from scorching and to deter spider mite. Calatheas prefer soft water. A well-drained soil is essential. Propagate by division.

C. lancifolia (C. insignis of gardens) The rattlesnake plant has narrow, neat leaves 6in(15cm) long with alternating long and short dark green markings either side of the midrib. Undersides are maroon.
55-60°F(13-16°C) H&S:9in(23cm)

C. majestica (C. ornata) Upright, dark green leaves are striped with pinkish-white lines along the lateral veins on both sides of the leaf. This is more pronounced in *C.m.* 'Roseolineata' and *C.m.* 'Sanderiana'. Undersides are purple.
55-60°F(13-16°C) H&S:18in(45cm)

C. makoyana The tall, striking peacock plant, or cathedral windows, has upright, papery leaves on long stalks.
55-60°F(13-16°C) H&S:24in(60cm)

C. roseopicta This small, neat calathea has almost rounded leaves, up to 8in(20cm) long, which sit flat. They are pink-edged and almost seem to have the picture of a second leaf etched in cream over the mid-green surface.
55-60°F(13-16°C) H:10in(25cm) S:12-15in(30-40cm)

C. zebrina The zebra plant is a handsome calathea of varying height; specimens grow taller when planted out than when confined to pots. Bright green leaves have even, symmetrical marks running parallel to the lateral veins. Undersides are purple.
55-60°F(13-16°C) H&S:24in(60cm)

Cordyline

(Agavaceae)

C. fruticosa (C. terminalis) The ti or goodluck plant comes from tropical Asia and Polynesia, where many uses are made of its ribbon-like, tapering green leaves. As greenhouse plants, the colored-leaved forms are more popular and are most effective when grouped together. Colors vary from crimson or crimson edgings to pink or green variegations. Plants do best in warm, constant temperatures with good humidity. Shade from scorching sun during summer. Propagate named varieties by cuttings of stem tips, 2in(5cm) stem sections, or basal shoots. Alternatively, remove a mature plant from its pot and look for fleshy, knobbly roots at the base. Cut them off 1-2in(2.5-5cm) long and plant horizontally 1in(2.5cm) deep. Plants, though not named varieties, can be raised from seed. Sometimes small reddish-white flowers are produced.
55°F(13°C) H:4ft(1.2m) S:30in(75cm)

Ctenanthe

(Marantaceae)

These clump-forming plants are mostly native to

Brazil. They are attractive but demanding: only grow them if constant warmth, humidity, and shade from hot sun can be provided. Spider mite can be troublesome, especially under hot, dry conditions. Propagate by division or cuttings.

C. lubbersiana Leaves 9in(23cm) long are dappled with dark, mid- and pale green with yellowish patches. They are useful for positioning around taller plants with dark green foliage.
55°F(13°C) H&S:30in(75cm)

C. oppenheimiana The never-never plant is an elegant species, H:48in(120cm) S:30in(75cm), with long leaf stalks and pretty silver markings, leaving arrow-shapes on the surface of mid-green, dull purple-backed leaves. This is more often represented by *C.o.* 'Tricolor', H&S:30in(75cm), where the leaf stalks are shorter, the blades strongly marked with cream, and the backs a brighter red. Three large plants together make marvelous "undergrowth" for more tree-like specimen plants.
55°F(13°C)

Dieffenbachia

(Araceae)

The dumb cane from Central and South America and the West Indies produces poisonous sap which causes swelling of the mouth and throat, and sometimes loss of voice. Handle with care and ensure that children and pets do not have access to them. All plants have the same cane-like stems, with large leaves.

D. seguine 'Maculata' (D. maculata, D. picta) The spotted dumb cane used to be the most popular but has recently been superseded by named cultivars like *D.* 'Camilla' with leaves that are largely white with a bright green edge, *D.* 'Veerie', with a lot of white, spotted with green and *D.* 'Janet Weidner' which has an even proportion of white to green. *D. compacta* tends not to get as leggy as some and *D.* 'Exotica' has creamy variegations. *D. seguine* 'Tropic Snow' has a wide, dark olive-green edge and midrib, with markings of cream and paler green toward the center. *D.s.* 'Tropic Sun' has a thinner edge of green, a bold green midrib and brighter, greenish-yellow and cream markings. *D.* × *bausei* gives an overall impression of bright, yellowish-green with small cream splashes and a darker edge. Provide a warm, even temperature, good humidity, and shade from hot sun. Propagate and prune when plants become leggy. Stem tips can be used as cuttings. Leafless sections of mature stem 2in(5cm) long, or containing at least two nodes, will root and sprout if nestled in horizontally until half-buried by loose potting mixture. Keep warm, moist, and out of direct sun. The pruned remains of old plants usually sprout successfully if placed in good light. Spider mite can be a problem.
55-60°F(13-16°C) H:18-36in(45-90cm)
S:30-36in(75-90cm)

Caladium bicolor 'Freida Hemple'

Caladium bicolor 'Gingerland'

Calathea makoyana

Calathea roseopicta

Ctenanthe oppenheimiana

Ctenanthe oppenheimiana 'Tricolor'

Cordyline fruticosa

Dieffenbachia 'Camilla'

Dieffenbachia 'Exotica'

Dionaea and other carnivorous plants

This specialized group of plants consists of a number of different genera from various families – of which *Dionaea*, the Venus fly trap, is perhaps the most popular example. These plants trap or hold insects and other small animals, from which they absorb nutritious fluid. This supplements or replaces the food which non-carnivorous plants usually obtain from water and soil. Plants can be grown individually, each pot standing in a wide saucer filled with ¹/₂-1in(1-2.5cm) of soft water. During winter, let the saucer (but not the soil) dry out before being refilled. Alternatively, for a lovely summer display, group plants together on water-holding plastic liners with an edging of long thin logs. Plants can remain in their pots, the gaps between being filled with peat and topped off with live sphagnum moss. Remove dead stems and matter to discourage fungal attacks. Most enjoy full sun, but some need light shade.

Darlingtonia (Sarraceniaceae)
D. californica, the cobra lily, from California and Oregon, really does resemble a cobra ready to strike. The pitcher is covered with nectar glands which guide insects into the domed head where they are trapped. They eventually fall to the bottom of the pitcher where digestion and absorption take place. In the wild, the roots of darlingtonia are kept cool by high altitude or by cool springs. It grows best in live sphagnum moss but equal quantities of orchid bark, peat, and perlite will do. Stand the plants in water, and also water from the top, at least once a day during summer and weekly during winter. Give the roots plenty of space, using an 8in(20cm) pot for a medium-sized specimen. Propagate by taking off the young plants produced by underground stolons. Flowers with arching green sepals and crimson-veined petals appear in spring. Seed can be sown. 27-45°F(-3-7°C) H&S:4-24in(10-60cm)

Dionaea (Droseraceae)
D. muscipula, the Venus fly trap, has green or red traps at the ends of the leaves which secrete nectar from the base of teeth that line each edge. Insects land on the trap, triggering sensitive hairs which cause it to close on them. Plants can be difficult to grow. Full sun is essential. Give them a cool winter's rest, with ventilation on warmer days and soft water. Even small plants have a surprisingly long root system and dislike being cramped. Repot during late spring or summer, using three parts of peat moss to one of sharp sand. Propagate by division, seed sowing, or leaf cuttings. In late spring or early summer, prepare a pot or tray of soil, overlaid with damp, live sphagnum moss, squeezed to get rid of excess moisture and chopped. Lay an entire leaf minus the trap horizontally on the moss with the top surface upward, then cover with the thinnest layer of moist sphagnum and water gently. Set the pot on a water tray and keep out of full sun. 38°F(3°C) H:4in(10cm) S:6in(15cm)

Drosera (Droseraceae)
Sundews trap their prey by small, usually red tentacles which cover the leaves. Each of these ends in a globule of sticky fluid. Plants appreciate full sun and like a potting mix of three parts peat moss to one of sharp sand. Propagate by spring-sown seed; germination usually takes six to eight weeks. Another method is by leaf cuttings. Prepare a seed tray as for dionaea. Cut off healthy, mature leaves and lay them down top side upward and cover with the smallest amount of live sphagnum. Stand in a water tray in a light, not too bright place. Some types, like *D. binata*, have thick fleshy roots which can be used as cuttings. Knock a mature plant from its pot, remove a large root and cut it into ¹/₂-1in(1-2.5cm) lengths. Bury them in shallow soil and stand in a water tray; they will sprout within ten weeks. Some of the many types and species of sundew are listed below. 38-40°F(3-4°C)

SUNDEWS THAT PRODUCE RESTING BUDS Some species from the northern Hemisphere die back to a tough

Dionaea muscipula

Darlingtonia californica

cluster of buds in winter. *D. rotundifolia*, the round-leaved sundew, is a small but common species found in Northern Europe (including Britain), Russia, Asia, and North America. It is easy to grow. Larger and more attractive is *D. filiformis*, the American thread-leaved sundew. Thread-like leaves unfurl in the spring. *D.f.* var. *filiformis* has leaves 8in(20cm) long and produces large, rose-pink flowers in summer. *D.f.* var. *tracyi* is similar but taller, with larger flowers. ROSETTE-FORMING SUNDEWS *D. spathulata*, named for the shape of its leaves, is mostly tiny but varies because of its wide geographical range. *D.s.* Kanto form is particularly nice with deep pink flowers and leaves that turn brilliant red when exposed to sun. *D. aliciae*, the Alice sundew from South Africa, is one of the easiest to grow. Circular, flattish rosettes 2in(5cm) wide of wedge-shaped, green leaves send up stems of rose-pink flowers.

PYGMY SUNDEWS These tiny plants of Australasian origin are very beautiful, some having flowers larger than the diameter of the whole plant. Shade from bright sun and watch for scale-like gemmae (winter buds) which form at the center and can smother the plants. Each of these is a potential new plant, so pick them up carefully on a fine brush. Space them out, about a dozen in a 4in(10cm) pot of new potting mix (three parts peat moss to one of sharp sand).

FORK-LEAVED SUNDEWS Mostly large, these Australian species are impressive. Viewed at eye level, their leaves make a forest of glistening branches. Foliage is forked, at least once, sometimes more. *D. binata* T form forks once, its olive-green, sometimes reddish leaves with red tentacles reaching 12in(30cm) high. Pure white flowers make an exciting contrast. In *D. multifida* leaves fork into six to eight points. Propagate from root cuttings.

OTHER SPECIES *D. capensis* from South Africa makes a showy plant about 6in(15cm) in diameter with robust, strap-shaped, green leaves bearing red tentacles. It adopts a trailing habit and has rose-pink flowers. There are also the shade- and humidity-loving sundews from Australian rainforests, tuberous kinds which can tolerate droughts, tree-like rainbow sundews, and fan sundews like *D. stolonifera*, the leafy sundew, which looks like a glistening bonsai tree about 6in(15cm) high.

Heliamphora (Sarraceniaceae)

Sun pitchers grow on rainswept table-top mountains which project out of the tropical rainforests of Guyana and Venezuela. Because these cool mountains are isolated from each other, the different species have evolved separately from a common ancestor. *H. nutans* is the species most found in cultivation. The red-tinged, apple-green pitchers have a spoon-like structure at the tip which holds nectar glands to attract insects. Flowers can appear at any time during

the year and are like nodding white or pale pink lilies. During summer, stand plants in water trays and sprinkle from above with soft water several times a day. Unlike most carnivorous plants, they benefit from a weekly high-nitrogen foliar feed applied at quarter strength. Plants appreciate light shade. Take care when potting as roots and pitchers are brittle. Use equal parts of live sphagnum moss and perlite. Propagate by dividing large clumps, carefully cutting through the rhizome with a sharp knife. Use a plant incubator to increase humidity.
40°F(4°C) H:6in(15cm) S:8in(20cm)

Pinguicula (Lentibulariaceae)

Butterworts are among the most attractive and useful of the carnivorous plants. Most make neat, golden-green, flat rosettes of glistening leaves covered with small glandular hairs which attract and trap their prey. Flowers stand out above the leaves on long stalks and often resemble violets. A suitable potting mix is four parts of peat moss to one of sharp sand. Propagate by division or seed.

P. grandiflora, the Irish or large-flowered butterwort, produces rosettes up to 5in(13cm) across decorated by violet-colored flowers. Propagate by gemmae, miniature resting buds which form around the main overwintering bud. Space them 1in(2.5cm) apart on the surface of new potting mix.
27-40°F(-3-4°C)

P. moranensis var. *caudata*, a Mexican native, is one of the most attractive butterworts, with rosettes of rounded, yellowish, olive-green leaves up to 8in (20cm) in diameter. In winter, these die off, to be replaced by smaller, more tightly packed leaves which are not sticky as there are few flies to catch. No winter resting bud is formed and warmer temperatures are required. Glorious salmon-pink flowers appear in summer and midwinter. These plants come from mountain forests which are bathed in mist for most of the year, so shade from hot summer sun. Propagate by division or leaf cuttings, best taken from the winter rosettes in spring. Pull down sharply to remove as much of the base as possible. Allow the break to heal before laying, surface upward, on a soil composed of equal amounts of peat and sharp sand. Stand the pot or box in a tray of water, then in a plant incubator until plantlets have developed around the leaf base. Do not disturb until the following spring.
45°F(7°C)

Sarracenia (Sarraceniaceae)

The fascinating pitcher plants from eastern North America make a number of new pitchers in the spring at the same time as sending up strange-looking but beautiful flowers in cream, yellow, and rich crimson. Pitcher plants catch vast quantities of insects which

Heliamphora nutans

Drosera aliciae

Drosera capensis

Dionaea and other carnivorous plants

are attracted by the intoxicating nectar secreted by the pitcher. As pitchers die off toward winter, trim them gradually from the top, leaving the nutritious fluid in the bottom to be absorbed.

S. purpurea ssp.*purpurea* is hardy but most of the other species need frost protection in a cool, well-ventilated greenhouse. Repot in spring, as the plants resume growth, using a potting mix either of equal parts of peat and sharp sand, or of four parts of peat moss, two parts of seed-grade perlite, and one part of sharp sand. Larger plants can be divided at the same time; cut through the rhizome where necessary with a sharp knife or pruners. Portions of healthy rhizome at least 1in(2.5cm) long can be used as cuttings. Tuck these into potting mix horizontally, so that they are half-buried and the right way up. Stand in a water tray and keep out of bright light. Propagation can also be by seed. Mature plants appreciate full sun and can be placed outdoors for the summer. Be vigilant against aphids and scale insect. There are many to choose from, including *S. leucophylla*, the white trumpet, with elegant white-topped pitchers traced with red veins, *S. minor*, the hooded trumpet, with rounded pitcher heads, and *S. psittacina*, the strangely shaped parrot pitcher.
40°F(4°C) H:4-30in(10-75cm) S:6-18in(15-45cm)

Sarracenia leucophylla

Episcia
(Gesneriaceae)
Some of these pretty relatives of the African violet have attractive foliage as well as flowers. *E. cupreata*, the flame violet, from Colombia and Venezuela, has bright red, 1in(2.5cm) wide flowers. Neat, hairy, oval leaves 2-4in(5-10cm) long are usually a coppery-green with striking silver veins and midrib. The veining can be less pronounced, sometimes pink or white. There are several named forms. A marvelous plant for a raised bed, it will creep across the surface and trail over the edge. A warm, moist atmosphere is crucial. Propagate by division, plantlets, or cuttings.
50-55°F(10-13°C) H:5in(13cm) S:indefinite

Farfugium
(Compositae)
F. tussilagineum (Ligularia tussilaginea) The species originates from Japan but is not a particularly showy plant. Evergreen leaves of interesting shape grow in a compact clump. Individually, they are rounded, with lobed edges like the feet of cartoon frogs. In fall, stems of bright yellow, daisy-like flowers rise above the foliage. More common is *F.t.* 'Aureomaculatum', liberally sprinkled with golden spots and blotches. *F.t.* 'Argenteum' has an irregular creamy edge to its gray-green leaves. Shade lightly and water well during summer, but keep plants drier and well ventilated during winter. Mealy bugs can be a problem. Propagate by lifting and dividing the crowns, as for herbaceous plants.
36-45°F(2-7°C) H&S:24in(60cm)

Fatsia
(Araliaceae)
F. japonica (Aralia japonica, A. sieboldii) The false castor oil plant (the true title belongs to *Ricinus*) comes from Japan and South Korea. The outline of the bold evergreen leaves, each composed of five to nine lobes, makes an impressive year-round feature in a cool greenhouse. To be effective, plants must be in top condition. Provide a cool, well-ventilated atmosphere with good but not scorchingly direct light. Avoid sharp temperature rises during summer. If plants become leggy, pinch growing tips in spring to promote bushiness. Propagate by spring-sown seed or by semi-hardwood cuttings in summer. *F. j.* 'Variegata', which has white-edged leaves, must be propagated by cuttings.
38-45°F(3-7°C) H&S:3-5ft(1-1.5m)

Fittonia
(Acanthaceae)
Fittonias are Peruvian natives useful for filling gaps on benches and in beds between larger plants. Small and creeping, they prefer a warm, moist, lightly shaded environment. Take care not to overwater as

their small root systems will soon suffer. Like many plants in the same family, they become straggly with age. Cuttings root easily. *F. verschaffeltii*, the painted net leaf or nerve plant, has 2-4in(5-10cm) long, pink-veined olive-green leaves. Upright spikes of green bracts bearing small yellow flowers appear during summer. *F. gigantea* is similar but taller, with slightly larger leaves. *F. verschaffeltii* var. *argyroneura* has leaves traced in silver; *F.v.* var. *a. nana* has smaller, 1in(2.5cm) long leaves and *F.v.* var. *pearcei* has carmine-veined leaves.
55°F(13°C) H:4-12in(10-30cm) S:indefinite

Gynura
(Compositae)
G. aurantiaca The velvet plant from Java is represented in cultivation by *G.a.* 'Purple Passion'. During summer they produce, at the expense of new foliage, bright orange, daisy-like flowers which smell awful and clash with the purple hairs which cover the leaves. Provide good, though not scorching light. Plants are upright at first, becoming trailing with age. Propagate by cuttings in spring and summer. Aphids can be a problem.
50-55°F(10-13°C) H&S:12in(30cm)

Hypoestes
(Acanthaceae)
H. phyllostachya (H. sanguinolenta) This plant from Madagascar is easily raised from spring-sown seed. By summer, small shrubby plants with pink-spotted leaves should be in full growth. Give good light, with shade against scorching sun. Under ideal conditions, plants grow quite tall before producing bright, lavender-purple flowers. Furry new shoots appear at the base at roughly the same time. After flowering, cut away old stems to make space for the new. Plants grow equally well in pots or planted into borders. They can either be discarded in the fall, and seed sown again the following spring, or overwintered. There is a variety with larger, brighter pink spots spreading into patches over the leaf and a similarly bold, cream-splashed variety. Propagate by cuttings.
50°F(10°C) H&S:24in(60cm)

Iresine
(Amaranthaceae)
These plants provide useful splashes of color especially when grouped together. They can become leggy, despite having their growing tips repeatedly pinched back. *I. herbstii* is known as the beefsteak plant, presumably on account of its red stems and leaves, though these are purplish rather than blood-red. Rounded in shape, they are notched at the tip. *I.h.* 'Brilliantissima' has larger leaves of deeper red, with luminous scarlet veins. *I.h.* 'Aureoreticulata' has red stems and bright green, pointed leaves with heavy

yellowish-cream markings over the veins. *I. lindenii*, the blood leaf, has lanceolate, deep red leaves. To maintain full color, a bright position is best. Propagate by cuttings in spring and summer.
50°F(10°C) H:24in(60cm) S:18in(45cm)

Ledebouria
(Liliaceae/Hyacinthaceae)
L. socialis (Scilla violacea) This native of South Africa has fleshy, 2-4in(5-10cm) long, evergreen leaves rising from bulbs which sit on top of the soil. The silvery surfaces of the leaves are blotched with deep olive-green. Undersides are purple. Spikes of small purple, green, and white flowers are produced in late spring. Grow in shallow clay pots or pans of sandy, well-drained soil. Give full sun and water generously except during winter. Propagate by dividing the clump of bulbs after flowering.
38°F(3°C) H:4in(10cm) S:12in(30cm)

Maranta
(Marantaceae)
Marantas make effective foliage clumps either in pots or borders. Used to the tropical atmosphere of Brazil, plants need constant warmth, high humidity, and shade from scorching sun. Spider mite can be a problem. Arguably the most striking is *M. leuconeura* var. *erythroneura* (*M. tricolor*), the herringbone plant, with red veins which make fish-bone patterns on dark green leaves with lighter patches running down the middle. Undersides are reddish-purple.

M.l. var. *kerchoveana* is the more familiar prayer plant or rabbit's tracks. Vivid, dark green blotches run down the middle of the leaves but fade to paler green as the leaf ages. Water sparingly at low temperatures. Propagate by cuttings or division.
50°F(10°C) H&S:12in(30cm)

Melicope
(Rutaceae)
M. hortensis (Euodia hortensis) This handsome foliage plant from Vanuatu (the New Hebrides) is relatively new to cultivation. Shrubby in nature, it has bright, light green foliage. Each leaf is held out from a main stem on a short stalk and is composed of three ribbon-like leaflets. Plants like good but not harsh sunlight. Avoid hot, dry air which tends to turn leaflet tips brown. Water regularly, even during winter. Young branchlets sprout readily from the base to hide older stems.
50°F(10°C) H:24-48in(60-120cm) S:12-24in(30-60cm)

Mimosa
(Leguminosae)
M. pudica A native of Brazil, the sensitive plant may lack size and substance but compensates for this with the novelty value of its folding leaves. Easily grown

Farfugium tussilagineum 'Aureomaculatum'

Fittonia verschaffeltii var. *pearcei*

Maranta leuconeura var. *erythroneura*

Pelargonium 'Chocolate Mint'

from seed, plants respond to warmth, humidity, and light shade from scorching sun. Delicate, fern-like foliage folds and bends at the lightest touch. After an hour or so, leaves return to normal but they usually fold up again for the night. Rounded heads of tiny purple flowers appear during summer. As plants do not always overwinter well, they are often best raised from seed again the following year. Spider mite can be a problem.
55°F(13°C) H&S:18in(45cm)

Oxalis

(Oxalidaceae)
These plants are popular for their delicate, shamrock-like foliage and dainty flowers. *O. tetraphylla* (*O. deppei*), H:6-10in(15-25cm) S:6in(15cm), is known as the rosette or lucky clover from Mexico. Growing from tubers beneath the soil, leaves are composed of four leaflets: in the cultivar 'Iron Cross', each is marked in the center with a chocolate-brown blotch. This coloring is more intense in good light but fades in the shade. Reddish-purple flowers appear in late spring and summer. The South African *O. purpurea*, H&S:6in(15cm), is another tuberous species which has purple foliage and pink flowers. Both plants will die down for the winter when kept at low temperatures, in which case they should be barely watered at all until spring. Propagate by

division in spring as growth resumes.
32-45°F(0-7°C)

Pelargonium

(Geraniaceae)
Most pelargoniums, or florists' geraniums, are grown for their flowers but some also boast scented, colorful, or ornamental foliage. Tricolors usually have striking leaves with emerald-green in the center, chocolate and coral zonal markings, and creamy edges. *P.* 'Happy Thoughts' has rather crinkled leaves with a broad, pale yellow blotch in the center and brightly contrasting crimson flowers. Varieties with silver-white and green variegated leaves include *P.* 'Frank Headley'. The sprawling growth of *P. tomentosum* is compensated for by the pleasant feel and smell of large, softly hairy peppermint-scented leaves. *P.* 'Chocolate Mint' has a dark blotch in the center of each leaf. These are among the more definite perfumes; others are less distinct. *P.* 'Attar of Roses' is said to be rose-scented, *P. odoratissimum* to smell of green apples, *P.* 'Prince of Orange' of oranges, and *P.* 'Lady Mary' of nutmeg. Sun-loving plants, pelargoniums make a major contribution to a bright greenhouse where masses of pretty leaves are needed to make a display between other plants. For cultivation see p.159.
38°F(3°C) H&S:6-18in(15-45cm)

Pellaea

(Adiantaceae)
P. rotundifolia The button fern from Australia, New Zealand, and Norfolk Island is easy to grow if cool, moist, lightly shaded conditions can be provided. Otherwise, they soon turn yellow and die. Fronds with hairy midribs radiate out from the center and are lined alternately with rounded, glossy, dark green pinnae. Propagate by spores in summer.
40°F(4°C) H:6in(15cm) S:9in(23cm)

Peperomia

(Piperaceae)
Known collectively as pepper elders, these small, neat plants are ideal for the fronts of tables and benches. There are two main groups, those with short, stumpy stems from which leaves arise in a rosette pattern, and those with a more open, either bushy or trailing habit. Flower spikes can be attractive or rather insignificant. Plants need warm conditions and light shading from hot sun. Do not overwater as roots die and the base of leaf stalks begins to rot if soil remains saturated for any length of time, particularly during low temperatures. Propagate by division, stem cuttings, or leaf cuttings (see pp.30-33).
P. argyreia (*P. sandersii*) The watermelon plant from tropical South America is one of the most handsome peperomias. Fleshy leaves up to 4in(10cm) long are

shining green, striped with silver between the veins.
50°F(10°C) H&S:8in(20cm)
P. caperata Thought to be a native of Brazil, this compact plant has neat, crinkled leaves puckered between the veins. Creamy flower spikes are attractive. There are several varieties with varying leaf color, leaf size, and height. *P.c.* 'Variegata' has wide, irregular white edges. When propagated by leaf cuttings, the plantlets revert back to green, so stem cuttings are needed to retain variegation.
50°F(10°C) H&S:6in(15cm)
P. fraseri (*P. resediflora*) The flowering mignonette from Ecuador is the only peperomia with truly attractive flowers. Borne on branching red stalks, they make fluffy white cones at the tips. Small heart-shaped, fleshy leaves are neat but unremarkable.
50°F(10°C) H:10-12in(25-30cm) S:9in(23cm)
P. obtusifolia The bushy, branching desert privet with rounded, glossy green leaves is not as popular as its handsome variegated varieties.
50°F(10°C) H&S:8in(20cm)
P. rotundifolia This South American peperomia has trailing stems of tiny, rounded, fleshy leaves patterned with a tracery of silver. Although flowers are insignificant, the profusion of upright spikes is not unattractive.
50°F(10°C) H:5in(13cm) S:10in(25cm)
P. scandens The cupid peperomia from Peru, usually represented by *P.s.* 'Variegata', has trailing stems with heart-shaped leaves.
50°F(10°C) H:10in(25cm) S:15in(40cm)

Pilea

(Urticaceae)
Useful display plants for small pots and pans, the dense-leaved pileas will lend splashes of leaf color where needed. Easy to grow. Propagate regularly by cuttings for new, fresh specimens. Shade from hot sun.
P. cardierei An upright, branching plant from Vietnam, the aluminum plant has dark, shining green leaves marked with silver on raised patches between the veins. Well-grown specimens are striking. *P.c. nana* is more compact.
50°F(10°C) H&S:12in(30cm)
P. involucrata The panamica or friendship plant from Panama to northern South America is a small branching plant with hairy leaves with deep veins and reddish undersides. In shade, leaves remain green, but when exposed to light turn metallic bronze-green. *P.i.* 'Norfolk' has silvery raised areas between the veins, although new leaves remain bronze. *P.i.* 'Moon Valley' has bright, almost lime-green leaves, extremely puckered, with dark chocolate-brown colored veins sunk between raised patches of leaf.
50°F(10°C) H&S:7in(17cm)
P. microphylla (*P. muscosa*) The tiny-leaved, low-

Pellaea rotundifolia

Pilea cardierei

Pilea involucrata 'Norfolk'

Pilea involucrata 'Moon Valley'

Pteris cretica 'Albolineata'

Selaginella martensii 'Watsoniana'

growing artillery plant has been widely used in what was called "bedding work" since Victorian times. Cuttings, which root easily, are best planted three in a pot. The common name comes from the puffs of pollen given off by insignificant flowers. Plants make a good, bright green edging in the greenhouse.
45°F(7°C) H:9in(23cm) S:12in(30cm)

P. peperomioides This peperomia-like pilea from China has unbranching stems which bear nearly round, fleshy, bright green peltate leaves. As specimens grow older and more straggly, leaves become crowded toward the tops of the stems.
50°F(10°C) H&S:12in(30cm)

Pogonatherum
(Gramineae)

P. saccharoideum (P. paniceum) The pretty house bamboo should suit any greenhouse owing to its diminutive size. Masses of thin stems bearing bright green foliage crowd the pot and begin to arch over the edges. Plants dry out rapidly and will suffer if not watered regularly. Propagate by division in summer and fall.
40°F(4°C) H&S:8-12in(20-30cm)

Polystichum
(Polypodiaceae)

P. falcatum (Phanerophlebia falcata, Cyrtomium falcatum) The holly or fishtail fern from Asia has a furry crown from which grow long stalks bearing opposite pairs of glossy, bright olive-green pinnae. They are unevenly toothed, 4in(10cm) long, and end in a curved point. Repot regularly to avoid root restriction. Provide shade and humidity. Propagate by spores or division in spring or summer.
32-45°F(0-7°C) H:24in(60cm) S:36in(90cm)

P. polyblepharum This native of Japan, Korea, and China benefits, in colder climates, from the protection of glass. It is useful for filling gaps under benches or for underplanting taller specimen plants. Light, golden-brown, scaly fronds unfurl in spring. Mature fronds have hairy midribs and glossy, olive-green pinnae. Provide shade and humidity. Propagate by spores in summer.
32-45°F(0-7°C) H:12in(30cm) S:24in(60cm)

Pteris
(Adiantaceae)

P. cretica The table fern, ribbon fern, or Cretan brake, H&S:12-24in(30-60cm), with its plain green ribbon-like pinnae, is fresh and attractive. There are many varieties. *P.c.* 'Albolineata' has a white central band marking each pinna. *P.c.* 'Wimsettii' is plain green but much crested, giving it a frilly appearance. Provide shade and humidity. Propagate by spores in summer or by division in spring or summer.
38-45°F(3-7°C)

Radermachera
(Bignoniaceae)

R. sinica (Stereospermum sinicum) This relative newcomer to cultivation would reach tree-like proportions in its native China, but as a pot plant remains small. The evergreen foliage of shiny green leaflets is attractive. Shade from hot sun, do not overwater but do not allow to dry out. It will tolerate very low temperatures but grows best at 55-60°F (13-16°C). If plants become ragged, prune hard back during summer. Propagate by seed. *R.s.* 'Kaprima' is a pretty variegated form with pale greenish-yellow edges. Whitefly can be a problem.
45°F(7°C) H:4ft(1.2m) S:3ft(1m)

Sansevieria

(Agavaceae)

These almost succulent plants, known as snake plants, are suitable for shade or full sun in the greenhouse. Easy to grow, they need a well-drained soil. Do not overwater, particularly during cold spells. Pot up in late spring or early summer. Propagate by cutting through the rhizomes to separate offsets. Leaf cuttings can be taken by chopping a healthy leaf into 2in(5cm) long sections (see p.32).

S. trifasciata Mother-in-law's tongue from South Africa has long, slightly wavy, sword-shaped leaves attractively marbled with dark and light green. Spikes of rather insignificant but night-scented greenish-white flowers are sometimes borne on mature plants. In cultivation, this species is mostly represented by its various forms.

S.t. 'Golden Hahnii' Unlike the long, sword-shaped leaves of common mother-in-law's tongue, these form a low rosette. Each leaf is marbled green down the middle but is bordered by a wide edge of pale gold.
50°F(10°C) H&S:7in(17cm)

S.t. 'Laurentii' This is the most familiar form, being exactly the same as S. trifasciata but with a vivid yellow stripe running down the leaf edges. This feature disappears when plants are propagated by leaf cuttings, with the resulting plants reverting back to the species.
50°F(10°C) H:18-48in(45-120cm) S:6-30in(15-75cm)

S.t. 'Moonshine' This sansevieria has an almost ghost-like appearance, being a shimmering, very pale green.
50°F(10°C) H:12in(30cm) S:7in(17cm)

Selaginella

(Selaginellaceae)

These delicate moss-like plants known as creeping moss have only limited use in the greenhouse. Lovers of cool, moist conditions, they find most environments too hot and dry. They are best used in a terrarium, bottle garden, an old fish tank, or close to water. They prefer soft water and should be misted frequently, but do not overwater. If pot grown, plunge them in a larger pot of permanently moist peat. Propagate by division or cuttings during spring.

S. kraussiana This South African species and its varieties are probably the most popular. Bright green leaves are robust when given the right conditions. Dwarf S.k. 'Aurea' is a golden-leaved form and S.k. 'Variegata' has creamy-yellow marks on its foliage. S.k. 'Brownii' is particularly attractive, forming hummocks, H:4in(10cm) S:6in(15cm), superficially resembling curled parsley. Avoid watering from above which might damage this dome-like shape.
40°F(4°C) H:9in(23cm) S:12in(30cm)

S. martensii This Mexican selaginella is a more erect, larger-growing kind, but still spreads, sending long brown roots into the soil. S.m. 'Variegata' has irregular white splashes on some branches. S.m. 'Watsoniana' is very pale, with almost silvery tips.
50°F(10°C)

Soleirolia

(Urticaceae)

S. soleirolii (Helxine soleirolii) Known as baby's tears or mind-your-own-business, this is a mat-forming plant from Corsica and Sardinia. It makes a pleasant mound of small leaves which eventually swamp their pot. Give shade and humidity but do not overwater. Water from below, to avoid scorching or discoloration of foliage on top of the mound. Plants do not last indefinitely, so take cuttings or carry out division to increase stock. Cuttings can consist of a small bunch of leafy stems, planted together into fresh soil. S.s. 'Aurea' has golden leaves and S.s. 'Variegata' has silvery edges.
45°F(7°C) H:7in(17cm) S:10in(25cm)

Solenostemon

(Labiatae)

Widely known as coleus, these colourful plants are easy to grow. They fall into two groups: those grown from spring-sown seed, which give color all summer and can then be thrown away in the fall, such as 'Fashion Parade' with fringed, serrated, and lobed leaves in gold, pink, and scarlet, and named varieties which are usually stronger and larger-growing. Propagate these by cuttings in fall or spring. Pinch back the tips of young plants at 3-4in(8-10cm) to encourage branching. The pinching of shoots should continue throughout the life of the plant, so that a large head of colorful leaves is formed and insignificant flowers are prevented from growing. Strong-growing varieties like S. 'Pineapple Beauty' will form tall standards. Keep out of cold drafts and give plenty of water and feed with liquid fertilizer throughout summer.
50°F(10°C) H&S:18in(45cm) or more

Strobilanthes

(Acanthaceae)

S. dyerianus The Persian shield from Burma is the only species in common cultivation. Not frequently seen for sale, it is propagated and spread among amateur growers. Leaves are lance-shaped and pointed. Midrib and vein areas are dark green, almost black, while between the veins is a shiny, silvery purple-pink. After a year or two, plants may become straggly but can easily be replaced by cuttings. Remove growing tips from young plants to encourage branching. Provide warm, humid temperatures but shade from hot sun. Spikes of pale lavender-blue flowers are sometimes produced.
55°F(13°C) H&S:24in(60cm)

Strobilanthes dyerianus

Smaller flowering and fruiting plants

If the greenhouse is like a stage on which specimen plants are the principal actors and those that climb and cascade make up the supporting cast, then the role of the crowd or "extras" is performed by plants that fill in the spaces. Although less distinguished than the "stars", the smaller flowering and fruiting plants are of interest themselves, adding seasonal color among foliage plants, creating handsome associations with their more distinguished companions, and making an important contribution to the overall effect you want to achieve.

People who prefer an uncluttered style of furnishing are likely to continue their minimalist theme in the greenhouse. When plants are grown for their architectural effect, smaller plants need to be chosen with particular care, for some have an abundance of flower that can confuse or even upstage the impact of the larger plants. Single plants in small pots run the risk of looking insignificant alongside stately subjects, and a miscellaneous collection could cancel out the dramatic effect of the focal point; however, a group of one impressive variety can make a real impact, perhaps making a shadow-like horizontal mass to balance the vertical of a large specimen.

Zebra plant (*Aphelandra squarrosa* 'Louisae'), for instance, with its bold, glossy green leaves striped with cream and showy yellow bracts and flowers, looks dramatic planted three or even five in a pot. *Capsicum annuum* cultivars or winter cherry (*Solanum capsicastrum*), both grown for their brightly colored fruit, appear suitably surreal when arranged in clusters. Several bulbs of *Lilium longiflorum* planted in a glazed pot make a good display. Well worth growing, their white flowers blend easily with the colors of other plants and are deliciously perfumed. The idea can be duplicated with bold *Hippeastrum* 'Red Lion', though in this case grow the bulbs separately and group them together when in bud, by plunging their pots into a larger container. For the warmer greenhouse, plants from the aroid family make bold clumps. Flamingo flower (*Anthurium scherzerianum*), with its origins in tropical Costa Rica, will send up a succession of extraordinary waxy scarlet spathes, each topped by a spiraling spadix. Other anthuriums have spathes of white, pink, or cream. Alternatively, spathiphyllums have elegant white spathes.

Well-chosen larger plants and climbers create impact in the greenhouse, but seasonal color is provided by smaller flowering and fruiting plants. Here, the massed summer display of streptocarpus (Cape primrose) and fuchsia seems easily contrived but, in fact, many of these smaller plants need frequent care and attention in order to give their best. They can be stood or planted in groups around larger plants or, as here, massed on benches.

For a less dramatic effect, smaller flowering plants can be grouped together with foliage plants in mixed arrangements. Make sure, however, that plants brought together on a purely aesthetic basis also enjoy the same cultural conditions. Preferences for light, frequency of watering, and minimum temperature must be similar. Very few plants flower continuously, so the best groups are often those composed of a good mixture of foliage plants to provide a permanent green structure, leaving gaps to be filled with a succession of flowering plants to suit the seasons. Small, low growers like *Viola hederacea* can even be planted in pots of taller plants to cover the soil. Candidates from the chapter on annuals, biennials, and bulbs can be brought in as short-term substitutes in their performing season.

Displaying smaller plants can pose a challenge, as suitable surfaces are needed to raise them off the floor. More easily appreciated at close quarters, they need careful arrangement to create the floriferous profusion required. Benches may be ideal in more functional greenhouses, but are often difficult to accommodate when sunrooms designed as home extensions are full of furnishings. The solution could be a collection of plant stands, carts, and small tables, largely hidden by the plants themselves. Include some plants with a sprawling, trailing habit to disguise the supports, or use jardinières and plant stands in keeping with this decorative style and make them part of the display. Care of a large number of smaller flowering plants is more difficult and demanding than caring for fewer, larger plants. In many cases (including *Peristrophe speciosa* and *Hypoestes aristata*), fresh batches of plants need to be raised annually or biennially from cuttings. Others, like boronia and *Cytisus canariensis,* need pruning or lopping back immediately after flowering to maintain shape and size.

Among the special types of plants that make appearances in this category are those bromeliads (see pp.45-8) that are small enough to be used as an underplanting for larger plants and do not object to a little shade cast from above. *Neoregelia carolinae* f. *tricolor* is suitable for a warmer greenhouse and a group of *Billbergia nutans* for cooler temperatures. A group of earth stars (cryptanthus) clustered around an old tree stump makes a wonderful natural-looking planting, growing either in beds of open soil or pots disguised with moss.

Healthy cacti will flower well and add seasonal color to their year-round display of interesting shapes. Of the desert cacti, mammillaria, rebutia, and echinopsis are particularly floriferous when small; among the epiphytic or forest-dwelling cacti, schlumbergera and the exotic epiphyllum are grown mainly for their flowers.

Achimenes

(Gesneriaceae)

These colorful plants originate from Central America and the West Indies. If bought as small rhizomes, pot up in early spring, setting them horizontally about ¹/₂in(1cm) below the surface of the potting mix, with five to seven in each shallow 5in(13cm) pot. Give an even temperature of 60-70°F(16-21°C), which may mean placing them in a plant incubator. Take care not to overwater at this critical stage, shade from hot sun during summer, and keep water off the foliage. Feed weekly, with a high nitrogen-fertilizer initially, then change to a high potash-formula as plants come into flower, giving weak doses regularly for the best results. Upright growers may need staking though there are naturally cascading varieties which are suitable for hanging baskets. The showy white, pink, salmon, pinkish-red, or blue flowers are between ¹/₂in (1cm) and 3in(8cm) across. A. 'Snow White', H:8in(20cm) S:18in(45cm), is somewhat trailing in habit. White blooms up to 1in(2.5cm) wide have mauve throats with a small yellow mark. A. 'Paul Arnold', H&S:18in(45cm), is upright, with large flowers 1¹/₂-2in(3-5cm) across, of blue with pale, whitish-yellow centers. A. 'Prima Donna', H&S: 6in(15cm), makes a neat, upright plant peppered with small pinkish-red flowers ¹/₂in(1cm) across. After flowering, plants die down in the fall and should be stored dry in their pots over winter. Divide and repot in early spring. Whitefly can be a problem.
55°F(13°C) H:9-15in(23-40cm) S:12in(30cm)

Aeschynanthus

(Gesneriaceae)

The trailing members of this genus are the better known (see p.106 and for cultivation) but there are others with more upright habit. For a spectacular show, plant three or five small plants in one large container. When they become straggly, take cuttings of shoot tips and prune back hard during summer. A. 'Big Apple' is compact and has clusters of red tubular flowers. A. hildebrandii makes a short plant with bright green foliage and large clusters of orange-red flowers. A. 'Topaz' is rather similar but with yellow flowers.
45-50°F(7-10°C) H:6-10in(15-25cm) S:8in(20cm)

Alstroemeria

(Liliaceae/Alstroemeriaceae)

Although mostly perceived as an outdoor plant, pots of alstroemeria, often called Peruvian lily for its origins in South America, will add spectacular flower color to a greenhouse planted mainly with foliage. Young plants obtained in spring can be planted into a border or potted up as required, preferably in a loam-based potting mix, until they fill an 8in(20cm) pot. Support with sticks or canes and string. Feed every two weeks with liquid fertilizer and shade from the hottest sun. Flowers are produced in summer. After flowering cut down the stems of withered flowers and dying leaves and water sparingly during winter to prevent the potting mix from drying out. Propagate by division of the tuberous roots in spring or by seed. Sow ¹/₄in(5mm) deep, place the pot inside a loosely tied plastic bag, and keep at 70°F(21°C) for three weeks. Place in the refrigerator for a further three weeks, then back to warm conditions until germination 10-14 days later. There are many species and varieties, including A. ligtu hybrids, H: 24-36in(60-90cm) S:18in(45cm), with superb flowers in shades of pink, yellow, orange, and flame; A. pelegrina from Chile, H:12-36in(30-90cm) S:10-18in(25-45), has white flowers, each petal marked with pink, while the two upper petals have yellow bases and are spotted with dark maroon. Look out for aphids on young shoots and buds.
40°F(4°C)

Anigozanthos

(Haemodoraceae)

The kangaroo paws from Western Australia make clumps of dark, evergreen foliage and, when established in beds or pots, long stems of unusual tubular woolly flowers in spring and early summer. They take their name from the way they are split at the mouth, ending in little claw-like segments. Propagation is easy by seed or division in spring. Keep cool and shade from the brightest sun. Ventilate well in summer and during warm winter spells.
A. flavidus In its native habitat, along the edges of rivers and creeks, the tall or yellow kangaroo paw can reach 10ft(3m). They make splashes of yellow-green when in bloom. Keep plants moist and well fed in summer, but water more sparingly in winter. They prefer an acidic soil mix and soft water. Forms with different colored flowers are available.
38°F(3°C) H:48in(120cm) S:18in(45cm)
A. manglesii The common green or Mangles' kangaroo paw is the floral emblem of Western Australia and has marvelous, emerald-green "paws" with bright red bases and red stems. The plant is susceptible to ink disease and is best re-raised regularly from seed.
38°F(3°C) H:36in(90cm) S:18in(45cm)
A. rufus In the red kangaroo paw deep red stems and exterior of the flowers contrast well with the pale green inside the petal segments. These come from sand heath habitats and need slightly drier conditions than A. flavidus.
38°F(3°C) H:36in(90cm) S:24in(60cm)

Anisodontea

(Malvaceae)

A. capensis (Malvastrum capense) This shrubby South African plant will provide pretty flowers throughout summer. Plants tend to become leggy so take cuttings in summer, shaping the young plants by pinching back the growing tips to encourage branching. These can be overwintered and grown on

Aeschynanthus 'Big Apple'

Anigozanthos flavidus

Aphelandra squarrosa

Anthurium andreanum

for next year's bloom. Propagate also by seed. At the end of summer, old plants can be tidied up and saved or thrown away. Prune old stock hard in spring, when more cuttings can be taken. Shape young plants by pinching back several times before they reach flowering size. Flowers are rosy pink and hollyhock-like, 1-1¹/₂in(2.5-4cm) across, with a striking tint of darker pink spreading from the center into the veins. Whitefly can be a problem.
38°F(3°C) H:36in(90cm) S:24in(60cm)

Anthurium
(Araceae)

These plants have an interesting flower structure consisting of a waxy, flattened spathe and an arched or twisted spadix which bears insignificant flowers and, later, the fruits. The two species regularly grown indoors for their flowers are epiphytic natives of the rainforests of tropical South America. Grow in a warm, humid greenhouse by fitting them to upright lengths of dead tree-branch secured to the floor. Remove the plant from its pot and shake off most of the soil, hold the roots to the branch with a handful of sphagnum moss, and bind in place with nylon fishing line. They will also grow in pots, using a

porous potting mix with some bark added, forming good clumps which can be divided during spring and summer. Shade from hot summer sun.

A. andreanum Given warmth and humidity, this plant will produce an impressive clump of lush, heart-shaped leaves to 9in(23cm) long and will rarely be out of flower.
55-60°F(13-16°C) H:24-30in(60-75cm) S:20in(50cm)
A. 'Lady Jane' This hybrid has distinctive, almost sagittate leaves and both these and the spathes have attractive pinkish-red stems. Both spathe and spadix are pink, with the 2-3in(5-8cm) spathe tapering to an elegant point. Plants seem more robust than *A. andreanum* at lower temperatures.
55-60°F(13-16°C) H&S:18in(45cm)
A. scherzerianum Although this flamingo flower is slightly more accommodating than *A. andreanum*, it still needs warm, humid conditions to succeed. Worth growing well, a healthy plant has glossy, lance-shaped leaves which are particularly attractive when young. The flower structure has a distinctive curly orange-red spadix spiraling from the top of the spathe. This is usually red but there are variations. *A.s.* 'Rothschildianum' is red, spotted with white.
55-60°F(13-16°C) H&S:12-24in(30-60cm)

Aphelandra
(Acanthaceae)

A. squarrosa The zebra plant from Brazil is grown as much for its striking foliage as for the bright yellow bracts which carry small yellow flowers. These are borne at the ends of shoots during fall. Even when not in flower, the shiny dark green leaves with bright, creamy-white veins are still attractive. *A.s.* 'Louisae' and *A.s.* 'Dania' are compact forms. *A.s.* 'Snow Queen' has bolder, almost silvery-white veining which seems to suffuse into the whole leaf. Provide warm, humid conditions and shade from hot sun. When plants become straggly, take cuttings during late spring or summer: take the shoot tip as a cutting then cut above and below each pair of leaves on portions of stem that are not too woody; split the stem vertically in half between the two leaves. Each portion of node with one leaf attached can be inserted as a cutting. Leaves can be reduced by half if necessary. Set in soil so that the new shoot from the axil between leaf and stem will grow upward. Cut remaining growth down to a stump of 2in(5cm) which, given good light, will sprout new shoots.
55°F(13°C) H:24in(60cm) S:18in(45cm)

Argyranthemum
(Compositae)

Paris daisies or marguerites used to be grouped under chrysanthemum but now have their own genus. these tender evergreen perennials are ideal for the greenhouse with their light, almost feathery foliage and daisy-like flowers. Flowers are produced mainly during summer but will appear intermittently throughout the year. Provide a cool, well-ventilated environment and bright light. *A. frutescens* has white flower heads with yellow centers contrasting well with fresh leaves. *A.* 'Vancouver' has large semi-double pink flowers and *A.*'wellwood Park' single pink blooms. *A.* 'Jamaica Primrose' is resplendent with large yellow daisies and *A.* 'Jenny' with slightly smaller ones. *A.* 'Mary Wootton' is pale pink with a mid-pink center. *A. frutescens* ssp. *foeniculaceum* bears profuse small white flowers and has almost succulent, much-divided, feathery blue-green leaves. Cultivation is simple: repropagate by cuttings and prune back. Cuttings taken in fall can be grown on during winter, giving large plants for summer flowering. A fresh batch of spring cuttings roots quickly and still makes good-sized plants. Prune old plants hard in spring. Standards are sometimes grown and, by pruning the head every spring, will last some time.
38°F(3°C) H&S:24-36in(60-90cm)

Arisaema
(Araceae)

Tubers of these plants should be potted about 3in (8cm) below the surface of the potting mix in spring. After flowering, they die down and should be kept dry with occasional watering to prevent shriveling. Feed with a well-balanced liquid fertilizer while plants are in active growth. Repot into fresh soil every other year. Shade from hot sun. *A. candidissimum*, H&S:18in(45cm), produces slightly fragrant pink-striped white spathes, up to 4in(10cm) long, in early summer. *A. sikokianum*, 12-20in(30-50cm), has 8in(20cm) long spathes of dark purple-brown. They are paler and green-striped on the hood and white inside the lower vase-like part, with white spadices.
38°F(3°C)

Asclepias
(Asclepiadaceae)

A. curassavica The blood flower from South America is easily raised from spring-sown seed saved from the previous year. Plants will reach flowering size, in pots or borders, by summer. Paired, lanceolate leaves act as a green foil to the umbels of bright orange flowers. Broken leaves and flower stalks release a poisonous milky sap. If plants become straggly by winter, trim them back and prune hard in spring. Propagate also by cuttings. Whitefly can be a problem.
45°F(7°C) H&S:36in(90cm)

A. physocarpa (*Gomphocarpus physocarpus*) This native of South Africa is much larger than *A. curassavica*, making a shrub grown primarily for its marvelous inflated seed pods. These pale green structures, about 2in(5cm) long, are covered with soft bristles and are much prized by flower arrangers. The flowers themselves are small, white, and attractive to butterflies. Propagate by seed or cuttings.
40°F(4°C) H:6ft(1.8m) S:36in(90cm)

Begonia
(Begoniaceae)

Begonias are such favorites that there are usually one or two in every collection of indoor plants. Many have attractive foliage as well as flowers. For cultivation see p.120. Shade lightly from hot sun.

B. × cheimantha The pretty Lorraine begonia has dropped in popularity since the introduction of B. × hiemalis hybrids. Although the B. × cheimantha hybrids are much daintier they are not easy to raise from cuttings or seed and are not widely sold. B. × c. 'Gloire de Lorraine', H&S:12in(30cm), used to be the most popular for its glistening pale pink flowers. Propagate by cuttings in spring and pinch back young plants to keep them bushy. Similar B. × c. 'Love Me', H&S:9in(23cm), is available in seed catalogs but needs a lot of warmth and cosseting to make good plants. Sow seed in spring and keep in a plant incubator to maintain the necessary humidity and bottom heat, especially when temperatures drop in fall. Only when the plants have almost reached full size can they be hardened off from the incubator and go on display. The reward is a profusion of beautiful single, icing-sugar-pink blooms. Discard after flowering and start again from seed.
55-60°F(13-16°C)

B. coccinea The shrubby angelwing begonia from Brazil is worth growing for its hanging clusters of coral-red flowers which appear in spring. The cane-like stems with swollen nodes can be tied onto canes as growth progresses. Leaves are neat, glossy green above, and reddish beneath. The common name refers to the winged ovaries of the flowers. This species has been used in hybridizing, giving rise to such favorites as spotty-leaved B. 'Président Carnot'. Propagate by cuttings. Prune old plants back hard during summer and they will sprout again in good light.
50°F(10°C) H:36-48in(90-120cm) S:12in(30cm)

B. fuchsioides The unusual-looking, upright fuchsia begonia does superficially resemble a fuchsia and has small, dainty, toothed leaves, borne on branching stems. Bright pink flowers open in winter. Plants need staking. Cut untidy plants back hard and they will sprout again. Cuttings root easily.
45-50°F(7-10°C) H:48in(120cm) S:18in(45cm)

B. × hiemalis These showy begonias are bought in

bud or flower to lend color where needed. The range of colors is wide with double flowers more prevalent but there are some single varieties. Flowers are profuse above deep green, glossy foliage. Give warmth, humidity, and good but not direct light. Plants are often discarded when they have finished flowering but if cut back hard they should regenerate, in good light, though they never quite repeat their original show. Propagate by cuttings. Mildew and botrytis can cause problems.
60°F(16°C) H&S:8-12in(20-30cm)

B. manicata This rhizomatous begonia from Mexico produces a mass of pretty pink flowers during winter. Several upright stems bear large, rather fleshy, red-edged, brittle leaves with red hairs on the undersides. Their stalks are mottled. Flower stems are much-branched, holding the dainty flowers clear of the foliage. Cuttings consist of 2in(5cm) chunks of thick stem taken during early summer. Push them horizontally into moist, loose potting mixture until two-thirds buried, water, and keep warm but not too moist until roots and new shoots have formed. The young plants will flower during late winter but if growth is encouraged by potting up and feeding with liquid fertilizer throughout the following summer, they will make fine specimens in their second winter.
45-50°F(7-10°C) H:24in(60cm) S:18in(45cm)

TUBEROUS HYBRID BEGONIAS Guaranteed to bring flamboyant color into the greenhouse, there are basically two types: upright and pendulous, the latter being suitable for hanging baskets and wall planters. Tubers are started into growth during spring. Nestle them hollow side up in a box of moist peat or peat alternative, so that just the upper surface protrudes. They need warmth, so a plant incubator or warm place in the house where 65°F(18°C) can be guaranteed will give good, even results. Once healthy shoots begin to grow, pot up into 4-5in(10-13cm) pots. For the largest, most spectacular blooms, remove all but the strongest growth (the others can be rooted as cuttings). Plants will need plenty of fertilizing and staking. Remove the two female flowers which flank the large double male flower to divert energy into the latter. Female flowers are easily identified by the ovaries behind the petals. At the end of summer, plants cease flowering and should be allowed to die down. They can be kept in their pots at 40-45°F(4-7°C); do not water during winter. In spring, remove from the pots, clean off old soil, and break off dead roots before repeating the procedure. Propagate also by seed or by cutting the tuber into two or more pieces, as long as each contains a growing tip.
50-55°F(10-13°C)

Boronia
(Rutaceae)

These beautiful but sometimes temperamental plants from Australia and Tasmania are ideal for the cool greenhouse, producing their delicate four-petaled flowers of surprisingly varied form and color in spring. Foliage can be pinnate, consisting of fine, almost needle-like leaves or leaflets which are attractive even when the plant is out of flower. The leaves of some have an aroma reminiscent of the herb rue. They like soft water, so if rainwater is not available, use boiled, cooled water and add a liquid fertilizer formulated for acid-loving plants. Trim back after flowering, without cutting into old wood. New stems will grow to produce next year's flowers and plants are prevented from becoming straggly. When repotting, use acidic soil mix. *B. citriodora* is a mountain species from Tasmania with lemon-scented leaves composed of three to seven leaflets. Pale pink flowers open quite wide. Rather similar is *B.* 'Southern Star', with four to six petals on each soft pink flower, reddish-green stems, and slightly bronze-tinged foliage. *B. heterophylla* has fine, bright green foliage with three to five leaflets and pendent, carmine-rose flowers with pointed petals. *B. megastigma* has three to five leaflets and fragrant pendent flowers of purple-brown on the outside and yellow inside. *B.m.* 'Heaven Scent' is a particularly good form. *B.m.* 'Lutea' has striking lime-yellow flowers with an intoxicating, but not sickly, sweet perfume. Propagate by semi-ripe cuttings in summer. 40°F(4°C) H&S:12-72in(30-180cm) depending on type and pruning

Argyranthemum 'Jamaica Primrose'

Argyranthemum 'Vancouver'

Begonia fuchsioides

Bouvardia

(Rubiaceae)

These Mexican plants were favorites in the nineteenth century when they were forced, under stove (tropical) conditions, to give winter flowers. Old varieties like double white *B*. 'Alfred Neuner', scarlet *B*. 'Dazzler', and double, deep pink *B*. 'President Garfield' were prized for their midwinter blooms. There now seems to be a resurgence of interest in bouvardias, which should restore their popularity and availability. Plants can be grown in pots, or planted into a greenhouse border. A thorough pruning, cutting last year's flowering stems back to within a node or two of older wood in spring, will keep them tidy. *B*. 'President Cleveland' is a beautiful red-flowered variety covered in bloom between summer and winter. *B. longiflora* (*B. humboldtii*) has elegant, perfumed white flowers with narrow 2in(5cm) long tubes, the four-petal lobes flaring out into a flat cross shape 1½in(4cm) wide. *B*. 'Roxanne' has semi-double, soft pink flowers. *B. ternifolia*, the scarlet trompetilla, has tubular scarlet flowers over 1in(2.5cm) long. Root cuttings can be taken. Whitefly can be a problem.
45-50°F(7-10°C) H&S:12-36in(30-90cm)

Canna

(Cannaceae)

Cannas are often used in subtropical bedding outdoors where the exotic foliage and blooms make a good show all summer, but also make first-class greenhouse plants. Most popular are the many hybrids with flower colors of red, pink, yellow, orange, warm peach, and apricot. Usually bought as rhizomes, planted in spring to flower during the first summer, plants can also be raised from large, hard seed, best soaked for 24 hours before sowing. Germination may take about one month in a plant incubator or on a warm windowsill. Flowering in the second season is normal. Plants die down for the winter. Keep them in frost-free conditions, in their pots, until spring, without allowing the potting mix to dry completely. Pot up in fresh potting mix as signs of new growth appear. Plants grown indoors are prone to spider mite. Mist the foliage regularly and take control measures as soon as the first mites are spotted.
40-45°F(4-7°C) H:36-48in(90-120cm) S:24in(60cm)
C. iridiflora This Peruvian species has pendent reddish-pink flowers, smaller than most of the showier hybrids. Plants will thrive grown as water-edge plants in the shallow water of a greenhouse pond 12-18in(30-45cm) deep as well as in pots or planted in the border. At temperatures of 55°F (13°C) and over, plants will grow throughout winter. Any lower and they will die down until spring. Remove from water during prolonged low temperatures.
40-45°F(4-7°C) H:7ft(2m) S:24in(60cm)

Capsicum

(Solanaceae)

C. annuum **Grossum Group** Sweet peppers are easily grown in the greenhouse by sowing seed in spring and growing on in 8in(20cm) pots. Four or five plants yield enough peppers for the kitchen and some to give away. There are plenty of varieties, yielding green, red, yellow, purple, or black fruits. Water well in summer and feed weekly with a high-potash fertilizer once established. Tall plants may need staking. Pests can be a problem, particularly aphids, whitefly, and spider mite. Introduce natural predators or parasites (see p.35) for pests as soon as they appear. Discard plants at the end of the season and raise fresh from seed the following year. Cultivation for hot chili peppers is exactly the same.
40°F(4°C) H:18-24in(45-60cm) S:15in(40cm)

Catharanthus

(Apocynaceae)

C. roseus (*Vinca rosea*) The Madagascar periwinkle has pretty flowers and is easy to grow, yet has never gained the popularity it deserves. Phlox-like flowers are either pink or white with a pink eye. Seed of single colors or mixtures is available. Sown in spring, it will yield compact plants with shiny leaves which flower all summer and fall. Cuttings root easily but the simplest option is often to throw old plants away in fall and sow again the following spring. If grown from cuttings pinch back shoot tips to

Capsicum annuum

Chorizema ilicifolium

encourage a good branching shape.
45-50°F(7-10°C) H&S:12in(30cm)

Centradenia

(Melastomataceae)

These pretty pink or white flowering plants are
unusual, but can occasionally be found for sale.
Flowers are short-lived but are produced over a long
period, mostly in winter and spring. Foliage is
perennially attractive, being deep green with
prominent, almost parallel veins running the length of
the leaf and violet or red undersides. Light is
important for good flowering, especially during
shorter days. Provide warm conditions, with humidity
in high temperatures. Propagate by cuttings, pinching
back the growing tips of young plants to keep a
compact, bushy shape with plenty of flowering
points. Trim older plants in spring. *C. floribunda* is
native to Guatemala and bears purplish-violet flowers
which match nicely with the purple undersides of the
leaves. There are named varieties, all of which need
similar treatment.
55°F(13°C) H&S:12in(30cm)

Chirita

(Gesneriaceae)

C. sinensis This unusual gesneriad from China makes
a rosette of softly haired leaves which can be
patterned with silver. In spring and summer lilac
flowers, up to 1½in(4cm) long, with an orange stripe
in the throat, are held above the foliage on long,
slightly curving stems. Propagate by leaf cuttings, as
for African violet (see pp.32-3). Keep water off leaves
and water carefully from below with water at room
temperature. Feed weekly with African violet fertilizer
and shade from sun.
55°F(13°C) H:4in(10cm) S:8in(20cm)

Chorizema

(Leguminosae)

These Australian shrubs are easy to grow, given good
light and a well-drained soil, preferably loam-based,
kept just moist during winter. Small plants look
flimsy and inconsequential, but once the stems have
matured and branched out, the result is a fine shrub,
liberally sprinkled with small vivid flowers. Prune if
necessary after flowering, if stems die back,
or if the plant begins to sprawl. Propagate from
spring-sown seed or short cuttings.
40-45°F(4-7°C)

C. dicksonii The yellow-eyed flame pea has small,
spine-tipped, thin leaves, and yellow-spotted red
flowers throughout summer.
H&S:24in(60cm)

C. ilicifolium The holly flame pea is the most
popularly grown, slowly building itself up into a
wispy but attractive bush of many thin stems strung

Catharanthus roseus

143

with small, holly-like leaves. Initially stems may need some support. The bright pink and orange flowers are appealing, opening during summer even on young plants.
H:48in(120cm) S:36in(90cm)

Chrysanthemum

(Compositae)

The chrysanthemum (correctly classified as dendranthema) is now sold throughout the year as a dwarf flowering pot plant, and will provide a cheerful splash of color which should last up to two months in bloom. After flowering, plants can be thrown away or planted out in the garden during early summer. They will grow up to their true height and flower during fall.

In a different category, there are the many varieties of winter-flowering florists' chrysanthemums available from nurseries in the spring as rooted cuttings. These are best grown outside all summer but should be brought in before fall. They then need a cool, dry, well-ventilated atmosphere in which to flower. After flowering, cut plants back, leaving 2-3in(5-8cm) stumps. Either leave them in their pots or shake the soil off their roots and plant in boxes. Following a short rest, these root stocks can be warmed up, thoroughly moistened, and will produce shoots to be used as cuttings. Pot up and feed when established in their pots (initially with a high-nitrogen fertilizer but twice weekly with a high-potash formula as they build up to flower). Pinching back is also necessary, to encourage a number of lateral shoots bearing flower buds. This is generally carried out in spring, then again in early summer, depending on variety. Remove unwanted shoots and flower buds as growth ensues. Disbudding will determine which type of bud and how many are allowed to flower; this varies according to variety and the number and size of blooms desired. Most will need staking and tying.

Cascade chrysanthemums make trailing plants which become an attractive mass of small dense flowers. Propagate named varieties from cuttings. When the plant is 1ft(30cm) tall, insert a fairly long 12-gauge wire next to the trunk; bend the wire to an angle of 45 degrees and train the stems along the wire. All laterals and sublaterals are then pinched back at every fourth leaf joint until mid-fall.
40°F(4°C) H:60in(150cm) S:30in(75cm)

Clivia

(Liliaceae/Amaryllidaceae)

Easy to obtain, grow, and flower, clivias make reliable greenhouse plants. Grown in pots, they can remain undisturbed for at least five years at a time. Roots protruding from the surface will do no harm and are usually a signal of good humidity. Shade clivias from hot sun, which can bleach the foliage. To be sure of

Clivia miniata

Clivia miniata var. *citrina*

Coronilla valentina 'Citrina'

flowers every year, give a general liquid fertilizer every three to four weeks throughout summer. After flowering, fruits form, taking roughly one year to ripen. The large seeds inside will germinate at 60°F(16°C), but plants take at least four years before flowering. Divide clumps at potting time.

C. miniata Kaffir lily from South Africa is the species most commonly grown. Showy orange flowers are a delight in early spring and there are some lovely, uncommon hybrids and varieties of pale yellow and shades of orange.

C. nobilis Also from South Africa, this less showy but still interesting species has smaller, green-tipped orange flowers.
50°F(10°C) H&S:18in(45cm)

Coronilla
(Leguminosae)

C. valentina ssp. glauca From southern Portugal and Mediterranean regions, this lovely small shrub has bright green leaves composed of five to nine glaucous leaflets. Clusters of golden-yellow, pea-like flowers appear in spring and have a delightful fruity perfume. *C.v.* 'Citrina' has lemon-yellow flowers and *C.v.* 'Variegata' cream-variegated leaves. Give good light. Propagate by cuttings during summer.
32°F(0°C) H:36-48in(90-120cm) S:36in(90cm)

Crossandra
(Acanthaceae)

C. infundibuliformis The firecracker plant from India and Sri Lanka will make a valuable addition to the greenhouse if given sustained warmth and humidity. The plant itself is slow-growing but spends its energy on producing a succession of long-lasting spikes of salmon-orange flowers from spring to fall. Shade lightly from the hottest summer sun but otherwise give maximum light, warmth, and humidity. Even when not flowering, the foliage is handsome and glossy. Propagate by cuttings in spring or summer.
55°F(13°C) H&S:12-24in(30-60cm)

Cucumis
(Cucurbitaceae)

There is no reason why crops cannot be slotted in amongst the ornamental residents of the greenhouse, and canteloupes and cucumbers are a good choice. Unfortunately, cucumbers are prone to mildew and both will suffer from spider mite attack. However, if the predatory mite phytoseiulus is introduced at the beginning of the season at the first sign of the pest, they will prevent a few mites from spreading into an epidemic (see pp.35-7 for biological control). Protection from high summer temperatures, good humidity, ample ventilation, and careful watering to prevent drying out will also help.

Crossandra infundibuliformis

C. melo Canteloupes can be grown in a border of rich soil or in large pots. They require time and effort in their training, the usual method being to secure horizontal wires 12in(30cm) apart up the sides and under the roof, but at least 12in(30cm) away from the glass. A vertical cane tied to the wires can support the main stem of each plant, which can be pinched back at about 6ft(1.8m). Fruit-bearing lateral shoots are tied to the horizontal wires and pinched back after two leaves beyond each flower. When fruit are still small, thin so that four develop per plant, with no more than one per lateral. Hand pollination, best carried out at midday, is necessary for good fruit set. Either take a male flower, strip off the petals, and push the center into female flowers (those with small melons swelling behind the bloom) or use a soft brush to carry pollen from one to the other. Support developing fruit with nets hung from the wires.
50-60°F(10-16°C) H:6ft(1.8m) S:30-36in(75cm-90cm)

C. sativus High temperatures of 70-80°F(21-27°C) are needed for good germination of cucumbers. From spring sowings, cucumbers can be planted in borders or growbags but a large 9in(23cm) pot is preferable aesthetically, and will also stay moist for longer. There are plenty of varieties, but choose a non-bitter, all-female greenhouse type. Secure each plant to a cane and pinch back the growing tip when plants are 36-48in(90-120cm) high. Lateral stems from the leaf axils should be pinched back after two leaves and sub-laterals after one leaf.
50-60°F(10-16°C) H:48in(120cm) S:24-30in(60-75cm)

Cyclamen persicum

Cuphea
(Lythraceae)

C. hyssopifolia This low shrub from Guatemala and Mexico is sometimes referred to as false heather but both leaves and flower structure are different. It produces small neat leaves and a sprinkling of pink or white flowers during summer and fall. Useful for making a low clump at the edges of borders, or to use in pots to fill gaps, this cuphea can be propagated easily by cuttings.
38°F(3°C) H&S:18in(45cm)

Cyclamen
(Primulaceae)

C. persicum A pretty species with toothed, silver-patterned, dark green leaves and fresh pink or white flowers. The flowers, with their peppery fragrance and elegantly twisted, narrow, swept-back petals, have a fineness which has often been lost in the quest for bigger, gaudier blooms borne in greater profusion on larger plants. It is available as plants or seed. Both this species and the hybrid florists' cyclamen are easy to keep if given a bright, cool position. Water from below, by filling the saucer with water, to prevent water from lodging in the top of the corm, thus rotting newly emerging leaves and flowers. Empty away any excess water after an hour so that the roots do not become waterlogged. By late spring, a cyclamen stops growing, with no more buds emerging from the corm. Stop watering and leave to dry out, removing pots to other quarters while

dormant. Keep an eye on the dry corms, as they begin to grow during mid- to late summer, signaled by a proliferation of pink buds on the corm. Begin watering again and repot if necessary (approximately every three years). As new leaves grow, begin feeding with liquid fertilizer and the plant will repeat its performance, flowering during fall and winter. Propagate by seed, sowing open-pollinated varieties during summer to flower the winter after next. F_1 hybrids come into flower faster, being sown in spring to flower the following winter. Seeds are best soaked for 24 hours to wash away germination inhibitors, then sown 1/4in(5mm) deep, which gives them the darkness they need to germinate at 60°F(16°C). Thin when the second leaf has appeared. There are also some lovely small varieties with scented flowers. Plants are prone to attack by vine weevil larvae which eat the roots (see p.37).
50°F(10°C) H&S:4-8in(10-20cm)

Cyrtanthus

(Liliaceae/Amaryllidaceae)

C. purpureus (Vallota speciosa) The beautiful Scarborough lily has its true origins in South Africa. It is an evergreen bulb with strap-shaped leaves, grown for its show of bright red, funnel-shaped flowers in late summer. Pot new bulbs in the fall, using clay pots if possible and a well-drained, sandy soil, so that the tips just protrude through the surface. Once established, plants will flower better if left undisturbed, so only repot when congested with offsets. These can be detached and potted separately to make new plants. Provide good light all year but shade from the hottest summer sun.
38°F(3°C) H:12-20in(30-50cm)

Cytisus

(Leguminosae)

C. canariensis (Genista canariensis) This and the beautiful hybrid C. × spachianus (Genista × spachiana) are useful for the cool greenhouse. Leaves are trifoliate on short stalks, bright green above, and slightly silvery beneath. During spring, racemes of bright canary-yellow, pea-like flowers are produced toward the ends of shoots. These have a delicate but quite pervasive sweet perfume and last for some six to eight weeks. After flowering, prune back all the young stems by two-thirds to three-quarters, otherwise plants virtually double their size each year until fully developed. Shade lightly from hottest sun or stand plants outside in full sun for the summer. Spider mite can be a problem. Propagate by 3-4in(8-10cm) heeled cuttings in summer. Good, straight young plants can be selected and grown on as standards.
38°F(3°C) H&S:6-10ft(1.8-3m)

Cytisus × spachianus and *Streptocarpus × kewensis*

Erica cerinthoides

Eucomis bicolor

Erica

(Ericaceae)

There are numerous South African heaths which make interesting pot plants and respond well to the bright, cool conditions of the greenhouse. Not easy to grow, they should never be allowed to dry out, need an acidic soil mix, with extra sand added, and prefer soft water. Stand plants on moist sand or shingle to prevent drying out; this will also help keep the air around them moist. Do not allow to become waterlogged. Shade lightly from hot sun and ventilate freely when possible, including warm wintry days. Propagate by short cuttings of young shoots in summer, inserting them close together in loose potting mixture with a layer of sand on the surface. When potting up the cuttings next spring, do not water immediately, but use moist (not soaked) potting mix and leave to rest for a few days first. When they begin to grow, pinch back the growing tips, making them branch from low down. Species with soft shoots should be trimmed after flowering. Pot up in spring. Some species are available from seed which takes about one month to germinate.

E. cerinthoides This species produces coral-pink flowers, 1in(2.5cm) long, which appear toward the tips of stems mostly in summer. These are clad with neat, needle-like leaves arranged in whorls of four to six.
40°F(4°C) H&S:24in(60cm)

E. gracilis A pretty heath with small reddish-purple flowers which open during fall and winter in great profusion.
40°F(4°C) H:18in(45cm) S:12in(30cm)

E. × hiemalis The well-known Cape heath or French heather is widely grown as a pot plant for its white-tipped pink flowers among mid-green, thread-like leaves.
40°F(4°C) H:24in(60cm) S:15in(40cm)

E. mammosa The red signal heath is an almost hardy species which produces showy red flowers a little over ½in(1cm) long, opening during late summer and fall.
40°F(4°C) H:24-48in(60-120cm) S:24in(60cm)

E. pinea Tubular flowers are soft yellow, which look pretty alongside some of the red-flowered species.
40°F(4°C) H:24-60in(60-150cm) S:16-36in(42-90cm)

Eucodonia

(Gesneriaceae)

E. andrieuxii 'Naomi' This charming plant, once classified under achimenes, makes tufts of growth consisting of rosettes of 3in(8cm) long leaves. These are a hairy gray-green above but underneath have dense pink hairs over veins and white between. Tubular, mauve flowers have white throats spotted with yellow and are held aloft by thin stems covered with reddish hairs. Shade from the sun and avoid hot summer temperatures. Give tepid water from below.

The plant will die back to its rhizomes for the winter. Keep dry, then in early spring repot and start the rhizomes back into growth. Propagate as for achimenes (see p.138) by rhizomes, which increase every year.
50°F(10°C) H:3-4in(8-10cm) S:6in(15cm)

Eucomis

(Liliaceae/Hyacinthaceae)

The South African pineapple lilies give great value as greenhouse plants with their fresh and attractive foliage, sometimes speckled flower stalks and long-lasting flowers under a pineapple-like tuft of leaf-like bracts. Pot bulbs in spring, with their tips just beneath the surface of a well-drained soil. After flowering in late summer, plants die down for the winter; leave in their pots and keep dry and frost-free. Repot every two years in spring, increasing the size of pot when necessary, or just shaking off the old potting mix and potting into new. Propagate by seed or by dividing the clumps. Several species are usually available: the most common is E. bicolor, which has pale green, maroon-edged flowers. E. fallalis has white flowers, while those of E. comosa are tinged with pink. There are hybrids for sale, some of which have attractive purple leaves. There is also a purple-leaved form of E. comosa. While most conform to the dimensions below, E. pole-evansii, the giant pineapple flower, reaches 36-72in(90-180cm) in height when its stems of greenish-white flowers are fully developed.
38°F(3°C) H&S:18-24in(45-60cm)

Eupatorium

(Compositae)

E. sordidum This Mexican plant has small pompons of fluffy mauve-blue flowers held in dense clusters during winter. These show up beautifully against 4in(10cm) long, serrated, softly hairy mid-green leaves. After flowering, prune back and take cuttings of fresh shoots in spring. Pinch back the growing tips at least twice to ensure a well-balanced, rounded shape with plenty of flower heads. If well cared for and fertilized throughout their growing season, plants should end up in 8-9in(20-23cm) pots. Whitefly can be a problem.
50°F(10°C) H&S:36in(90cm)

Euphorbia

(Euphorbiaceae)

E. fulgens The Mexican scarlet plume is a more elegant plant than the poinsettia. At the ends of long, slender stems, clusters of flowers with scarlet, petal-like bracts are produced naturally in winter. Stems are sometimes sold in florists and can be a good source of cuttings material.
55°F(13°C) H:48in(120cm) S:24-36in(60-90cm)

E. pulcherrima Better known as poinsettia or

Freesias

Euryops
(Compositae)

E. pectinatus This sun-loving shrub from South
Africa is very useful for the cool greenhouse. Rarely
out of flower, it will grow quite large if planted in
beds or can be restricted in pots. Deeply cut, almost
fern-like, silvery-green, down-covered leaves crowd
together, making a dense backdrop for bright yellow,
daisy-like flowers held away from the foliage on
slender, 5in(13cm) long stalks. Prune older plants
hard after flowering or in early spring, to keep them
compact. Propagate by cuttings in summer.
40°F(4°C) H:48in(120cm) S:36in(90cm)

Fortunella
(Rutaceae)

Kumquats share their cultivation requirements with
citrus (see p.53). Best grown in containers, plants
remain compact in the greenhouse and make
charming free-flowering and fruiting specimens. The
tangy and slightly bitter fruits are eaten without being
peeled or can be made into marmalade.
50°F(10°C)

F. hindsii The Hong Kong kumquat comes from
southern China and is distinctive in its upright, tidy
habit. Foliage is neat and bright green, while the
plant is studded with bright orange-red fruits
¹/₂in(1cm) in diameter. Plants are armed with sharp
spines.
H:6ft(1.8m) S:3ft(1m)

F. japonica F.j. 'Meiwa' has round yellow fruit
1in(2.5cm) in diameter. Plants can be trained into
most attractive dwarf trees on short or long stems.
There is a pretty variegated variety.
H&S:24-48in(60-120cm)

F. margarita The Nagami or oval kumquats from
southern China are among the most decorative. The
oval fruits 1¹/₂in(4cm) long are a rich orange-yellow
and are sometimes on sale in supermarkets: try
sowing their pips. There are varieties with variegated
leaves.
H:5ft(1.5m) S:3ft(1m)

Freesia
(Iridaceae)

A few pots of freesias add color and fragrance to the
greenhouse early in the year. Several species came
originally from South Africa, but now it is mostly the
hybrids with flowers of white, pink, yellow, orange,
purple, and blue, as well as some double-flowered
kinds, which are grown. Plant corms in late summer
for the earliest flowers, though they can be started
during the fall for a later spring display. Set them
2-3in(5-8cm) apart, five to seven in a 5in(13cm) pot,
so that the tops are just covered with potting mix.
Initially, grow outside in cold frames, only bringing
them into the greenhouse when frosts are likely.

Christmas star, these showy plants are grown mainly
for their bracts. They originate from Mexico where
they make large shrubs. The plants we buy are either
dwarf varieties or have been treated with growth
regulators to keep them small. Plants have become
traditional Christmas pot plants and are available in
red, pink, white, cream, and apricot. Bracts are long-
lasting if plants are given a light spot, warm constant
temperature – 50-55°F(10-13°C) – and not
overwatered. When plants have finished, either
discard or prune down all the stems to within about
4in(10cm) of the base. Water carefully, and new
shoots will begin to grow. Thin down to between

three and five shoots. Water, fertilize and shade
lightly from sun throughout summer. Given high
temperatures, bracts should be fully developed by
early winter. To ensure this, from early fall place the
plant in a dark place or cover it up for fourteen hours
each day for about three weeks. Cuttings taken at the
time of thinning out the young shoots will root best
given bottom heat. They are very soft and leak white
sap, so take during morning or evening to avoid
excess water stress. Cut with a sharp blade, use
hormone rooting compound, then insert immediately
to minimize sap flow.
50-55°F(10-13°C) H&S:12-36in(30-90cm)

148

Keep moist but not too wet, gradually increasing the water as they grow and adding liquid fertilizer every two weeks when growth is strong and flower buds start to form. Support the leaves and stems with twigs or split canes tied with string. As the flowers fade, gradually stop watering and allow plants to die down for the summer, leaving them in their pots until late summer, when the process can repeat itself. Propagate by small corms which take a year or so to flower, or by spring-sown seed. Freesias can be susceptible to spider mite. They are also liable to show signs of stress as a result of too much fluoride in their water. This manifests itself as scorch marks at the tips and edges of leaves. As this is exacerbated by acidic soil mixes and hot dry weather, symptoms can be alleviated by adding lime to raise the pH of the soil mix, and by controlling the temperature and humidity of the greenhouse. Alternatively, use bottled or rainwater.
40°F(4°C) H:18-24in(45-60cm)

Fuchsia
(Onagraceae)

Small fuchsias in 4-6in(10-15cm) pots can be dotted around the greenhouse or arranged together to give color in summer. Both upright and trailing varieties (see p.111) are suitable. Good cultivation is essential for strong plants. Take cuttings in spring from stock plants that have overwintered. For larger plants, cuttings can be rooted the previous summer but the young plants need a warmer temperature, 45-50°F (7-10°C). Short, soft cuttings 2-3in(5-8cm) long root best. A few weeks after potting, pinch back the growing tip. For short-jointed varieties, do this after three pairs of leaves but for long-jointed kinds, pinch after just one pair to avoid legginess. Four axillary growths are usually produced, and these should be pinched back again after another two pairs of leaves. Two pinchings are normal but more can be made depending on variety and when flowers are needed (allow six to eight weeks between the last pinching and flowers opening). Provide good light, with only the lightest shading from hot sun. Too much exposure will turn white-flowered varieties a dirty pink. Give plenty of water in summer but do not allow to become waterlogged. Feed at least once a week with a well-balanced liquid fertilizer. This will encourage plants to flower without their shoots becoming woody and mature. If plants appear exhausted by midsummer, feed with a high-nitrogen fertilizer. In the fall, cut back old plants by as much as a third, and keep frost-free during winter. Under cold conditions – 38-40°F(3-4°C) – give only enough water to keep the rootball moist, not wet. In early spring, prune hard, then about ten days later repot by scraping away old potting mix and dead roots and potting back to a smaller-sized pot.

Cuttings can be made of the new shoots. Subsequent growth is pinched back in the same way as for a new cutting.

F. 'Winston Churchill', of upright, bushy growth, has prolific, medium-sized, double flowers with broad, pink, reflexed sepals tipped with green. The corolla is lavender-blue, maturing to pale purple. F. 'Swingtime' has double blooms with red sepals and white petals. Small-flowered varieties with a profusion of neat blooms include F.'Graf Witte' in carmine and purple and F. 'Saturnus' with recurved red sepals and purple corolla. New trends in breeding include flowers that look up, rather than down. These include F. 'Upward Look' and F. 'Plenty'. Triphylla types, bred from F. triphylla, have distinctive leaves and tubular flowers usually clustered in terminal bunches. These normally require slightly higher minimum temperatures.
40°F(4°C) H:18-36in(45-90cm) S:12-24in(30-60cm)

Geranium
(Geraniaceae)

Two shrubby Madeiran geraniums make fine plants for the cool greenhouse, ideal for pots or planting straight in the border. G. palmatum (G. anemonifolium) comes also from Tenerife and has deeply cut leaves 6in(15cm) across and rich pink flowers in early summer. G. maderense is a fine plant with large, dissected, palmate leaves which are held out on long pinkish stalks from a trunk-like stem. It needs plenty of space to produce its masses of bright purple-pink flowers during spring. It is important to save seed, as plants usually die after flowering. Both have a habit of supporting their trunk-like stems with the old leaves, which, folded back and stiffening with age, act like props. As well as being useful, they are very much a part of the plant's outline, so it is not advisable to remove them.
38°F(3°C) H&S:24-36in(60-90cm)

Gerbera
(Compositae)

G. jamesonii The gerbera or African daisy from South Africa is easy to grow from spring-sown seed and will produce long-stemmed, daisy-like flowers during summer. Overwintering at frost-free temperatures, plants stay green but dormant, coming to life again in spring. Once growth has started, repot into fresh potting mix, splitting plants that have made several crowns. Provide a bright position and do not overwater, particularly during winter. Flowers are yellow to orange-red, up to 4in(10cm) wide, on stalks 18in(45cm) high. Leaves are shaped like those of the dandelion, only thicker and densely hairy. However, it is mostly hybrids which are grown from seed, giving a wider range of colors'including pink, red, orange, yellow, cream, and white. Dwarf hybrids

Gerbera jamesonii

Fuchsia 'Graf Witte'

149

are available which make compact pot plants but without the beauty of the long flower stems. Red spider mite can be a problem.
38°F(3°C) H:7-24in(17-60cm) S:7-18in(17-45cm)

Gloxinia

(Gesneriaceae)

The showy, large-flowered plants which used to belong under this name are now included in *Sinningia* (see pp.161-2). However, *G. perennis* (*G. maculata*), a species from Colombia to Peru, remains and merits close inspection for the beauty of its tubular, lavender-blue flowers, 1-1½in(2.5-4cm) across, with deep purple throats. These appear during summer in the upper axils of the bright green toothed leaves. Shade from hot sun and keep water off the foliage. Plants die down to rhizomes in the fall and should be overwintered virtually dry, with just a little water to keep the rhizomes plump. Resume watering in spring and repot and divide rhizomes. Propagate also by spring-sown seed. Stem or leaf cuttings will root during summer.
50°F(10°C) H&S:12-24in(30-60cm)

Heliotropium

(Boraginaceae)

H. arborescens (H. peruvianum) Heliotrope, or cherry pie, is invaluable for its purple flowers and delicious fruity fragrance reminiscent of cherries. It is a shrubby plant whose flower color can vary from purple to white. There are several named varieties, which have to be propagated by cuttings, although there are also some very good seed strains which give rise to compact plants with lovely deep purple flowers. Seeds sown in early spring will yield a crop of plants to flower all summer. Heliotropes enjoy light and dislike too much fertilizer, which causes growth at the expense of flowers and sometimes gives rise to blackened leaf edges. Plants from cuttings will need to be pinched back twice to encourage branching. Prune back old plants hard in spring, to give a flush of fresh shoots. Plants confined to containers seem to flower more profusely. Aphids and whitefly can be a problem.
40°F(4°C) H&S:18in(45cm)

Hibiscus

(Malvaceae)

H. esculentus (Abelmoschus esculentus) Although not showy (for hibiscus with beautiful flowers see pp.62-3), this hibiscus bears edible fruit known as okra or ladies' fingers. Originally from West Africa, this annual plant can be grown from spring-sown seed. Tie the main stem into a cane, enjoy the pale yellow flowers and harvest the erect, ribbed fleshy pods when 3in(8cm) long. Pick regularly to encourage pods to develop from midsummer into the fall.

Discard plants after fruiting and raise fresh from seed each year.
50-60°F(10-16°C) H:36in(90cm) S:18in(45cm)

Hippeastrum

(Liliaceae/Amaryllidaceae)

These showy bulbous plants, also known as amaryllis, are easy and fun to grow. Bulbs of large-flowered hybrids become available in the fall, often being sold in "kit" form complete with pot and potting mix. Larger, more expensive bulbs will give a more stunning initial display, usually with two flower stems carrying up to four blooms each. *H.* 'Apple Blossom' and vivid *H.* 'Red Lion' are popular varieties. For daintier plants with several shorter stems bearing smaller but more numerous blooms, choose the gracile varieties. Soak the fleshy roots at the base of the bulb for an hour or two prior to planting. Then bury the bulb by two thirds, keep moist, and stand in a bright, warm position. A flower stem will soon begin to grow, followed by strappy leaves. As these are responsible for re-fueling the bulb for next year's flowers, they need careful treatment. Use a high-nitrogen fertilizer initially, followed by high potash to encourage flowering. If a hippeastrum is given enough light, moisture, and warmth, it will retain its leaves and produce at least one flower stem a year, usually during summer. Most growers prefer their plants to become dormant, in order to start them into growth during fall for winter flowers. To achieve this, stop watering during early summer, so that the leaves die back. A warm winter minimum of 55°F(13°C) will give the best results. In a frost-free greenhouse, bulbs which have been allowed to grow all summer will die down naturally as the temperature reduces in the fall. Keep these dry all winter and let them flower during spring and summer as the temperature warms up. Repot every three years.
40°F(4°C) H:12-20in(30-50cm) S:12in(30cm)

Hydrangea

(Hydrangeaceae)

H. macrophylla During spring, potted specimens of hydrangea varieties can be bought in bud. Kept cool and bright, they will remain in flower for up to eight weeks. Take cuttings from mid spring, selecting non-flowering shoots. When rooted and potted singly, they can be grown outside in a cold frame for the rest of the summer: pinch back the growing tip and pot in 5in(13cm) pots as new shoots begin to break. They will lose their leaves in the fall. Protect from the severest of winter cold, either in a frost-free greenhouse or inside a cold frame covered with burlap cloth or old carpet. Toward late winter, move the plants into a warmer temperature of 45-50°F(7-10°C), misting the shoots regularly to encourage growth.

Once the buds begin to break, start feeding with a well-balanced liquid fertilizer. Blue-flowered varieties need an acidic soil mix, soft water, and liquid fertilizer containing sequestered iron to help them retain their color, or aluminum sulfate is sometimes used. Pink-flowered varieties prefer a slightly alkaline soil but do not require special treatment. After flowering, prune back to a healthy pair of leaves, pot up, and repeat the process. Otherwise, plant in the garden and start again from cuttings.
45°F(7°C) H&S:12-36in(30-90cm)

Hymenocallis

(Liliaceae/Amaryllidaceae)

The fragrant white or yellow flowers of this attractive genus bear an exotic resemblance to those of daffodil, with a corona composed of fused, membranous stamen filaments and spidery, reflexed petals. Most commonly grown is *H.* × *festalis* (*Ismene* × *festalis*), a deciduous hybrid very similar to one of its parents, Peruvian *H. narcissiflora*. Flowers are 4-5in(10-13cm) wide, creamy-white, and gloriously scented. Pot bulbs in spring, with the necks just above soil level. Shade lightly from hot sun and feed regularly with liquid fertilizer. Flowers are borne during spring or summer, those plants kept warmer blooming earlier. Keep deciduous kinds dry when dormant in winter. Do not allow evergreen types to dry out but water sparingly in winter. Repot every three or four years. Propagate by offsets. Mealy bugs can be a problem.
45°F(7°C) H:30in(75cm) S:18in(45cm)

Hypoestes

(Acanthaceae)

Although this genus is mostly represented by the polka dot plant *H. phyllostachya* (*H. sanguinolenta*) – see p.130 – there is a little-known relative, *H. aristata* from South Africa, which deserves wider recognition. Its pretty mauve and white flowers brighten the greenhouse during winter. After flowering, prune hard and take cuttings from the ensuing growth during summer. Pinch back young plants twice to make bushier specimens.
50°F(10°C) H:36in(90cm) S:24in(60cm)

Impatiens

(Balsaminaceae)

The number of impatiens or busy Lizzie hybrids available for bedding and container planting is almost bewildering. In white, all shades of pink, orange, and red, as bicolors, doubles, or rosebuds, these compact floriferous plants can also bring color to the greenhouse. Keep plants cool and shade from hot sun. Prune hard when necessary, usually in spring and summer. Seeds need light to germinate but tend to dry out when surface-sown. One solution is to sow them in shallow drills across the soil surface but cover with a thin layer of vermiculite. This inert substance will keep them moist while letting light through. Maintain a warm temperature of 55-60°F (13-16°C) during winter, but plants will tolerate 50°F(10°C). Propagate by cuttings. Spider mite, western flower thrips, and cyclamen mite can be a problem, especially in hot, dry air.

I. New Guinea hybrids Following a plant-collecting expedition, some of the species collected were crossed to give rise to a group called New Guinea hybrids. With large scarlet, pink, or lilac flowers and lush, often brightly colored, sometimes variegated leaves, they have become popular indoor plants ideal for the greenhouse. Their stems are strong and fleshy, making sturdy, rounded plants covered with bloom from spring through fall. They can be raised from seed.
50°F(10°C) H&S:18in(45cm)

I. niamniamensis The Congo cockatoo, a showy species from central Africa, has yellow flowers 1½in(4cm) long with inflated red spurs which look like the curved beaks of exotic parrots. Leaves, which can be up to 8in(20cm) long, tend to be clustered at the tops of sturdy stems, with the flowers held out on thin stalks among them during summer and fall.
50°F(10°C) H:24in(60cm) S:12in(30cm)

I. pseudoviola This unusual impatiens with a distribution from Kenya to Tanzania makes a delicate plant bejeweled with dainty violet-like flowers during spring, summer, and fall. It makes a draping mound of growth and is useful for plugging gaps between plants on benches. Planted in a bed, several plants will knit together to make a pleasant carpet of bright green studded with violet.
50°F(10°C) H&S:9-12in(23-30cm)

I. repens An unusual yellow-flowered species from India and Sri Lanka which is little known but deserves wider cultivation. Its creeping habit is useful for covering the front of tables or benches. Reddish, brittle stems are furnished with small, rounded but pointed leaves and pretty bright yellow spurred flowers 1½in(4cm) long during summer.
50°F(10°C) H:4in(10cm) S:12in(30cm)

I. walleriana This busy Lizzie from Tanzania and Mozambique with its pale green stems and pale pink flowers used to be widely grown before the advent of modern hybrids. It has now been superseded by more compact, floriferous, or showy hybrids. Flower color can vary to include scarlet, orange, and white. There are variegated forms with pink or orange flowers. Plants can flower year-round in warm temperatures.
50°F(10°C) H&S:24in(60cm)

Impatiens New Guinea hybrids

Hydrangea macrophylla

Hippeastrum hybrids

151

Kohleria digitaliflora

Jatropha

(Euphorbiaceae)

J. podagrica The gout plant or Guatemalan rhubarb from Central America makes a fascinating specimen. From a swollen woody stem which narrows toward the top grow a cluster of long-stalked, three-lobed leaves. During cold periods, growth stops and the leaves yellow and fall. Water sparingly during dormant spells. When temperatures and light increase, growth resumes. Sometimes the growing tip dies away to be replaced with one or two more, so that the plant slowly becomes branching. While temperatures are warm, a succession of long-lasting flower heads bearing small red flowers are produced. Water regularly while in leaf. Feed with a well-balanced liquid fertilizer two or three times during summer. Propagate by seed. Repot in spring about every four years.
50°F(10°C) H:18-36in(45-90cm) S:12-24in(30-60cm)

Jovellana

(Scrophulariaceae)

J. violacea This small shrubby plant from Chile is covered with dainty flowers during summer. Individually helmet-like in shape, flowers, 1/2in(1cm) across, are pale lilac with purple-spotted, yellow throats. Leaves are so coarsely toothed they appear lobed. Prune back after flowering to reduce size and retain a compact shape. Propagate by cuttings in summer.
40°F(4°C) H&S:2-6ft(60-180cm)

Justicia

(Acanthaceae)

The main drawback with these useful greenhouse plants is that their rapid growth soon results in untidiness. They respond well to pruning and cuttings root easily throughout spring and summer. By regularly replacing old stock with new, fresh compact plants can be enjoyed. When pruning, cut hard back so that old growth is almost completely replaced by new. Whitefly can be a problem.

J. brandegeeana Still widely known by its old name of *Beloperone guttata*, the shrimp plant from Mexico is probably the best-known species. Each flower head consists of salmon-colored, overlapping bracts from which protrude white tubular flowers. Well fed and cared for, plants in pots will last several years before bareness at the bottom of stems necessitates propagation, pruning, and renewal. Planted in a bed, individual species barely need any attention and will flower virtually year-round. They prefer warmer temperatures, but will tolerate temperatures almost down to freezing, although they will lose most of their leaves.

J. b. 'Yellow Queen' has yellow bracts.
50°F(10°C) H&S:30in(75cm)

***J. carnea* (*Jacobinia carnea, J. pohliana, J. velutina*)**
The king's crown or Brazilian plume is a showy
plant with sturdy stems furnished with large leaves,
up to 10in(25cm) long, crowned by 4-5in(10-13cm)
long, plume-like spikes of rose-pink flowers in
summer.
50°F(10°C) H:48in(120cm) S:30in(75cm)
***J. rizzinii* (*J. pauciflora*)** A pretty gap-filler whether
planted in the border or grown in pots, this Brazilian
species makes sprawling, shrubby growth and is
peppered with tubular flowers 1in(2.5cm) long.
Scarlet at the base and yellow toward the tip, they
make a bright and cheerful sight from fall, through
winter to spring.
50°F(10°C) H&S:12-24in(30-60cm)
***J. suberecta* (*Diclipteris suberecta*)** This species from
Uruguay with soft, velvety leaves covered with silvery
gray hairs tends to be straggly. This is offset by a
show of delicate orange tubular flowers 1in(2.5cm)
long, produced in summer and fall.
50°F(10°C) H&S:12-24in(30-60cm)

Kohleria
(Gesneriaceae)
Attractive hairy-leaved plants from the highlands of
Colombia. Water sparingly when growth stops
during winter. If they become untidy, repropagate by
cuttings in spring and summer and cut down the
older stems. Healthy, well-fed plants will soon grow
sturdy new shoots. Alternatively, pot pieces of the
underground rhizomes separately in spring.
K. digitaliflora This kohleria has foxglove-like
flowers in summer and fall which are a festive
combination of pink tubes with turned-back,
maroon-spotted, pea-green lobes. *K.* 'Hannah Roberts'
has a coral tube with maroon-spotted cream lobes.
50°F(10°C) H:24in(60cm) S:18in(45cm)
K. eriantha Although probably the straggliest
species, it compensates by having showy, orange-red,
tubular flowers during summer. Provide the support
of canes as stems grow.
50°F(10°C) H:36in(90cm) S:30in(75cm)

Lachenalia
(Liliaceae/Hyacinthaceae)
Known as Cape cowslips, a reference to their South
African origins, these bulbous plants are wonderful
for the cool greenhouse. Given frost-free
temperatures they will grow throughout winter and
open their unusual flowers from midwinter. Flower
spikes, bearing cylindrical or bell-shaped flowers, rise
up from between strap-shaped leaves. Most common
flower colors are yellow, orange, and green but there
are lesser-known purple- and white-flowered species.
L. aloides var. *luteola* (*L. tricolor*) has mottled leaves
and pretty red, yellow, and green flowers. *L.a.* var.
aurea is taller with lovely golden bells. *L.a.* 'Nelsonii'

Justicia rizzinii

Justicia brandegeeana

Kohleria eriantha

Lilium auratum

Lilium nepalense

Lachenalia aloides var. quadricolor and L.a. var. luteola

has green-tipped, yellow flowers, while those of *L.a.* 'Pearsonii' are similar but tipped with reddish-purple. *L.a.* var. *quadricolor* manages to combine almost all the colors by having red, yellow, green, and purple flowers. *L. bulbifera* 'George' is very fine, having unusual pinkish flowers with green tips. Pot bulbs during late summer or early fall, setting five to seven in a 5in(13cm) pot and covering them with 1in (2.5cm) of soil with a little added sharp sand. Water in well, but sparingly thereafter, until leaves are visible. After flowering, allow to die down, leaving them dry in their pots until repotting in summer. 38°F(3°C) H:6-12in(15-30cm) S:2-3in(5-8cm)

Lagerstroemia
(Lythraceae)
L. Little Chief Hybrids These make admirable pot plants. Branching into a small shrub, they lose their leaves in winter. For cultivation see p.63.
32-45°F(0-7°C) H&S:12in(30cm)

Lantana
(Verbenaceae)
L. camara The yellow sage is a shrubby plant with hairy, almost scratchy leaves and compact heads of flowers which open yellow in the center but age to bright orange-red. There are various named forms, with flower colors of yellow, pink, red, and white, most exhibiting some color variation in the same head. Restricted in pots or planted in beds, shrubs tend to become leggy but respond well to pruning. They are useful for unshaded greenhouses, being tolerant of full light. Propagate in summer by cuttings. Whitefly are a problem.
50°F(10°C) H&S:24-48in(60-120cm)

Ledebouria
(Liliaceae/Hyacinthaceae)
L. socialis (Scilla violacea) The South African wood hyacinth needs cool conditions and good light for the leaves to retain their compact shape and strong color. Each bulb has about four highly decorative leaves at one time. These are silvery green with irregular green spots and brownish-purple beneath. During late spring, spikes of small flowers are produced, each with six white petals striped down the middle with green, surrounding a bunch of bright purple filaments topped by yellow anthers. Grow in shallow pots or pans. Propagate by division of bulbs. (See also p.131.)
38°F(3°C) H:4-5in(10-13cm) S:indefinite

Lilium
(Liliaceae)
Although most lilies are hardy, they can also be grown indoors. The best time to plant is late fall. A 6in(15cm) pot will hold a single bulb, or three

bulbs can be planted in a 10in(25cm) pot. Cover with 1in(2.5cm) of potting mix. Stem-rooting lilies are best planted lower down in the pot so that, as they grow, another 2-3in(5-8cm) layer of potting mix can be added to encourage healthy roots. Water in well, then water sparingly until growth begins. Stand in a protected cold frame or inside a cool, well-ventilated greenhouse. Begin feeding as the flower buds appear. Stake the flower stems. After flowering, lilies can be dried out, then planted in the garden or repotted, although freshly bought bulbs usually give better results. Propagate by offsets in fall, seed in spring or fall, scales in summer and sometimes stem bulbils in fall. Aphids can be a problem.

L. auratum The gold-rayed lily from Japan is a summer-flowering, stem-rooting species with huge, open white flowers 10-12in(25-30cm) across. Each petal is stroked with a band of yellow down the center and spotted with red and yellow. The intense perfume could be overwhelming in a small space. The large bulbs each need a 10in(25cm) pot.
32°F(0°C) H:36-60in(90-150cm) S:18in(45cm)

L. longiflorum The Easter lily, white trumpet lily or Bermuda lily is a stem-rooting species from Japan. Its trumpet-shaped white flowers, with orange stamens, appear in late spring.
32°F(0°C) H:24-36in(60-90cm) S:18in(45cm)

L. nepalense This unusual Himalayan stem-rooting species is best planted in a greenhouse border, as the stems run underground. Elegant pendent flowers are an unusual green color with maroon centers.
38°F(3°C) H:12-36in(30-90cm) S:indefinite

Limonium

(Plumbaginaceae)

L. latifolium The sea lavender from Russia and Bulgaria makes an admirable pot or border plant for the cool or even unheated greenhouse. A reliably frost-hardy perennial, it produces a cloud of tiny blue flowers in summer, above large rosettes of dark green leaves. Propagate by division in spring.
27°F(-3°C) H&S:24in(60cm)

Liriope

(Liliaceae/Convallariaceae)

Lily turf makes an unusual plant for a container or border. Provide a cool, humid atmosphere and shade from hot sun. Stress shows itself as brown tips to the leaves, which can be removed for tidiness. *L. muscari* from China and Japan produces spikes of rounded, bell-shaped purple flowers in summer and fall. Named cultivars like *L.m.* 'Majestic' have larger, bolder spikes. *L.m. variegata* has cream-edged leaves and *L.m.* 'Monroe White' has white flowers. Propagate by dividing the rhizomes in spring, or by seed in fall.
32°F(0°C) H&S:15-20in(40-50cm)

Lycopersicon

(Solanaceae)

A few tomato plants make an interesting contrast to the ornamentals in the greenhouse. Choose greenhouse varieties and sow in early spring. Young plants can be planted in borders but after a few years there might be a build-up of diseases in the soil. If so, revert to growing in large pots or growbags. Most varieties need to be staked and the side shoots removed as plants grow. Pinch back growing tips after about six trusses have set fruit. To achieve a good set, tap the cane to vibrate the flower and cause the pollen to shake out over other flowers. Once fruit starts setting, feed weekly with a tomato fertilizer. The range of choice is exciting – including yellow cherry-fruited 'Mirabelle'. 'Tumbler' needs no staking and has been specially bred for growing in containers. 'Dombito' and 'Super Marmande' have huge "beefsteak" fruits. 'Gardener's Delight' has small, flavorsome fruits. Whitefly can be a problem. Use biological control as soon as this pest appears (see p.35).
50-60°F(10-16°C) H:1-6ft(30cm-1.8m) S:12-24in(30-60cm)

Nematanthus

(Gesneriaceae)

These compact, almost trailing Brazilian natives are useful for hanging baskets as well as pots, where they will make mounds of shiny foliage decorated in spring and fall by tubular flowers, their bottom halves inflated and pouch-like. *N. gregarius* (*Hypocyrta radicans*), often known as clog plant, has orange flowers. *N.g.* 'Golden West' (*N.g.* 'Variegatus') has yellow centers to the leaves. *N.* 'Black Magic' has dark, glossy green leaves and orange yellow-tipped flowers and *N.* 'Freckles' has red-spotted, yellow flowers. Provide warm temperatures with good humidity and a well-drained soil. Propagate by cuttings in spring and summer, ultimately planting three in a large shallow pot or basket.
50°F(10°C) H&S:9in(23cm)

Nertera

(Rubiaceae)

N. granadensis The bead plant from Mexico and Central America looks somewhat unreal when bearing fruit. The compact, mat-forming growth with masses of small rounded leaves resembles *Soleirolia soleirolii* until insignificant flowers are followed by spherical, bright orange berries (strictly drupes) in fall. It requires a moderately shaded position. Grow several plants in a pan of well-drained peaty potting mix, watering carefully from below. Never allow roots to dry out. Propagate by division, seed, or small tip cuttings in spring.
32°F(0°C) H:¹⁄₂in(1cm) S:4in(10cm)

Nertera granadensis

Nematanthus 'Black Magic'

155

Miltoniopsis hybrids

Orchids

Orchids (members of the family Orchidaceae) can make an interesting addition to a collection of greenhouse plants, as long as they are chosen so that their minimum temperature and other requirements are generally the same. Many orchids are epiphytic and their leaves and flowers often arise from swollen water storage structures known as pseudobulbs. Terrestrial orchids grow in the ground, often under trees where soil is made light by leaf mold. In both habitats, there would be shade from strong sun and a moist atmosphere.

Mainly because of their epiphytic nature, orchids require a well-drained soil. The usual main constituents are bark chips and charcoal, Styrofoam beads, or perlite. Orchids growing in pots need watering less frequently than other plants. The surface of orchid potting mixes containing bark can appear deceptively dry, even when the rest is soaking wet. As a result the weight of the pot is a safer guide to whether water is required. This might be twice a week during summer but only once every two weeks during winter. Epiphytic orchids can also be grown in hanging baskets made out of slatted wood. Slabs of cork or tree fern fiber make ideal mountings as the aerial roots will cling to their irregular surfaces. Soak every day during hot summers but only every week or two during winter. High humidity and misting are important but not during late afternoon and night in summer or after midday in winter, as a combination of damp with lowering temperatures can prove fatal. Bowls and tanks of rainwater will help raise humidity during hot weather, as well as providing an ideal source of water at the right temperature. Add a half- or quarter-strength orchid fertilizer to every watering except the fourth, which should be pure water to flush out excess salts. Most orchids can be propagated by division or removal of offsets at potting time. Scale insects, mealy bugs, spider mites, and aphids on flower buds can be a problem.

Cattleya

These epiphytic orchids with showy blooms generally grow well in pots using three parts fir bark to one part charcoal, styrofoam beads, or perlite. Such a mixture provides an ideal balance between organic matter and coarse aggregate for good drainage. Pot up between early spring and summer and feed regularly with high-nitrogen fertilizer.

C. bowringiana, H:18in(45cm), the cluster cattleya from Central America, has club-shaped pseudobulbs, usually bearing two long, oval, stiff leaves and rose-purple flowers in fall.
50-55°F(10-13°C)

Coelogyne

Himalayan *C. cristata*, H:9in(23cm), is quite an easy epiphytic orchid to grow and will expand into an impressive clump of pseudobulbs and leaves. In winter and spring, pendulous racemes of lovely white flowers are produced evenly over the clump, giving a trailing appearance shown off to best effect on a stand. The fragrant blooms are 3-4in(8-10cm) wide, marked with yellow inside. Provide high humidity and water sparingly during winter. Use the same potting mix as for cattleya.
50°F(10°C)

Cymbidium

One of the most commonly cultivated orchids, H:24-36in(60-90cm). Most plants in cultivation are hybrids. Linear leaves arise from often large pseudobulbs, to be joined by long spikes of showy, long-lasting flowers in winter and spring. Plants can be stood in the garden in spring and summer, choosing a position of light shade. It is crucial to keep the plant cool at night, below 58°F(15°C), during spike development. Avoid overwatering and add fertilizer at half strength. Use a high-nitrogen formula during late winter and spring, none at all during spike initiation in midsummer, a high-potash formula in early fall and a well-balanced fertilizer during winter. Move back into the greenhouse before temperatures drop too low in early fall but give light shade and keep cool during hot periods. Plants seem to flower better when slightly pot-bound. When growth has reached the edge, pot up in spring after flowering, dividing the clump when it becomes too large. Throw away old growth and split the rest so that each new plant has two to three pseudobulbs behind new growth. Position the oldest pseudobulb against the edge of the pot, leaving maximum room for new growth. Great care is required not to overwater at the critical stage after division and repotting. An ideal potting mix consists of three parts peat substitute (adding chalk and dolomitic lime to achieve a pH of 6.2), one part of coarse perlite and one part of bark. Alternatively, use the absorbent type of rock wool.
50°F(10°C)

Dendrobium

This large, mostly epiphytic genus has a wide distribution and consequently varied cultural requirements.

Upright species, like *D. kingianum*, H:8in(20cm), from Australia, grow best in pots. This has long, stem-like pseudobulbs producing 4in(10cm) long leaves and, in late winter, spikes of delicate 1in(2.5cm) wide, pale purple-pink flowers.

The trailing growth of larger flowered, purple-pink and white, semi-deciduous *D. nobile*, H:24in(60cm), from the Himalayas to Taiwan, and its hybrids, are better accommodated in baskets or attached to cork bark or osmunda fiber. This is also true of beautiful semi-deciduous *D. aphyllum* (*D. pierardii*), H:36-72in(90-180cm), from the Himalayas to Malaysia, which bears exquisite white and pale mauve blooms. Keep cool and almost totally dry in winter but water regularly in summer and feed to encourage new growth. The more tropical dendrobiums require greater warmth and moisture throughout the year.
45-55°F(7-13°C) depending on species

Encyclia

Within this large genus of epiphytic orchids, *E. cochleata* (*Epidendrum cochleatum*) the cockle-shell orchid from Mexico to Brazil, H:12in(30cm), is perhaps best known. It has smooth oval pseudobulbs and produces racemes of strange, upside-down flowers with cockle-shell-shaped maroon and cream lips. Long thin greenish-cream sepals sweep away from the base. Use the same potting mix as for cattleya.
50°F(10°C)

Laelia

Epiphytic *L. anceps*, H:10in(25cm), from Mexico and Belize, is a good orchid for beginners and flowers in winter. One thick leaf grows from each pseudobulb and the long-lasting, decorative flowers are purple-pink. Water all year but take care not to overwater during winter. Brazilian species exhibit a wide range of flower colors, including orange, yellow, and pink. Use the same potting mix as for cattleya.
50-55°F(10-13°C)

Masdevallia

The diminutive size of most of these epiphytic orchids from Mexico and Peru means that a great variety can be accommodated. Correct watering

Coelogyne cristata

Cymbidium Pontac

Miltoniopsis Anjou 'St Patrick'

Odontoglossum × andersonianum

Paphiopedilum insigne

Phalaenopsis hybrid

Phalaenopsis Stadt Trier

Pleione formosana

Zygopetalum Artur Elle

Orchids

during winter is essential to prevent the neat cluster of stems and leaves from rotting. Avoid temperatures above 75°F(24°C). Use the same potting mix as for cattleya. Provide good humidity and air circulation and water carefully during winter. "Flowers" are in fact ornamental sepals which can, in the case of commonly grown *M. coccinea*, H:6in(15cm), from Colombia, be orange, yellow, pink, red, or white.
50°F(10°C)

Miltoniopsis

The beautiful pansy orchids, H:8in(20cm), have large, brightly colored flowers. The highland species usually tolerate cooler temperatures than lowland species but the majority in cultivation are hybrids. Keep moist year-round. Use the same potting mix as for cattleya.
58°F(15°C)

Odontoglossum

The mostly epiphytic species in this group have given rise to a large number of hybrids with spectacular flower spikes mainly flowering between fall and spring, with each spike lasting five to seven weeks. They grow best in pots. Cool summer temperatures, ideally below 75°F(24°C), are needed for healthy growth. Provide good air circulation, keep moist and humid throughout the year, and never overwater. Fertilizer should be diluted to quarter strength. Following nearly a century of hybridization, they are now available in all the colors of the rainbow, H:5-9in(13-23cm). Pot in early spring or fall, using the same potting mix as for cattleya.
50°F(10°C)

Paphiopedilum

These slipper orchids with their fan-like foliage and characteristically pouched flowers are mostly terrestrial. The many species have attractive, delicately shaped flowers, mostly in reddish-purple, green, yellow, and brown. Many of the plants commonly cultivated, however, are hybrids. Complex types, which have plain green leaves, flower mostly during winter. Mottled or tessellated types produce most of their flowers during summer but occasionally flower at other times of the year as well. Each individual bloom can last up to three months. Keep plants moist, though not waterlogged, year-round and make sure that water does not lodge in leaf bases since this causes rotting. Liquid fertilizer should be diluted to quarter strength. Use the same potting mix as for cattleya, potting in spring. The easiest to grow is probably Himalayan *P. insigne*, which can tolerate a minimum of 45°F(7°C). Mottle leaf: 45-55°F(7-13°C)
Green leaf: 65°F(18°C)

Phalaenopsis

The pretty epiphytic moth orchids from tropical Asia are relatively easy to grow if care is taken not to overwater them. Keep moist, but not waterlogged, year-round as they do not have pseudobulbs to store water. Feed with liquid fertilizer at half strength. Provide humidity and shade. When the last flower in a spike has faded, never cut the whole flower spike off but prune just above the second node back from the last flower. The stem should branch and produce more buds, so that one plant can be in flower for up to six months. Spikes rise 12-36in(30-90cm) high. Potting should take place in spring and early summer, using the same potting mix as for cattleya.
60°F(16°C)

Pleione

Less demanding than some other orchids, pleiones, H:3-8in(8-20cm), are ideal for the cool greenhouse. They are semi-epiphytic, growing on slopes and on rocks in high forests. Their natural soil is very crumbly and well-drained. A good potting mix consists of eight parts of orchid-grade bark to four parts of peat, and three parts of coarse-grade perlite. One dormant bulb should be potted in a 3in(8cm) pot, or several in a larger, wide shallow pot so that one-third to half the bulb protrudes from the surface. Delay watering, only doing so when the flower bud grows, to make the new roots search for moisture. When leaves grow, water normally and begin liquid feeding with a low-nitrogen, high-potassium, and high-phosphate fertilizer at half strength every other watering, which is roughly weekly. As leaves begin to yellow in fall, stop watering. Repot every year in winter while plants are dormant. Propagate by removing bulbils from the sides of older bulbs. These should reach flowering size in two to three years.

P. bulbocodioides Limprichtii Group have pretty rose-purple flowers but there are yellow- and lilac-flowered species as well as a host of exquisite and often very expensive hybrids. *P. formosana* has magenta, lilac, or white flowers.
32°F(0°C)

Zygopetalum

Although not often seen, these epiphytic orchids, H:12in(30cm), are quite easy to grow and flower. They originate from upland forests in tropical South America and grow from pseudobulbs, producing leathery leaves and stems of quite large flowers with similar dramatic coloring and fragrance. Sepals and petals are pale green marked with dark maroon, which contrast with a pretty white lip striped or flushed with violet. Use the same potting mix as for cattleya.
55°F(13°C)

Pachystachys lutea

Pachystachys
(Acanthaceae)

In common with other members of this family, quick-growing pachystachys have attractive flowers but after a couple of years individual plants become leggy. As cuttings root easily, propagate regularly, replacing old stock with new. Pinch back the growing tips of young plants to help develop a branching shape. Prune older plants hard in spring or summer. Provide good light and feed with liquid fertilizer when new shoots appear. Shade lightly from hot sun. Whitefly can be a nuisance.

P. coccinea Cardinal's guard from northern South America and the West Indies produces 2in(5cm) long, scarlet flowers protruding from green bracts in winter.
55°F(13°C) H:60in(150cm) S:24-36in(60-90cm)

P. lutea More popular than *P. coccinea*, the lollipop plant or golden candles, from Peru, is grown for its 4in(10cm) long candles of bright yellow bracts, from which emerge pretty white flowers. Flowering continues until the depths of winter. Grow in pots or in greenhouse borders.
55°F(13°C) H:36in(90cm) S:30in(75cm)

Pavonia
(Malvaceae)

P. multiflora An erect-growing plant from Brazil which produces several very upright stems hung with narrowly oval, pointed leaves. Red and purple-blue flowers are produced at the ends of stems. Prune back old plants to produce new shoots. Give warmth and humidity, although plants will tolerate a lower winter resting temperature. Propagate by seed or in summer by cuttings. Whitefly can be a problem. 50°F(10°C) H:36-72in(90-180cm) S:24-36in(60-90cm)

Pelargonium
(Geraniaceae)

This attractive group of plants contributes color and interest to the greenhouse while needing little special cultivation. Most pelargoniums have their origin in South Africa, where they are adapted to poor soils and hot sunshine. There are many different types and varieties. Most common are zonal pelargoniums, often referred to, confusingly, as geraniums. Trailing ivy-leaved pelargoniums are popular for hanging baskets and wall planters (see p.113). Most pelargoniums flower profusely during summer and some will carry on during winter if temperatures are high enough and the light good. Late summer is the best time for rooting cuttings. Take them about 3in(8cm) long, trimming them under a node with a sharp knife and inserting them without hormone rooting powder into 3½in(9cm) pots of loose potting mixture. Do not cover, but stand on the greenhouse

benches under light shade to root. Water in well but carefully thereafter. If the greenhouse is only heated to keep the frost off during winter, then leave these cuttings undisturbed in their pots until spring. Once they have been potted separately, removing the growing tip will encourage those with a leggy habit to branch. If a minimum of 45-50°F(7-10°C) can be maintained, rooted cuttings can be potted separately in fall. Prune back old stock plants in spring to retain a compact shape. Once they begin to grow, repot into a same-sized or larger pot. Cuttings root well in spring too. Never overwater pelargoniums, as this damages their roots and makes leaves turn red or yellow. Propagate zonal pelargoniums by seed sown early in the year. Rust and whitefly can be a problem (see p.37).

ZONAL PELARGONIUMS Marvelous summer flowerers for terracotta pots, characterized by darker zonal markings on their leaves. There is great variety in flower shape and color. Basic types are either single or double. Among doubles are *P.* Irene varieties which tend to have large blooms and leaves. *P.* Deacon varieties, also doubles, produce abundant flowers on compact plants. Recent introductions

include speckled varieties like *P.* 'Magda', pale pink splashed and speckled with red. Finger-flowered kinds are of American origin and have quilled petals and distinctively lobed leaves. Cactus-flowering kinds, like scarlet *P.* 'Fire Dragon' and double white *P.* 'Noel' are quilled and pointed. Popular Rosebud varieties such as *P.* 'Apple Blossom Rosebud' date from Victorian times but are enjoying a resurgence of popularity. Stellar varieties such as *P.* 'Apricot' and pink *P.* 'Supernova' have distinctively lobed, often heavily marked leaves and feathery petals. The tulip-flowered varieties salmon *P.* 'Patricia Andrea' and *P.* 'Red Pandora' from North America are very unusual as their flowers never fully open. The dwarf and miniature varieties like pale pink *P.* 'Denebola', deep red *P.* 'Goblin', and lavender-pink *P.* 'Jayne Eyre' are useful where space is restricted, but are prone to the bacterial disease leafy gall (see p.37). 38°F(3°C) H:4-24in(10-60cm) S:4-18in(10-45cm)

UNIQUES These shrubby varieties often have the added bonus of aromatic foliage. *P.* 'Scarlet Unique' has soft stems and leaves which combine well with beautifully shaped, bright scarlet flowers with darker marks on the two larger upper petals. The petals of 'Hula' are

Pelargonium 'Cherry Orchard' and *P.* 'Fringed Aztec'

Pelargonium 'Catford Belle'

Salvia leucantha

rich rose-pink with maroon blotches. Those of 'Mystery' are a deep velvety red with black markings.
38°F(3°C) H&S:18-36in(45-90cm)

REGAL PELARGONIUMS Their main flowering period is in early summer, when large blooms mass together so that hardly any foliage can be seen. Slightly more demanding than most other pelargoniums, they need more moisture at the roots and warmer minimum temperatures during winter. Propagate as soon as flowers fade. 'Country Girl', 'Lavender Grand Slam', and 'White Glory' are reliable cultivars.
45-50°F(7-10°C) H:12-18in(30-45cm) S:12in(30cm)

ANGELS These petite versions of regal pelargoniums flower all summer. *P.* 'Catford Belle' is an upright grower with purple-pink blooms marked with dark maroon. Overwinter cuttings and stock plants at frost-free temperatures.
38°F(3°C) H:9in(23cm) S:6in(15cm)

SPECIES Some species are grown for their scented leaves but others have attractive, if usually rather small flowers. *P. echinatum*, H:20in(50cm) S:12in(30cm), the cactus geranium from Southern Africa, produces white flowers with reddish blotches on the upper petals throughout winter. Plants seem to rest during early summer, then begin flowering again. Naturally branching stems are succulent and bear neat, sage-green leaves and prickle-like stipules. *P.e.* 'Miss Stapleton' is a pretty pink form. The more succulent species with swollen stems or woody bases require careful watering and sandy, well-drained soil.
45-50°F(7-10°C)

Pentas
(Rubiaceae)

P. lanceolata The pretty Egyptian star cluster from tropical East Africa to southern Arabia is a shrubby plant that will thrive in a pot or planted in the greenhouse border. Heads of usually pink but sometimes white, red, or mauve flowers appear during summer and fall. When pot-grown, plants tend to be leggy. This is easily solved by pruning in late winter. As shoots begin to sprout, they can be used as cuttings or the plant potted to make a larger specimen. Propagate also by seed. Shade lightly from hot sun. Whitefly can be a problem.
50°F(10°C) H&S:36in(90cm)

Peristrophe
(Acanthaceae)

P. hyssopifolia (P. angustifolia) This species from Java is usually represented by *P.h.* 'Aureovariegata', whose leaves, heavily marked with yellow in the center, clash with small purple-pink flowers in summer. Plants tend to be straggly, so propagate frequently and replace old stock with new. Pinch back shoot tips of young plants as they grow to encourage bushiness. Shade lightly from hot sun.
50°F(10°C) H:12-24in(30-60cm) S:18-36in(45-90cm)

P. speciosa This Indian species has a much neater habit than its relative and grows into a well-formed bushy shrub. Bright, pinky-purple flowers 1½in (4cm) long open during winter. After flowering, prune hard back and wait for new shoots to grow in spring. Root these as cuttings, pinching back the growing tips several times as they grow, to encourage a bushy shape. Well-grown, well-fed plants will end up in 7-9in(17-23cm) pots. Once the cuttings are growing successfully, the old plants can be thrown away. Whitefly can be a problem.
50°F(10°C) H:36in(90cm) S:24-30in(60-75cm)

Plectranthus
(Labiatae)

P. thyrsoideus (Coleus thyrsoideus) This plant from central Africa is rather like a plain-leaved coleus with slightly fleshier, strong-smelling leaves and spikes of blue flowers produced in winter. Take cuttings from stock plants in spring, pinch back the growing tips to keep them bushy, pot up as needed and you'll be able to enjoy large plants by winter. A second batch of cuttings can be rooted during summer to produce smaller plants. Whitefly can be a problem.
45°F(7°C) H:12-36in(30-90cm) S:12-24in(30-60cm)

Polygala
(Polygalaceae)

P. × dalmaisiana (P. myrtifolia var. grandiflora) An attractive shrub which can grow tall enough to earn itself space as a specimen but is more often kept small by pruning in late spring. Elliptic gray-green leaves are attractive year-round and are joined by ridged, pea-like pinkish-purple flowers from spring to fall. Prefers an acidic soil mix and soft rainwater. Propagate by seed in spring or by cuttings in summer.
40°F(4°C) H&S:24-48in(60-120cm)

Saintpaulia
(Gesneriaceae)

African violets are widely cultivated as houseplants but are also suitable for the greenhouse provided there is shade from hot sun and temperatures above 85°F(29°C) can be avoided. The wide variety of plants grown today come from a handful of species collected originally from the Usambara Mountains of Tanzania. The first (*S. ionantha* and *S. confusa*) were introduced into Europe in 1892 and almost immediately gave rise to hybrids. As rooms became warmer, so more African violets were grown, increasing the incidence of interesting sports. Soon there were doubles, varieties with white-edged flowers known as Genevas and star-shaped flowers different from the classic violet shape. *S. groetii*, which was a later introduction, has a trailing habit and was used to create pendent varieties suitable for hanging baskets. There are even miniature and micro varieties, such as 'Pip Squeak' which has pale blue flowers and is only 2½in(6cm) across. Now there are varieties to suit every taste: 'Maria' has pink frilly petals, 'Rococo Pink' is a double, 'Fancy Pants' is a bicolor with maroon-edged, white blooms, and 'Blue Nymph' has more violet-like, blue and white flowers.

In the wild, saintpaulias flourish under the shade of tree canopies, often at high altitudes, enjoying a stable temperature of 65-77°F(18-25°C). They might tolerate a short period of temperatures as low as 40°F(4°C) but will languish until warmth returns. Never overwater. The easiest method is to fill the plant's saucer with 2in(5cm) of tepid water for half an hour, drain and return the plant to a dry saucer. Never splash water onto leaves, as it can leave ugly marks. During periods of active growth, feed virtually at every watering using a special African violet fertilizer at quarter or half strength. Occasionally, give pure water from the top to flush out any excess fertilizer from the soil. Propagation is usually by leaf cuttings (see pp.32-3). The aim is to produce a single-crowned plant with just one rosette of leaves. Divide congested, multi-crowned plants by cutting through thick mats of roots if necessary. Side shoots can be severed from the main plant. Propagate also by sowing the tiny seed onto moist potting mix. Germination takes three to four weeks; do not cover with potting mix or place in the dark. Mealy bugs and cyclamen mites can be a problem.
60-65°F(16-18°C) H:4in(10cm) S:10in(25cm)

Salvia

(Labiatae)

There are several tender salvias, mostly with their origins in Mexico, which, while they can be grown outside during summer in cold climates, need winter protection from frost. They also make excellent greenhouse plants throughout the year, either planted in borders or grown in pots. Most are shrubby plants and need regular pruning in early spring. Flowers are usually interesting in shape and color but even when plants are not flowering, aromatic foliage is attractive. Pinch back the growing tips of young plants to encourage a bushier shape. Old, ragged plants can be replaced by new. Propagate by spring-sown seed or cuttings taken in spring or late summer. Whitefly can be a problem.

S. buchananii This species has large, furry magenta-colored flowers which appear toward the end of summer. Leaves are dark grayish-green with a leathery texture.
40°F(4°C) H&S:18in(45cm)

S. discolor Possibly the most striking salvia, with near-black, violet-hued flowers projecting downward from almost hooded, pale bluish-green calyces in winter. Foliage is silvery and reminiscent of blackcurrant when crushed.
40°F(4°C) H&S:24in(60cm)

S. fulgens Soft, hairy, scarlet flowers 2in(5cm) long are borne in summer.
40°F(4°C) H:36in(90cm) S:24in(60cm)

S. involucrata Racemes of magenta flowers in late summer and fall are enveloped by showy pink bracts. S.i. 'Bethellii' has larger flowers and bracts.
40°F(4°C) H&S:36in(90cm)

S. leucantha The beautiful Mexican bush sage has long spikes of flowers that appear purple and white. In fact both calyces and stems are covered in violet-purple hairs, so that the ¾in(2cm) long white flowers make a fine contrast. Flowers appear in late summer and fall.
40°F(4°C) H:36-48in(90-120cm) S:30-36in(75-90cm)

Scadoxus

(Liliaceae/Amaryllidaceae)

These African bulbs need plenty of room in a large (preferably clay) pot. Repot every two years in late spring. Even if they are not to be given a larger pot, shake away the old soil with dead roots and replace with a soil-based potting mix with extra sand. A layer of gravel over the surface sets them off and helps water pass quickly away from the bulbs. Water evergreen species sparingly when almost dormant during winter. Deciduous species should have no water at all while resting. During summer when growth is active, keep moist and give liquid fertilizer every three weeks or so. This is particularly important after flowering if seeds are to set. Shade lightly from

Pentas lanceolata

hot sun. Propagate by removing offsets in spring, or sowing seed when ripe in spring or fall. These are borne inside berry-like fruits which take up to one year to ripen.

S. multiflorus The fireball lily or blood flower is a tropical African species usually obtained as a bulb in spring. Plant just under the surface of the soil and water thoroughly. Water sparingly afterward until growth is well established. The flower stem bearing a spectacular spherical head, up to 6in(15cm) wide, of beautiful red flowers, usually appears before the maroon-spotted basal leaves. As these fade, longer green leaves grow up. Eventually these too begin to turn yellow and the plant dies down again until the following spring. H:18in(45cm) S:12in(30cm). By contrast, *S.m.* ssp. *katherinae* is virtually evergreen, with leaves persisting throughout winter and only just beginning to die off as the new growth bud bursts through the old stem at the top of the bulb. Flower heads are 6-10in(15-25cm) across in summer. Fruits eventually turn red and hold up to four seeds each, which often begin to germinate before the fruit falls.
50°F(10°C) H:30in(75cm) S:18-24in(45-60cm)

S. puniceus The royal paint brush from southern Africa has small, dark maroon basal leaves. Later, larger, wavy-edged leaves sheath the stem with handsomely maroon-speckled bases. The flower stem rises above the foliage and in spring holds an umbel of tightly packed orange-red flowers with yellow anthers. Held in by greenish-maroon bracts, they resemble a red paint brush dipped lightly into yellow

Scadoxus multiflorus

paint. The plant dies down in fall and stays dormant all winter.
38°F(3°C) H&S:18in(45cm)

Scutellaria

(Labiatae)

S. costaricana The scarlet skullcap from Costa Rica is a shrubby plant which bears heads of tubular orange flowers, each with a hooded upper lip and bright golden lower lip, from midwinter to midsummer. It can be planted into borders or grown in pots. Shade from direct sun. Propagate and prune to replace and rejuvenate stock. Whitefly can be a problem.
55°F(13°C) H:24-48in(60-120cm) S:12-24in(30-60cm)

Serissa

(Rubiaceae)

S. foetida This shrub from southeast Asia provides useful ground cover in a greenhouse border between larger specimens, or to grow in pots. Wiry stems bear small, shiny, deep green leaves and small white flowers between spring and fall. Trim back pot-grown specimens after flowering to retain a compact shape. A double-flowered form and a variegated form with cream-edged leaves can also be found. Propagate in summer by cuttings.
45°F(7°C) H:18in(45cm) S:24in(60cm)

Sinningia

(Gesneriaceae)

Sinningias, including plants which used to be called gloxinias, grow from woody tubers and can be kept

Sinningia cardinalis

Solanum capsicastrum

Sutherlandia frutescens

from year to year. In the fall, flowers stop forming and leaves turn yellow and die off as temperatures drop and light fades. Allow plants to become dry and leave in their pots until the following spring. Then shake free of old soil and pot up so that the surface of the tuber is just level with the peat-based or peat-alternative potting mix. Water carefully while new roots are growing. During active growth, provide temperatures between 65 and 70°F(18 and 21°C). Keep water off their sensitive leaves, particularly when light is bright. Shade from sun and avoid hot summer temperatures. Propagate by cuttings of young stems in early summer or by leaf cuttings. Tubers can be cut into portions, each containing potential growing tips. Dust cut surfaces with a fungicide before potting into loose potting mixture to grow roots and shoots. Seed is very small and should be surface-sown.

S. cardinalis The attractive cardinal flower from Brazil is readily available from seed. Soft, hairy, bright green leaves are topped by 2in(5cm) long, tubular red flowers during summer. Only repot every three years or so, to avoid disturbing plants. Simply water to start them into growth in spring.
50°F(10°C) H:4-10in(10-25cm) S:6-7in(15-17cm)
SINNINGIA HYBRIDS The commonly grown hybrids, generally referred to as gloxinias, make lovely greenhouse plants which, raised from seed sown in late winter, will flower during late summer and fall. If temperatures are still low during the early part of

the year, grow the tiny seedlings on in a heated plant incubator with a temperature of 65°F(18°C). Keep them warm during thinning and first pot stage, by which time natural temperatures will have risen. Tubers are also available. Plant in spring and repot each year into fresh potting mix. There are also miniature hybrids, many of them with *S. pusilla* as a parent. The stems of this diminutive species are only ¹/₂in(1cm) high and the leaves ¹/₂in(1cm) across. Tiny lavender-colored flowers appear almost continuously.
50°F(10°C) H:¹/₂-12in(1-30cm) S:1-16in(2.5-42cm)

Smithiantha
(Gesneriaceae)
Sometimes referred to as temple bells, this interesting group of Mexican species are generally represented in cultivation by their hybrids. These tend to be compact and offer an interesting range of flower colors, usually involving red, yellow, and orange. Plants grow from underground scaly rhizomes, which can be separated and repotted in spring. After flowering, plants die down; keep dry until growth resumes in late winter. Shade lightly from full sun and keep water off the foliage.
50°F(10°C) H&S:8-12in(20-30cm)

Solanum
(Solanaceae)
S. capsicastrum The winter cherry from Brazil is valuable for its cheerful orange-red winter fruits.

Plants can be made to last for several years. Usually raised from spring-sown seed, young plants can be grown on outside, where there are more insects to pollinate the small white flowers. Choose a light position, but protect from midday sun. Feed with a liquid fertilizer and water throughout summer and move plants indoors before temperatures drop in the fall. Berries should have begun forming and will gradually turn from green to orange-red. Aphids can be a problem while plants are in the greenhouse. When the display of fruit is over, keep plants growing well until spring, then prune back by two-thirds. Place outside when all danger of frost has passed. Despite their common name, fruits are not edible.
40°F(4°C) H&S:12-18in(30-45cm)

Spathiphyllum
(Araceae)
The beautiful peace lilies with their lush foliage make a lovely underplanting to larger plants in a warm greenhouse in pots or borders. To grow well, they need shade, warmth, and humidity. In a dry atmosphere, spider mite can be a problem. *S. wallisii* from Colombia and Venezuela used to be the most commonly grown. White arum-like spathes rise above lance-shaped leaves. Then *S.* 'Mauna Loa', a vigorous, slightly larger hybrid with bigger flowers, was produced. There are now several hybrids, all similar but varying in size. *S.* 'Petite' grows

12in(30cm) high, while S. 'White Queen' is similar but has strange spathes which clothe the flower stems for some way below the spadix. S. 'Mauna Loa' and S. 'White Moon' are about 18in(45cm) high. S. 'Viscount Prima' reaches 24-30in(60-75cm) and S. 'Sensation' 36in(90cm) with massive leaves. Propagate by dividing the clump in late spring. Pot each portion separately and water very carefully. If plants need to withstand lower temperatures for a short period, keep them drier.
55-60°F(13-16°C) H&S:12-36in(30-90cm)

Streptocarpus
(Gesneriaceae)

There are two different types of Cape primrose: caulescent (stem-forming) and stemless. Most of the plants grown are derived from the stemless species and make a rosette of wrinkled, hairy leaves. Flower stems are produced almost continuously from spring to fall. Rosette-forming species originate from the steep wooded sides of the Drakensberg mountains in South Africa and like good light but shade from hot sun. A sunless greenhouse would be ideal. Plants are either mixtures raised from seed, or selected named sports and hybrids. In 1826, S. rexii, a pretty species with mauve-blue flowers marked with darker stripes, was dispatched from South Africa. Other species followed and hybridization took place using mostly rosette-forming plants. There are some strange one-leaved species and one of these, S. dunnii, was used to introduce red color. By the early 1900s there was a complex mixture of hybrids known loosely as S. hybrids. In the 1940s the John Innes Institute in England bred S. 'Constant Nymph', using S. johannis as a parent to achieve a multiflowered habit. In Holland S. 'Maassens White' occurred as a sport on S. 'Constant Nymph', and they encouraged more sport formation, arriving at S. 'Blue Nymph', S. 'Albatross', and S. 'Snow White'. More crosses at the John Innes Institute in the 1970s gave rise to pretty pink S. 'Tina', blue S. 'Paula', and others. New varieties are still being raised at a nursery in Wales. S. 'Kim' is a hybrid with profuse, dark, inky-blue flowers. S. 'Ruby' is a sport with large, rich pinkish-red blooms. There are double varieties like pink S. 'Rosebud' which has its origins in America. S. 'Falling Stars' has masses of delicate lavender-blue flowers and 'Gloria' is similarly dainty with lilac-pink flowers. Streptocarpus are easy to propagate from leaves (see p.32).
50°F(10°C) H:6-10in(15-25cm) S:12-16in(30-42cm)

S. glandulosissimus This attractive caulescent species has sprawling growth, small leaves, and small blue flowers. As well as thriving in pots, these plants do well in a bed of peat-based or peat-alternative potting mix, where several will knit together, making an eye-catching rich blue underplanting.
50°F(10°C) H:12in(30cm) S:18in(45cm)

Sutherlandia
(Leguminosae)

S. frutescens This shrub from South Africa is rather straggly in habit but has attractive pinnate, fern-like foliage of a dark, bluish-green, contrasting well with silvery stalks and stems. Bright red pea-shaped flowers appear in late spring to be followed by 2in(5cm) long inflated green seed pods which take on a pink flush as they dry. The seeds inside germinate easily and plants thrive in pots of well-drained potting mix and good light. They will need the guidance of one or two canes and are prone to attack by spider mite. Prune untidy plants in winter, or raise fresh plants from seed or summer cuttings.
40°F(4°C) H&S:4ft(1.2m)

Thunbergia
(Acanthaceae)

T. natalensis This pretty, low-growing sub-shrub from southern Africa is almost frost-hardy when grown in a well-drained soil. If left in low temperatures, it will die down in winter, behaving more like a herbaceous perennial. Flowers are a delightful combination of soft blue with a yellow tube and appear in summer, carrying on well into the

Streptocarpus 'Falling Stars'

Streptocarpus 'Gloria'

163

Veltheimia bracteata

Viola hederacea

fall. Propagate by shoot cuttings in summer or by dividing the root stock in spring.
40°F(4°C) H&S:24-36in(60-90cm)

Tibouchina
(Melastomataceae)

T. urvilleana (T. semidecandra) The Brazilian spider flower or glory bush has exotic purple flowers, 3-4in(8-10cm) wide, each bearing a set of stamens that looks like a spider lying on its back in the middle. Plants can grow tall but are rather straggly. They can be trained as wall shrubs or allowed to make taller specimens. However, a succession of smaller plants can be maintained by pruning and taking cuttings. Propagate also by seed, which sets freely. Although tolerant of cool minimum temperatures, plants given 55-60°F(13-16°C) during winter will flower almost continuously. Shade from hot sun. Whitefly can be a problem *T. organensis* has even larger flowers on more compact plants and *T. 'Jules'* has an extremely dwarf habit, making a neat shrub, H:36-48in(90-120cm) S:36in(90cm). Smaller flowers have petals set farther apart and are purple tinted with pink.
45-50°F(7-10°C) H:2-8ft(60cm-2.5m)
S:2-5ft(60cm-1.5m)

Tulbaghia
(Liliaceae/Alliaceae)

These plants from the tropics and South Africa form clumps of evergreen, grass-like leaves. Propagate by division, during which a certain amount of bruising and crushing of leaves and roots is inevitable, releasing an unpleasant smell. *T. violacea* is the worst offender, yet is the most often grown. Provide good light. Pot up into well crocked clay pots, using a well-drained potting mix.

T. cominsii A lovely neat tulbaghia whose scented white and pale lilac flowers can be produced year-round.
38°F(3°C) H&S:6in(15cm)

T. leucantha This diminutive plant has broader leaves than *T. violacea*. Flowers are narcissus-like with a nearly white perianth and orange cup.
38°F(3°C) H:3-4in(8-10cm) S:3in(8cm)

T. simmleri (T. fragrans) The sweet garlic has fragrant, lilac-colored, tubular flowers during summer. Extra warmth in winter may encourage a few flower stems.
38°F(3°C) H:16in(42cm) S:12in(30cm)

T. violacea Long stems of lilac-hued, pink tubular flowers are produced between spring and fall, above a clump of grass-like leaves about 12in(30cm) in height. *T.v. 'Pallida'* is a white-flowered form, while *T.v. 'Silver Lace'* offers the added interest of variegated leaves.
38°F(3°C) H:24in(60cm) S:12in(30cm)

Veltheimia
(Liliaceae/Hyacinthaceae)

Forest lilies are beautiful South African plants which produce their pink, tubular flowers during late winter and early spring. These are held aloft from clumps of wavy-edged leaves by 12in(30cm) long, maroon-speckled stems. Pot new bulbs in late summer, planting three to a medium-sized clay pot, so that their tips are just visible above the soil. Use a loam-based potting mix with added peat and sand for good drainage. Keep cool throughout winter, providing ventilation on warm days. After flowering, leaves gradually turn yellow and die off for the summer. Leave them quite dry until early fall then water to restart growth. Renew the potting mix every two years. Propagate by removing offsets and potting separately. There are two very similar species, *V. bracteata* (*V. undulata, V. viridifolia*) and *V. capensis* (*V. glauca, V. viridifolia*), which are often confused. *V. bracteata*, probably the more common in cultivation, is evergreen, though treated as deciduous. *V. capensis* is truly deciduous and has a narrower leaf.
40°F(4°C) H:12-18in(30-45cm) S:12in(30cm)

Viola
(Violaceae)

V. hederacea The Australian or ivy-leaved violet is a petite plant which thrives in semi-shade. Fresh-looking purple and white flowers, produced chiefly in spring but sporadically throughout the year, are held above a dense growth of kidney-shaped leaves. Grow in wide, shallow clay pans, use to cover the soil in pots of larger plants or to cover soil under benches. Propagate by division.
32-40°F(0-4°C) H:2in(5cm) S:indefinite

Zantedeschia
(Araceae)

Z. aethiopica The arum or calla lily from South Africa is prized for its exquisitely formed "flowers", which consist of a white spathe surrounding and tapering away from a yellow spadix which holds the true flowers. Greenhouse plants reach 36in(90cm) and usually begin flowering in midwinter, possibly carrying on until spring. Stand plants outside for the summer. Although dormant, they need not die down completely and can be watered occasionally. Before temperatures begin to drop, ease old plants out of their pots, shake old soil from the rhizomes, divide if necessary, and repot into a rich, preferably loam-based potting mix. Water in but allow the top third of the potting mix to dry out again before repeating. Bring newly potted plants into the greenhouse and give bright light. When new growth has started, feed with a well-balanced liquid fertilizer every two weeks. Although tolerant of temperatures as low as 38°F(3°C), plants will not flower until summer. A temperature of 55°F(13°C), is required to produce winter flowers. Once in flower, this could drop to 45-50°F(7-10°C). Z.a. 'Green Goddess' has green-backed spathes tipped and flushed with green on top. 50-55°F(10-13°C) H:36in(90cm) S:18-24in(45-60cm)

Z. albomaculata The spotted calla with a distribution from South Africa to Zambia has handsome white-spotted leaves and creamy-white spathes with a reddish-purple, sometimes pink throat and base. Smaller than *Z. aethiopica*, it prefers warmer conditions and should be started into growth in early spring, potting the rhizomes so that they are just covered with soil. If necessary, start them in a plant incubator to achieve 55-60°F(13-16°C). Shade lightly and feed regularly with liquid fertilizer during growth. After flowering, which starts in early summer, allow the leaves to die down. They will remain dormant throughout winter and should be watered occasionally to prevent the rhizomes from withering. Repot into fresh, rich potting mix in early spring. Propagate by offsets.
50°F(10°C) H:12-24in(30-60cm) S:12in(30cm)

Z. elliottiana The golden calla from South Africa has attractively silver-spotted leaves. Cultivation is similar to *Z. albomaculata*.
50°F(10°C) H:24-36in(60-90cm) S:18-24in(45-60cm)

Z. rehmannii This exotic-looking species from South Africa bears delicate, dusty-pink spathes almost curling around a creamy spadix. Cultivation as for *Z. albomaculata*.
50°F(10°C) H:12-24in(30-60cm) S:12in(30cm)

HYBRIDS There are increasing numbers of hybrids available with different-colored spathes. Z. 'Bridal Blush' is light pink, Z. 'Harvest Moon' yellow, and Z. 'Cameo' orange. Bound to become more popular for greenhouses, unusual colors are also prized by flower arrangers. Grow as for *Z. albomaculata*.

Zephyranthes

(Liliaceae/Amaryllidaceae)
Pot these pretty South American zephyr lilies in spring, covering them with 1in(2.5cm) of well-drained, preferably loam-based potting mix. Rush-like foliage is joined, in late summer and fall, by the delicate flowers. Zephyranthes can stand outside for the summer in a warm, sunny spot and be brought in when flowers form. They will die down after flowering. Protect from frost in winter. Repot into fresh potting mix every two to three years. Propagate by seed or offsets. *Z. candida*, the flower of the western wind or wind flower from Argentina and Uruguay, has crocus-like white flowers up to 2in(5cm) long. *Z. citrina* has slightly smaller, bright golden-yellow flowers while those of *Z. grandiflora* are like deep pink lily flowers 2¹/₂-4in(6-10cm) long.
38°F(3°C) H&S:6-12in(15-30cm)

Zantedeschia rehmannii

Annuals, biennials, and bulbs

Once a permanent structure of planting has been worked out, space can always be made for a succession of seasonal performers. This category of plants can very easily be raised from fresh seed or bulbs planted at the appropriate time. With careful planning there can always be an abundance of bloom, but there is particular merit in concentrating on plants which will bring the greenhouse to life during dull periods. The right planning will ensure a spectacular display for a special occasion. Stocks, cineraria (now correctly pericallis), primula, calceolaria, and schizanthus can bring bright color in late winter and early spring. Mimulus, digitalis, and antirrhinum will perform in early summer, followed by campanula, celosia, eustoma, trachelium, and fragrant nicotiana. Late summer brings the blue of exacum, fall the fruits of capsicum, and midwinter, the first flowers from forced bulbs like paper-white narcissus (*N. papyraceus*) and hyacinths.

Annuals will provide the bulk of the plants raised from seed, though some annuals can be persuaded to behave like biennials, which require two growing seasons to come to flower, by sowing them toward the end of summer or fall and growing them throughout the winter. The result will be considerably larger and sturdier plants than those acheived from spring sowings.

Also included are some of the plants which, though perennial in nature, grow so easily from spring-sown seed that it is simpler to throw old plants away at the end of the year and start again: subjects like browallia, *Cuphea ignea,* and alonsoa.

The process of raising plants from seed is straightforward, but there are some golden rules. Never allow young plants to become pot-bound until they reach their final pot size, or they will flower prematurely. Annuals sown during summer and fall, to flower in late winter or spring, should be grown as cold as one dares. Ventilation should be adequate and opened as often as possible. Maximum winter light is crucial to success, but shade lightly from hot sun during summer. Loam-based potting mix works best for plants which grow over winter. Feed regularly with liquid fertilizer once plants have settled in their pots and are making active growth. Never cram plants together, and dead-head assiduously in order to prolong flowering.

As far as spring bulbs are concerned, a colorful display could include narcissus, crocus, hyacinths, and tulips. Ordinary bulbs can be planted at any time in the fall but those which have undergone temperature treatment in order to shorten the time span of the bulb's year should be planted as soon as they become available, to take advantage of their early flowering. They will require special bulb fiber if you are using bowls with no drainage holes, but in ordinary pots will grow happily in any good potting mixture. After planting, bulbs should be watered thoroughly and kept cool – not more than 48°F(9°C) for at least twelve weeks – and dark while a good root system forms. The best place for this is out in the garden, preferably at the base of a sunless wall. Shovel a good 5-6in(13-15cm) layer of garden soil, peat, or orchid fiber on top of the bulbs, or, alternatively, wrap the pots with black plastic. Check to make sure they remain moist but protect bowls with no drainage holes from rain as the bulbs will rot if they become waterlogged. Leave them, through frost, wind, and rain, for the eight to twelve weeks required before the shoots are 1-2in(2.5-5cm) high, then unwrap them or clean away the covering, and bring them, full of promise, into the sunroom. Where this outside treatment is not possible, a cool, dark shed or cabinet will do.

Bright light and cool temperatures, 40-50°F(4-10°C), will keep bulbs sturdy, but if canes and string are needed they should be put in place before leaves and stems start to flop. For a spectacular display, individual pots of bulbs can be amalgamated, either on their own or mixed with foliage plants, into larger bowls or containers. Plunge them in soil or expanded clay pebbles, and place moss over the soil surface to add the finishing touch. Informal "landscapes" can also be created using rocks, driftwood, moss, pebbles, and pine cones.

After flowering, ordinary varieties of hyacinths, crocus, tulips, and narcissus can eventually be planted in beds, but may miss a year's flowering while recovering from their indoor experience. The more unusual species bulbs (crocus, tulips, and narcissus for instance) can be treated differently, with the same bulbs being brought into flower for the sunroom year after year. Pot them into a well-drained but fairly rich potting mixture and top off with a layer of gravel. Keep cool in a shady cold frame, but bring into the sunroom before any danger of frost. Feed them well with liquid fertilizer while in growth. During their dormant season in summer, place them under the benches or outside in a shaded spot. An occasional watering will keep them plump. In fall, repot the bulbs into fresh potting mix.

Sunrooms, like well-planned gardens, are enhanced by the seasonal presence of bedding plants and bulbs, and there is always room to accommodate a few small pots of these bright, colorful, though comparatively short-lived plants. They can be bought in bud and discarded when their display is over, but keen gardeners will want to raise their own from seed or by planting bulbs. Young plants will add vibrancy and liveliness, as in this collection of narcissus, hyacinths, lachenalia, primroses, and irises.

Alonsoa

(Scrophulariaceae)

A. warscewiczii The perennial mask flower from Peru is usually bright scarlet, though some seed mixtures produce plants with paler, peach-colored flowers (the latter known as *A.w.* 'Peachy Keen'). Spring sowings will result in ³/₄-1in(2-2.5cm) wide flowers throughout most of summer. The rather spindly plants will need the support of twigs or canes if they are not to flop. Cuttings of one's favorite color can be rooted in summer and overwintered for the following year.
38°F(3°C) H:12-24in(30-60cm) S:12in(30cm)

Browallia

(Solanaceae)

Neat, rounded plants covered with white or blue flowers 2in(5cm) across.
B. speciosa The bush violet from Colombia is really a perennial, and has been replaced in catalogs by more compact varieties. 'Blue Bells' and 'Silver Bells' are taller, while 'Blue Troll' and 'White Troll' are more dwarf. *B.s.* 'Major' has large, showy flowers. Sow in spring for summer flowers and in summer for a winter display.
50°F(10°C) H:8-10in(20-25cm) S:6-8in(15-20cm)

Calceolaria

(Scrophulariaceae)

The vibrant and brightly colored slipper flowers,

C. × herbeohybrida, with their inflated blooms of red, orange, and yellow forming a dome over the top of flattish leaves, might be too overpowering for some tastes. Seed mixtures like Jewel Cluster and Growers' Pride are mainly sown in early to midsummer to flower the following spring. The mixture Anytime should flower in 18 weeks from seed sown at virtually any time of the year, but will not bloom when nights are too warm.
40°F(4°C) H:8-9in(20-23cm) S:6in(15cm)

Calendula

(Compositae)

A summer sowing of the pot or English marigold will provide a display of bright orange, yellow, or cream flowers in late winter. There is plenty of choice, including the pastel blooms of Art Shades. Seedlings should eventually grow in 5-6in(13-15cm) pots.
38°F(3°C) H&S:12-24in(30-60cm)

Campanula

(Campanulaceae)

C. isophylla The Italian bellflower will bloom in summer from a spring sowing. Neat, trailing stems carry large, bell-shaped flowers and can be used to drape over the edges of tables or shelves or to burst from hanging baskets or wall planters. There are varieties with blue, white or mixed flowers. *C. fragilis* and its varieties are similar.
45-50°F(7-10°C) H&S:12in(30cm)

Capsicum

(Solanaceae)

The ornamental peppers are grown for their bright, usually cone-shaped, inedible fruit which decorate the plants. They can be green, violet, yellow, orange, or red, sometimes tapering and twisting into interesting shapes. Dwarf varieties like 'Inferno' or 'Fireworks' are popular. Sown during spring, plants flower in summer and fruit in fall. Misting the plants while in flower will assist fruit set. Spider mite and aphids can be a problem.
40°F(4°C) H&S:6-24in(15-60cm)

Celosia

(Amaranthaceae)

C. argentea Cristata Group (**C. cristata**) The astonishing cockscomb is either loved or hated: indifference is hard to maintain when faced with an enormous crested head of flower with brain-like convolutions in red, yellow, pink, and apricot. Really large heads are favored by florists, and in arrangements can look like stemmed fans of coral.
C. argentea Plumosa Group (**C. plumosa**) These have the more familiar plumes of flower in a similar color range. Sow in spring for summer flowering in 5in(13cm) pots.
38°F(3°C) H:12-24in(30-60cm) S:8-12in(20-30cm)

Crocus

(Iridaceae)

Originally from mountain regions of Europe and Asia, crocus appreciate a well-drained soil, with extra sand added if necessary. Although they will grow quite happily in ordinary plastic pots, try them in clay pans. Smaller species produce their perfect flowers several weeks earlier than the large-flowering types. There is plenty of choice, including *C. biflorus* (purple and white), *C. sieberi* (pale mauve and yellow), *C. chrysanthus* 'E.A. Bowles' (rich yellow with darker base), and *C.c.* 'Zwanenburg Bronze' (dark bronze and yellow). Plant the corms ¹/₂in(1cm) deep and 1in(2.5cm) apart, cover with a layer of sand, water in, and place in a cold frame or cool greenhouse.

The larger, more popular Dutch hybrids come into flower a little after the earlier species. Plant them close together but not touching, and just cover with soil. Water well, and place outside in a plunge bed or other cool, dark place until the shoots start to grow. Place them outside after flowering, and keep them dry in summer after the foliage has died down; they can be planted out in the garden in fall.
38°F(3°C) H:4-5in(10-13cm) S:3in(8cm)

Cuphea

(Lythraceae)

C. ignea The cigar plant from Mexico will flower

Calceolaria × herbeohybrida

during summer from a spring sowing. Small orange-red tubular flowers have a dark, then light ring at the tip, resembling a lit cigar. Although perennial, they are best sown fresh each spring.
40°F(4°C) H&S:12in(30cm)

Digitalis

(Scrophulariaceae)
The common foxglove makes it perfectly feasible to create a woodland glade in the greenhouse for a special occasion. Grow some small birches in pots, and then add half a dozen pot-grown foxgloves to complete the scene. Sow these at the end of spring, leave them to spend the summer in cold frames and overwinter in an unheated greenhouse or cold frame; alternatively, lift plants from the garden and pot up in early fall. There are many different sorts of foxglove but *D*. Excelsior Hybrids Mixed are probably the most reliable.
32°F(0°C) H:5-6ft(1.5-1.8m) S:15in(40cm)

Eustoma

(Gentianaceae)
Prairie gentians have recently become popular. They are mostly hybrids of *E. grandiflorum* (*Lisianthus russellianus*), native to Colorado, Nebraska, Texas, and northern Mexico. Sow early in the spring for summer flowers. Grow one in a 4in(10cm) pot or four in a 6in(15cm) pot. They like a well-drained soil and will not tolerate being overwatered. The color range of the 3in(8cm) diameter flowers is fantastic, including blue, shades of pink, yellow, white, and cream. There are singles, doubles, and bicolors. *E*. Double Eagle Mixed offers a particularly good range.
45°F(7°C) H:9-24in(23-60cm) S:6-12in(15-30cm)

Exacum

(Gentianaceae)
The Persian or gentian violet makes a compact mound of small glossy leaves which become studded with slightly fragrant, yellow-centered, lavender-blue or white flowers. The original *E. affine* came from the island of Socotra in the Indian Ocean, but useful dwarf varieties are available. Sow in spring for a lovely late summer display. In a warm greenhouse, plants from a summer sowing can be overwintered for earlier flowering.
50-55°F(10-13°C) H&S:6-9in(15-23cm)

Hyacinthus

(Liliaceae/Hyacinthaceae)
There are two sorts of hyacinth bulbs. The Dutch hyacinths, which are commonly grown, descend from *H. orientalis*, a native of central and eastern Mediterranean regions. There are now plenty of Dutch hyacinths to choose from, including yellow, cream, white, pink, blue, and orange-red ones. *H.o.*

Exacum affine

Browallia speciosa 'Major'

Eustoma grandiflorum

var. *albulus* is the Roman hyacinth from southern France, which differs in having several stems of smaller flowers. To have flowering plants by midwinter, choose specially prepared bulbs (which have undergone cooling treatment) as soon as they become available in summer. If this is delayed by more than about a month they will flower later, in which case one might just as well have bought cheaper, ordinary bulbs. Several bulbs of the same variety can be planted in one container, but they may grow at slightly different rates, giving an uneven result. Far better to pot bulbs individually into 3½in(9cm) pots, so that the nose of the bulb is just protruding above the potting mix. Water in and stand in a cool spot for the roots to grow. After about twelve weeks, when the flower shoots are 2in(5cm) above the neck of the bulb, they can be brought into their flowering positions. Group several in larger containers for maximum impact of color and perfume. Three can be tied to a single cane in the middle. Special hyacinth vases are ideal for single bulbs. Simply fill with water and sit the bulb in the top part so that the base is just above the water. Keep somewhere dark, but above all cool, until roots have grown to fill the bottom part of the vase. Once the required 2in(5cm) long flower bud has emerged, the plant can take up position in the greenhouse. Keep topped up with water.
40°F(4°C) H:8in(20cm) S:3in(8cm)

Iris
(Iridaceae)

Small, bulbous Reticulata irises will produce their exquisite flowers in late winter. Plant the bulbs 1in(2.5cm) deep and about six in a 5in(13cm) pot. Water well and place them outside, well covered with soil until growth begins. After flowering, plants can be transferred to the garden, where they are likely to miss a year's flowering while settling down. Most popular is *I. reticulata* itself, a native of Turkey, Caucasus, Iran, and Iraq. Deep purple-blue flowers with orange markings are 3in(8cm) across and blessed with a faint violet perfume, but many similar iris for sale are forms or hybrids with slightly larger flowers. Some of these have *I. histrioides* 'Major' as a parent. This is a really early flowerer, often opening in midwinter to reveal large royal-blue flowers. *I. danfordiae* from east Turkey has honey-scented flowers which are bright lemon-yellow.
38°F(3°C) H:2½-6in(6-15cm) S:3in(8cm)

Kalanchoe
(Crassulaceae)

K. blossfeldiana This small bushy plant, H&S:12in (30cm), topped by heads of red flowers, comes originally from Madagascar. Today, it has been largely superseded by smaller hybrids with red, pink, white, or yellow flowers. Sow in spring for a lovely winter display. Plants can also be propagated by cuttings.
50°F(10°C) H&S:6-9in(15-23cm)

Linaria
(Scrophulariaceae)

L. maroccana The pretty Moroccan toadflax is an ideal subject for the greenhouse. Fall sowings will yield spring-flowering plants, while those from spring sowings will flower during summer. A favorite variety of this purple- and yellow-flowered species is the neat *L.m.* Fairy Bouquet whose dainty spurred flowers open in a variety of jewel-like colors. Plant three or five seedlings in one 4 or 5in(10 or 13cm) pot for a bushy effect.
38°F(3°C) H:8-15in(20-40cm) S:6-8in(15-20cm)

Matthiola
(Cruciferae)

There are several different types of stock which are useful for their color and perfume. Many of these have been developed from *M. incana*, native to coastal southwest Europe. Some are known as "selectable stocks," meaning that those seedlings which will have double blooms can be selected for thinning. Sow between 55-60°F(13-16°C), but after germination, move to temperatures below 50°F(10°C) when the color difference between the singles and doubles

Matthiola

Kalanchoe blossfeldiana

becomes more obvious. Weed out the paler, yellow-leaved double seedlings and discard the green singles. Sow during summer for winter-flowering plants and in early spring for summer flowers.
38°F(3°C) H:8-30in(20-75cm) S:9-12in(23-30cm)

Mimulus
(Scrophulariaceae)
The monkey flower makes a compact pot plant. If the plants are placed on tables or benches it is easier to inspect the lovely shape and markings of the flowers. M. Calypso has large flowers of yellow, wine, orange, red, and gold. M. Malibu is similar. *M. aurantiacus* has glossy leaves and tubular orange or deep yellow flowers. Sow during late summer for large plants flowering in early summer. Spring sowings will yield smaller summer-flowering plants.
40°F(4°C) H:6-9in(15-23cm) S:6-12in(15-30cm)

Narcissus
(Liliaceae/Amaryllidaceae)
The slightly tender, multi-flowering tazettas are popular for early forcing. They include two fragrant favorites, the glistening paper-white narcissus (*N. papyraceus*) and deep yellow N. 'Soleil d'Or'. These take about eight weeks to flower. You can pot them up in potting mix or they can be grown in a bowl of pebbles. Fill a glass bowl with attractive pebbles, planting the bulbs into the top. Water in, so that the water level settles to within ½in(1cm) of the base of the bulbs. Stand in a cool, though not necessarily dark, place and move into position as the flowers open.

Many daffodils and narcissi can be forced. Pot them in late summer or early fall, with the tips of the bulbs just protruding from the potting mix. Set as many as possible in one pot but make sure they are not quite touching. You can also plant them in layers, with the top bulbs sitting between the lower ones, to allow space for the shoots to develop. Water well and stand outside, covering the tops with a good layer of orchid fiber or soil. Alternatively, stand somewhere dark but, above all, cool. When 3in(8cm) of growth shows, they can be brought into the greenhouse. Of the tall yellow daffodils, H:18in(45cm), old favorites like N. 'King Alfred' and N. 'Carlton' are reliable. N. 'Mount Hood' has creamy-white flowers. N. 'Hawera', H:12in(30cm), a popular Triandrus type with small nodding lemon-yellow flowers and slightly thrown-back petals, is very dainty. Short, bright yellow N. 'Tête-à-Tête' is a Cyclamineus type, H:8in(20cm). Smallest of all are the tiny species like fragrant, pale primrose N. romieuxii, H:4in(10cm), and N. bulbocodium, the golden yellow hoop-petticoat daffodil, H:4-12in(10-30cm). Plant these in a well-drained but rich soil; for N. bulbocodium the soil should be acidic. Top with 1in(2.5cm) of sand,

Mimulus aurantiacus

water in and stand in the cool, well-ventilated greenhouse. Feed well during growth. When the leaves have died down, either stand beneath the benches or outside in a shaded place. Water occasionally to keep the bulbs plump and in fall repot into fresh potting mix.

Pericallis
(Compositae)
These floriferous late winter and spring flowerers, derived from various Canary Islands species, are not the easiest plants to grow well. There are numerous varieties from which to choose; they vary in height and color but all have an abundance of daisy-like flowers. Popular *P.* Spring Glory, 10in(25cm) high, has fresh-colored flowers with pronounced eyes.

P. Moll Improved, 15-18in(40-45cm), contains nine colors and is packed with bright flowers. If small plants are required, Mini Starlet Mixed reach only 6in(15cm). Some worthy hybrids can be propagated by cuttings in spring, among them *P. × webbii,* grown for its electric blue flowers and silvery gray foliage. Sow them during the summer and grow cool throughout the winter. Give each plant plenty of space and be on guard against aphids and leaf miner. Good air-circulation is essential.
40°F(4°C) H&S:6-15in(15-40cm)

Petunia
(Solanaceae)
It is not worth giving greenhouse space to petunias if you can grow them in the garden, but they do

Primula × kewensis

Primula malacoides

Rehmannia elata

Schizanthus

provide reliable summer flower. A few plants, potted up and well cared for, can be dotted about, grouped in a block, or arranged on tables and benches. Any bedding varieties will do, but Grandiflora and Cascade types are possibly the best. Some, surprisingly, have a powerful scent which tends to go unnoticed outdoors. This applies particularly to Multiflora types with indigo coloring. Sow in spring for summer flowers.
50-55°F(10-13°C) H&S:8-9in(20-23cm)

Primula
(Primulaceae)
Primulas provide reliable color during winter and spring. The tiny seeds are not always easy to germinate, and surface sowing is usually recommended. Press the seeds gently onto the potting mix surface, then add another sprinkle of potting mix so that they nestle among the moist particles. A temperature of 60°F(16°C) is required for germination; warmer temperatures can sometimes be detrimental. Although perennial, they are best raised from seed each year.

HYBRID PRIMROSES These bright, colorful plants may not be the subtlest of flowerers but are extremely good value. Plants brought into flower during early winter will continue to flower throughout spring. When no more buds appear as summer approaches they can be transferred to the garden. Sow in spring for the best results. The bright colors of F1 varieties like Show Mixture or Husky Mixed include purple, pink, red, yellow, and white with yellow eyes. The mixture Countrywide includes some fetching pastel shades and has a contrasting inner ring of red.
38°F(3°C) H&S:6in(15cm)

P. × kewensis This interesting hybrid originated at Kew Gardens in England, and is well worth growing for its fresh green foliage (although some forms are dusted with a white powder) and its bright yellow flowers. Sow during spring for flowering the following winter and spring. After flowering, plants can be kept cool, shaded, and moist. They will flower again as larger specimens.
38°F(3°C) H&S:12in(30cm)

P. malacoides The fairy primrose has slender stems rising above hairy leaves. These bear a profusion of light, airy flowers which appear during winter and spring after an early summer sowing. There is now a wide color range, encompassing pink, lilac, red, and white.
38°F(3°C) H&S:8-12in(20-30cm)

P. obconica The only disadvantage of these pretty primulas, which originated in China, is that the hairs on their leaves can give some people a nasty rash. Sow from late winter to early summer for clustered heads of large, lasting flowers produced from the following winter to summer. Plants are

worth keeping for two to three years, after which they become weakened. Flower colors include purple-blue, red, white, salmon, and pink.
45-50°F(7-10°C) H&S:6-12in(15-30cm)

P. sinensis Although this primula has been grown in China for centuries, it is no longer known in the wild. The leaves are slightly lobed and toothed and flowers of purple, pink, or white with yellow eyes are produced in whorls from winter to spring from an early summer sowing the previous year.
40°F(4°C) H&S:10in(25cm)

Psylliostachys
(Plumbaginaceae)

P. suworowii (Limonium suworowii) Known as sea lavender, rat's tail, or Russian statice, this plant comes originally from Caucasus and Iran to central Asia. Sow during fall and grow on in 5in(13cm) pots. Tiny rose-pink flowers packed into long panicles grow up from the rosette of wavy leaves in spring.
40°F(4°C) H:24in(60cm) S:12in(30cm)

Rehmannia
(Scrophulariaceae)

R. elata (R. angulata) The Chinese foxglove is a lovely plant, not widely grown. From a rosette of leaves rise stems that bear purple-pink foxglove-like flowers with spotty yellow throats in late spring. Sow seed in spring for flowering the following year and grow the plants on in at least 6in(15cm) pots. Stand outside for the summer in a slightly shaded spot; their winter quarters must be frost-free. The plants will flower again but it is easier to sow batches each year.
38°F(3°C) H:30in(75cm) S:18in(45cm)

Salpiglossis
(Solanaceae)

These showy plants, originating in Chile, make good splashes of color. Most of the 2in(5cm) wide flowers are heavily stencilled with a contrasting color, and there are some good varieties to choose from. Try Bolero Mixed, Casino Mixed, and Friendship, which give rich red, yellow, blue, gold, pink, and purple flowers. Sow in fall for the best early summer show; early-spring sowings tend to produce later, spindlier plants. Be prepared to stake.
40°F(4°C) H:12-30in(30-75cm) S:12in(30cm)

Schizanthus
(Solanaceae)

The poor man's orchid or butterfly flower from Chile should be sown at the end of summer and overwintered at low temperatures for really large-flowering specimens in spring. Smaller, later-flowering plants will result from early-spring sowings. The frilly, beautifully marked flowers, mainly in shades of pink, reddish-pink, beige, and salmon,

open amidst and above bright green ferny foliage.
38°F(3°C) H:8-20in(20-50cm) S:8-18in(20-45cm)

Trachelium
(Campanulaceae)

T. caeruleum Now popular as a florists' flower, the blue throatwort from west and central Mediterranean regions has long been considered a reliable plant for providing late-summer color under glass. Its lovely long-stemmed heads of hazy blue flowers are well worth having. Sow at midsummer for strong plants the following summer. They will benefit from cool growing conditions in a cold frame until fall.
38°F(3°C) H:24-36in(60-90cm) S:18in(45cm)

Trachymene
(Umbelliferae)

T. caerulea (Didiscus caeruleus) The blue lace flower from Australia is sown in spring for dainty domed heads of tiny soft blue summer flowers. These superb plants blend well with any planting and are in no way distracting or dominating.
40°F(4°C) H:18in(45cm) S:10in(25cm)

Tulipa
(Liliaceae)

The bright color of tulip flowers can be dramatic. Most originate from central Asia but many available today are hybrids. Choose the earlier-flowering varieties, either double or single. Darwin types are also of merit. Pot in fall, planting the bulbs close together but not touching, so that their tips are just visible above the surface of the potting mix. Water well and place outside, under a 5-6in(13-15cm) layer of soil or orchid fiber until growth begins, when they can be taken into the greenhouse. Provide canes for support as they grow.
40°F(4°C) H:4-24in(10-60cm)

Verbascum
(Scrophulariaceae)

V. arcturus (Celsia arcturus) The Cretan bear's tail is grown for its soft, downy, gray-green leaves and spikes of large clear yellow flowers. Sow in summer for sturdy plants to flower early next summer. Alternatively, plants will flower later from an early-spring sowing.
38°F(3°C) H:18-30in(45-75cm) S:10in(25cm)

Primula obconica

Aquatic plants

A pond in the sunroom or greenhouse enables a greater range of plants to be grown, it helps raise humidity, and it is in itself potentially of great aesthetic value. If you are considering a pond for such an area, it is best to do so at the planning stage, to avoid disruption later on. However, if the trouble and extra expense seem too great, or if the sunroom or greenhouse is already crowded with plants and features, an aquatic tub garden is the easiest to install.

A tub garden can be a large glazed or plastic pot, ideally 18in(45cm) high and wide without a drainage hole, or a lined wooden half-barrel. Although barrels are capable of holding water, the wood often contains toxins which might affect plants. Repeated soaking and draining is one solution, but an even better method is to line the barrel with a sheet of strong plastic or rubber. Drape this over the barrel, fill it with water, then secure to the edge with carpet tacks or builder's staples, and cut off any excess material. The beauty of tub gardens is that they can be emptied and moved at whim. Plants grown in containers can be switched around to give seasonal variation.

Larger ponds, whether sunk into the ground or raised above, will need to have a minimum depth of 18-24in(45-60cm) to accommodate larger tropical or hardy waterlilies. Building techniques are identical to those used for outside ponds. The job is messy, complicated, and involves reinforcement with a grid of steel. By far the simplest method is to line the pond with butyl rubber, which has a twenty-year guarantee. Unlike cheaper PVC, this is not sensitive to heat or light. Such liners can also be used to give an attractive, irregular outline to the pond, which may fit in much better with the surroundings than the shape of a premolded plastic or fiberglass shell.

Decide on the size and shape of the pond before digging it out, leaving shelves 9in(23cm) wide and deep for water-edge plants. Cut the edge out to accommodate the overlap of the liner, which will need to be anchored and perhaps covered by an edging of rock slabs or pebbles set in mortar. A cushion of damp builder's sand ¹/₂in(1cm) deep laid around the bottom and sides will cushion the liner against stones, but extra matting might be needed on very stony ground. Place the liner over the hole and push it in, then fill with water, attempting to smooth out creases as they occur. Once the hole is full, trim off any surplus liner leaving an edging of 4-5in

(10-13cm). This can be secured into the ground with long nails.

It is not necessary to heat the water for all plants but it is advisable where tropical waterlilies are to be grown and enjoyed at their best. They require 75-85°F(24-29°C) to grow properly and become dormant when temperatures drop below 70°F(21°C). Nevertheless they are well worth growing, if only for their wide range of vibrant colors, including many fine blue varieties and others with beautiful pink blooms. Some are night bloomers, a distinct advantage for gardeners who are out at work all day as the sight and perfume of these tropical lilies can be enjoyed all evening. Choose rose-pink, fragrant Nymphaea 'James Gurney' whose flowers are 10-12in(25-30cm) across, or ghostly white N. 'Missouri' with blooms up to 14in(34cm) across and mottled, indented leaves. Day bloomers include scented, pink N. 'General Pershing' whose flowers project 12in(30cm) above water.

Leaves of the giant waterlilies (Victoria cruziana and V. amazonica) can reach 6ft(1.8m) in diameter. Size is governed by the amount of soil available to the roots and they can be grown in small ponds. Adequate light is the most difficult requirement to satisfy, with powerful supplementary lighting necessary in northern latitudes.

Whether installing an aquarium heater for a small pond or heating a large volume of water, consult a licensed electrician to make sure the installation conforms to local safety codes.

Clean away dead leaves regularly in order to prevent plants from rotting and decaying. A balance of submerged oxygenating plants and some floating leaves will help aerate and shade the water, thus deterring algae. Baskets lined with burlap cloth and aquatic plant crates make ideal planters. Use either a heavy loam fortified with bonemeal, or a ready-to-use aquatic plant potting mix. Feed at least once a season with aquatic plant fertilizer tablets.

As well as tender aquatic plants, almost all hardy aquatics can be grown under glass. Most will need good light and can become prone to pests not usually encountered outside. Water hawthorn (Aponogeton distachyos), S:24-48in(60-120cm), has almost oblong floating leaves and V-shaped prongs of white, scented flowers. This will bloom in sun or shade and is ideal for a greenhouse pool which does not get full sun. An adaptable plant, it will even open some flowers during winter. Sagittaria latifolia, the American arrowhead or duck potato, is a water-edge plant with beautifully shaped, arrowheaded leaves held above water and white flowers, H:12-24in(30-60cm) S:24in(60cm). Typha minima, H:18in (45cm) S:12in(30cm), is a miniature bulrush and could be used to give height to a tub. Bolder, taller, and very dramatic is zebra rush, Scirpus lacustris ssp. tabernaemontani 'Zebrinus', H:36in(90cm) S:indefinite. The narrow, cylindrical, green stems are attractively striped horizontally with white and make an effective background to other plants. Arum lilies, Zantedeschia aethiopica (see p.164), can stand in water up to 9in(23cm) over the planting container.

In the sunroom as elsewhere in the garden, water can be used to create either excitement or an oasis of tranquillity. This large pond offers calm reflections, as well as a home for aquatic plants and added humidity for the surrounding plants. Here, the day-flowering Cape blue waterlily (Nymphaea capensis) can grow to full size, its exotic blooms thrusting up out of the water and its floating leaves radiating outward in a pleasing pattern. While the waterlilies have their roots anchored in the soil of a container, those of the water hyacinth (Eichhornia crassipes) dangle freely from the base of the plant. The foliage of the plants around the pond is particularly lush and beautiful.

Canna 'Endeavour', *C.* 'Ra' and *C.* 'Erebus'

Cyperus papyrus

Azolla

(Azollaceae)

A. caroliniana A native of the American Carolinas, this quick-spreading plant is now naturalized in many warm and tropical areas of the world. Known as fairy moss, mosquito plant, or water fern, the last name is most apt, as it is closely related to ferns. Seen from afar, this floating aquatic provides a green covering over the pond but closer inspection reveals divided fronds floating on the surface, with dark roots hanging in the water. In shade, plants remain green but they take on a reddish-purple color in full light. Although they spread, growth can easily be controlled by skimming off excess with a net. These water ferns can be used to provide some of the shade necessary for keeping the water cooler and reducing the light that encourages algae.

38°F(3°C) S:1in(2.5cm) for one individual but spread indefinite

Canna

(Cannaceae)

Water cannas make an unusual and striking choice for the greenhouse pond. Grow them in pots or planting baskets in a depth of 0-6in(0-15cm). At temperatures of 55°F(13°C) and over, even when the water is unheated, plants are likely to remain evergreen and will grow and bloom sporadically throughout winter as well as in summer. At lower temperatures, leaves and stems die back to their tuber-like rhizomes. Remove from water and keep moderately dry until spring. Peruvian *C. iridiflora* bears nodding, reddish-pink flowers which are smaller than the more popular hybrids.

C. 'Endeavour' has red flowers, *C.* 'Ra' yellow, and *C.* 'Erebus' pink. Propagate by division in spring. These cannas can be grown successfully out of water. 40-45°F(4-7°C) H:7ft(2m) S:24in(60cm)

Colocasia

(Araceae)

C. esculenta This plant from southeast Asia is ornamental yet has edible tubers; its common names include taro, cocoyam, dasheen, and elephant's ear. Heart-shaped leaves 18in(45cm) long and 12in (30cm) wide are deep green, with veins often picked out in contrasting white. This water-edge plant could be grown in a pot or basket container standing in shallow water. Grown in cooler temperatures, it will die back for the winter and can be removed from the pond. At warmer temperatures – over 70°F(21°C) –

the foliage remains evergreen. Shade lightly from hot sun. Propagate by division of tubers in spring.
40°F(4°C) H:36-48in(90-120cm) S:24-30in(60-75cm)

Cyperus
(Cyperaceae)
Although cyperus do not have to be associated with water features, they need high humidity and regular watering. They often do best when standing in shallow water constantly. Dryness in the air or at the roots eventually results in yellow-looking plants. In the wild, they originate from swampy areas and look their best planted by a pond, standing in shallow water, or planted as water-edge plants. Propagate by seed or division in spring or summer.

C. albostriatus (C. diffusus) This umbrella plant from South Africa makes a clump of strap-shaped basal leaves, from which rise short "umbrellas" of bright green leaf-like bracts topped by pale brown flowers. Shorter, and with broader, paler green leaves than *C. involucratus*, it is useful where space is restricted. Propagate by seed or division, or cut off an umbrella, trim stalks and leaves, then up-end the leaves into a container of water. Once roots and new shoots have established, the new plant can be potted as desired.
45-50°F(7-10°C) H:36-48in(90-120cm) S:indefinite

C. involucratus (C. alternifolius of gardens**)** This umbrella plant from Mauritius has clumps of long stems furnished with leaves which project, umbrella-like, around the top. In a pot, they often need staking, but planted in a bed the stems become stronger. Pale, grass-like flowers in the center of the "umbrella" show up clearly against the dark green leaves. This plant can also be propagated by rooting in water, in the same way as *C. albostriatus*.
45-50°F(7-10°C) H:36-48in(90-120cm) S:indefinite

C. papyrus The Egyptian paper sedge is the most spectacular cyperus in cultivation. Originally from Nile areas, stems were used by the ancient Egyptians to make paper. Long stems, graced by tufts of leaves and grass-like flowers at the top, grow from thick root stocks. Warmth, ideally 65-70°F(18-21°C), humidity, and moisture are crucial. Grown in pots, this species needs to stand in wide containers of water at all times.
50°F(10°C) H:10ft(3m) S:indefinite

Eichhornia
(Pontederiaceae)
E. crassipes The water hyacinth, with a distribution from southern North America to Argentina and the West Indies, is considered a menace in sub-tropical waterways, where it forms an almost impenetrable mat, but is welcome in the indoor pond. A fascinating plant, it floats by means of its inflated leaf stalks. The leaf blades are rounded or kidney-shaped unless the atmosphere is very warm and humid, when they become longer and overcrowded. If there is a bed for water plants at the edge of the pond, they will root and produce longer, thinner leaf stalks. Spikes of mauve flowers with a yellow-orange spot on the upper petal project above the leaves in summer. They are valuable for discouraging algae, as they provide shade and also use up excess nutrients in the water. Warm water temperatures of 80°F(27°C) suit them best but they can be overwintered at lower temperatures. Plants spread by rhizomes, which can be cut to separate individual plants.
40°F(4°C) H:4-12in(10-30cm) S:12in(30cm) for one individual but spread indefinite

Iris
(Iridaceae)
I.ensata (I. kaempferi) The pretty Japanese iris with its exotic-looking purple flowers grows well in the greenhouse. There are many varieties with single or double flowers and colors of blue, mauve, purple, pink, and white. Keep the toes of the iris wet but its ankles dry. Elevate the crown 2in(5cm) above the surface of the water. To avoid an ugly pot showing, use an attractive container. This iris will enjoy good light. Spider mite can be a problem.
32°F(0°C) H:24-36in(60-90cm) S:indefinite

Marsilea
(Marsileaceae)
Closely related to ferns, the pretty water clovers are grown for their fronds which resemble four-leaved clover. These will stand proud in shallow water or float on the surface where it becomes deeper. Plant in pots, aquatic plant baskets, or a soil bottom with about 2in(5cm) of soil over the roots. There are many species including warmth-loving *M. drummondii* from Australia and *M. quadrifolia* from Europe and Asia which can tolerate temperatures just above freezing. Propagate by division in spring.
38-45°F(3-7°C) H:4-9in(10-23cm) S:indefinite

Myriophyllum
(Haloragidaceae)
M. aquaticum The pretty parrot's feather from South America makes a lovely show of feathery, bright green foliage whether allowed to romp around the edges of a large pond, or used to trail effectively over the edge of a tub. Rampant plants, they will need controlling (by pinching back to encourage branching) on ponds where stems up to 6ft(1.8m) long make a mat of pretty growth. Easy to grow, several shoot tips 6-8in(15-20cm) long, well anchored in a pot of soil in spring, then submerged, will soon root and grow.
38°F(3°C) H:4in(10cm) S:indefinite

Eichhornia crassipes

Marsilea quadrifolia

Nelumbo
(Nelumbonaceae)
Lotus grow from rhizomes in rather the same way as waterlilies, except that their large 12-24in(30-60cm) wide, rounded, peltate leaves and flowers are held above the water. Exotic blooms are followed by attractive seed pods. The rhizomes resemble smooth bananas with a brittle, easily damaged growing tip. Fill a large container with heavy topsoil tightly packed to within 6in(15cm) of the surface, adding two large handfuls of aquatic fertilizer halfway down. Set the rhizome on top and peg in place with sturdy U-shaped pieces of wire. Cover with 2-3in (5-8cm) of water and leave, winding the rhizome around the top of the container and pinning it down as it grows. Lotus may need extra light in regions where light levels are generally low. Lights suspended

above the plants should entice them into bloom.

N. lutea, H&S:36in(90cm), the American lotus, has blue-green leaves and fragrant yellow flowers in summer. The slightly taller sacred lotus (*N. nucifera*), H&S:36-60in(90-150cm), has superb pink flowers with yellow centers, with even taller *N.n.* 'Alba Grandiflora' producing white blooms, *N.n.* 'Alba Striata' fragrant pink-edged, white flowers, and *N.n.* 'Rosea Plena' huge double pink flowers. One of the prettiest and most easily contained is *N.* 'Mrs Perry D. Slocum', H&S:36-48in(90-120cm), whose flowers, up to 12in(30cm) wide, are peach-yellow at the base, shading to pink at the tips. Ideal for a tub pond would be the smaller *N.* 'Momo Botan', H&S:18-24in(45-60cm), which has double cherry-pink flowers resembling fluffy peony blooms up to 6in(15cm) wide. Divide and pot large plants in spring. Propagate also by seed. Sow individually, each seed in its own pot, top with gravel, then submerge carefully in water at 70°F(21°C) to germinate.
32°F(3°C)

Nymphaea
(Nymphaceae)

HARDY WATERLILIES Any of the small to medium species can be used effectively in a greenhouse pond or tub. Reliable *N.* 'Marliacea Chromatella' will spread 36-60in(90-150cm) in a pond but will remain as small as 18in(45cm) when restricted in a tub. Yellow blooms which might reach 6in(15cm) will shrink to 4in(10cm). *N.* 'Aurora', *N.* 'Indiana',

and *N.* 'Sioux' are "changeables" whose fall-toned colors will vary during the three days they are open. Another waterlily that changes color is *N.* 'Comanche'. When young the flowers are much paler than the sunset shade attained after several days of flowering. Most suitable of all for tub gardens are pygmy waterlilies which can have white, pink, or yellow flowers. *N.* × *helvola* is a lovely soft yellow and has green leaves mottled with maroon. Natural spread is only 18in(45cm) and the flowers are tiny. These can be grown without any water heating and enjoy good light. Plant rhizomes in spring or early summer, using large containers of good loam with a handful of added bonemeal. Plant so that the growing tip of the rhizome is just above soil level and top with gravel or sand. Submerge pygmy waterlilies 8in(20cm) below the surface, other species 12in (30cm) or more below. After about three years, thin out and repot. All waterlilies need to be fed two or three times during one growing season. Use aquatic plant fertilizer tablets.
32°F(3°C)

TROPICAL WATERLILIES A greenhouse pond or tub will need a water heater if tropical waterlilies are to be grown successfully. Ideally, they also need about 18in(45cm) depth of water. *N. capensis*, the Cape blue waterlily from South Africa, and others have been used to produce superb hybrids. They send their flowers up out of the water by 2-4in(5-10cm) or more and are often highly scented. Some are night bloomers and tend to be more robust with pointed, coarser, wavy-edged leaves prominently veined

beneath. Flowers are closed during the day. Night-blooming *N. lotus* has scented white flowers with yellow centers. *N.* 'Red Flare', S:1-8ft(30cm-2.5m), has deep mahogany foliage and intense, ruby-colored flowers. *N.* 'Sir Galahad' has superb white flowers which appear soft and powdery instead of shiny. Day flowerers include *N. colorata* whose soft blue flowers have yellow centers and *N.* 'Margaret E. Randig', S:2-8ft(60cm-2.5m), with purple flowers and maroon-marbled leaves; *N.* 'Director George T. Moore', S:6-7ft(1.8-2m), is deep blue with a golden-yellow center and *N.* 'Persian Lilac' has yellow-centered pink flowers.

Despite their size, all but the largest can adapt to life in a tub pond warmed by an aquarium heater. They become smaller as a result of their restriction. The tubers of tropical waterlilies are unlike their hardy counterparts in looking more like a walnut. Instead of branching, they make a proliferation of small new tubers around the old one. When repotting, these can be removed and potted separately to grow on. Plant one mature tuber of 1-2in(2.5-5cm) diameter into a large – up to 18in (45cm) wide – container with drainage holes to allow escape of gases. Pack the soil in firmly, adding a good handful of aquatic fertilizer, to within 1in(2.5cm) of the top. Pot the tuber centrally, so that the tip is just visible, and cover with gravel, keeping the growing tip exposed. Fertilize regularly as for hardy waterlilies. Repot every other year. Where tropical lilies are grown in unheated water in cool greenhouses, it may be best to store them out of the water during winter. They will go dormant as temperatures drop. Take off remaining small underwater leaves, clean soil and roots off carefully. Float for two days in tepid water to get rid of debris, then store in a large jar of moist, drained sand, with the tip facing upward and the lid punctured with holes to keep moisture in but allow gases to escape. Place in the dark at 55°F(13°C) until spring. Check periodically for correct moisture and to stop rotting before damage occurs.
50°F(10°C)

Nymphoides
(Menyanthaceae)

N. peltata 'Bennettii' (Villarsia bennettii) The fringed waterlily or water fringe from Europe and Asia grows from small rhizomes, making a spreading mat on the surface. Small maroon-mottled floating leaves and fringed, bright yellow flowers combine to make an attractive plant during summer. Very good for a tub pond, it likes good light. Propagate by division in spring. As the rhizomes are very small, pot in a basket as for any of the other water-edge plants.
38°F(3°C) S:indefinite

Nelumbo nucifera 'Rosea Plena'

Nelumbo nucifera 'Alba Grandiflora'

Pistia

(Araceae)

P. stratiotes The water lettuce grows in tropical and subtropical countries all over the world. Rosettes of light green, finely hairy leaves will float in deep water or root in the muddy bottom of shallows. Flowers are insignificant. Light and warmth are essential for healthy growth. Propagate by separating plantlets which are joined together by stolons.
50-60°F(10-16°C) H:4in(10cm) S:4in(10cm) for one individual but spread indefinite

Salvinia

(Salviniaceae)

These strange plants, known as floating mosses, are closely related to ferns. They appear as masses of hairy leaves roughly arranged into pairs, although for every two there is a third, modified underwater leaf. This is dissected and takes the place of roots. Upper leaves are usually green but can turn purplish-brown in strong sun. *S. auriculata*, from Mexico and South America, sends out fingers of leaves on branching stems. *S. natans*, with a wide distribution including central and southern Europe, North Africa, and Asia, can tolerate cooler conditions and has smaller, oval floating leaves. Propagate by division.
50°F(10°C) S:indefinite

Thalia

(Marantaceae)

T. dealbata This species from southeastern North America is an aquatic relative of the prayer plant (maranta). A superb plant for the indoor pond, it makes a sheaf of blue-green leaves not unlike those of strelitzia. These reach 3-4ft(90-120cm) but flower stalks rise up to some 6ft(1.8m) in summer and end in a panicle of strange purple flowers held by powdery, silvery-gray bracts. Stand the pot in up to 6in(15cm) of water or keep the soil very moist, in good light. Propagate by division in spring.
T. geniculata is similar but prefers warmer water. The red-stemmed cultivar is particularly attractive.
45°F(7°C) H:6ft(1.8m) S:24in(60cm)

Trapa

(Trapaceae)

T. natans The floating water chestnut has prettily marked, toothed leaves in the shape of oriental fans. These spread out in a loose floating rosette, but under water there are submerged, dissected leaves growing off the thick stems rather like roots. White flowers are borne in summer and, where conditions are right, are followed by horned fruit containing a large, edible seed (this is not the edible water chestnut used in Chinese cookery). Propagate by seed and rhizomatous division.
40°F(4°C) S:9in(23cm)

Pistia stratiotes

Salvinia auriculata

Nymphaea 'Persian Lilac'

Nymphaea lotus

Choosing the right plants

Plants for specific temperatures

These lists will help people who know the temperature range of their greenhouse or sunroom and want to be able to see at a glance what plants they can grow. Note that plants are listed here according to their ideal temperature categories. Discrepancies between these temperatures and those included in individual entries in the text are due to the fact that these lists suggest *optimum* temperatures, whereas the text indicates the *minimum* temperatures tolerated. Some plants, of course, are eligible for more than one temperature range, and appear in several temperature categories.

Unheated: below 38°F (3°C)

Abutilon megapotamicum
 A.m. 'Variegatum'
 A. × suntense
Acacia dealbata
Acca sellowiana (Feijoa sellowiana)
Actinidia deliciosa (A. chinensis)
Agapanthus Headbourne Hybrids
Aloysia triphylla (A. citriodora, Lippia citriodora)
Ampelopsis brevipedunculata 'Elegans'
Bambusa multiplex 'Alphonse Karr'
 (B. glaucescens 'Alphonse Karr')
 B. ventricosa
Beschorneria yuccoides
Billardiera longiflora
Camellia
Campsis grandiflora
 C. radicans
 C. × tagliabuana 'Madame Galen'
Clematis cirrhosa ssp. balearica
Cupressus macrocarpa
Daphne odora 'Aureomarginata'
 D.o. 'Walburton'
Drosera rotundifolia
Eccremocarpus scaber
Eucalyptus gunnii
Fascicularia bicolor
 F. pitcairniifolia
Fatsia japonica (Aralia japonica, A. sieboldii)
Ficus carica
Hedera algeriensis 'Gloire de Marengo'
 H. colchica 'Dentata Variegata'
 H. helix varieties
Laurus nobilis
Limonium latifolium
Liriope muscari
 L.m. 'Majestic'
 L.m. variegata
Musa basjoo
Myrtus communis
 M.c. var. tarentina
M.c. 'Variegata'
Nandina domestica
Olea europaea
Oxalis tetraphylla (O. deppei)
Passiflora caerulea
 P. incarnata
 P. 'Incense'
Phormium cookianum (P. colensoi)
 P. tenax
Phyllostachys aurea
 P. nigra
Pittosporum tenuifolium
Polystichum polyblepharum
Sarracenia purpurea ssp. purpurea
Solanum crispum 'Glasnevin'
Soleirolia soleirolii (Helxine soleirolii)
Vitis 'Alicante'
 V. 'Black Hamburgh'
 V. 'Buckland Sweetwater'
 V. 'Syrian'
Yucca whipplei

Frost-free: 38-40°F (3-4°C)

Acacia baileyana
Adiantum capillus-veneris
Agave americana
 A. filifera
Aloe arborescens
Alstroemeria pelegrina
Ampelopsis brevipedunculata 'Elegans'
Anigozanthos flavidus
 A. manglesii
Argyranthemum frutescens
 A.f. ssp. foeniculaceum
Arisaema candidissimum
 A. sikokianum
Asparagus densiflorus 'Meyers'
 A.d. 'Sprengeri'
 A. falcatus
 A. setaceus (A. plumosus)
Billardiera longiflora
Billbergia nutans
Bomarea caldasii
Buddleja asiatica
 B. auriculata
 B. lindleyana
 B. officinalis
Cacti and other succulents (most)
Callistemon citrinus 'Splendens'
 C. speciosus
Camellia
Campsis grandiflora
 C. radicans
 C. × tagliabuana 'Madame Galen'
Canna
Cestrum elegans
 C. 'Newellii'
Chamaerops humilis
Clematis cirrhosa ssp. balearica
 C. napaulensis
Clianthus puniceus
Cobaea scandens
Cordyline australis
 C.a. purpurea
 C. indivisa
Coronilla valentina ssp. glauca
Correa alba

C. backhouseana
C. 'Mannii'
C. pulchella
C. reflexa
C.r. virens
Crinum bulbispermum
 C. × powellii
Cupressus macrocarpa
 C. torulosa 'Cashmeriana' (C. himalaica var. darjeelingensis)
Cytisus canariensis (Genista canariensis)
 C. × spachianus (Genista × spachiana)
Dregea sinensis (Wattakaka sinensis)
Eccremocarpus scaber
Echium candicans (E. fastuosum)
 E. pininana
 E. wildpretii
Erythrina crista-galli
Eucomis autumnalis
 E. bicolor
 E. comosa
 E. pole-evansii
Farfugium tussilagineum 'Argenteum'
 F.t. 'Aureomaculatum'
Fascicularia bicolor
 F. pitcairniifolia
× Fatshedera lizei
Fatsia japonica (Aralia japonica, A. sieboldii)
Ficus carica
Fuchsia (all)
Furcraea foetida 'Mediopicta'
Gordonia axillaris
Hardenbergia violacea
Hedera algeriensis
 H. colchica 'Dentata Variegata'
 H. helix cultivars
Jasminum mesnyi (J. primulinum)
 J. polyanthum
Kennedia coccinea
 K. macrophylla
 K. rubicunda
Lachenalia (all)
Lagerstroemia indica
 L. Little Chief Hybrids
Ledebouria socialis (Scilla violacea)
Leptospermum
Limonium latifolium
Liriope muscari
 L.m. 'Majestic'
 L.m. 'Monroe White'
Livistona chinensis
Metrosideros kermadecensis 'Variegatus'
 M.k. 'Radiant'
Mitraria coccinea
Mutisia decurrens
 M. ilicifolia
 M. oligidon
Nerium oleander
Nertera granadensis
Oxalis purpurea
 O. tetraphylla (O. deppei)
Paraserianthes distachya
Passiflora caerulea
 P. incarnata
 P. 'Incense' (P. incarnata × P. cincinnata)
Pelargonium
Pittosporum crassifolium

P. eugenioides
P. tenuifolium
P. tobira
Podocarpus latifolius
 P. macrophyllus
Polystichum falcatum (Phanerophlebia falcata, Cyrtomium falcatum)
Prostanthera cuneata
Pteris cretica
Punica granatum
 P.g. var. nana
Rhododendron ciliicalyx
 R. 'Countess of Haddington'
 R. 'Fragrantissimum'
 R. 'Lady Alice Fitzwilliam'
 R. lindleyi
 R. maddenii
 R. 'Princess Alice'
Sarracenia (all)
Sedum morganianum
 S. sieboldii
Senecio rowleyanus
Solanum jasminoides
Soleirolia soleirolii (Helxine soleirolii)
Tetrapanax papyrifer (Fatsia papyrifera)
Thunbergia natalensis
Trachelospermum jasminoides
Tulbaghia cominsii
 T. fragrans
 T. simmleri
 T. violacea
 T.v. 'Silver Lace'
Viola hederacea
Yucca elephantipes
 Y. whipplei

Cool: 40-50°F (4-10°C)

Abutilon hybrids
 A. pictum 'Thompsonii'
Acacia baileyana
 A. dealbata
 A. paradoxa (A. armata)
 A. podalyriifolia
 A. pravissima
 A. retinodes 'Lisette'
Adiantum capillus-veneris
Agapetes serpens
Aloysia triphylla (A. citriodora, Lippia citriodora)
Alstroemeria ligtu hybrids
Alyogyne huegelii 'Santa Cruz'
Ampelopsis brevipedunculata 'Elegans'
Anigozanthos flavidus
 A. manglesii
Araucaria heterophylla (A. excelsa)
Araujia sericifera
Argyranthemum frutescens
 A.f. ssp. foeniculaceum
Arisaema candidissimum
 A. sikokianum
Aspidistra elatior
Asplenium bulbiferum
Beaucarnea recurvata (Nolina recurvata)
Begonia sutherlandii
 B. (tuberous)
Billardiera longiflora
Bomarea caldasii

Boronia heterophylla
  B. megastigma
  B.m. 'Heaven Scent'
  B.m. 'Lutea'
  B. 'Southern Star'
Bougainvillea (all)
Brugmansia (all)
Buddleja asiatica
  B. auriculata
  B. lindleyana
  B. officinalis
  B. tubiflora
Cacti and other succulents (most)
Callistemon (all)
Campsis grandiflora
  C. radicans
  C. × taglibuana 'Madame Galen'
Canarina canariensis
Ceropegia linearis ssp. woodii
Cestrum elegans (C. purpureum)
Chorizema dicksonii
  C. ilicifolium
Clematis cirrhosa ssp. balearica
  C. indivisa
  C. napaulensis
Clianthus puniceus
Cobaea scandens
Coronilla valentina ssp. glauca
Cryptanthus bivittatus
  C. bromelioides var. tricolor
  C. fosterianus
Cycas revoluta
Cyperus albostriatus (C. diffusus)
Cyrtanthus purpureus (Vallota speciosa)
Cytisus canariensis (Genista canariensis)
  C. × spachianus (Genista × spachiana)
Dicksonia antarctica
Dregea sinensis (Wattakaka sinensis)
Eccremocarpus scaber
Erica canaliculata
  E. cerinthoides
  E. gracilis
  E. × hiemalis
  E. mammosa
  E. pinea
Eriobotrya japonica
Eucalyptus citriodora
  E. ficifolia
  E. globulus
  E. gunnii
  E. moorei nana
Eucomis autumnalis
  E. bicolor
  E. comosa
  E. pole-evansii
Euryops pectinatus
Farfugium tussilagineum 'Argenteum'
  F.t. 'Aureomaculatum'
× Fatshedera lizei
Fatsia japonica (Aralia japonica, A. sieboldii)
Freesia
Fuchsia (all)
Furcraea foetida 'Mediopicta'
Gelsemium sempervirens
Geranium maderense
  G. palmatum (G. anemonifolium)
Gerbera jamesonii

Hardenbergia violacea
Hedera (all)
Heliamphora nutans
Heliotropium (all)
Hoya carnosa
  H. fusca 'Silver Knight' (H. 'Silver Pink')
  H. globulosa
Hymenocallis × festalis (Ismene × festalis)
Ipomoea indica (I. learii, I. acuminata,
    Pharbitis learii)
Jacaranda mimosifolia
Jasminum mesnyi (J. primulinum)
  J. polyanthum
Jovellana violacea
Kennedia coccinea
  K. macrophylla
  K. rubicunda
Lablab purpureus (Dolichos lablab)
Lachenalia
Lagerstroemia indica
  L. Little Chief Hybrids
Lapageria rosea
Ledebouria socialis (Scilla violacea)
Limonium latifolium
Liriope muscari
  L.m. 'Majestic'
  L.m. 'Monroe White'
  L.m. variegata
Lonicera sempervirens
Lotus berthelotii
  L. maculatus
Lycianthes rantonnetii (Solanum rantonnetii)
Maurandya barclayana (Asarina barclayana)
  M. erubescens (A. erubescens)
  M. scandens (A. scandens)
Michelia figo
Mitraria coccinea
Mutisia decurrens
  M. ilicifolia
  M. oligodon
Nerium oleander
Nertera granadensis
Oxalis purpurea
  O. tetraphylla (O. deppei)
Paphiopedilum insigne
Paraserianthes distachya
Passiflora alata
  P. × allardii
  P. amethystina
  P. 'Incense' (P. incarnata × P. cinnata)
Pelargonium
Pellaea rotundifolia
Pilea microphylla (P. muscosa)
Pinguicula grandiflora
  P. caudata
Pittosporum crassifolium
  P.c. 'Variegatum'
  P. eugenioides
  P.e. 'Variegatum'
  P. tenuifolium
Pleione tobira
Podocarpus latifolius
  P. macrophyllus
Polygala × dalmaisiana (P. myrtifolia var.
    grandiflora)
Polystichum falcatum (Phanerophlebia falcata,
    Cyrtomium falcatum)

Prostanthera cuneata
  P. lasianthos
  P. melissifolia
  P. nivea
  P. rotundifolia
Pteris cretica
Punica granatum
  P.g. var. nana
Rhodochiton atrosanguineus
Rhododendron (indoor azalea)
  R. brookeanum
  R. 'Countess of Haddington'
  R. ciliicalyx
  R. 'Fragrantissimum'
  R. 'Lady Alice Fitzwilliam'
  R. lindleyi
  R. maddenii
  R. 'Princess Alice'
Salvia buchananii
  S. discolor
  S. fulgens
  S. involucrata
  S. leucantha
Sarracenia (all)
Saxifraga stolonifera (S. sarmentosa)
Scadoxus puniceus
Schlumbergera
Sedum morganianum
Selaginella kraussiana
  S.k. 'Aurea'
  S.k. 'Brownii'
  S.k. 'Variegata'
  S. martensii
  S.m. 'Variegata'
Senecio macroglossus 'Variegatus'
  S. morganianum
  S. rowleyanus
Senna alata (Cassia alata)
  S. artemisioides (C. alata)
  S. corymbosa (C. corymbosa)
Serissa foetida
Solanum jasminoides
  S. wendlandii
Soleirolia soleirolii (Helxine soleirolii)
Sollya heterophylla (S. fusiformis)
Strelitzia reginae
Streptosolen jamesonii
Sutherlandia frutescens
Tetrapanax papyrifer (Fatsia papyrifera)
Thunbergia natalensis
Tibouchina organensis
  T. urvilleana (T. semidecandra)
Tolmiea menziesii 'Taff's Gold'
Trachelospermum jasminoides
Tradescantia sillamontana
Tropaeolum majus 'Hermine Grashoff'
Tulbaghia cominsii
  T. simmleri (T. fragrans)
  T. violacea
  T.v. 'Silver Lace'
Tweedia caerulea (Oxypetalum caeruleum,
    Amblyopetalum caeruleum)
Veltheimia bracteata (V. undulata,
    V. viridiflora)
  V. capensis (V. glauca, V. viridiflora)
Viola hederacea
Yucca aloifolia

Y. elephantipes
Y. whipplei

Temperate: 50-60°F(10-16°C)

Acalypha wilkesiana
Achimenes (all)
Adiantum raddianum (A. cuneatum)
Aechmea fasciata
Aeschynanthus marmoratus
  A. 'Mona Lisa'
  A. speciosus
Agapetes macrantha
  A. serpens
Alpinia purpurata
  A. vittata (A. sanderae)
  A. zerumbet (A. speciosa, A. nutans)
Alsobia dianthiflora (Episcia dianthiflora)
Amomum compactum (A. cardamomum)
Anemopaegma chamberlaynei
Ardisia crenata (A. crenulata)
Argyranthemum frutescens
  A.f. ssp. foeniculaceum
Asclepias curassavica
  A. physocarpa (Gomphocarpus physocarpus)
Aspidistra elatior
Beaucarnea recurvata (Nolina recurvata)
Beaumontia grandiflora
Begonia (most)
Bignonia capreolata
Billbergia nutans
  B. × windii
Blechnum gibbum
Bougainvillea
Bouvardia longiflora (B. humboldtii)
  B. 'Roxanne'
  B. ternifolia
Brachychiton rupestris
Brunfelsia pauciflora 'Macrantha' (B. calycina
    'Macrantha')
Buddleja madagascariensis (Nicodemia
    madagascariensis)
Callisia repens
Cestrum aurantiacum
  C. elegans (C. purpureum)
Chamaedorea elegans
Chlorophytum comosum 'Vittatum'
Chrysalidocarpus lutescens (Areca lutescens)
Cissus antarctica
  C. rhombifolia
× Citrofortunella microcarpa
Citrus aurantiifolia
  C. aurantium
  C. limon
  C. medica
  C. reticulata
  C. sinensis
Clerodendrum speciosissimum
Clivia miniata
  C. nobilis
Codonanthe gracilis
Coelogyne cristata
Coffea arabica
Columnea × banksii
  C. 'Krakatoa'
  C. microphylla
  C. 'Stavanger'
Cryptanthus bivittatus

C. bromelioides var. tricolor
C. fosterianus
Cuphea hyssopifolia
C. ignea
Cyclamen
Cymbidium
Cyperus albostriatus (C. diffusus)
C. involucratus (C. alternifolius of gardens)
C. papyrus
Cyphomandra crassicaulis (C. betacea)
Dendrobium nobile
Dioscorea elephantipes (Testudinaria elephantipes)
Dombeya burgessiae
D. × cayeuxii
D. wallichii
Encyclia cochleata (Epidendrum cochleatum)
Eucodonia andrieuxii 'Naomi'
Eugenia brasiliensis
E. uniflora
Euphorbia pulcherrima
Ficus benghalensis
F. benjamina
F. deltoidea (F. diversifolia)
F. elastica
F. longifolia
F. lyrata
F. microcarpa
F. pumila (F. repens)
F. religiosa
F. sagittata (F. radicans)
Fortunella hindsii
F. japonica
F. margarita
Gloriosa superba
Gloxinia perennis (G. maculata)
Grevillea banksii
G. robusta
Hedychium coronarium
H. gardnerianum
Hibbertia cuneiformis
H. scandens (H. volubilis)
Hibiscus rosa-sinensis
Hippeastrum
Howea belmoreana
H. forsteriana
Hoya australis
H. carnosa
H. fusca 'Silver Knight' (H. 'Silver Pink')
H. globulosa
H. lanceolata ssp. bella
H. macgillivrayi
H. multiflora
H. pubicalyx 'Red Buttons'
Hypoestes aristata
H. phyllostachya (H. sanguinolenta)
Impatiens New Guinea hybrids
I. niamniamensis
I. pseudoviola
I. repens
I. walleriana
Ipomoea indica (I. learii)
Iresine herbstii
I. lindenii
Jasminum nitidum
J. sambac
Jatropha podagrica

Justicia brandegeeana (Beloperone guttata)
J. rizzinii (J. pauciflora)
Kalanchoe manginii
K. pumila
K. 'Wendy'
Kohleria digitaliflora
K. eriantha
K. 'Hannah Roberts'
Laelia anceps
Lantana camara
Lonicera hildebrandtiana
Luculia gratissima
Lycianthes rantonnetii (Solanum rantonnetii)
Macfadyena unguis-cati (Doxantha unguis-cati)
Mandevilla × amabilis 'Alice du Pont'
M. boliviensis
M. laxa (M. suaveolens)
M. splendens
Manettia luteorubra (M. inflata)
Mikania dentata (M. ternata)
Miltoniopsis
Mitriostigma axillare (Gardenia citriodora)
Monstera deliciosa
Nematanthus 'Black Magic'
N. 'Freckles'
N. gregarius (Hypocyrta radicans)
N.g. 'Golden West' (N. g. 'Variegatus')
Neodypsis decaryi
Nephrolepis exaltata
Nerium oleander
Ochna serrulata
Odontoglossum
Pandorea pandorana
P. jasminoides
Paphiopedilum hybrids
Passiflora alata
P. × allardii
P. antioquiensis
P. × belotii (P. × alatocaerulea, P. 'Empress Eugenie', P. 'Impératrice Eugénie')
P. × caeruleoracemosa
P. edulis
P. ligularis
P. manicata
P. mollissima
P. quadrangularis
Pelargonium (Regal)
Pellaea rotundifolia
Pentas lanceolata
Peperomia argyreia (P. sandersii)
P. caperata
P. fraseri (P. resediflora)
P. obtusifolia
P. rotundifolia
P. scandens
Peristrophe hyssopifolia 'Aureovariegata'
P. speciosa
Petrea volubilis
Phoenix dactylifera
P. roebelinii
Pilea cadierei
P. involucrata 'Moon Valley'
P.i. 'Norfolk'
P. microphylla (P. muscosa)
P. peperomioides
Platycerium bifurcatum

P. superbum (P. grande)
Plectranthus forsteri 'Marginatus' (P. coleoides 'Marginatus')
P. madagascariensis 'Variegated Mintleaf'
P. oertendahlii
P. thyrsoideus (Coleus thyrsoideus)
Podranea ricasoliana
Psidium guajava
P. littorale var. littorale
P. littorale var. longipes (P. cattleianum)
Pteris cretica
Punica granatum
Pyrostegia venusta
Radermachera sinica (Stereospermum sinicum)
Rhapis excelsa
R. humilis
Rhododendron (indoor azalea)
Salvia leucantha
Sansevieria trifasciata
S.t. 'Golden Hahnii'
S.t. 'Laurentii'
S.t. 'Moonshine'
Saxifraga stolonifera (S. sarmentosa)
Scadoxus multiflorus
S.m. ssp. katherinae
Schefflera actinophylla (Brassaia actinophylla)
S. arboricola (Heptapleurum arboricola)
Schlumbergera
Scirpus cernuus (Isolepis gracilis)
Selaginella kraussiana
S.k. 'Aurea'
S.k. 'Brownii'
S. martensii
S.m. 'Variegata'
Senecio confusus (Pseudogynoxys chenopodioides)
Serissa foetida
Sinningia cardinalis
S. hybrids
Smithiantha
Solandra maxima
Solanum capsicastrum
Solenostemon
Sparmannia africana
Stenotaphrum secundatum 'Variegatum'
Stephanotis floribunda
Strelitzia reginae
Streptocarpus
Streptosolen jamesonii
Tecomaria capensis
Thunbergia grandiflora
Tibouchina organensis
T. urvilleana (T. semidecandra)
Tradescantia fluminensis 'Albovittata'
T.f. 'Quicksilver'
T. pallida 'Purpurea' (Setereasea purpurea)
T. sillamontana
T. zebrina (Zebrina pendula)
Veitchia merrillii
Yucca elephantipes
Zantedeschia (all)

Warm/Tropical: 60°F (16°C) and over
Acalypha hispida
A. wilkesiana
Adiantum trapeziforme

Aechmea (all)
Aeschynanthus marmoratus
A. 'Mona Lisa'
A. speciosus
Aglaonema (all)
Allamanda cathartica
A. schottii (A. neriifolia)
Alocasia × amazonica
A. cuprea
Ananas bracteatus var. tricolor
A. comosus var. variegatus
Anthurium andreanum
A. crystallinum
A. 'Lady Jane'
A. scherzerianum
Aphelandra squarrosa 'Dania'
A.s. 'Louisae'
A.s. 'Snow Queen'
Aristolochia littoralis (A. elegans)
A. gigantea
Asplenium nidus
Begonia masoniana
B. rex
Caladium bicolor
Calathea (all)
Calliandra haematocephala
Carica papaya
Caryota mitis
Cattleya bowringiana
Centradenia floribunda
Chirita sinensis
Chrysalidocarpus lutescens (Areca lutescens)
Cissus discolor
Clerodendrum philippinum (C. fragrans pleniflorum)
C. splendens
C. thomsoniae
Codiaeum variegatum var. pictum
Columnea × banksii
C. gloriosa
C. 'Krakatoa'
C. microphylla
C. 'Stavanger'
Cordyline fruticosa (C. terminalis)
Crinum asiaticum
Crossandra infundibuliformis
Cryptanthus bivittatus
C. bromelioides var. tricolor
C. fosterianus
Ctenanthe lubbersiana
C. oppenheimiana
Cycas circinalis
Cyperus papyrus
Dieffenbachia (all)
Dracaena cincta
D. deremensis
D. fragrans
D. reflexa (Pleomele reflexa)
Epipremnum aureum (Scindapsus aureus)
Episcia cupreata
Eupatorium sordidum
Ficus benjamina
F. deltoidea (F. diversifolia)
F. elastica
F. longifolia
F. lyrata
F. microcarpa

F. pumila (F. repens)
F. religiosa
F. sagittata (F. radicans)
Fittonia (all)
Guzmania 'Amaranth'
G. 'Gran Prix'
G. lingulata var. minor
G. musaica
Gynura aurantiaca
Hibiscus rosa-sinensis
H. schizopetalus
Howea belmoreana
H. forsteriana
Hoya multiflora
Impatiens New Guinea hybrids
I. niamniamensis
I. pseudoviola
I. repens
I. walleriana
Ixora coccinea
Jasminum rex
J. sambac
Juanulloa mexicana (J. aurantiaca)
Justicia carnea (Jacobinia carnea, J. pohliana, J. velutina)
Lagenaria siceraria (L. vulgaris)
Latania loddigesii
Leea coccinea
L. guineensis 'Burgundy'
Licuala grandis (Pritchardia grandis)
Ludisia discolor (Goodyera discolor, Anoectochilus discolor)
Luffa aegyptiaca (L. cylindrica)
Mandevilla × amabilis 'Alice du Pont'
M. boliviensis
M. laxa (M. suaveolens)
M. splendens
Manettia luteorubra (M. inflata)
Mangifera indica
Maranta leuconeura var. erythroneura (M. tricolor)
Medinilla magnifica
Melicope hortensis (Euodia hortensis)
Mimosa pudica
Monstera deliciosa
Musa acuminata 'Dwarf Cavendish'
M. uranoscopus (M. coccinea)
Nematanthus 'Black Magic'
N. 'Freckles'
N. gregarius (Hypocyrta radicans)
N.g. 'Golden West' (N. g. 'Variegatus')
Neoregelia carolinae 'Flandria'
N.c. f. tricolor
N. marmorata
N. sarmentosa
Nepenthes
Nephrolepis exaltata
Nidularium billbergioides
N. fulgens
Pachystachys coccinea
P. lutea
Passiflora cirrhiflora
P. coccinea
P. coriacea
P. racemosa
P. vitifolia
Pavonia multiflora

Peperomia argyreia (P. sandersii)
P. caperata
P. fraseri (P. resediflora)
P. obtusifolia
P. rotundifolia
P. scandens
Peristrophe hyssopifolia 'Aureovariegata'
Persea americana (P. gratissima)
Phalaenopsis
Philodendron angustisectum (P. elegans)
P. bipennifolium (P. panduriforme)
P. bipinnatifidum
P. erubescens
P. melanochrysum (P. andreanum)
P. scandens
Pilea involucrata 'Moon Valley'
P.i. 'Norfolk'
P. peperomioides
Piper ornatum
Pisonia umbellifera 'Variegata'
Platycerium superbum (P. grande)
Plumeria rubra (P. acuminata)
Polyscias scutellaria 'Balourii' (P. balfouriana)
P. filicifolia
P. guilfoylei
Radermachera sinica (Stereospermum sinicum)
Ravenala madagascariensis
Saintpaulia
Schefflera elegantissima (Heptapleurum elegantissimum, Aralia elegantissima)
Scutellaria costaricana
Sinningia cardinalis
Smithiantha
Spathiphyllum
Stephanotis floribunda
Strobilanthes dyerianus
Tecomanthe speciosa
T. venusta (T. dendrophila)
Tetrastigma voinerianum (Cissus voinerianus, Vitis voineriana)
Thunbergia mysorensis
Tillandsia argentea
T. caput-medusae
T. cyanea
T. ionantha
T. usneoides
Vigna caracalla (Phasaeolus caracalla)
Vriesea hieroglyphica
V. × poelmanii
V. splendens

Plants with special features

Other useful lists to help people furnish their greenhouse with plants that share particular attributes indicate scented plants, those that bloom in winter, and a few favorites to grow for variegated foliage.

Plants with scented flowers or foliage
(Unless otherwise indicated, the plants listed below have scented flowers)
Acacia baileyana
A. dealbata
A. retinodes 'Lisette'

Amomum compactum (A. cardamomum) (foliage and roots)
Araujia sericifera
Beaumontia grandiflora
Begonia solananthera
Boronia megastigma
Brugmansia arborea
B. × candida
B. chlorantha
B. suaveolens
Brunfelsia americana (at night)
B. undulata
Buddleja asiatica
Callistemon citrinus (foliage)
Citrus
Clerodendrum philippinum (C. fragrans pleniflorum)
Crinum asiaticum
Cytisus canariensis (Genista canariensis)
Daphne odora 'Aureomarginata'
D.o. 'Walburton'
Dregea sinensis (Wattakaka sinensis)
Epiphyllum oxypetalum
Eucalyptus citriodora (foliage)
E. ficifolia (foliage)
E. globulus (foliage)
E. gunnii (foliage)
E. moorei nana (foliage)
Freesia
Gardenia augusta (G. jasminoides)
Hedychium coronarium
H. gardnerianum
Heliotropium
Hoya australis
H. carnosa
H. lanceolata ssp. bella
Hyacinthus
Hymenocallis amancaes
Jasminum nitidum
J. polyanthum
J. sambac
Laurus nobilis (foliage)
Luculia gratissima
Mandevilla laxa (M. suaveolens)
Matthiola
Michelia figo
Mitriostigma axillare
Murraya paniculata
Myrtus communis (foliage)
Narcissus papyraceus
N. 'Soleil d'Or'
Pandorea pandorana
Pelargonium 'Attar of Roses' (foliage)
P. 'Chocolate Peppermint' (foliage)
P. 'Lady Mary' (foliage)
P. odoratissimum (foliage)
P. 'Prince of Orange' (foliage)
P. tomentosum (foliage)
Pereskia aculeata
Pittosporum eugenioides
P. tobira
Plumeria rubra
Prostanthera cuneata (foliage)
P. lasianthos (foliage)
P. melissifolia (foliage)
P. nivea (foliage)
P. rotundifolia (foliage)

Rhododendron 'Countess of Haddington'
R. 'Fragrantissimum'
R. 'Lady Alice Fitzwilliam'
R. lindleyi
R. maddenii
R. 'Princess Alice'
R. taggianum
Rosa 'Maréchal Niel'
R. 'Niphetos'
Solandra maxima
Sansevieria trifasciata
Stephanotis floribunda (at night)
Trachelospermum jasminoides
Vigna caracalla (Phasaeolus caracalla)
Yucca whipplei

Winter-flowering plants
Acacia baileyana
A. dealbata
A. paradoxa (A. armata)
A. podalyriifolia
A. retinodes 'Lisette'
Agapetes macrantha
Aloe arborescens
Anthurium andreanum
A. 'Lady Jane'
A. scherzerianum
Begonia procumbens (B. limmingheana, B. glaucophylla)
B. solananthera
Browallia
Buddleja asiatica
B. officinalis
B. tubiflora
Camellia sasanqua
Canarina canariensis
Centradenia floribunda
Citrus
Clematis cirrhosa ssp. balearica
C. napaulensis
Clerodendrum speciosissimum
Correa 'Mannii'
C. pulchella
Daphne odora 'Aureomarginata'
Dombeya wallichii
Erica gracilis
E. × hiemalis
Eupatorium sordidum
Euphorbia pulcherrima
Freesia
Grevillea banksii
Hardenbergia violacea
Hyacinthus
Hypoestes aristata
Jasminum mesnyi (J. primulinum)
J. polyanthum
J. rex
J. sambac
Justicia brandegeeana (Beloperone guttata)
J. rizzinii
Kalanchoe pumila
Lachenalia
Luculia gratissima
Matthiola
Narcissus papyraceus
N. 'Soleil d'Or'
Pachystachys coccinea

Pericallis
Peristrophe speciosa
Plectranthus thyrsoideus (Coleus thyrsoideus)
Primula × kewensis
  P. malacoides
  P. obconica
  P. sinensis
Rhododendron (indoor azalea)
Scutellaria costaricana
Senecio grandifolius (Telanthophora grandifolia)
Senecio macroglossus 'Variegatus'
Senna alata (Cassia alata)

Sparmannia africana
Thunbergia mysorensis
Veltheimia bracteata (V. undulata, V. viridifolia)
  V. capensis

Variegated evergreens
Aichryson × domesticum 'Variegatum'
Aphelandra squarrosa 'Dania'
  A.s. 'Louisae'
Chlorophytum comosum 'Vittatum'
Coprosma 'Beatson's Gold'
  C. repens 'Marble Queen'

  C.r. 'Picturata'
Coronilla valentina 'Variegata'
Epipremnum aureum (Scindapsus aureus)
× *Fatshedera lizei* 'Variegata'
Ficus benjamina 'Starlight'
  F.b. 'Golden King'
  F. microcarpa 'Hawaii'
Hedera colchica 'Dentata Variegata'
  H. helix 'Goldchild'
  H.h. 'Luzii'
Hibiscus rosa-sinensis 'Cooperi'
Metrosideros kermadecensis 'Variegatus'
  M.k. 'Radiant'

Myrtus communis 'Variegata'
Nerium oleander 'Variegatum'
Pittosporum crassifolium 'Variegatum'
  P. eugenioides 'Variegatum'
  P. tenuifolium 'Irene Paterson'
  P. tobira 'Variegatum'
Polyscias scutellaria 'Marginata'
  P. scutellaria 'Pennockii' (*P. balfouriana* 'Pennockii')
Schefflera arboricola (Heptapleurum arboricola)
Senecio macroglossus 'Variegatus'
Trachelospermum jasminoides 'Variegatum'

Glossary

Aerial root Root borne above ground
Annual Plant completing its life-cycle within one growing season
Anther Pollen-bearing part of the stamen
Areole (on cactus stem) Small cushion bearing a spine or tuft of hairs
Awn Slender point, or the bristle-like tip found especially on flowering parts of grasses
Axil Upper angle between leaf or leaf stalk and stem
Basal Growing from or constituting the base (of a plant); the lowermost part (of leaf)
Biennial Plant requiring two growing seasons to complete its life-cycle
Bifoliate Having two leaves
Bipinnate Both stems and leaflets following a pinnate pattern (e.g. mimosa)
Bract Modified leaf, usually protecting flower or inflorescence
Bromeliad Plant of the family Bromeliaceae
Bulb Underground storage organ usually consisting of layered fleshy inner leaves surrounding a stem and shoot and thin outer leaves
Bulbil Small bulb-like organ growing from leaf axil or flower stalk
Calyx (pl. calyces) Collective name for sepals forming the outer part of the flower
Caulescent Having a properly developed stem growing above ground
Coir Fibrous planting medium derived from outer husk of the coconut
Cold frame Low glazed structure without artificial heating used for plant protection outdoors
Coralloid Bearing similarity to the structure of coral
Corm Bulb-like solid swollen underground stem base, usually covered by papery skin, acting as a storage organ
Corolla Collective name for petals forming inner part of the flower
Corona Crown- or cup-like structure of petals or filaments between corolla and stamens (e.g. *Narcissus, Passiflora*)
Culm Stem of a grass
Cultivar (cultivated variety) Distinct variant of a plant which has arisen in cultivation or in the wild, maintained in cultivation by propagation
Dead-head To remove spent flowers to tidy a plant or prevent seeding
Deciduous Shedding leaves or petals after the growing season is complete
Dibble To make holes in the planting medium for seeds, plantlets, etc.
Dormant Suspending active growth during unfavorable conditions such as cold
Drupe Fruit consisting of a soft fleshy covering surrounding a single stone-like hard seed
Epiphyte (adj. epiphytic) Plant growing on another plant without being parasitic
Ericaceous Pertaining to the Ericaceae (heather) family; also describing its preferred growing medium
Evergreen Retaining foliage through more than one growing season
Fasciation Abnormal fusing of stems, etc., to produce flattened, misshapen growth
Filament Anther-bearing stalk of a stamen
Foliar feed Liquid fertilizer sprayed onto, and absorbed through, leaves
Forma (abb. 'f.') Distinct variant of a plant
Gesneriad Plant of the family Gesneriaceae
Glaucous (of leaf) Coated with a fine bluish or whitish waxy bloom
Groundsel Weed from the genus *Senecio,* with little yellow flowers
Heel Small section of the parent plant that remains connected to a young shoot cut for propagation and which helps to ensure successful rooting
Herbaceous Having soft, leafy growth; not forming a persistent woody stem

Hybrid Plant produced by crossing two dissimilar plants
Hydroculture, hydroponics Cultivation of plants in liquid nutrient solutions rather than in solid planting medium
Inflorescence A plant's flowering part
Internode Length of stem between two nodes
Keel Ridge formed by the two lower united petals of a pea flower
Lanceolate (of leaf) Lance-shaped, tapering to a pointed tip
Lateral On or at the side
Leaflet Separate part of a compound leaf
Lenticel Pore on the surface of fruit or bark allowing gas penetration or exchange
Lithophyte (adj. lithophytic) Plant surviving on rocks or stony ground by taking nutrients from the atmosphere
Loam Fertile soil containing balanced proportions of clay, sand, silt, and organic matter
Lobe (of leaf, petal, etc.) Rounded division or segment
Node The point on the stem where leaves, flowers, or shoots are attached
Offset Plantlet or runner growing from the base of the parent plant
Panicle Branching inflorescence with each branch producing more than a single flower
Peltate (of leaf) Attached to its stalk from its center rather than from an edge
Perennial Non-woody plant with a life-cycle of at least three growing seasons
Perianth Term for the corolla and calyx combined, mainly used when these are not obviously differentiated
Perlite Granular planting medium derived from volcanic rock
Petiole Leaf stalk
pH Degree of soil acidity or alkalinity
Phylloclade Flattened stem performing the functions of a leaf
Phyllode Enlarged petiole functioning as a leaf-blade
Pinna (pl. pinnae) Leaflet(s) (see pinnate)
Pinnate Resembling a feather, with veins or leaflets arranged on opposite sides of a main stalk
Pinnule One of the individual leaflets of a bipinnate leaf
Pip Seed of a fleshy fruit (e.g. lemon)
Plunge bed Frame containing sand, peat, or ash, in which plant pots are buried to the rim to protect roots from temperature fluctuation, drying out, etc.
Pseudobulb Expanded stem resembling a bulb, able to store water; generally found in orchids
Raceme Simple elongated inflorescence on a single stem, the oldest flowers nearest the base (e.g. foxglove)
Reflexed (of petal) Abruptly bent downward or backward
Rhizome (adj. rhizomatous) Enlarged, horizontal stem lying underground or near the surface and which produces aerial parts, resulting in new plants
Rockwool Synthetic fibrous substance derived from molten rock, usable as planting medium
Rootstock The crown and root system of herbaceous perennials and suckering shrubs
Runner Trailing stem which produces roots and shoots at its tip or nodes, resulting in new plantlets
Sagittate (of leaf) Arrowhead-shaped, with downward-pointing basal lobes
Semi-evergreen Normally evergreen but losing some or all foliage in cold conditions
Sepal Segment of the calyx
Spadix Spike-like inflorescence bearing many small stalkless flowers and commonly surrounded by a spathe (e.g. arum)
Spathe Large leaf or bract enclosing the spadix

Spore (in lower plants, e.g. ferns and mosses) Unit of reproduction, able to develop into a new plantlet
Sport Individual plant (or shoot) spontaneously deviating from typical growth of the species that produced it, usually due to mutation
Spur Short bud-bearing branchlet of tree; tubular nectar-producing projection at base of flower petal, etc.
Stamen (adj. staminal) Male floral reproductive organ, consisting of an anther usually held up by a filament
Stipule Leafy, generally paired growth at base of leaf stalk
Style Elongated part of the female reproductive organ
Succulent Thick, fleshy; water-storing plant adapted to dry conditions (e.g. cactus)
Terminal (leaflet, bud, etc.) At the tip or apex of a stem
Tessellated (of leaf) Marked with checkered, mosaic-like pattern

Top-dressing Application of fertilizer, fresh potting mix, etc. to soil surface only, without digging in
Trifoliate Having three leaves
Tripinnate Bipinnate with each division pinnate
Tuber (adj. tuberous) Fleshy underground stem used for storing food
Tufa Porous rock used as a planting medium
Umbel Flat-topped inflorescence with all flower stems growing from a single point
Variegated Irregularly marked with color/s, often due to uneven distribution of chlorophyll
Varietas (botanical variety, abb. 'var.') Distinct variant of a plant species which has arisen naturally, in the wild
Vermiculite Sterile crumb-like planting medium made from expanded mica

Useful addresses

UNITED STATES AND CANADA

A Fleur d'Eau Inc., P.O. Box 118, Stanbridge Est, QC, J0J 2H0 (Specializing in indoor and outdoor aquatic plants)

Aimers Seeds and Bulbs, 81 Temperance Street, Aurora, ON, L4G 2R1 (Specializing in rare seeds)

Altman Specialty Plants, 553 Buena Creek Road, San Marcos, CA 92069 (Specializing in rare and unusual succulent plants)

Bluestone Perennials, 7201 Middle Ridge, Madison, OH 44057 (Over 400 varieties of sturdy seedlings)

Brite-Lite Ltd., 2215 Walkeley, Montreal, QC, H4B 2J9 (Specializing in indoor gardening and hydroponic supplies)

Canadian Hydroponics Ltd., 8318 120 Street, Surrey, BC, V3W 3N4 (Specializing in vegetables for the home gardener)

Charley's Greenhouse Supply, 1569 Memorial, Mount Vernon, WA 98273, 800/322-4707 (Everything for the greenhouse, conservatory, and sunroom gardener, except plants)

Clargreen Gardens, 814 Southdown Road, Mississauga, ON, L5J 2Y4 (Specializing in orchids, bonsai, and tropical plants)

Cruikshank's Inc., 1015 Mt. Pleasant Road, Toronto, ON, M4P 2M1 (Importers of customary and rare bulbs, and specialists in garden accessories)

Dutch Gardens, P.O. Box 200, Adelphia, NJ 07710 (Close-to-wholesale prices on Dutch-grown bulbs)

The Fragrant Path, P.O. Box 328, Fort Calhoun, NE 68023 (Seeds for vines, trees, shrubs, perennials, and herbs)

Gardener's Supply, 128 Intervale Road, Burlington, VT 05401, 800/688-5510 (Large selection of tools and supplies for natural pest control)

Gardenimport Inc., P.O. Box 760, Thornhill, ON, L3T 4A5, 800/565-0957 (Specializing in imported bulbs and seeds. Mail order to Canada and USA)

The Green Escape, P.O. Box 1417, Palm Harbor, FL 34682 (Extensive collection of tropical and hardy palms)

Grisby Cactus Gardens, 2354 Bella Vista Drive, Vista, CA 92084 (Unusually large selection of cacti and succulents)

Hortico, Inc., 723 Robson Road, R.R. 1, Waterdown, ON, L0R 2H1 (A varied selection of roses, perennials, shrubs, and vines)

J. L. Hudson, P.O. Box 1058, Redwood City, CA 94064 (Rare and unusual seeds from the far corners of the globe)

Janco, 9390 Davis Avenue, Laurel, MD 20723, 800/323-6933 (Over 100 models of freestanding and lean-to greenhouses)

The Lily Pool, 3324 Pollock Road, R.R. 2, Keswick, ON, L4P 3E9 (Specializing in aquatic plants (hardy and tropical varieties), bog-type plants, and planting mediums)

Lilypons Water Gardens, 6800 Lilypons Road, Lilypons, MD 21717, 800/723-7667 (Quality aquatic plants and water gardening supplies)

Limerock Ornamental Grasses, Inc., R.D. 1, Box 111C, Port Matilda, PA 16870 (A fine source for greenhouse grasses)

Logee's Greenhouses, North Street, Danielson, CT 06239 (Huge selection of begonias, citrus trees, orchids, jasmine, and ferns)

Moore Water Gardens, Highway 4, P.O. Box 340, Port Stanley, ON, N0L 2A0 (Aquatic plants, specializing in waterlilies)

Mountain Maples, P.O. Box 1329, Laytonville, CA 95454 (Over 100 Japanese maples and bonsai for the conservatory)

Nor'East Miniature Roses, 58 Hammond Street, Rowley, MA 01969 (Selected miniature roses in every shade imaginable)

Patio Garden Ponds, P.O. Box 890402, Oklahoma City, OK 73189 (Specializing in aquatic plants, pond liners, pumps, and filters)

W.H. Perron & Cie Ltée, 2914 Curé-Labelle, Chomedey, Laval, QC, H7P 5R9 (Specializing in seeds and a variety of bulbs)

Peter Paul's Nurseries, Canandaigua, NY 14424 (Carnivorous plants and the supplies to keep them happy)

Pickering Nurseries, 670 Kingston Road, Pickering, ON, L1V 1A6 (Specializing in heirloom and species roses)

Plumeria People, Box 820014, Houston, TX 77282 (Over 300 varieties of flowering vines, fragrant plants, and tropicals)

The Sandy Mush Herb Nursery, Rt. 2, Surrett Cove Road, Leicester, NC 28748 (Very large selection of herbs and scented-leaf geraniums)

Springwood Miniature Roses, R.R. 3, Caledon East, ON, L0N 1E0 (More than 100 varieties of miniature roses)

Superior Growers Supply, Inc., 4870 Dawn Avenue, East Lansing, MI 48823 (Lighting, irrigation, hydroponic systems, and high-tech greenhouse supplies)

Texas Greenhouse Company, 2524 White Settlement Road, Fort Worth, TX 76107 (Kits for building do-it-yourself greenhouses plus gardening-under-glass supplies)

Van Well Nursery, P.O. Box 1339, Wenatchee, WA 98801 (One-stop shopping for standard and dwarf fruit trees)

Les Violettes Natalia, 124 Chemin Grapes, Sawyerville, QC, J0B 3A0 (Over 2,000 varieties of African violets and 700 gesneriads)

Wayside Gardens, P.O. Box 1, Hodges, SC 29695, 800/845-1124 (Large assortment of choice perennials, shrubs, and vines)

Woodlanders, 1128 Cooleton Avenue, Aiken, SC 29801 (Extensive stock of exotic trees, shrubs, and perennials)

Index

Page numbers in *italics* refer to illustrations or their captions.

Author's acknowledgments

Every gardener has a store of information gathered by working closely with plants. In writing this book, I have become deeply aware of how much this has been tempered and improved by thoughts and comments from fellow enthusiasts, both professional and amateur. My warmest thanks go to all those with whom I have discussed sunroom plants, who have challenged my opinions, or added a vital ingredient which has found its way into this book.

There have been categories of plants where I knew that specialist knowledge would be superior to my own. I would like to add particular thanks to Barbara Dobbins-Davis from Stapeley Water Garden, Ray Bilton from McBeans Orchids, and Martin Gibbons from the Palm Centre.

It has been a luxury, while writing, to know that a photographer and plantswoman as capable as Deni Bown has been out and about taking beautiful pictures of the plants. These, more than my words, should encourage even the most conservative of sunroom gardeners to experiment. Reassurance has also been provided by Dr Tony Lord and Patrick Nutt who have checked the text with meticulous care, although any inaccuracies that may exist are my responsibility.

Family and friends deserve thanks, too, for their understanding, support, and encouragement. Especially my parents, who have given much of their time to remove some of the domestic pressures that might have prevented me from writing.

Final thanks must go to Diana Loxley, who has patiently coaxed *The Sunroom Gardener* from me and who, together with Penny David, Caroline Hillier, Erica Hunningher, and others at Frances Lincoln, has molded it into a fine book.

Photographer's acknowledgments

I would like to thank the following people and places for allowing me to take photographs, and for helping to locate plants: staff at the Royal Botanic Garden, Edinburgh; Jenny Evans and staff at the Royal Botanic Gardens, Kew; Richard Schnall and staff at the New York Botanical Garden; staff at the US National Arboretum, Washington DC; John Ravenscroft, Bridgemere Nurseries, Nantwich, Cheshire; staff at Bodnant Garden, Gwynedd; Christopher Fairweather at Christopher Fairweather Ltd, Beaulieu, Hampshire; Tony Jackson at the Welsh Mountain Zoo and Botanical Garden, Colwyn Bay, Clwyd; Chris Colbourne at Newington Nurseries, Oxford; Ray Waite and staff at the RHS Garden, Wisley; Joanne Miles at Castle Ashby, Northampton; Len Salt at Birmingham Botanic Gardens; staff at the Canal Gardens, Roundhay Park, Leeds; Noel Kingsbury at Sunbeam Nurseries, Frampton Cotterell, Avon; Brian Rittershausen and staff at Burnham Nurseries, Newton Abbot, Devon; Rex Dibley and family at Efenechtyd Nurseries, Ruthin, Clwyd; Susan Briggs (and friends) at Gwynyndy, Clwyd; Oliver Menzel at Long Man Gardens, Wilmington, E. Sussex; Terry Hewitt and staff at Holly Gate Cactus Nursery, Ashington, W. Sussex; staff at Torbay Palm Farm, Newton Abbot,

Devon; Ray Hubbard at Hill House Nursery and Gardens, Ashburton, Devon; managers and staff at Frost's Garden Centre, Woburn Sands, Milton Keynes, and Millett's Garden Centre, Abingdon, Oxfordshire; Barry Findon, Wyld Court Rainforest, Newbury, Berkshire; staff at Chessington Nurseries, Chessington, Surrey.

Picture credits
Photographs
All photographs by Deni Bown except for the following: (*l*=left *r*=right): Boys Syndication/Michael Boys: 136; Garden Picture Library/Tommy Candler: 10; Garden Picture Library/Ron Sutherland: 11*l*, 116; John Glover: 19*r*; Jacqui Hurst © FLL: 21; Michèle Lamontagne: 174; Marianne Majerus © FLL: 11*r*; Clive Nichols © FLL: 2, 19*l*; Fritz von der Schulenburg: 6, 14
'Pests and Diseases' (pp. 36 and 37, numbering 1-25 from left to right and top to bottom): B & B photographs/Dr S T Buczacki: 1, 3, 6, 10, 14, 16, 17, 20; Ron and Christine Foord: 2, 4, 5, 7, 12; Holt Studios International: 8, 11, 13, 18, 22; Horticultural Research International: 9, 15, 19, 21, 23, 24, 25
Illustrations
Liz Pepperell:17; Jim Robins: 15, 26, 32-4; Sarah-Jayne Stafford: 24-5, 27-31; Mitch Stuart: 8, 12-13

Publishers' acknowledgments
The Publishers would like to thank the following people and institutions for their help in producing this book: Ruth Carim, Joanna Chisholm, Jo Christian, Lorraine Dickey, the late Hilary Dickinson, Sue Gernaey, Gareth Richards, Caroline Taylor, Louise Tucker, Anne Wilson; Camden Garden Centre for the loan of plants; Karen Stafford for her speed and efficiency.

Horticultural consultants Tony Lord, Patrick Nutt

Project editor Diana Loxley
Editor Penny David
Coordinating editor (N.A.) Barbara Jacksier
Design Karen Stafford
Picture research Sue Gladstone
Picture editor Anne Fraser
Art director Caroline Hillier
Editorial director Erica Hunningher
Production Adela Cory